Social Control

The Production of
Deviance
in the Modern State

Social Control
The Production of Deviance in the Modern State

Nanette J. Davis
Portland State University
and
Bo Anderson
Michigan State University

✳ IRVINGTON PUBLISHERS, INC.
740 BROADWAY NEW YORK, N.Y. 10003

Library of Congress Cataloging in Publication Data

Davis, Nanette J.
  Social control.

  Includes bibliographical references.
  1. Social control. 2. Social structure. 3. Deviant behavior. 4. Self-help groups. 5. Social policy.
I. Anderson, Bo. II. Title.
HM291.D339 1983   303.3'3   83-136
ISBN 0-8290-0727-X

Printed in the United States of America

DEDICATION

To My Family—Jim, Katherine, Susan, Elizabeth, Timothy, Michael, and Patricia.

—N.J.D.

To My Father, the Memory of my Mother and my Daughter, Sara

—B.A.

Contents

Tables

FOREWORD

Few will dispute the central place that social control holds in the effort to understand and eventually to influence the course of society. In this book by Nanette Davis and Bo Anderson, the authors reassert the concept for contemporary readers that the study of society is the study of social control. Social control involves the processes by which people are taught, urged, or coerced into being a part of an intricate reticulation of relationships, statuses and roles that involve patterns of behavior, and expectations from self and others. Society can be thought of as networks of control, sometimes visible yet more binding when they are less apparent to eye and ear.

Many social thinkers have rejected, or at least found overstated, the image of humanity harbored by Thomas Hobbes. He postulated that without some force external to the individual and threatening punishment for those who step out of line, human life would deteriorate to a war of all against all. Nonetheless, even those most skeptical of this vision concede that the control of human behavior by something other than natural instinct is essential to survival. Only the most utopian amongst us, neo-Marxists, anarcho-Marxists, or whatever label they choose to apply to themselves, cling to the image of a state that will wither away and in which people will merge into one great cooperative mass.

Davis and Anderson remind us that control over our lives and fate by forces that originate outside of ourselves is a fact of life. Although we may strive as individuals for a maximum escape from that control, and some of us may find this in the existential concept of freedom, we are doomed if we do not embrace social control as beneficial, as something not merely inevitable but desirable, as not merely preventing freedom of action by ourselves but as presenting it against ourselves, and as not merely restraining us but liberating us from fear by restraining others. Ideally, social control channels us in directions that we would have chosen by our own volition, had we more wisdom.

Fëdor Dostoevsky, perhaps a better sociologist than any among his contemporaries in his or the century or more that followed him, understood that we are all both doomed and blessed because we live in a world in which we are so completely and thoroughly circumscribed. When Rodion Raskolnikov in *Crime and Punishment* seeks to establish the fact that there is an elite sector of humanity — of which he is a part — which by virtue (an ironic phrase, indeed) of its superiority can rise above ordinary laws that are created for ordinary people, he chooses to become a murderer. One reads that he chooses with some hesitation; yet it is a choice not the less so because he cringes from making it. He claims to himself both that he had the right to make the choice and that it was not he who made it, but some inner force, no longer under his command.

It is the lesson of Dostoevsky, or at least one of the many lessons of this rich and stimulating oeuvre, that in seeking to establish his right to be free from the control imposed by his inferiors, and to rise above the moral laws created by ordinary humans, Raskolnikov did not establish that he was superhuman, but only that he was human and mortal; and not that he was above others, but that he had fallen below them. In attempting to shift the responsibility for his action from himself to a force within him over which he had no control, he was responsible for having made the choice of relinquishing his freedom to choose.

Davis and Anderson demonstrate that in this juxtaposition of inner and outer restraints, most of us prefer the reduction of the forces that are formal, openly coercive, and repressive. We envision a free society as one to which people conform because of a desire to do so, because of agreement with the surrounding norms, a society in which our behavior patterns would be unchanged if coercive powers were to disappear. In one sense, as this book emphasizes, we are all prisoners of our culture, which has taught us to distinguish between the most rudimentary forms of acceptable and unacceptable behavior, at so early an age that most of us could not step out and challenge our teachers. It is a society that has given us only limited choices and has then kept us in ignorance of choices that were absent, so that we did not even know what was being missed or what we might have done had we not during our earliest years been so completely socialized. (Some would say "brainwashed," but that word has another, although not unrelated, meaning.)

Accordingly, we often become acculturated to what Alfred Schutz called — in a simple phrase that illuminated so much because of its utter simplicity — our taken-for-granted world. We come to accept the behavior patterns dominant in our culture as the way things naturally are, or at least ought to be—albeit with flexibility, a bit of skepticism, some protest, occasional opposition and plaintive cries that Pangloss is not to be interpreted literally. (After all, Voltaire was a satirist, was he not?) And thus we are often muted by the very large amount of social control, which we see as liberating rather than constraining. Seldom, in fact, do we even stop to consider that we may be living a contradiction in terms.

What is confusing about the problem of social control is that a society wants a great deal of it, and at the same time needs considerable freedom from it. Deviance and conformity are seen as opposite sides of a two-sided coin; and if deviance is defined as patterns of behavior that are unacceptable and negatively sanctioned in society (formally or informally or both) then we are confronted with the apparent contradiction that neither the rejection of deviance nor the acceptance of conformity is satisfactory to a modern society. There is another option: it is nonconformity, innovation, iconoclasm—what André Gide referred to as the activities of people who shake their fists at humanity. They shake their fists, not their bayonets: they act rather with ideas, no matter how unpopular—especially when unpopular.

If we live in what some have conceptualized as a great prison—a prison that is culture or society or some interweaving of the two—then we can think of ourselves as entwined in a network of social control made up of rules that we believe in so thoroughly, that we love so fully, that we have become oblivious to the prison created by them. The cage in which we move is too big, the arrangements apparently so logical (a characteristic of the system to which we have been acculturated: namely, that the arrangements always appear to be so logical), and our movements so frequently voluntary that (if I may be permitted to stretch the metaphor) we have become unaware of the fact that it is a cage at all. We become aware of this cage only when we are brought back to some shocking realities, which is what Nanette Davis and Bo Anderson have done for us in this book.

Of course, we did not need Davis and Anderson to tell us that there is another form of social control in addition to the external one that imposes itself through the state, its military and police force and its monopoly on legitimate violence (perhaps we should call it a legitimate monopoly on violence, for this would lead to the question of whether violence itself is ever legitimate). We see men and women in blue with whistles, billyclubs, guns, badges and handcuffs that are symbols and agents of a society that controls by force rather than by the persuasion of intellect and an appeal to ethics and morality, righteousness and justice. And how can it be otherwise, when it takes so little sophistication to see that righteousness and justice are not distributed evenly in society?

Behind the men and women in blue, we see a system of juvenile detention centers, hospitals in which people are involuntarily confined, jails, prisons and other walled and locked enclosures with neither entrance nor exit at the will of the inmate. Many Americans believe that there are too few dangerous people in these ultimate bastions of social control, and at the same time they deride societies thousands of miles away whose inmate populations are as high as ours in proportion to the total population, give or take a few tens of thousands, which is no mind-boggling task when we are talking in frighteningly high figures.

It can be said that social control has two faces. Like Janus, one is pleasant to contemplate, except when we are the victim, while the other is less so. Like Janus, the latter is unpleasant or tragic; but unlike Janus, the first face is not comic, except in the Pagliaccian sense in which the comic artfully conceals the tears behind the mask, until they rush in such volume that even the supposedly insoluble circus paint is washed away. These are the two faces of formal and informal social control. In the first we are all controlled, and in the second we are all controllers. We are part of countless conspiracies, which are not the less effective because we self-righteously and indignantly deny their existence. In fact, on contemplation, it is difficult to imagine how we could organize our lives without efforts to control others. We are part of a society that controls through the creation of outcasts, upon whom we heap ridicule, despite the fact that as ladies and gentlemen (and professors, too) we like to feel that we have never joined in this game, except against those terrible people who deserve it. We judge others and are constantly engaged in formulating such judgments. Nor is this less true when we abjure the term judgmental, claiming that this does not apply to ourselves—although in making this claim we become judgmental of those we see as judgmental. Compare all this to the other type of social control, which comes forth without fineries that would mask its purpose or make its mode of operation difficult to recognize. This is the control of the police-man and the prison guard, or even the teacher or employer. Keep in line or take the consequences, whether they are dismissal and poverty, a failing grade and suspension or confinement behind walls. The message is firm, but not without ambiguity, for society is so often benefited precisely by those who step out of line.

Davis and Anderson have shown us in an analysis that I find disturbing (in the very positive sense of this word) that social con-trol operates through many forms. Some of them are even more assiduous and insidious than the subtle inculcation of culture into the helpless infant as both victim and beneficiary. In their own way, physicians are agents of control in society as much as are police officers. The former use different but not less lethal instruments. Our bodies are controlled, as are our lives, by the medical profes-sion, by social workers and psychologists, by tradition and tradi-tionalists. Nevertheless, a few people have not only called for alter-natives, but have also paved the way for them. They have experi-mented, walked lonely paths and sought to recapture control over mind and body for themselves, or for a cohort with which they could identify and to which they belonged. It is not the abandon-ment of social control that feminist health centers and voluntary associations of alcoholics and other deviants are seeking; in fact, it may even be the strengthening of it. Above all, it is the restructur-ing of it, the necessary shift from control that is outside of oneself to control within one's own power—or at least a power in which each of us can participate.

In this intellectually exciting and erudite work, Davis and Ander-son have brought together several of the major themes that have informed social thought in the past few decades: structuralism, phenomenology and democratic Marxism. They have infused a newly synthesized outlook with their own commitments to feminism, to self-help, and to the causes of all who are oppressed and despised. Not satisfied with drawing on Foucault, Rothman and others among our contemporary thinkers, they have used the work of these and others as points of departure, so that they could weave their own intricate design.

This is a book that makes a distinct contribution to the understanding of social control, and hence of society itself. The careful reader will often be puzzled and will frequently be engaged in a quarrel with the authors, but these are the hallmarks of an important work in a very important area of human thought.

Edward Sagarin
City University of New York

PREFACE

This is a book about institutional social control and the oppressions and reactions it creates. The theme, social control, is both old and new. As one of the dominant ideas of the founding fathers of sociology, the term social control usually evoked a negative set of images about problems of urban order, mass society and unassimilated proletariats that included loss of faith in institutions, collective unrest and widespread anomie. The focus was on the *effects* of change: institutions and persons dislocated by often invisible social forces that only time and gradual, preferably noninterventionist accommodation could correct. The overall image is the inevitability of social disorder as a temporary state; hence, the fatalistic embrace of the *status quo*.

The contemporary meaning of social control, mainly articulated by European critical theorists, and used in this book, is opposed to the older, inherently conservative one. Here the spotlight is on master institutions, primarily the state, that use and abuse power without the general consent of the populace. And because modern states practice a covert style of governing, citizens invariably have little or no influence in shaping their collective destinies. Conflict and oppression are embedded in the social structure, not because social change invariably makes it so, but because the technologically advanced state denies genuine and effective power sharing, and the enhanced level of knowledge such sharing creates. Accordingly, our economic and political knowledge is retrograde. The closed mind has given way to the closed society, and we are threatened with becoming captives of our collectively created prison.

Such a loss of significant information implies that our public and private lives are increasingly separated. The way in which society functions appears more and more mythlike, at the same time that politicians are calling for simple, anachronistic, if not stupid, solutions to our complex economic and social ills. For example, when President Reagan proposes that Americans must produce more business entrepreneurs to offset the widespread malaise, he apparently sees a "spirit" that is "still there, ready to blaze into life" if only we "stimulate our economy, increase productivity, and put America back to work" (quoted in Rothschild, 1981:12). This *laissez-faire* ideology perpetuates the economic problems, inasmuch as it ignores the role of business and state interests in systematically using fiscal policies that undermine full employment and encourage inflation (e.g., import policy). The real problems of gross economic mismanagement and inequality here and abroad in advanced capitalistic states, and the systematic exploitation of third world people are never mentioned. When times are tough, the governing elite can always blame citizen apathy and lack of patriotism. This suffices to close off debate and restricts public criticism to trivialities or technicalities.

The pervasive public silences about the real problems of social order are one reason we wrote this book. We believe social control is a necessary human invention; it is the style and focus of control that we take issue with.

Another reason we offer this study in institutional control is to emphasize certain paradoxes in modern life: Social control can be just as oppressive when there is not enough—when it is ambivalent, overly permissive or indifferent—as when it plays the bully or the cop. Bureaucracies are as essential for distributing human services for large populations as they are inadequate in humanizing their products. And self-help, the people-to-people solution to massive bureaucratic indifference, contains its own potential tyrannies.

The third motive for our writing this book is to use our critical perspective to communicate some survival skills for our bureaucratic age. The message is simple: look behind the myths to uncover the underlying reality, despite the fact that the methods for accomplishing this unmasking remain inchoate, still to be systematized. Thus, while this book addresses some institutional causes of our collective discontent, and proposes initial policy steps for altering the growing deterioration, it is hoped that others will follow who will demonstrate more specifically what can be done.

Plan of the Book

The Book has four parts. The Introduction has three chapters: the first presents the social and historical context for the book; the second chapter discusses the main concepts; and the third chapter offers a model of social control used in subsequent chapters.

The social control and deviance field is dominated by sociologists in the symbolic interactionist tradition (the "Chicago School") whose representative works include Erving Goffman's *Asylums* (1961) and Howard Becker's *Outsiders* (1962). We have felt it necessary to point out the serious limitations of this perspective in understanding social control in large-scale societies. Another theoretical source is the work of sociologically-oriented lawyers, represented by such studies as Herbert L. Packer's *The Limits of the Criminal Sanction* (1968) and the essays of Johannes Andenaes (1974). These writings are closer to the traditional sociological treatment of social control than to the approach of the symbolic interactionists. In short, we have outlined our own theory of social control and a procedure for the modeling of the structurally significant features of the three types of social-control organizations described in this chapter. We will make use of these concepts and this modeling procedure throughout the remainder of the book.

Chapters 4, 5, and 6 form Part II, which is devoted to total institutions. Chapter 4, a theoretical analysis of total institutions, traces the origins of the use of confinement and the social processes inside custodial organizations. Chapter 5 deals with the special case of asylums for the mentally ill, and chapter 6 considers women prisoners as "symbolic offenders," an example of inept state control over powerless populations.

Part III examines the bureaucratic modes of control, loosely called community-based care. Chapter 7 focuses on the state and institutions that have been set up as substitutes for the traditional custodial institutions (e.g., mental health centers replacing the asylum). Total institutions have been attacked by a number of critics, such sociologists as Goffman or members of political-pressure groups concerned with mental health or the civil rights of prisoners and patients. Budgetary considerations on the part of legislators and administrators also play a role in "deinstitutionalizing" problematic groups. This moves the treatment and control from confining institutions into the community. Chapters 8 and 9 analyze welfare and community mental health, respectively, and deal at some length with the control structures that result from this shift.

The section on self-help and mutual-help organizations in Part IV extends through chapters 10, 11, and 12. Here we analyze commitment organizations that spring out of social movements. Such groups have arisen largely independently of the mainstream political and administrative attempts to deal with deviance or problematic groups. Their bias is antiprofessional in that they mobilize the energies, talents, and resources of afflicted persons to develop and run rehabilitation organizations. Representative examples are Alcoholics Anonymous, alternative health "collectives" that are often outcroppings of the women's movement, and poor people's movements. As we describe at some length, these organizations differ in significant ways from both custodial and community-care systems. Here we study more intensively the cases of Alcoholics Anonymous and feminist health organizations to learn about the strengths and limitations of this mode of social control.

The final chapter, 13, examines the implications for policy of the sociological discussions. The three modes of social control treated throughout this book—total institutions, community systems, and self-help networks—all have severe limitations. Even if society makes use of all three for varying control tasks, a good deal of "slippage" will occur. Hence we address ourselves to two main questions. What should reasonable policies of social control consist of? How should they be formulated? In the interest of value neutrality, many sociologists have shied away from issues of policy formation and the contents of policy. We reject this academic timidity. We believe that it is possible to develop policy guidelines that are informed by sociological analysis and that take into account both the issues of values in policy formation and the politics of implementation. At the same time we hope that wiser minds will go beyond our tentative conclusions and offer a more complete set of working blueprints for applied policy.

In concluding this project, we begin to realize how deeply indebted we are to persons who have sponsored, supported and aided us. Stanford University provided Nanette Davis with a NIMH Fellowship in Sociology through the Research Training Program on Organizations and Mental Health in 1978-1979, where she enjoyed enormously supportive colleagueship with Professors Joseph Berger, W. Richard Scott and John Meyer. At Michigan State University, Jay Artis not only encouraged and supported Bo Anderson in undertaking the enterprise, but also made possible our joint work by arranging a one-year teaching appointment for Davis during the fall and winter of 1979-1980. Marilyn Lovell, executive secretary par excellence, and her able staff kept the typewriters humming during that year. At Western Washington University, where Davis spent two writing terms, Patty Houtchens generously provided typing services beyond the call of duty. Thanks to a leave of absence for Davis from Portland State University, this perambulating style of teaching, research and writing was possible.

In addition we are grateful to a number of colleagues for suggestions, discussion of theoretical points and empirical studies: Frederick B. Waisanen, William A. Faunce, Peter K. Manning and Peter Lyman at Michigan State University; David Willer, University of Kansas; and Manuel L. Carlos, University of California at Santa Barbara. The Willer-Anderson new theory book, *Networks, Exchange and Coercion* (1981), written about the same time as this book, helped greatly in formulating our own structural approach.

Our three editors deserve special, if not extraordinary, mention. Clarice Stasz, Sonoma State University, whose seminal article, "Images of Man and Social Control," (published under Stoll) initially stimulated our thinking, worked through our various versions of these chapters with patience, skill and insight. Edward Sagarin, who contributed the Foreword, gave us extensive and excellent feedback after reviewing the manuscript for his own write-up. Both Stasz and Sagarin are masters of English writing, so we feel very fortunate to have had their help (even if we did not take all of their suggestions). James Davis, Nanette's husband, took time from his own demanding administrative duties to critique, edit, comment and wisely suggest. What he prefers to call "only my layman's insights" into the control process have contributed greatly to our attempts to think through these slippery, invariably paradoxical, problems of contemporary social control.

Nanette J. Davis
Portland State University

Bo Anderson
Michigan State University

I. Introduction

Chapter 1
The Center Cannot Hold:
An Overview of Social Control

Things fall apart; the center cannot hold,
Mere anarchy is loosed upon the world,
The blood-dimmed tide is loosed, and everywhere
The ceremony of innocence is drowned;
The best lack all conviction, while the worst
Are full of passionate intensity.

William Butler Yeats, *The Second Coming* (1921)

Law and order as an essential sign of the times appears to be breaking down in American society. Institutions established to guarantee stability are perceived as not working or collapsing altogether. Political parties and candidates in their search for "campaign packages" have raised the law and order issue as a priority item. Party professionals believe this slogan has wide appeal. Mass media give daily coverage to reports of muggings, riots, murders, and personal injuries. "Long hot summers" of unrest are predicted in cities unless the federal government provides funding for jobs for the urban unemployed. Alcoholism and drug addiction are rampant and spreading even among groups once considered uncontaminated. In all major cities people report fear about going out at night. And some of the leading law and order advocates (e.g., cabinet members and members of Congress) who were found to have broken the law themselves have gone to jail as a result of the Watergate and Abscam scandals. Opinion polls report a drastic decline in the faith of citizens that society's institutions are doing their proper job. The public has demanded that politicans "do something," but there is widespread scepticism about politician's ability or even desire to make the needed changes. It is out of this moral turmoil that the concept of social control becomes a central concern for citizens and social scientists.

3

Origins of the Social Control Concept

This book does not contain proposals for new "fix-it" policies. Rather, our task is to try to understand the often contradictory issues. We can begin by raising some pertinent questions: What are some reasons why some formerly very effective restraints on people's behavior are not working, or working less well than before? What different, sometimes underutilized and frequently misused organizational resources are available for society's control of deviance and disorder? How do they work? How well can they be expected to work? What accounts for the widespread perception that the control institutions are decaying or being overwhelmed?

Still other questions are: Why are some problematic behaviors and practices subjected to controls or control attempts while others are tolerated or even relished? Why, for example, is homosexuality frowned upon and why are homosexuals harrassed, whereas violence is institutionalized in sports and the media? Why is alcohol tolerated and popularized, while marijuana is declared illegal?

What do the control practices of a society tell us about its structures, troubles and values? What changes occurred in American society within a decade to transform abortion from a crime into a right? To shift to an earlier epoch, what were the institutional concerns and fears that lay behind the European institution of the 15th- and 16th-century Inquisition that caused it to track down heretics or to organize witch trials and the extermination of women labeled as deviants? These inquiries tell us that we need to see social control practices in light of a larger social and historical context.

Questions of a normative import also belong in the context of social control. For instance, how do we establish a rational social control policy? Which behaviors and practices need to be societally controlled, and which ones should be left completely to individual preference? What sanctions serve best to discourage those practices that are deemed to be harmful? How are those who have made them into habits "rehabilitated."

In the social sciences questions such as these have traditionally beloned to the study of *social control*. This area has been of central concern in the sociology discipline from the time it emerged as a field of study in the latter half of the nineteenth century. In the present era Neomarxists and structuralists have reopened many of the old questions, offering new and often innovative theoretical angles.

Sociologically oriented lawyers have made important contributions. "Legal realists" in the United States and Scandinavia, for example, have studied law enforcement practices and functions.[1] Moral philosophers, especially those working within the fields of jurisprudence, have analyzed the logic of concepts and arguments used by legal and political institutions to offer new approaches to discourses about social controls (for example, Hart, 1968, Dworkins, 1977). Major contributions to the study of social control have been made and continue to be made by social historians.

As sociologists, we approach the study of social control from the perspectives of social organization and the sociology of knowledge. The sociologists' concern with social control is rooted both in intellectual tradition and in social and cultural conditions. The latter two are, we believe, the most important. In social philosophy there has been a vigorous debate among English thinkers from the 17th century to our time about how any social order and cooperation could arise if, as was postulated, each individual naturally pursued a course of self-interest. First discussed by Thomas Hobbes in *Leviathan,* this fundamental question has been the absorbing preoccupation of the authors of some of the most influential "systems" of social thought, including Durkheim, Alfred Schutz and Talcott Parsons.[2]

Social conditions of nineteenth-century societies in Western Europe and the Unites States lent great urgency to social control as a topic for social theory. The population of industrial countries grew dramatically, and as a result of improved transportation, were more mobile than before. Large cities contained burgeoning working classes that vastly outnumbered those who owned the property or had claims to higher status. From the point of view of the higher classes, the workers were "the dangerous classes," uprooted, without social discipline and sometimes invested with revolutionary sentiment. Serious riots and attempts at social revolution occurred in several major industrial countries. The most dramatic events were the armed uprisings in Paris in 1848 and 1871 (the Paris Commune) and the disturbances in eastern cities in the United States in the early 1860's as a reaction to the Civil War draft. Similar to today, crime, intoxication, vagrancy and normlessness were seen to be growing beyond control. In the United States a major problem was how the millions of new immigrants were to be absorbed and Americanized.

Under these conditions, agendas for political and administrative action (from the point of view of those who ruled) gave high priority to the following concerns: (a) How were the interests of private property, which formed the basis of capitalist accumulation, to be safeguarded against the demands of the propertyless? (b) How could reform legislation gradually and safely incorporate the masses into society and pacify them with acceptable concessions? (c) How could public order and safety be maintained? (d) How were the energies of the masses to be mobilized for the benefit both of capital accumulation and the imperial power of the state?

Vast networks of institutions and social practices gradually developed in different countries in response to these societal issues. The police, the traditional prison, the asylum, compulsory school attendance, social work and the modern factory discipline were all developed in reaction to these concerns. Donzelot (1979) has shown in detail how in France the state gradually organized a system of social control of and through the family to deal with juvenile offenses, vagrancy and insubordination among the young. In the political arena suffrage was gradually extended, but in the big cities whose masses particularly were feared to be volatile—Paris, London and New York—citizens were prevented from the full self-government enjoyed by other municipalities (Yearley, 1973).

The emergence of sociology as an organized field of study occurred against the background of these institutional and administrative developments.[3] Durkheim's teaching and research at France's most distinguished institution of higher learning, the Sorbonne, examined the sources of morality and social solidarity. In his view, modern order was problematic and required a neutral agent that could ride herd over conflict. At that time, the French state was in the throes of having its liberal and secular republican policies threatened both by the right (Monarchists, Bonapartists) and the socialist left.[4] Among Durkheim's students were those who would become France's notables. Their loyalties had to be captured in competition with the rival ideologies. Durkheimian sociology was to become a guiding belief for society's guardians. We do not intend any "institutional reductionism" here, nor are we arguing that Durkheim's sociology was "nothing but" an administrative ideology. Durkheim and his disciples were more sympathetic to socialism than to the establishment, and their proposed plans for developing social control were similar to syndicalism or "guild socialism."[5]

No sociological system equal in intellectual scope and institutional prestige to that of Durkheim's ever developed in England. Still, English thinkers were not backward in constructing significant social control doctrines, such as those developed by John Austin's jurisprudence, based upon common law, and by utilitarian social philosophers.[6] Important empirical investigations into the conditions of the London working classes were carried out by Charles Booth and his collaborators. This work was continued by Sidney and Beatrice Webb and other Fabian socialists, (see Webb, 1979, and Cole, 1961). The Fabians never developed an abstract sociological system. Their contributions through social reform and investigations into concrete social and administrative issues helped generate proposals for reform measures. Like the Durkheimians, the Fabian socialists believed in reform through a political and administrative elite of civil servants (see MacKenzie, 1977).

Founders of modern American sociology, for example, Ross, Cooley and Park, did not work in a centralized university system teaching a highly selected, future political administrative elite. They were deeply concerned with the *community*, which became their dominant metaphor for social life. This led them to a very broad conception of social control.[7] Theorists whose primary orientation is to administration and legislation tend to restrict social control to those official practices and institutions specifically set up to control, for instance courts, the police and the asylum. But if the *community* is the basic metaphor, then social control also becomes a byproduct of a variety of social institutional activities. For example, any primary group may serve to enforce compliance with some subset of society's norms. E. A. Ross (1901) distinguished between the narrow and the broad uses of the social control concept. The broad meaning of the concept continues to be employed in American sociology, for example in Richard LaPiere's (1954) influential textbook. For the purposes of our study, we use social control mostly in its narrower sense of deliberate action for control. We do not want the term to be synonymous with social action in general. Also, since our focus is *organizational*, the narrower sense is the natural one. The distinction should not be pressed very far, however. It is often not easy to decide what is "intentional," since institutions more often than not hide their intentions behind ideological screens. Indeed, if our analytical frame of reference stresses *unmasking* and the study of the signs by which ideological fronts are created by institutions, then the distinction becomes hard to maintain. In this book we study institutions as ideological and power systems.

Ideology is a major topic in the study of social control conducted by Marxists, critical theorists, and structuralists. By "structuralism" we mean the school of sociologists, originating in France, who have made discourses, rhetorics and other linguistic and sign practices a main focus of study. Levi-Strauss, Foucault, and Barthes are some leading proponents. "Critical theory" originates in Germany, in the "Frankfurt School."[8] Both structuralists and critical theorists are indebted to Marx and akin to the branch of Western Neomarxism that has been influenced by the Italian theorist Antonio Gramsci.[9]

The study of ideologies, their structures and the institutions and practices that sustain them became a major focus for the sociology of social control at a time when the discipline attempted to comprehend the various cultural movements challenging the prevailing conceptions of sexuality, gender and ethnicity. Sociologists had for a long time believed theoretically that our conceptions of sex roles and ethnicity are matters of convention and culture. But it was only after women and minority groups created social movements that demanded equality, legalized abortion and so on that the accepted norms became suspect. Scholars began to inquire how social arrangements were *made* to look natural and transparent while masking inequality and oppressions. Concepts such as *hegemony* (see Williams, 1977) and *discourse* (Foucault, 1972; Deleuze, 1972) were developed to study the mechanisms by which ways of thinking, perceiving and speaking about social phenomena become established as being "in the nature of things," how these systems come to be viewed as legitimate and why they go unchallenged for long periods, even in part (but rarely in total) by those whom they suppress. Much of the scholarly work on social control at the present time is heavily influenced by this perspective. For example, the historical work of E.P. Thompson (1975) and others provides detailed insights into how a ruling class, by controlling key legal institutions, maintained its hegemony on law and how it was subsequently challenged. Foucault's work on mental illness and the punishment of criminals has become a major influence for sociologists and historians studying social control (Foucault, 1973, 1978).

It is still not possible today to present a complete sociological theory of social control, as LaPiere attempted in 1954. Important contributions are being made from different theoretical perspectives; yet it is not possible to integrate them into a simple formulation.[10] The nature of social control has shifted, making some of the older approaches less relevant. Theory has not caught up with social change. Organizations play an increasing role while the local community has been diminished. These organizations range from complex Weberian bureaucracies to less bureaucratic and more ideological professional systems. The state has created some of the organizations and influences the actions of most of them through its legislative and funding activities. Organizations and the state control in the name of legitimating ideologies, for instance, medicine, efficiency or education. At the same time these ideologies are being resisted by "alternative" social movements. A combination of the *organizational* and *sociology-of-knowledge* perspectives therefore seems imperative to study modern social controls.

The development of sociology as a discipline from the utopian socialists Saint-Simon and Fourier, to Talcott Parsons and Herbert Simon has paralleled, influenced and been influenced by the changes in society's techniques of social control. A future history of sociology should see the field as part of a larger discourse of administrative, political and professional practices that have shaped the ways that the various populations of industrial societies are controlled. We use "discourse" in the sense of Foucault (1972):

> Discursive practices are not purely and simply ways of producing discourse. They are embedded in technical processes in institutions, in patterns for general behavior, in forms for transmission, and diffusion, and in pedagogical forms which, at once, impose and maintain them.

Organization theory is largely a rationalization—in both the Freudian and Weberian senses—of the practices of management and administration. But branches of the subfield—for instance, the human relations school—have also influenced these practices. Methods of sociological inquiry, such as the use of documents or the interview, developed by such pioneers as Charles Booth in England and Thomas and Znaniecki in America, became incorporated into the techniques of professional social work (see, for instance, the influential, model-setting book by Mary Richmond, 1917). Small-group studies in sociology have influenced the development of group therapies as important tools of the mental health professions, and also of the various human growth movements. Organizations, casework, therapy and encounter groups are, from our point of view, techniques of social control. The rhetoric that surrounds them—efficiency, help and melioration, treatment, and human liberation, respectively—are of course different. Control techniques are not all legitimated in the same manner; their targets have to be constituted differently. This is not an attempt to debunk these various techniques: societies have to be ordered, social controls are necessary. Some contemporary techniques and rhetorics (for example, those that center around environmental causation and treatment) are probably more benign than those that stress degeneracy and incarceration.

This book is written from an eclectic point of view and owes a good deal to Foucault and critical theory, as well as to pragmatic considerations about different types of control organizations in modern society: the asylum, the community-care organizations and the movements and organizations for self-help and mutual aid. We see these organizations as discourses, that also contain ideologies, myths and beliefs about human behavior. Some of these ideologies are drawn from variants of sociology, psychology or psychiatry. Others derive from beliefs about proper and productive principles of organizational work and practices, documentation and bodies of evidence that support these principles. Thus, the organizational analyses of structures and functions have to be complemented with analyses of ideologies.

The Deviance Problem: Social Construction and Sentiment

Deviance, crime and disorder pervade modern society. Yet most persons in America and other modern societies probably live in environments that are relatively safe. What accounts, then, for the perception that crime and deviance have gotten worse or even out of hand? This perception represents, it seems, more than a realistic appreciation of the dangers that undoubtedly exist. The historical evidence seems to indicate that the present era in many ways is less violent and crime-ridden, is safer and publicly more peaceful than past periods in the histories of the same societies in North America and Western Europe. Accounts of Dickens's London, as well as for nineteenth-century Paris and New York, speak of riots, public drunkenness and areas into which one could not venture without armed escort. A hundred years ago, many rural areas in the same countries were policed inadequately or not at all. Banditry was not uncommon, and travel was hazardous. Protests involving ethnic minorities, assassination of prominent political figures and urban riots all occurred in the nineteenth century.

And yet, as we reiterate, there exist sincere and widely held beliefs that things have gotten worse. What accounts for the preoccupation with and fear of deviance and disorder?

There are some immediate answers to the question. In many localities, violence, visible deviance and disorder are less contained than before; they spill into areas that used to be safe or "straight." The media instantly make known such dramatic "newsworthy" events to mass audiences. That the day passed without incident in many neighborhoods of varying compositions is not newsworthy.

Richard Sennett (1970, 1974) argues that people in contemporary society live their lives less publicly and seek more bounded and homogeneous environments than at earlier times. The home and the suburb shelter people from the multitudes of varied encounters and bewildering stimuli that are found in public places and at the crossroads, for instance, of large cities. If Sennet is right—and we find many of his detailed arguments plausible—then it becomes a little easier to understand how people come to believe that there is increasing deviance and disorder. People who are accustomed to a homogeneous environment will readily notice the deviant, and will define whatever is different as deviant. Therefore, as privatization spreads, more deviance will be recognized. Add to this that some of the deviant acts have become more visible than before (for example homosexual activity and drug use are symbolically and emotionally loaded).

Drawing on the classical sociological tradition, we can point to a deeper source for the preoccupation with deviance and disorder. Some of the classical writers, for example, Burckhardt, Nietzsche and Max Weber, spoke in various ways about *disenchantment* and spreading nihilism. Institutions have lost much of their legitimacy, orginally based on traditional beliefs, and are viewed as incompetent and malfunctioning (from the various perspectives used to evaluate the current scene). At the same time, for reasons that will be dealt with later in this book, we have come to rely more on the same institutions and demand that they solve more social problems than before. A malaise has set in, a feeling that "nothing works." Yet politics and public administration are on the average probably more honest and competently managed now than in the past, though there are always enough instances of corruption and questionable performances to sustain the malaise.

A few years ago Lillian Breslow Rubin published an insightful book entitled *Worlds of Pain* (1976) that dealt with working-class family life. The author pictures a world of dejection, disillusionment, resentment and bewilderment. Life is not what it was promised to be. Yet, in a modest way, these families seemed well off. Still the malaise remained. The many statements quoted by Rubin reveal some of the anatomy of the common sentiments that most of us share. There are the poorly defined expectations about what adult life is supposed to be like. There are the myths of romantic love and its modern sequel, liberation through sexual fulfillment and thence through the simultaneous conjugal orgasm, which culminates later in the inevitable disappointments and the feelings of failure and self-blame.

The process is a self-fulfilling prophecy. Institutions require much sustained work to function even moderately well. A widespread feeling of "what is the use" will inevitably produce institutions that do not work very well. Then the malaise and indifference becomes justified. And the vicious cycle goes on.

Malaise often breeds a taste for authoritarian solutions, as various social theorists have pointed out (for example Fromm, 1941). Let a bureaucracy worry about the social problem and leave *me* alone is a typical reaction. Bureaucracies in modern societies are almost inevitably distant and impersonal. This again nourishes the indifference, the malaise, the powerlessness.

The Societal Pervasiveness and Unease of Social Controls

Modern societies do not feel at ease with their institutionalized social controls. In some areas—for example, abortion, some sexual practices and the use of "soft" drugs like marijuana—social control produces bitter value conflict, generating topics of one-issue movement politics. In other areas, notably the field of criminal justice, there is much consensus that a repertoire of control measures are appropriate, either to rehabilitate offenders or preserve the respect for law and order. There is some evidence that criminal sanctions affect the crime rate. For example, crime went up in Copenhagen and Montreal when the police in those two cities were on strike for substantial periods (Andeneas, 1974). Generally, criminologists argue that the criminal sanction should be selected rationally, in analogy with treatment for diseases. But the empirical evidence available about the crime-preventive effects of the various criminal justice measures cannot be relied upon in sentencing and other decisions because it lacks detailed content, conflicts with other evidence or is hard to interpret. A judge cannot use the data to decide, for instance, whether someone should be sentenced one or two years in jail or get a suspended sentence. To make such decisions rationally, the judge would need prognostic tables similar to the actuarial tables used to set insurance rates.

Social controls vary in acordance with norms, ideologies and strongly felt values. Social control practices of a society say more about its normal institutions than about its offenders. We have included a cross-cultural illustration on variations of imprisonment rates in Table 1:1 to clarify this. The Norwegian criminologist Nils Christie presents the following table concerning the average number of inmates in Nordic prisons:

Table 1:1   Average Number of Inmates in Nordic Prisons

	Absolute Numbers	Per 100,000 Inhabitants
Denmark, 1970	3,458	70
Finland, 1971	4,992	107
Norway, 1972	1,807	46
Sweden, 1971	4,606	57
Iceland, 1973	Not Available	19

(Christie, 1975, vol. 2, p. 309)

The five countries are culturally similar, have been intimaely tied to one another historically and have influenced one another's institutions. It stretches the imagination to believe that the great differences shown in the table reflect the rational reactions of decision-makers in the criminal justice systems to objective conditions. It is unlikely that the differences shown between Norway and Finland, say, reflect objective differences in the severity and prevalance of crime or the prognoses for rehabilitation of offenders or the needed protection of law and order. Differences among countries such as those in the table represent deepseated differences in ideology and unreflected institutional processes. If we go back in history briefly, we notice that there have been major changes in social controls. The reasons for the changes are, however, often obscure. Why, for example, were homosexuality or masturbation regarded as severe deviancies until quite recently? And why are they now regarded as "normal" expressions of sexuality? It is hardly because society has become more enlightened as a result of medical or psychological evidence. If evidence played a major role, we would have decriminalized soft drugs some time ago, and probably instituted tight controls over the sale of alcohol.

In the 1950's one of the authors of this book worked for a summer in the alcohol branch of social services in a city in Sweden. Alcohol was rationed at that time, and even minor episodes of repeated public drunkenness led to a strong societal reaction. The person would be called in, reprimanded and put under obligation to report regularly to a social worker. At present alcohol is not rationed, and the abuse has been decriminalized in Sweden. Not surprisingly, there is a good deal of drinking and drunkenness in public. Chronic alcoholics, even young ones, are often put into early retirement under social security. All the evidence shows that alcohol-induced injuries have increased dramatically. Treatment facilities are inadequate. In effect, society subsidizes the drinking of the alcoholics until their early deaths. It would seem obvious that the current laissez-faire policy makes less sense in the light of evidence and humanitarian values than the earlier repressive one. But it would be a mistake to assume that the present policy represents an unfortunate consequence of a conscious decision by Swedish society to decontrol its citizens and increase the scope of personal choice. As a matter of fact, Sweden spends a great deal of energy on other control matters. It is, for example, against the law for parents to spank their children. Much effort goes into detecting and punishing tax evasion and into combating "underground," no-receipt transactions in services.

One plausible hypothesis about social control is that the main agenda of societies is regimentation and control and that they only decriminalize some behaviors when better bases of regimentations have been developed. The control of sexuality in the nineteenth century was, from this point of view, *not* primarily concerned with sexuality per se, but with regimentation. For this, sexuality provided a convenient focus. Much energy was devoted to organized suppression of "unclean" habits and thinking. Purity crusades, youth work, conduct-of-life literature and medical theories and practices designed to control the dangerous sexuality of youth and women were primary control tools (see Kett, 1977, Chapter 7; and Szasz, 1970; especially chapters 11-13). If sexuality is being decontrolled today, it is because other avenues of regimentation have become available through modern data management. Files accumulated by the state, our banks and credit institutions, unions and large-scale employer organizations keep track of our lives. Permits, credentials and certifications are necessary for a variety of activities. These controls are impersonal but very effective. Sexuality and other personal habits are therefore obsolete as bases for social control. Moral sentiments lag, however, and many people feel uneasy about decontrolling habits that were viewed as evidence of a person's moral worth. The abolition of controls leads many people to perceive a breakdown of standards of law and morality.

Bureaucratic controls make use of the rapidly developing technologies for recording, filming, storing, processing and retrieving of data. "Bugging" files can be kept on us all, and can be combined with cradle-to-grave personal data. A surveillance technology is "in place" that surpasses George Orwell's *1984* nightmares (see Smith, 1980, and Rule, McAdam, Stearns and Uglow, 1980). Constitutional and other legal guarantees have so far prevented the equipment from getting totally "hooked up." But is it not likely that the control machinery will be used by the state in a major national emergency? The impersonal controls of bureaucracies contribute to or reinforce the disenchantment discussed above. They accomplish this by deindividuating humans. Some of the old-fashioned control techniques that assumed individual moral responsibility and the person's struggle for God against sin, and against Evil helped build identities. Deviants were real people. But he or she that is the target of bureaucratic controls is not a moral agent and becomes only an object. One could feel at home with a wrathful God, but not with the databank.

Unlike the old-fashioned control techniques that relied on stigmatizing the deviant, the bureaucratic and medicalized ones are presented as *benign*. They claim to promote social justice, as for example, when the revenue authorities are given access to private information, ostensibly for "higher ends" (e.g., national security). When psychological tests are given to job applicants for the "person's own good," or when a taciturn employee is sent to counseling as a condition for keeping the job, "good" reasons can be piously produced. Self-control wanes in the context of official evaluations.

In our lifetime, the control revolution has shifted from body to mind. Once the body was the focus of the most intense social regulation: sexuality and alcohol control, discussed in chapter 12, are merely examples of the typical forms regulation took. The body was a natural object of intervention. It was visible, it expressed the moral state of its occupant (remember Oscar Wilde's nineteenth-century morbid picture of "Dorian Grey") and it was fairly easily intimidated. The whip, enforced hunger, hanging by the thumbs, the "iron cage," beating with paddles, the "water crib" and other monstrous inventions used in post Civil-War American prisons and asylums (Rothman, 1980: 19-22) kept exernal order. In any event, such external regulation signified internal order. Mind intervention had not yet been discovered or lacked the technology to be effective. In our age, the mind has become the chief object of control. Hence, the extensive use of official secrecy, womb-to-tomb data coverage on all aspects of our personal life and the use of depth psychology to correct wrong thinking or attitudes.

A potentially pervasive control actually serves a reverse set of goals. Instead of confidence in our institutions and leaders, it undermines public faith. Rather than buttressing self-control and community order, it breeds mistrust and lost hopes. And in impersonalizing social regulation in the interests of uniformity, it encourages strong individual reaction against important but constraining norms. We are at the beginning of a new and possibly dangerous epoch of social control; hence, the need to document the past and present societal efforts. This book presents three models of social control: total institutions, community care, and self-help, and shows the evolution of new forms emerging from discontent and the rejection of older ones.

In the next two chapters we treat the concepts and offer a theory of social control. Three large sections follow, each one examining one mode of control and examples of it. The last chapter raises some enduring questions about social policy and offers some politically unorthodox solutions.

CHAPTER 1—NOTES

[1] See, for example, Friedmann (1949), chapters 17, 18, and Packer (1968). The intensive and important Scandinavian discussions can be studied in Aubert (1954), Strömholm (1972), Andenaes (1974), Forslund (1978).

[2] Parson's first major work. *The Structure of Social Action* (1937) focused on Hobbes's problem. See also O'Neil (1972).

[3] Durkheim's sociology has its roots in the utopian socialists Saint-Simon and Fourier. These systems were compulsively concerned with how human populations could be organized into "natural" classes and segments. See Manuel (1956) and Barthes (1976).

[4] See, for instance, Zeldin (1973) for a good acount of modern French history. For Durkheim's place in French society see Lukes (1973).

[5] See E. Durkheim's Preface to the second edition of *Division of Labor*.

[6] For the utilitarians and Austin, see Friedmann (1949), chapters 15, 18.

[7] Comprehensive analyses of the conceptions of deviance and control in the various American schools of sociology are given in Davis (1980).

[8] The Frankfurt School, which evolved in part out of reaction against the specter of totalitarianism in Europe in the 1930's and 1940's, has the warranted reputation of being a Marxist heresy. It is genuinely a critical scholarly tradition that uncovers myths and ideologies, whether they represent the political right or left.

[9] For an introductory orientation in critical theory see Connerton (1976). For the French structuralists see, for example, Jameson (1972). Williams (1977) gives a good account of Gramsci's key concepts.

[10] See Roucek, ed. (1980) for a recent attempt to integrate past and current theoretical directions in social control theory.

[11] For a history of sexuality see Foucault (1978).

Chapter 2
Perspectives and Paradigms

The moral order and the knowledge that sustains it are created by social conventions. If their man-made origins were not hidden, they would be stripped of much of their authority. The conventions themselves are, therefore, not merely tacit but often extremely inaccessible to investigation.

Mary Douglas, *Rules and Meanings*

This chapter sets out the major perspectives of social control and provides a paradigm for identifying key features of regulatory systems. Here we address how social control is constructed, how it is linked to larger institutional structures, how it affects policies and practices, and how it is organized in divergent ways.

In one sense, social control is ubiquitous. It involves every ideology, action and sentiment that restrains and guides human behavior. This totalistic definition, often used by early American sociologists, has little current sociological utility. Therefore, we offer a more limited definition. by *social control* we mean those *policies, practices and institutional arrangements that a society designs in order to deal with groups or social situations that are defined as "problematical," "troublesome" or "deviant."* In most instances, then, we are referring to institutionalized organizations and occupations that are specifically mandated to carry out control tasks: police, psychiatrists, social workers and so forth.

Collective Definitions and the Control Task
What is problematic, troublesome or deviant depends on the collective definitions, beliefs, sentiments and values that are taken for granted and enforced in a society or in a segment of a society. What is problematic in one society or segment of society, say, open homosexual relations in small-town America, may not be problematic in another, for instance, a gay couple sharing a household in San Francisco. And what was problematic at one time may not be in a later period, as when the law recently decriminalized abortion. When conduct or arrangements are defined as a "problem," they are viewed as dangerous to the social order. This means that they

threaten those institutions seen as fundamental to society or that they jeopardize deeply held sentiments, beliefs or values.

A good deal of societal work is always involved in recreating, articulating and demonstrating the collective definitions of a social act as right or wrong. The definition of social control used in this book, therefore, implies that a major issue in the study of social control must be the study of *who* it is in a society that creates and upholds collective definitions of behaviors and situations as problematic, as well as *what* is being done to enforce the prevailing concepts, (see Olson, 1971).

Certainly, some areas of conduct or social arrangements are seen as problematic by most societies requiring sanctioned interventions. Sexuality, for instance, seems rather universally to be subject to control and regulations. The differences among societies and historical periods, though, are much more important than the similarities. The sexuality of children or single women, quite recently problematic in Western societies, is now taken for granted. But death, once familiar and taken for granted as a normal, everyday occurrence, has become surrounded by practices that imply denial, fear and mystification. Consequently, social institutions have developed to keep death out of the sight of most people most of the time. Almost all societies define certain behavior as criminal or delinquent or as symptomatic of mental illness and, therefore, as a social problem. But cultures vary enormously in how these phenomena are specifically defined and remedied. "Hidden" problem areas occasionally emerge into the open and become defined as social problems: recent examples are child and spouse abuse, obesity and environmental pollutions. Once problems become visible, we find that control organizations also emerge: women's centers, Parents Anonymous groups, the Weight Watchers movement, antipollution watchdogs, legislative-action groups, and so on.

Social institutions have a number of features of special significance to social control. Here are some areas of inquiry we consider essential for understanding regulatory orders.

Structure. Structure refers to the social organization of an institution. Thus, education and medicine are institutions; schools and hospitals are their organizational extensions. This analysis entails relationships among various tasks that the institution performs as well as relations among the categories of persons or organizations that carry out such tasks. Questions of structure include: What is the division of labor? In what order are tasks performed? How do status, power and authority relations work, and with what implications for organizations, professions, clients and collaborative or constituent groups? Interdependencies between organizational units are crucial issues. For example, when control organizations that are meant to be interrelated in a single control task adopt divergent ideologies and practices, offenders learn to manipulate the system rather than to come to grips with their negative behavior. Overly complex structures, such as the criminal justice system and the mental health system, that are subjected to such cleavages may recognize failures in coupling between units, but in the interests of other values and demands (e.g., professional careers, politics, civil liberties, inertia), they often succumb to the revolving door or client loss.

Function. The results and accomplishments of institutional activities are termed their functions, regardless of whether these outcomes were intended or simply evolved. A functional analysis of an institutional activity deals with what happens as consequences of the activity. Institutions often perform conflicting functions. For instance, prisons may promote crime control by incarcerating some offenders and deterring others. At the same time, prisons also serve as training camps for future criminal activities.

Environments. Institutions are shaped by environments that include other institutions and that provide a context within which organizations operate. An organization must appraise its environment in terms of the constraints and opportunities that exist for actions to be successful. A school system that wishes to incorporate a mental health unit within its domain must, because of particular ethnic or class problems, first examine the local mental health system as well as national resources that may be available (e.g., special federal funding for Indian mental health). Even when organizations prefer to ignore their environment, they do so at their own risk. For instance, the activities of police departments or mental hospitals are influenced by legal decisions concerning the rights of suspects or patients as well as by media reports about their organization's successes or failures. Fiscal decisions by legislative bodies affect the budgets of hospitals, schools, welfare programs and other public institutions, which determines what activities can be maintained, dropped or altered. Social movements dealing with the rights of minorities, women, the elderly and other disenfranchised groups force changes in many organizations, even where legislative actions and budgets remain static.

Recruitment and Socialization. Institutional activities are shaped by the recruitment and ongoing socialization of personnel and clients. Organizations that serve high-status clients recruit from higher-status professional groups and insure their continuity as high-prestige service systems by access to better budgets and more effective legal and political protection than those that serve low-status clients (Larson, 1977). All these factors help determine the day-to-day operations of its activities and the success of its programs. A typical case of this dual-status structure is the mental health system. Consider how clients enter the system. One pathway leads from criminal justice and welfare and focuses on coercive therapy (although it may be termed "voluntary" because clients must be willing to give signed consent to avoid prison). Therapy sessions are nonindividualistic, sometimes highly ritualistic, and the outcome is often failure; i.e., the client returns to prison or welfare. The second pathway, emanating from schools, families or businesses, conducts middle- and upper-status offenders into private psychiatry and intensive relational programs, teaching persons significant skills for independent living. Rewarded with high levels of success, professionals and clients treat this as a positive, people-regenerating system.

Ideology and Myths. Institutions distinguish themselves as separate entities by ideologies and myths. These are complexes of beliefs, often centered around some central images, verbal phrases, narratives or symbols that serve the institutions in a variety of ways (Barthes, 1975). The beliefs make plausible the activities of participants by inspiring confidence, diverting criticism, and interpreting relevant events as they occur. Thus, police officers may believe that long-haired college students are radicals and "hippies" who avoid hard work, deal in drugs and have their minds bent by their unorthodox life styles. Any legitimate "bust" of a student with long hair serves to confirm this imagery. Conversely, some students believe that police are working-class authoritarians, violence prone, arbitrary, and trigger happy. Shorthand stereotyped verbal phrases often serve to condense beliefs and images. "Cops are pigs," was used frequently by college protesters in the 1960s and even today remains a rallying call among the younger, pot-smoking generation. "Free abortion" or "abortion on demand," means women's absolute right to have total control over their bodies. "The right to life of the fetus" posits the prior importance of the unborn over the woman's voluntary decision to have a child. "Criminals need treatment, not punishment," is a common cry among prison reformers, while "law and order" is the stock phrase of those citizens who fear the increasing lawlessness and lack of protection against urban street criminals.

Social Change. Although we study institutions as though they were static, institutions are subject to multitudinous processes of institutional change. A time perspective is essential to understand an institution's mandate (or to use the vernacular of service organizations, its "mission"), its division of labor within and among organizations, its personnel categories, the clientele, the particular ways work is done, its functions accomplished or attempted, its recruitment patterns and its ideologies and myths. Two major sources of change are *drift* in response to changing institutional environments and *transformations* as a result of deliberate reform. Like persons, institutions can be said to have careers—to go through stages of relative stability, and phases of crisis, self-doubt and disruption (see Hughes, 1972). In the latter part of the twentieth century, almost all social control institutions are going through various crises of confidence. Traditional divisions of labor, status, power and relations of authority are being challenged; new mandates are being added and old ones scrutinized, as excluded groups demand entrance into positions formerly denied to them. Beliefs and myths that used to be unquestioned are being undermined. These changes produce a good deal of disorientation among participants.

As a result of the women's movement, a well-known case, an inevitable dichotomy that fosters disorientation is taking place. From a civil-liberties perspective, the women's movement is long overdue. Yet resistance is pervasive. Persons, families and organizations, struggling with issues of sex inequality and injustices, are often perplexed about the "right" thing to do in many situations, although they do not deny altogether that something is drastically "wrong." Since there are few reliable guideposts for reinstituting balance and order once disruption occurs, contemporary society tends to mythologize and ritualize equality demands (e.g. affirmative action), rather than to confront the hard reality of changing inequality practices.

Social Policy. A recent perspective is the study of the implications for *social policy* of institutional structures and processes. Social policy is the deliberate attempt by societies to shape their long-term futures. During periods of stability, the institutional arrangements and agendas *de facto* determine the social policies of the society. But during periods of sudden change and crisis, new arrangements and agendas may be tried and institutionalized, although some of these new forms may have virtually no impact on shaping future social policy. The students' movement that peaked about a decade ago offers a notable example of institutional pressure for changing patterns of authority, but this movement has had virtually no significant impact on university and college policies. Not only are hierarchies as entrenched as ever, but lower-level faculty and research workers may also have lost ground because of increased administrative prerogatives over this ten-year period.

The systematic study of social control within sociology, jurisprudence and social psychology has resulted in a variety of general policy discussions and statements of conclusions. Like deviance theories, social control theories will inevitably acquire political and ideological overtones. It is, of course, true that both deviance theories and social control theories are used by scholars to explain in disinterested and detached ways why deviance occurs, or why control measures are successful or fail to work (see Gibbs and Erickson 1975). But such theories also become incorporated into the training and practice of professionals (e.g., police officers, social workers, or psychiatrists) who staff the institutions that deal with problematic groups. In this way, social control and deviance theories become part of the belief systems that legitimate and guide the day-to-day practices of these institutions. When the theories serve these functions, they are no longer subjected to the rigorous critical scrutiny of the scholar, but rather to institutional demands for continuity, including routines and maintenance work in an often politicized environment.

This is not to say that institutions are arbitrary or uncritical when they evaluate their performance. Increasingly, institutions engage in rigorous assessments of their activities, as evidenced by the rapidly growing utilization of evaluation research, which attempts to put these activities on a scientific footing. Under economic and political pressure, though, such an enterprise precludes a detached analysis of successes and failures. The scientific premise of suspen-

sion of personal belief and the systematic use of experiment that is
at the heart of the scholar's conception of objectivity are not possible in these action settings. This is because organizations exist to get
things done. A court must render a decision; a legislature must vote
for or against a bill; a social worker or parole agent must decide
what to do with a client. Action must be taken even though evidence is flimsy or dubious.

Theorizing in ideologically charged contexts is methodologically
risky. Pragmatic criteria of truth and evidence are invoked: the
theory works, hence it is true. The trouble with this point of view is
that negative evidence gets explained away or is termed irrelevant.
At the same time, any supportive evidence is readily accepted. For
instance, in mutual-help groups like Alcoholics Anonymous, members are presented with many stories about how rehabilitation has
been possible by faithful adherence to the organization's program
(Cahn, 1970). Cases of failure are also told, but then evidence is
always presented to show that the person had failed to practice the
necessary prescriptions. In many instances, this is undoubtedly the
case. And it is also true that many persons who follow the rules stay
sober. But is clear that AA members, when confronted with failures, are more likely to accept evidence of noncompliance with the
rules than they are apt to critically scrutinize the evidence for compliance with the same rules when told a success story. Generally
speaking, the burden of proof is on the skeptic in ideological contexts. In scientific method, on the other hand, the burden of proof
is always on the proponents of a theory.

Sociologists confronted with a field of study that contains a multi-
plicity of ideologically influenced formulations need to work with a
critical sociology-of-knowledge perspective. For myth and ideology, while often calling attention to important facts and connections, also serve to create stereotyped and narrow perceptions and
reasonings. To understand social control theories, both academic
logic and those theories embedded in institutional practices, distortions and biases must be identified. The sociology-of-knowledge
study of social control theories involves the following interrelated
steps:

1. The fit betwen the institution and theory have to be
   described and examined. Relevant questions are: What kinds of
   institutional structures and practices are justified by the
   theories? What problems in the institution are left unattended

because the theory is silent about them? What are the tensions recognized by those who staff the institution between things predicted and prescribed by the theory and the practical demands of institutional work?

2. The biasing role of the theories, metaphors, beliefs and myths must be studied. In what ways do they screen out uncomfortable information, creating silences around questions and problems that society needs to face rationally and critically? In what ways do they serve to maintain stereotyped views of client groups by arranging the evidence? How do established theories, beliefs and myths impede or distort measures that aim toward institutional reform?

3. In what ways are beliefs, myths and theories about social control related to other salient beliefs, myths and ideological themes in the society? These relationships in a complex society are likely to vary. There will be *congruences* (for instance, between the total institution's ideology and patriarchal dominance in family and kinship); and *reversals* (e.g., countermyths of liberation will spring up in populations subjected to regulating institutions, as when the success of the proabortion movement generates a right-to-life antiabortion movement).

Societal Regulation of Deviance

In order to study the main complexes of control ideologies and organizational practices, we propose a paradigm. This summarizes three prevailing definitions of problematic behavior and control practices, and shows how social regulation intervenes to discourage, protect, enhance or penalize behavior. We distinguish three control modes: (1) custodial control in institutions that are more or less *total*, e.g., prisons, mental hospitals and certain therapeutic communities; (2) community care organizations in which state-funded agencies carry out regulatory activities, including such service groups as family planning organizations, community mental health centers, crisis intervention organizations and others; and (3) self-help and mutual-help organizations that are sponsored and staffed by deviants or deprived groups, including Alcoholics Anonymous, alternative health clinics and shelters for abused women or runaway teenagers.

Kuhn's (1962) notion of paradigm applied to organizational analysis enables us to identify five features of regulatory systems:

(1) theory of society and human behavior; (2) dominant metaphor; (3) methods for regulating social conduct; (4) reflexivity; or the fit between organizational theory and practice; and (5) the "politics" of organizational regulation—as in public appeals and positive and negative reactions among citizen and client groups to policies.

The paradigm approach avoids artificial distinctions between institutions or organizations based on function, type of clientele, social ecology or degree of organizational hierarchy. Instead the approach focuses on *common* structural features in organizational concepts, diagnoses, treatments and outcomes. For example, mental hospitals, work camps, prisons, and homes for the elderly have distinct spatial and social identities. What they share is a common control mandate that involves institutionalizing relatively powerless social groups whose deviation presents a fundamental threat to cherished values and life styles of dominant groups.

Similarly, "community corrections" diversion programs in the criminal justice system, "community-care" projects for the mentally ill, alcoholic and methadone programs and local welfare agencies distribute significantly different services to different segments of urban populations. These programs are linked, however, by a quasiinstitutional mandate that meets various personal and social needs "from a distance." Those persons with blemished moral records, who are deemed unsuitable for full integration into the community, are kept on the bureaucratic string to be pulled into the total institutions if conduct significantly varies from bureaucratic norms. In both regulatory modes, negative identity-building and dependency tend to freeze the deviant identity, rather than to liberate the person from a morally problematic state.

Self-help networks reveal important variations from bureaucratic approaches for regulating members' conduct. Rejecting formal models of control, such groups as Alcoholics Anonymous, Parents Anonymous and feminist and gay consciousness draw on self-labeled deviants to shape new meanings and practices for social renewal. A transcendent ethic of personal liberation substitutes for the classical sin-punishment model of deviance—guilt, incompetence, deterrence and vengeance. Networks are personal; hierarches are group-ordained, not imposed; and positive identity-building transforms the despised self into a morally renewed self. Unlike the stratified professional-client relationship, self-help groups engage in status leveling or suppression of class and educational differences. This facilitates in-group solidarity, or a "we" conception among members.

Applying the paradigm to the three regulatory systems, Table 2:1 shows systematic variations in organizational features and processing.

By focusing on alternative modes of controlling deviance, we emphasize essential properties of deviance as (1) politically constructed reality, (2) shaped and given expression by social policies aimed to reduce or eliminate it, (3) mediated by organizations and groups, and (4) surviving in opposition to the contradictory rules and standards of governing and administrative elites and professional experts.

As we stress in Chaper 13, social policy values are an essential element in thinking about social control and in proposing remedies for social problems that will ameliorate human misery. This book uses critical theory not as a debunking exercise, but rather to decipher general social tendencies that erode and destroy freedom of choice and collective participation in dominant institutions. We reject authoritarianism, expressed in omnibus state strategies to control deviance, regardless of whether such absolutism derives from the political left or political right.

There are no final and orderly solutions to the dilemmas and contradictions of advanced industrial societies. But as we argue in the last chapter, policy guidelines can be developed that are consistent with humanistic values and societal survival.

Table 2:1 Alternative Regulatory Models: Total Institution, Community Care and Self-Help Network

Organizational Features	Custodial Institutions	Community Care	Self- and Mutual-Help
Theory of Society	Highly structured stratification and normative order two-class system: controllers and controlled; conspiracy theory of social order; rigid classification system; class and status authority; punitive theory of correction of moral failures	Social structure lacks coherence; conflicting hierarchies (e.g., government bodies, citizen groups, clients, partisans); structural options articulate, but limited to formal bureaucratic directives; moral anomalies tacitly rejected.	Ideology and commitment as basis of social structure; moral order sustained by "true believer" posture and moral authority of the "saved"; sense of formal organization; underlying organizational principle bonds members; rejection of pluralistic order; recognition of moral anomalies, but suppressed in favor of unconditional acceptance of organizational "program"; consistent classification system; differences resolved by organizational "fission."
Theory of Human Behavior	Mechanistic view of persons; distrust of out-groups; rejection and denial of moral diversity; two-logic moral order: persons as good or bad; deviance as antisocial or pathological; deviants as nonhuman or "animals" that lack standard claims to legal rights and obligations.	Contradictory classification system; asymmetrical relations; mechanistic and individualistic view of self tempered by "transference," or client identification with professional or agency; human "goodness" confined to persons with education and status; middle class work ethic identifies "winners" from "losers"; Client noncoping requires resocialization, typically by masked coercive techniques.	Symmetrical relations; organic conception of humans; group dependence; rejection of class and status differences; often status reversal; virtue achieved through submission and mortification; sponsor system fosters group identification.
Dominant Metaphor	Law and Order.	Rehabilitation, adjustment.	Revitalization, liberation, ego development, solidarity and bonding.

Reflexivity	Good fit between punitive theory and practice; relatively low intellectualization among gatekeepers regarding theory and practice.	Poor fit between theory and practice; highly intellectualized theory; incoherent and conflicting practice; institutional maintenance in jeopardy as programs shift focus and form, depending on support and funding.	Good fit between theory and practice; "performative" or praxis criterion for theory (Does it work?): self-consciousness among partisans regarding practice or "program"; low intellectualization regarding theory.
Politics	Appeals to highly threatening nature of incarcerated groups; negative reactions among public to institutionalized persons; exclusion justified on deterrence grounds.	Appeals to inclusion of deviant groups ("community-care" approaches) that remain unconvincing and resisted by elites and citizenry. Virtual isolation of the needy reduces their visibility; bureaucratic accountability limited to "numbers game" and fiscal responsibility.	Partisan appeals to alternative consciousness; negative social reaction from dominant groups; occasional alliances between self-labeled deviants on specific issues (e.g., feminists, gays and blacks support affirmative action in employment).
Representative Type of Organizations	Prisons, mental hospitals, alcoholic wards, homes for the aged, schools for the blind.	Halfway houses, welfare agencies, methadone programs, mental health out-patient clinics.	Alcoholics Anonymous, Parents Anonymous, Black Muslims, feminists, "gay" groups.
Methods of Control			
Diagnosis	Deviance as pathological; "patient" requires isolation to prevent spread of disease.	Deviance as inadequate socialization; "correctable" through official intervention.	Deviance as "wrong" living; revitalize self through radical change in identity and ideology.
Treatment	Coercive medical model; surgery, drugs, behavioral modification; negative-identity building.	Modified medical model; out-patient care; impersonal bureaucratic programs; negative-identity building.	Acceptance of movement "program"; self-labeling as deviant ("I am an alcoholic"); positive-identity building.
Prognosis	Frozen deviant identity adaptation to total institution implies maladaptation to outside world.	Sporadic deviant career; shift to total institutions depends on official discretion.	Successful outcomes for committed persons; failure cases muted, ignored or denied.

Chapter 3
Modeling the Structure of Social Control

> But society is not only something attracting the sentiments and activities of individuals with unequal force. It is also a power controlling them. There is a relation between the way this regulative action is performed and the social suicide rate.
>
> Emile Durkheim, *Suicide*

This chapter develops a structuralist theory of deviance and social control. Specifically, we discuss the three basic types of social control—total institutions, community care and commitment organizations—and what they mean in terms of sociological analysis. We begin by defining the structuralist viewpoint in sociology, and contend that it implies a holistic way of looking at deviance, social control and social policy. Next, we introduce a typology of social control systems.

There are two fundamental ways of controlling people's social behavior: one controls them morally by having them *internalize* certain norms, the other controls them externally through positive and negative *sanctions*. Control systems vary with respect to the emphases they place on moral and external controls. A second basic consideration is the range of behavior that a control system attempts to regulate. By combining the emphases placed on moral and external controls, on the one hand, and the degree of pervasiveness of the attempted regulations, on the other, we develop a useful typology of control systems. We illustrate the typology using cases from historical and sociological studies. In the last section of the chapter we develop a couple of hypotheses about social control that build on the typology.

Structuralism

Since Durkheim's study of suicide, we recognize that social regulation has dual phases that present both objective and subjective realities. From the structuralist perspective these two varieties include structuralism "on the ground" and structuralism "in the head." The structures on the ground are the historically given

30

social relations that order how persons interact and are able to interact with one another in the social situations that commonly occur. The contents and functions of these relations possess an overwhelming historical force—the individual is born into them, socialized to them and can negotiate and influence them, if at all, only in very minor ways. Much of sociological theory has been concerned with the workings of these social relations: classical theorists Karl Marx, Emile Durkheim, Max Weber, Robert E. Park and Talcott Parsons, the great founders of sociological analysis, all make this their central concern in long series of investigations. The argument that unites these very diverse theorists is that it is the *structures,* the ordered arrangements of basic and diverse social relations, which are taken for granted as part of the *natural* order of things. These set the narrow limits for social behavior that will occur regardless of the good or bad intentions, wishes and aspirations of the various groups or individuals involved in the relationships. In contemporary analyses of social problems, this perspective is still a minority position. Our culture is still deeply committed to legal and moral reasoning in terms of individual choice and responsibility. This stresses individual motivations, sustaining a variety of therapeutic regimes and other social control organizations that treat the isolated individual. This book builds on the classical structuralist tradition.

The structures in the head are the shared categories in terms of which members of a society conceive of and reason about social issues. In Power/Knowledge (1980), Foucault, the French structuralist, uses the term *discourse* to help us grasp the mental and ideological activities of a society or an entire epoch in the life of a society. The discourse of a society or social group is a complex of categories: ways of speaking, habits of perceiving and rules about what aspects of phenomena must be emphasized and spoken about. It also includes prohibitions, that is, rules about what must *not* be dealt with in open speech, and also societal *institutions,* for instance, schools, academies, churches and mass media that indoctrinate members to see and speak in given ways and that create, maintain and deny legitimacy (Foucault, 1972). Members of societies, by and large, take the discourses for granted as the natural, inevitable ways of speaking, seeing and thinking.

Foucault and other structuralists argue that the reigning legal and moral conception of the autonomous individual who personally shapes his or her destiny on the social scene is a grand illusion. It is created by the discourse of our particular historical epoch, which is dominated by capitalism, modernity and an ethic of possessive individualism. Building on Foucault and other structuralists, we shall in this book pay special attention to how deviance and social problems come to be defined and acted upon within the institutional discourses.

Sociology and Social Problems

Social-problems analysis, once viewed as a main task of sociology, has long languished. Problems like suicide, crime, urban conflict and change, class struggle and revolution, and intergroup tensions were not seen as separate problems by the classical thinkers in sociology. Marx, Durkheim, Weber, Park and Simmel attempted to demonstrate how given problematic situations in society serve as windows through which we catch glimpses of basic processes in society. The classical thinkers treated social problems—for example, unemployment, suicide and crime—as *significant signs* of fundamental, but normal, social processes.

Scientific sociology, developing its own theoretical and methodological claims, gradually split off from its all too vulgar ancestor social problems, leaving that field to a motley collection of *ad hoc* formulations. None of these have been successful in organizing the field. American social-problems theories have long consisted of loose, amorphous, many-faceted sets of concerns with no clear lines of demarcation between testable theory and speculation, hypothesis and evaluation data, and ideology and research design. No tightly knit groups spearheaded the competing orientations, and no specific research programs have thought-out, systematically pursued and gradually cumulative research developments. It is true that attempts have been made in labeling theory and other variants of symbolic interactionist sociology to develop systematic research on social problems. For reasons stated in the last section of this chapter, we believe these efforts to be inadequate. The resulting micro-perspective, a small-groups concern, cannot provide the comprehensive analysis that is needed.

Putting the study of social control, deviance, and social problems back on sociology's central agenda enriches both sociology and social policy. Sociologists will have to modify their habits of thinking and research enormously. In important ways the existing theory and methodologies fail to illuminate social problems.

1. Social problems by definition depend conceptually on values and ideology. The analysis of a social problem must elucidate relevant ideological themes in terms of their original formation and transformation. Problems emerge as a distinct set of meanings, but these are often dramatically transformed over time. They have one identity at one time period and get absorbed into different definitions and institutional processes in a later period, reemerging with still different forms at another time period. For instance, abortion, racial discrimination and poverty take on distinct and multiple meanings as we follow their histories in post-World War II America.

2. Social problems are obviously independent of any group's subjective definitions of situations and values. For the sociological analyst, it makes sense to argue that although social arrangements like racial discrimination, poverty and sexism may in some period appear to be *normal* features of the social structure and hence unproblematic, they are nevertheless festering sores on the social body, even though no one in an influential position has so defined them. However, policy making presupposes that the issue becomes *defined* as problematical in the context of existing values and social categories. Values, shared cognitions and beliefs constitute an ideology. An important aspect of the emergence of a social issue as a problem is that it represents a *shift* in the discourse of the society.

3. For any identifiable social problem, a host of different conceptions, definitions, action plans, conflict parties, resolutions and solutions of the problem exist. These are determined by the varying social placements of the participants. Thus, for example, prostitution is an entirely different reality depending on whether the perspective taken is that of the police, social workers, social reformers, courts, pimps, conventional parents or the "working girls" themselves. To claim that *one* single reality of prostitution exists, and that one can apply a standard methodology to find it, is likely to do violence to the complex, multifaceted realities and meanings that are involved.

The failure to take account of the variations in realities and meanings among individual persons or groups often leads to policies that aggravate the problem. For instance a law-and-order policy, when implemented against prostitution, will make the women increasingly dependent on pimps, and work at cross-purposes with attempts at rehabilitation and training.

For the sociologist, constructing a social problem entails a threefold activity: (1) studying the various perspectives taken by the different participants (group or persons), (2) understanding how the perspectives lead to actions, and (3) modeling how the actions *combine* to form the structure of the social problem. Hardcore social problems, for instance, street prostitution and some kinds of alcoholism, are formed in part by collective definitions. This is one reason why they are hard to treat. Routine treatments neglect the collective, systematic problem by focusing on the isolated deviant, the prostitute or drinker. This leads to blaming the victim, which is not only morally reprehensible, but also inefficient if our aim is to develop well-grounded policy proposals.

A Typology of Social Control Systems

In chapter 2 we described three different forms of social control that are found in modern societies: the custodial, the community-care and the self-help systems. We shall now attempt to get a fuller understanding of how social control operates by describing the three forms in terms of some basic sociological concepts. Each type will be found to have variants. The typology gives us six ideal or "model" types of social control, and also suggests some hypotheses about changes in social control in modern society.

The models are somewhat idealized, since ongoing control systems are usually mixtures of the different models we describe. Nevertheless, in empirical systems one of the theoretical models tends to dominate over less significant arrangements that correspond to other models. Sometimes a model is a product of social reform that remains of secondary importance because it has to adapt to the dominant model (see, for instance, Riska and Buffenbarger, 1980). In adapting to the dominant structure it comes to closely resemble it in significant ways. For example, nursing homes remain asylums or total institutions, regardless of their claims as community-care facilities.

Persons comply with norms, either because they believe the norms to be *right* or *legitimate*, or because they *fear* the negative sanctions that result from noncompliance and *desire* the positive ones that come with compliance. The first reason for compliance is usually called *internalization*, and the second we shall call *external*

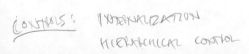

control. From a theoretical point of view, this distinction primarily concerns the *source* of the positive or negative sanctions. A person who has internalized a norm sanctions *himself or herself* positively or negatively for compliance or noncompliance. In external control, on the other hand, compliance is achieved because of sanctions that are seen to come from outside superiors, God or the community. When control is external, it can be more or less *hierarchical;* i.e., there is social distance between controller and controlled.

All social control systems rely on both internalization and hierarchical control. But it is fruitful to classify them with respect to the differing emphases they put on each of the two modes of control. Prisons, for instance, rely predominantly on external, strongly hierarchical control, whereas small communities and voluntary organizations rely on members' commitments to norms and values (although a moral, rather than positionally legitimated, hierarchy often exists). Organizations exist that emphasize *both* internalization and external control. Militant religious orders (for instance, the Jesuits in Counter-Reformation times), military elite groups (the Prussian general staff, parts of the Nazi SS corps) and underground resistance groups are examples of organizations that stress *both* external hierarchy and internalization.

PERVASIVENESS

Social control systems vary a good deal in *pervasiveness,* that is, with respect to how much of persons' lives they attempt to regulate (Etzioni, 1961). Modern business organizations are *low* in pervasiveness; they demand compliance with the rules that apply to the work situation, but do not attempt to regulate what the employees do in their free time—whom they marry, what their religion is or how they furnish their homes. Organizations that are high in pervasiveness, for instance, religious orders, fundamentalist churches and totalitarian political movements, attempt to regulate in considerable detail *all* the important spheres of their members' lives. Most universities and colleges formerly acted *in loco parentis* and were much more pervasive in their controls than they are today (Hofstadter, 1963). Traditional business enterprises, often located in company towns, exercised more pervasive controls over employees than modern corporations.

We shall now make use of the two criteria or characteristics to develop a six-fold classification of social control systems. We give examples of each type, and discuss how conformity with social norms is achieved.

Table 3:1 A Classsification of Social Control Systems

Mode of Control	High Pervasiveness	Low Pervasiveness
Externalized Control	I Asylums, Prisons, Fundamentalist Schools	II Bureaucracies, Businesses
Internalized Norms and Values	III Transformative Community Groups e.g., Alcoholics Anonymous, Synanon, Feminist Health Collectives	IV Specific Self-Help Groups, Weight Watchers, Parents' Anonymous
Externalized Control and Internalized Norms and Values	V Traditional Families and Kin Groups; Militant Religious and Military Orders	VI Professions (Law, Medicine, Social Work)

Let us now discuss these six types in order.

I. Asylums and penitentiaries are typical examples of the high-pervasive, external-control system type. Those at the top of the hierarchy have a total monopoly on both the positive and negative sanctions, and their actions are subject to few effective rules. The inmates are kept in line through negative sanctions and also by making them compete for the few available positive rewards and resources. Whether the inmates internalize any norms or not is unimportant from the point of view of officials or those on top of the hierarchy. There are well formulated rules for every sphere of behavior the inmates encounter, and they "only" have to conform and obey. The *Gulags* and other prison camp systems of totalitarian regimes have perfected this mode of control (see, for instance, Solzhenitsyn, 1978; Kogan, 1960). Conformity is in this case defined in terms of acceptable behavior routines; the controlled are expected not to venture outside these boundaries. The authorities deal with each inmate separately, and any attempts by inmates to form coalitions are strongly suppressed.

II. The nonpervasive, exernally controlled hierarchy is a well-studied control type. It is dealt with at length in texts on formal organizations (for instance, Crozier, 1953; and Perrow, 1978). The system *only* demands compliance with those norms that are relevant to *specific* work performances. The importance of this type of organization for the broader issues of social control is in a sense a negative one. If it is becoming the dominant form of social organization as is often argued, and if pervasive structures like family and kin groups and small communities are becoming less important, then social control is becoming fragmented, limited to task-related specifics and disconnected from everyday life. Bureaucratic organizations may have depended for a long time on values of workmanship, unquestioning loyalty, docility and honesty that were acquired in traditional pervasive structures—old-fashioned families and communities that are now being systematically weakened.

III. Some traditional, highly cohesive communities fall within the transformative community groups that depend upon internalized norms and values. For example, the historian Michael Zuckerman (1970) described small New England communities in the early part of the Colonial era. Such communities were highly egalitarian, but regulated the members' behavior in detail. Harmony, that is, the absence of difference, was a primary value. Transgressors were subjected to community censure, ostracism or expulsion. The public confrontation of deviants was the commonly used means of control and often led to confessions of guilt and repentance (see Zuckerman, 1970, especially chapter II).

Many movements of social and moral reform have attempted to model themselves on the example of the traditional community. In 19th-century industrial America, many small communities were founded by people seeking refuge from social upheavals and, in their view, the corrupt new ways of life. The Shakers, the Oneida Experiment and the Owenites of New Harmony were examples of such moral and religious utopian experiments (see Nordhoff, 1875, 1966, ed., for an early classic description; and Kanter, 1972, for a recent comparative sociological study). In the twentieth century, Alcoholics Anonymous is an example of a redemptive, transformative movement that shares some features with the utopian experiments. These movements have currency today. Contemporary political transformations that have occurred after revolutions have developed control practices identical to those used in the Puritan and utopian communities (see for instance, Lindbloom,

1977, chapter 4). The emphasis is on moral, communitarian confrontation and guidance that is said to lead to complete transformation of persons' life ways. The attainment of salvation, whether it is the recovery from alcoholism or the building of socialism, are viewed as requiring conversions, dramatic breaks with the past. Methodical, step-by-step procedures prescribe how the transformation is to come about. The Puritan and the Maoist programs show a good deal of resemblance to the twelve steps of Alcoholics Anonymous (discussed in chapter 11).

The transformative accomplishments of this type of organization are its major source of strength. Many persons who have gone through the conversion of their beliefs, values and life ways in such programs as Alcoholics Anonymous emerge as zealous, highly motivated, often self-righteous, but selfless AA activists.

Yet compared to the hierarchical organizations, the self-help systems are structurally weak. Leadership depends entirely on the individual's moral standing, and on rewards given out by persons of doubtful or shaky legitimacy. By contrast, if a hierarchical organization, for instance, an army unit or a government agency, goes through a period of defeat, uncertainty about its goals or the means of achieving them, the organization's chain of command remains ordered. It is usually clear who has the right to give orders and who has to follow them. Leadership is based on hierarchical position, and leaders need not embody the norms and values of the failed organization any more than other members.

IV. The specific self-help system is, in reality, a muted form of type III. Persons get help with specific problems they are having, for instance, obesity or child abuse, but no major transformation of their beliefs, values and life ways occurs. The moral zeal that one finds, for instance, in Synanon or feminist health collectives appears to be lacking, and the organizations have a high turnover of members.

V. The traditional family and kin group and religious or military organizations use both internalization and hierarchical control. This may be the most effective type of social control devised in human societies. For instance, monasteries regulate and sanction all the behavior of members. The Rule of St. Benedict, which became the model for all Western monastic orders, sets out in explicit detail how much food and drink the brothers are to have, when they get up in the morning, how they are to sleep or comport themselves during meals and even the details of their clothing. The abbott and other superiors are to be promptly obeyed (see *The Rule of St. Benedict,* Meisel and del Mastro, 1975).

In many organizations of this type, members may not belong to any other group or organization. If this rule is violated, explusion is irrevocable and entails the loss of all social identity. High discipline and single-minded, fanatical commitment to the organization's goals are common. In modern times Hitler's SS elite corps was an almost pure case of this type of organization. Unquestioning obedience to superiors was demanded, the prospect of social mobility was visible and ideological indoctrination was total. From the historical records it has become clear that the SS did not kill millions of Jews and other "undesirable" people because they "merely followed orders." They exterminated because they saw the elimination of Jews, Gypsies and Slavs as a duty and a calling (Rhodes, 1980). The SS believed completely in Hitler's ideology. The Deathhead Division, recruited among concentration camp guards, was (according to professional German officers who despised what it stood for) one of the bravest fighting units on the Russian front in World War II and also a highly efficient executor of the Nazi program of subjugation and extermination of civilians. Missionary religious orders and underground revolutionary political parties or resistance groups, imbued with radically different and, for us, more acceptable values and goals, have exhibited similar disciplined devotion, courage and fanaticism.

VI. Most of us have some direct experience with the professional type of social control structure. Members of professional groups, for instance, doctors and other medical workers, lawyers, scientists, teachers and police officers, are regulated (at least when on their jobs) both by internalized norms and values and by superiors' actual and potential sanctions. Their jobs form only a part of their lives, and the norms and values that pertain to the jobs do not combine into anything approaching the total ideology or world view that members of the type-V system possesses. Members of professions have more than one social world. Unlike the member of a highly pervasive organization, they have to balance a variety of commitments and trade off professional rewards or encumbrances against those that they gain from being parents, spouses, sports enthusiasts, church members and so on. Thus, both in terms of ideology or world view and role performances, the professional leads a fragmented life. To be sure, there is much competence and devotion to craft and duty among modern professionals, but most professionals do not possess the sense of an overriding calling that members of the totalitarian type-V organizations have.

Social Control Hypotheses

The three social control forms introduced in chapter 2 can be described in basic sociological terms. The custodial type is hierarchical and highly pervasive and relies primarily on external controls. The community-care form is specialized, i.e., not pervasive and only moderately hierarchical in its relations to clients, and it possesses few positive or negative sanctions for controlling them. Internalization is desired, but since the clients have limited contacts with the organization and the sanctions are limited, this is hard to accomplish. Self-help organizations rely mostly on internalization, and the most successful ones are more pervasive than community-service organizations. The latter, however, have in some cases developed halfway houses that are highly pervasive, almost total institutions (e.g. Synanon).

Modern communities—families, kin groups and organizations—are less pervasive in their efforts to regulate members' behavior than their traditional counterparts and predecessors. Developing ideas about civil liberties, legal and moral conceptions of privacy, the rights of children and young people to their own "life styles" (for instance, the right to obtain contraceptives without parental consent), the separation between the place of work and residence and the refusal of schools and universities to act *in loco parentis* are all symptoms of the trend away from pervasive regulations. The lessening of pervasiveness has led to a weakening of social control in industrial society. But in order to state more precisely what we mean by this hypothesis, we must first briefly separate ourselves from certain popular ideas that we do *not* support or incorporate into our argument.

We are not saying that people who live in urban industrial settings are contactless, isolated, alienated or deindividuated persons. The mass society thesis, as this idea has come to be called, is not an accurate sociological description of modern American conditions and has been amply and searchingly criticized (for instance, see Claude Fischer, 1972, 1975). Studies show that urban and industrial people are embedded in social networks (see for instance,

Wellman, 1979; Young and Wilmott, 1957; Laumann, 1973). The urban networks do not, however, form *tightly knit* communities, but rather, tend to exhibit low *density;* many of the individuals who form the network of a given person do not, in turn, have direct contacts with one another. The links between persons in the urban networks are often weak or specialized. One contacts different persons depending on what need or activity one has in mind. In weak-linked, low-density networks there is no reason why anyone should care much about how a given person performs in his or her transactions with other persons. The reason for this is entirely *structural:* in a network of high density where most links are strong, one is likely to know and have direct ties to most persons affected by the misbehavior of a member of one's network (see Granovetter, 1973, for an extensive discussion of this point). In a dense network any transaction therefore becomes one's concern. Network relations are thus likely to become pervasive. This is the basis for group confrontations, shunning and other forms of community social control. In a weakly connected network, on the other hand, there are few reasons why we should care about anyone else's relationships to others.

We are, of course, not denying that norms and values are to some extent internalized even in weak networks. Nor are we saying that members fail to sanction or censure members for compliance or noncompliance with important norms, for instance, norms of fairness, honesty, reciprocity, helpfulness. Yet, since the networks are often of low density, there is not likely to occur much organized community control of deviants. Also, the visibility of deviance is low. If a norm has been violated in one network transaction, the person's other network contacts often remain unaware of it, and the transgression and rupture of one network tie may have no effect on other ties. The upshot is that social control gets to be fragmentary, limited in scope and ineffective.

Our guiding hypothesis can now be formulated as follows: *As the pervasiveness of social organization declines, most persons will spend their lives in social structures of low density in which the network ties are weak and specialized. In such structures much deviance is invisible or defined as no one's concern; sanctions for compliant or noncompliant behavior often do not happen at all or are limited in scope.*

This hypothesis will be elaborated and qualified in later chapters of this book. We intend it to capture some basic consequences for social control in the social evolution of the organization and value system of the modern liberal, industrial and bureaucratic state. Social control is weakening because small communities become suburbs or "bedroom" communities, because corporations no longer recruit their labor force from company towns, because young people, convicts, the mentally ill, and elderly, are recognized to have civil rights and hence cannot be dispatched into total institutions without their consent, because organizations and procedures are set up to protect these rights, because schools and colleges are expanding in size and have to cease to operate *in loco parentis* and so on. We think that most of these changes are positive, but they still weaken social control. And even if we were to lament the passing of the tightly knit, small community, or the paternal employer or college, which we are not, we must argue as sociologists that the process is irreversible. Any useful thinking about the future of social control policies has to begin with this recognition.

Pervasiveness, Control and Socialization

Some socialization, including the internalization of norms, occurs in all groups and organizations, but pervasiveness is a determinant of what kind of socialization can be accomplished. Bureaucratic organizations, stressing norms of technical efficiency, will concern themselves with a small part of the employee's personality and behavior. As long as the employee learns to deploy the skills and conform to the rules that pertain to his or her work and develops a minimal commitment to the organization as a whole or at least to the segment of it where the job is located, it matters little to superiors and fellow workers what the remainder of the person's life is like. Pervasive organizations, on the other hand, are concerned with the member "as a whole" and stress loyalty over technical competence. In Talcott Parson's terms, bureaucratic systems encourage and reward affective neutrality toward tasks and focus the employee's or client's attention on a small number of very specifically defined jobs (see, for instance, Parsons, 1951, 1954). Pervasive groups or organizations, on the other hand, stress and reward *diffuse* and *affective* orientations to roles and role incumbents (Parsons, 1951). Social norms that are task- and situation-specific are obviously norms learned in bureaucracies and other low-pervasive organizations. But *many* important rules, for instance, loyalty, reciprocity, altruism, honesty, and the caring and responsibility for others, are not and cannot be task- and situation-specific. Their enactment cannot be routinized or become part of any technical rule book. They are best learned in pervasive systems.

In the previous section we argued that the decline of pervasiveness weakens social control in society. If the present argument is correct, then a related guiding hypothesis follows: *The decline of pervasiveness leaves much socialization undone.* Some sociologists (Strömholm, 1972; Habermas, 1975) have argued that modern bureaucratic, nonpervasive societies have benefited from vanishing modes of socialization that stem from older forms of communities, families, and other pervasive organizations. These are now being rapidly dismantled, often in the name of the right to privacy, due process or other values.

There are some signs, however, that communitarian forms of social life are reappearing in new forms, although with a limited scope of control. It is almost as if they were created in reaction to the reigning fragmentation. The 19th-century utopian movements tried to reconstruct the traditional community. Later, labor unions, religious revivals, youth movements, communes and temperance organizations provided part-time, pervasive havens in a heartless world. Some of the communitarian agitation of the two recent decades echoes the movements of the nineteenth century. Much of this recurring communitarianism is nostalgia. But new forms of viable social life may evolve from the experiences with communes and other alternative organizations. Recent emphases on urban neighborhood building may represent progressive developments (see, for instance, S.M. Miller and others, 1980). And older organizations, for instance, the Chicago Area Program, contain much organizational experience that should be salvaged (see Sorrentino, 1977, for a history of this project). The discussion of these topics will be resumed in chapters 10, 11, and 12.

Symbolic Interactionism: The Inadequacy of a Micro-Perspective

We believe that it is necessary to study deviance and social control from a macro-sociological perspective. The failure and inconsistencies of control are rooted in the contradictions of those major political, ideological and economic social processes that shape the social structures that we live in. By contrast, the treatments of social control that dominate contemporary American sociology ignore the larger social structure in order to focus on interactions in smaller units, such as neighborhoods (Suttles, 1968; Whyte, 1955; Gans, 1962 are good examples), small-group settings (Emerson, 1970) or more abstractly conceived "encounters" between social actors in culturally stereotyped roles (The works of Erving Goffman, 1959, 1967, 1971, are excellent examples.) In these writings we gain much insight into how behavior in social situations becomes "normalized," that is, brought into line with largely implicit norms and definitions. The relationships of competition and boundary maintenance among ethnic and other subcultures, so much in evidence on the American urban scene, are spelled out and documented.

However, in concentrating on how individuals manage their social roles, on how they go about creating and maintaining various legitimate or deviant identities and on their constructions of shared images and beliefs about social reality, symbolic interactionists ignore the "iron cage" of social structure. This keeps the subcultures in their place and stratifies the actors in terms of prestige, income and, above all, power, The decisions that shape those social processes in communities that Gans, Suttles and others so interestingly and movingly write about are made in outside political offices or in federal and state bureaucracies, most often for reasons that are unrelated to the needs of the local communities.

Most symbolic interactionists are committed to participant observation as their main research method. This is not merely a practical methodological commitment, but also a metaphysical one. It reflects the view that only by sharing the lives of the group studied and learning to see it from the insiders' point of view can the sociologist provide a comprehensive, concrete account. The working style will necessarily limit the sociologist to small segments of the society. But in identifying the sociological explanation of social behavior with the accounts collectively constructed by those involved in the action, symbolic interactionists remain parochial. In accounting for their actions, participants are limited to what they know or think they know. In addition, they often resort to stock accounts or clever, verbal games in order to cover bewilderment, lack of information, and their resentment against outside forces that are seen to control much of their lives. Participants' accounts are often interesting data, but should not be confused with sociological analysis.

Symbolic interactionism typically studies groups that occupy "niches" in the social structure that are far removed from the centers of power and authority. These niches are often inhabited by people who are looked down upon by "respectable" citizens. Symbolic interactionists, by stressing the methodology of participant observation, attempt in their research to learn to see the social world from the point of view of these groups. Implicit in this theory and their writings is the argument that the groups studied are much more like the "respectable" groups than often thought. The debunking point is often made in a subtle, deadpan manner. One may, for instance, argue that the prostitute is much like the doctor in that she attends, for a fee, to the needs of her clients. The doctor's role is used to illuminate metaphorically that of the prostitute. Then the argument is turned around; if the prostitute is like the doctor, then obviously the doctor is also like the prostitute. The reader is now covertly invited to think about how the prostitute's role may be used to explore metaphorically that of the doctor.

It is clear that a good deal is gained by this rhetorical device. Persons with deviant roles are drawn close to us: we learn to see them as fellow humans. Like the doctor, lawyer and professor, they too manage on a day-to-day basis, often under stress and adversity, their relations with colleagues, peers, clients, control agents and superordinates. And like the others, they try to balance their "professional" roles with their "straight" roles as parents, spouses, homeowners and so on. Participant observation makes the sociologist identify with the group that he or she studies. Symbolic interactionist writings are filled with understated, sometimes sneering "between-the-lines" advocacy and with leveling pathos. There is no doubt that symbolic interactionists have helped remove prejudice, condescension and estrangement. They have also taught us much about how people, given their understanding of the situations they are in, go about accomplishing their jobs.

Yet much of symbolic interactionism in the field of social control must be viewed as escapist and irrelevant. Doctors, lawyers and politicians, unlike prostitutes and other victims and underdogs, have power or access to those who do have it. They also have high status that can be converted into power or economic "clout." It would be ironic if the social-leveling commitments experienced by many sociologists combined with an ontology and methodology that rendered inaccessible those realities that shape the conditions of the local group that could benefit from realistic reform policies. A structural perspective avoids this false identification between unlike groups to recognize essential status and power differences. Even more, the structural model proposed here addresses how varying social control regimes fit different social situations.

II. Total Institutions

Chapter 4
Total Institutions:
The Confinement Solution to Social Control

> Reification can be described as an extreme step in the process of objectiva-
> tion, whereby the objectivated world loses its comprehensibility as a human
> enterprise and becomes fixated as a non-human, non-humanizable inert
> facticity. [Humans are] apprehended as its product, and human activity as
> an epiphenomenon non-human processes...the reified world is, by defi-
> nition, a dehumanized world.
>
> Peter L. Berger and Thomas Luckman
> *The Social Construction of Reality*

How is the principle of confinement legitimated in a society
where the dominant ideology is permissive individualism? From all
evidence, total institutions—prisons, boarding schools, asylums,
work farms—are outmoded relics that violate our most cherished
beliefs in due process and personal responsibility. In actuality, they
amplify individual deviance and incur a damage that far outweighs
their avowed people-changing mission. But most dangerous for
the human enterprise is the way in which the total institution
assumes a thing-like, normal and everyday appearance (Berger
and Luckmann, 1967). We shall argue that the peculiar social formation of these institutions enhances their de-human qualities,
making them especially unfit in their existing organizational form
to perform their correcting, caring and socializing functions.

Whether total institutions represent society's last-ditch effort to
separate the socially dangerous for its own protection and survival,
as advocates argue, or whether they are archaic residues of a barbaric control mentality, as the new critics attest, may be at the basis
of significant ideological issues.[1] Neither view offers an adequate
explanation of how the confinement process depicts a prototypical
mode of ordering reality in the modern epoch. Highly differentiated, the total institution is characterized by rigid hierarchy,
caste-like authority relations, and a plethora of externally imposed
rules and roles designed for the "expelled" (Mathieson, 1965)—the
old, sick, poor, young, minority and deviant populations. Confine-

ment provides the ultimate organizational form of social power. Unaccountable in any real sense to either civilians or clients, taxpayers or reformers, total institutions express the traditional bureaucratic form. Their survival in an age of permissiveness testifies to the dominance of an outmoded form of rational-legal authority.

As legally enforced monopolies, total institutions draw their legitimacy from the capitalist institutions they serve. How can we reconcile the persistence of these rigid organizations with the more general "loosening" trends in recent years—flexibility, egalitarianism, leveling, and openness of social life. Placing these structures in their cultural, historical and political context clarifies this contradiction as surface reality only. Involuntary confinement—as process, structure and outcome—is the base line against which all normative control structures operate. Misbehavior, disease, deviance and human miseries—whatever their genetic, physical, psychological or social sources—have their final solution or destiny behind locked doors.

Numbers tell part of the story. By 1975, there was a total of 3,234,069 Americans in four major types of federal and state institutions including mental hospitals, adult correctional facilities, juvenile detention or correctional centers (includes public and private), and nursing homes. Mental institutions actually house the largest number of inmates, annually holding an in-patient population of 1,791,171 (1975). In addition, there are 131 Americans in prison for every 100,000 citizens. And if present trends continue, there will be 380,000 Americans in prison by 1985 (compared with 275,578 in 1975). These figures exclude the local lockup or jail population, which usually accounts for the poorest and least sophisticated offenders. And these structures are costly. For example, the annual expenditure for all state correctional activities (e.g., prisons, jails, juvenile corrections, probation, parole and so on) runs well over two and one half billion dollars and is still rising (*Sourcebook of Criminal Justice Statistics,* 1979; see, also *The World Almanac,* 1979).

I. HISTORICAL BACKGROUND

Origins and Blueprints

One can envisage social life as a series of Chinese boxes, progressively smaller boxes enclosed within larger ones, a systematic metaphor for the levels of control. The largest box is culture, the next, institutions, then organizations and interaction, and finally, the self. This approach stresses both interdependence and autonomy for each system, but emphasizes the more significant role played by larger social forces—culture, institutions, organizations and interactions—over the individual self. While behavior and personality represent distinct elements, they are also subjected to the larger environment within which they are contained. This is not to deny that persons cannot be active agents of culture and institutional formation, only that the self is encapsulated within a social collectivity (see Mary Douglas, 1966).

Prisons, asylums, nursing homes, work camps and formerly the poorhouse, workhouse and orphanage are among those institutionalized organizations whose cultural blueprints for action were set in a premodern epoch.[2] These earlier structures form a "trace," or residue, on more recent structures, irrevocably shaping the inmate by stripping him or her of power, will and responsibility. In this way the system replicates its social product, producing what Marcuse (1968) and members of the Frankfurt School assert is the "one-dimensional man." Private and ultimately powerless, the individual is expected to conform as the well-socialized worker, parent, citizen or the reverse—a useless nonentity fit only to be recycled through institutions. In either case the tracking requires the political economy of confinement. This disciplinary method asserts more rigorously the rules and boundaries of everyday life. Where did the idea of the lock-up come from? And where does it fit into the control scheme of things? The changing form and function of the regulatory order is a logical starting point for clarifying the shift in forms of regulations—from household to institution—induced by urbanism and industrialism and their attendant social ills.

Premodern to Industrial Control Orders

The confinement solution to social problems is a recent one, historically speaking. Prior to the fourteenth century, European social order depended on two key organizations that were largely village based—the household and the church. What the household could not manage—indigent widows, orphans, unemployment, disease, sexual license—was dealt with at the parish level through moral support, an *ad hoc* alms system or banishment. In any event, social order was more thoroughly casual among these smaller populations. Life was on the whole "nasty, brutish and short," to quote Hobbes's famous phrase in *Leviathan*. Exceedingly high mortality, a domineering theology and limited social opportunities conspired to keep community order. Begging and leprosy, twin scourges of the period, symbolized the dreaded evidence of human fate and were used as sources of powerful myths to restrain individual and collective impulses. Crime as a secular concept had not yet developed in this theological order. The invention of various modern deviancies—juvenile delinquency, mental illness, property crime, pornography and others—required different ingredients to give them life. This was an epoch where religious excommunication, community banishment or self-imposed withdrawal into monastery life could consign persons to nonpersonhood (inasmuch as social identity had no relevance outside of the established estates). Social order, while inevitably imperfect, was more secure, because of its solid symbolic basis (see Cohn, 1970; 1975).

By the sixteenth century, Europe could no longer be characterized as an assemblage of villages. Instead, urban development went hand in hand with a number of cataclysmic changes that altered the face of the Continent. This cultural turbulence facilitated the rise of the total institution.

In the first place, the Reformation was a social revolution as well as a religious one. Popular classes rose up against corrupt dogma and clergy, but at the same time against poverty and injustice. Secondly, the undercutting of the artisan class by capitalism, the draining of the countryside of workers for the new factories and the concentration of the poor and unemployed in urban centers diminished and often eliminated parish and kinship structures as institutional buffers for poverty, illness and old age. And thirdly, displaced populations were increasingly drawn not only from the alienated, rootless poor, but also from city women and teenagers (Cohn, 1970). Marginal groups were often instrumental in fomenting crowd violence and terrifying peaceful citizens (N.Z. Davis, 1975). In Poitiers, France, in 1559 and again in 1562, ten- to twelve-year-old Protestant youngsters and older students took the initiative in smashing statues and overturning altars, disturbances repeated in the Netherlands, in Rouen and elsewhere. These violent actions were drawn from a storehouse of current punitive or purificatory traditions. What was also evident in the regular Catholic-Protestant outbreaks that culminated in St. Bartholomew's Massacre in 1572 was the breakdown of religious traditions for ordering daily life and the increase in nonreligious sanctions and techniques to influence social actions.

In France, the diminishing household was obviously no equal for the swelling crowd of unattached and chronically needy *menu peuple,* the "little people." A twofold impulse—humanitarian concern and street safety—initiated the first systematic poor-relief measures. The movement to enclose the poor in disciplinarian "hospitals," led by the pious orders, was carried out enthusiastically by the citizens under the growing belief that the only hedge against the twin scourges—plague and famine—was some form of institutional aid. The entries and deaths at the *Hotel Dieu* in Lyons, France, between 1530 and 1540 show how an institution set up initially for a single purpose—care of the very poor—expanded to accomodate more general social needs—feeding and hospitalizing the working class, particularly unemployed artisans. Since about 30 percent died in hospital each year, it also becomes clear that death itself, once an intimate household function, was relocating into large-scale impersonal settings. Importantly, under a centralized administrative system (e.g., census), welfare reform extended accounting and measuring into an enlarged area of social life. In Lyon, France, for example, foundlings and orphans raised in the *Hotel Dieu* graduated at age seven into the *Aumône Général,* where they were adopted by the rectors. Boys and a few bright girls were taught to read and write, males were apprenticed to craftsmen, and females were dowered for marriage. During economic recessions, the same formerly institutionalized population could tap back into the community largesse for bread and sous, a poor relief program that, despite its mixed motives, was exemplary for its epoch (N. Z. Davis, 1975).

Ushered in by the new humanism of the fifteenth century, the Great Confinement was dominated in the classical age by a wholly different world view: the disciplinary society. What fundamental break in the order of things shifted the discourse from concern over "famished" cities, wherein a centralized administration was brought to bear to better perform its distributive task, to an obsession with order? This rule fixation would lead to the wholesale production in the eighteenth and nineteenth centuries of massive human warehouses throughout Europe, and by the age of Jackson, in America. Where did the faith in rules come from? It is apparent that institution building was merely the sign of a larger social preoccupation—the search for certainty.

On the face of it, the myth was simple: everything that occurs is because of a rule, and for everything that could occur, there should be a rule. But the cultural impulse was far from simple. There were at least four very distinct streams that spilled into the ideological reservoir: the plague, state building, science and factory organization.

"Inspection functions ceaselessly; the gaze is alert everywhere... " Foucault (1977) observes of plague-stricken towns. Control of contagion, first applied to leprosy, was now adapted to the new spectacle of death that swept Europe. Entire towns were segregated. All individuals were under surveillance, their every motion monitored to enhance their visibility, destroy their mobility and eradicate disorder. Whereas the leper colony upheld the image of the pure, undifferentiated community, the arrest of the plague became linked to a highly differentiated power; "a power that multiplied, articulated and subdivided itself" (Foucault, 1977:198). Leprosy was defined by exclusion, the branded deviant cut off from all human contact. Plague victims, though, were marked by their individualization, as each person in every household became transformed into *objects of an all-seeing, omniscient control order.* Foucault interprets this changing control as the first significant step into modernism. Society replaced God and social order was ubiquitous.

The plague may have served as the initial impetus to change: catalogue, classify, coerce and inevitably freeze urban populations into hierarchically imposed status groups. But the massive state-building that occurred during this same period carried its own built-in regulatory imperative. The single center of authority came into its own under the aegis of a highly technologized military. Here the notion of correct training, hinted at in medieval religious tracts by mystics (Meisel and Mastro, 1975), was transmuted by the new economy of power into a more rigorous military organization.

The utilitarian model of a balanced social order, a lawlike regime where individuals were like soldiers—hierarchically distributed, registered and regulated—entailed what Foucault (1977:ch. 3) terms the vision of the "panoptic scheme."

Bentham developed an architectural figure, now so familiar in the maximum prison plan, that had a central tower surrounded by identical cells. Here deviants were for the first time both excluded and differentiated, Foucault (1977:200) says:

> All that is needed, then, is to place a supervisor in a central tower and to shut up in each cell a madman, a patient, a condemned man, a worker or a schoolboy... Visibility becomes a trap.

Since all light converges on the cell, making its inhabitant seen but never able to see, the object of information but never a subject of communication, power became absolute in a sense never before imagined. And what made its spread so pervasive is that Bentham's panoptic scheme was not an isolated idea but a disciplinary mechanism that spread over an ever enlarging surface until it became a unitary model. Foucault (1977) observes:

> The regulations characteristic of the Protestant and pious armies of William of Orange or of Gustavus Adolphus were transformed into regulations for all the armies of Europe; the model colleagues of the Jesuits, or the schools of Batencour or Demia... provided the outlines for the general forms of educational discipline; the ordering of the naval and military hospitals provided the model for the entire reorganization of hospitals in the eighteenth century.

It was to prevent looting, desertion or failure that military training and work disciplines tightened up. Instead, discipline had its own rationale: to increase the utility of the individual for the new economic machine. Requiring high levels of aptitudes and skills, disciplined workers could be readily transferred and adapted from one institutional sector to another: work, knowledge or war. And supervision was the essential component that made order and obedience possible.

Science was not an idle bystander in this general tightening-up process. What Newton had shown as probable—the lawlike organization of nature—became for the utilitarians the axiom for social action. The age was fascinated with mechanics—clocks, for instance, were the emblem of the period. The human body, too, came under scrutiny as an object for observation and intervention. The machine metaphor acted to expose not only the public, visible parts, but the private ones as well. During this same period, de Sade liberated sexuality from its secret shame. Under the impulse of a maniacal obsession with technology, the libertines reduced the body to a mere stimulus-response object (see the Marquis de Sade in Seaver and Wainhouse, 1966). In the nineteenth and twentieth centuries, the institutionalized body as passive, mechanical object would serve as the natural laboratory for scientific experiments— behavior modification, drugs, surgery, electroshock. These treatments would become standard in mental institutions, prisons, boarding schools for delinquent youth, old age homes or wherever the powerless were forcibly congregated. The rise of the primary individual in modern European societies, highly differentiated and self-conscious to an extent unknown in other cultures, has occurred against a background of acute sensory discipline and deprivation.

What is the connection between this old discipline inherited from the Puritans and the militarists and the new, ostensibly liberated one, adapted from science? Both regimes eliminate human will. Indeed, will and responsibility do not figure in the social psychological schemata of the utilitarians and their updated professional and lay counterparts. What the panoptic vision reveals is the capacity of a world society to transform an ethos (Puritanism) into a vastly different economic process. Even more, this ethos is so adept at constructing social reality for members that alternative forms of social power are deemed virtually impossible. This is the hegemony process: politics becomes a hierarchical, unitary process, a mechanization of the most fundamental collective activity (see Habermas, 1973).

The factory system accomplished this end. The penetration of machines into the moral sector of human activity proved devastating (see Friedmann, 1955). From the nineteenth century on, our image of these early processes has been informed by photographic documents of the fatigued faces of female textile workers, child coal miners or men standing in bread lines when the machine fails, and more recently, wire press accounts of feudal labor prectices in the Third World. Machine technology has created an abundance of wealth and power, unlike anything the world has known before. It has also shaped humans in its image. The rhythms of the factory have penetrated western consciousness and shaped our common language and experience. "Human motor," an expression first used in the eighteenth century, treats the body in terms of the laws of the supply, expenditure and functioning of a machine. Encouraging mass-production meant low worker-control, strict output requirements, segmented task, semiautomatic process and exclusion of human personality.

Today the factory image pervades bureaucratic planning and treatment for incarcerated populations. Ironically, while the factory is being phased out as the prototypical organization in corporate state societies, its spirit lingers on. It remains the dominant model of the economic-political order.

Europe led the way in this mechanization process, but North America was not far behind. In fact England and North America show clear divergencies from the Continent in their cultural development, which stymied the full expression of the mechanized service institution in England and temporarily slowed it down in America.

Composition of households, Peter Laslett (1977) demonstrates, may be a critical indicator of social structure. Comparing southern France, the German-speaking lands and Sweden, family households were as likely to be extended or multiple as nuclear, compared with England and Colonial America, where they were almost uniformly nuclear. In parts of France, Germany and Sweden sentiment supported the senior-male, large, multigenerational, kin-enfolding, servant-retainer household. In the preindustrial era, these European families were larger, authoritarian and patriarchal and their households were highly stable. Marriages were fairly early for women, males were older than their wives, female fertility and infant mortality were fairly low (compared with England and America), and there was little movement of people. By contrast, England and Colonial America had a nuclear family tradition in which marriages were late, the wife was older than her husband and children were born of mature women, usually in their late 20's or early 30's. This household composition supported companionate marriage, individual responsibility, and independent control by adults and children.

England had different structural conditions than Europe. The British institution of the servant kept nearly 10 percent of the population on the move and, with high mortality, resulted in the English village having a turnover population of nearly two thirds of all persons within a twelve-year period. Servants in England shifted households frequently, their average stay usually being about one year, and political patriarchalism, codified in the 1630s, appeared to have little impact on regulating their mobility. Service in England was a stage in the life cycle for large numbers of people. "Life-cycle servants," as Laslett (1977) calls this largest single occupational group up to the early 1900s (when they died out as a class), involved over 30 percent of English households over three centuries. Whereas France retained its immigrants, the population in French towns rising steadily during the seventeenth century, in England entire households emigrated, settled and dispersed, along with the movement in and out of servants.

The extraordinary instability of part of the population in the English villages, we may speculate, contributed to a more fluid labor market and high levels of individualism. These factors decreased dependence on the total-service institution and, although not necessarily reducing poverty and its attendant ills, contributed to a more passive underclass. The greater volatility of the French *déclassé*, especially dislocated peasantry and artisans, could be explained by the "steam kettle" theory. Instead of diffusing discontented populations to reduce their collective outbursts, France contained them. The total institutions, initially developed to feed the famished, became warehouses for surplus populations, eventually producing a double movement. Institutions became a sign of power, symbols of the despised regime and the focus for revolutionary activity.

What features in North America constrained the rush toward large-scale institution building until after 1825? Certainly, abundant space was a critical factor, enabling populations to move. So was the youthfulness of the populace, a condition that facilitated large numbers of newly married couples and unattached men to take on the frontier and the Indians rather than remain unemployed in eastern mill towns. Canada and Colonial America shared another tradition that absorbed unattached persons, the boarding and lodging practice. Lodging involved renting part of one's residence, sometimes a room, at other times a bed. Boarding implies lodging as well as the provision of one or more meals for the lodger. For young people who came in search of work from either the rural countryside or from another country to a rapidly growing industrial city where they had no kin, boarding and lodging were highly adaptive devices (Modell and Hareven, 1978:51-68). Providing an inexpensive place to stay, this invention was an important socializing experience for the young, and income and company for couples whose children had been launched. Other evidence on rural American family patterns in the seventeenth century shows the influence of paternalistic authority in stabilizing family life and community. For example, in Massachusetts, land deeds were held by the father until his death, keeping sons in prolonged dependence (Greven, 1978:20-37).

The Rise of the Total Institution in America
  The specter of institutional control hovered in Colonial America. Rothman (1971, 1980) analyses the discovery of the asylum and concludes that America's asylum assumed a unique charactaer. In comparison with the English, and especially the French investment in the asylum, America relied more upon the settlement and poor-relief laws to deal with vagrancy and to support the needy. When these early Colonial legislatures enacted punitive measures to control strangers, as Connecticut did, they required houses of correction primarily for the "rogue vagabond"; afterwards "other lewd, idle, dissolute, profane and disorderly persons, that have no settlement in this colony" (Rothman, 1971:27) were added to the list. Striving to reduce costs and take care of local need, citizens were more likely to merge the various functions into one building, for example, to combine the almshouse and the workhouse, rather than to erect multiple institutions. Church wardens gave greater attention to supporting the poor than to detecting abuses (Rothman, 1971:34).
  In any event, the poor in this era were not invisible. They were next door or possibly boarding in a neighbor's household. The standard almshouse built in the eighteenth century was modeled in the style of an ordinary residence; internally and externally it followed the organization of the family. At first, the sick made up a sizable proportion of the almshouse population. But by the end of the Colonial period, this institution followed the European pattern. It had become a dwelling place for the poor.
  Colonial penal law remained very strict. A wide range of criminal codes provided for fines, whippings, mechanisms of shame like the stocks, pillory and public cage, and banishments and the gallows. Jail served then, as now, as a detention center for those awaiting trial. It was not for those who had already been judged, since the

jail was also constructed along the lines of the household and was not intended for long-term detention. In the older colonies, witch-hunting also played a crucial role in social control, as it clarified the sources and centers of power against potential heretics and other threatening groups (see Erikson, 1966).

The age of prisons moved into institution building in a gigantic way (Allen and Simonson, ch. 3). Three distinct phases occurred commensuraste with different vocabularies of control: penitence, punishment and rehabilitation.

Beginning with the Pennsylvania system at the advent of the nineteenth century, the radically new prison concept of reform through isolation was proposed as the sole reformatory process. This was believed to be a superior corrective to enforced labor, and the design, based on a poor imitation of Bentham's Panopticon, was an octagonal monstrosity comprised of small dark cells for solitary confinement and silence. This harsh system killed more than it cured and was eventually abandoned by the United States (while wholeheartedly adopted by many European countries). Men, women and children, sane and insane, young and old, criminals and victims, all occupied one building.

The Auburn experiment included congregate work in the shops in the daytime, separation of prisoners, lock-step formations, a congregate mess at which the prisoners sat back to back and the use of solitary confinement for rule infraction. Because verbal exchange was believed to be contaminating, conversation was prevented by liberal use of the whip. The story of punishment under the guise of disciplinary penitence is sharply demarcated in a letter from the most vocal advocate of this system.

> The whole establishment, from the gate to the sewer, is a specimen of neatness. The unremitted industry, the entire subordination and subdued feelings of the convicts, has probably no parallel among an equal number of criminals. In their solitary cells they spend the night, with no other book but the Bible, and at sunrise they proceed, in military order, under the eye of the turnkeys, in solid columns, with the lock march, to their workshops; thence, in the same order at the hour of breakfast, to the common hall, where they partake of their wholesome and frugal meal in silence. Not even a whisper is heard; though the silence is such that a whisper might be heard through the whole apartment. The convicts are seated, in single file, at narrow tables, with their backs towards the center, so that there can be interchange of signs. If one has more food than he wants, he raises his left hand; and if another has less, he raises his right hand, and the waiter changes it. When they have done eating, at the ringing of a little bell, of the softest sound, they rise from

the table, form the solid columns, and return, under the eye of the turnkeys, to the workshops. From one end of the shops to the other, it is the testimony of many witnesses, that they have passed more than three hundred convicts without seeing one leave his work, or turn his head to gaze at them. There is the most perfect attention to business from morning till night, interrupted only by the time necessary to dine, and never by the fact that the whole body of prisoners have done their tasks, and the time is now their own, and they can do as they please. At the close of the day, a little before sunset, the work is all laid aside at once, and the convicts return, in military order, to the solitary cells, where they partake of the frugal meal, which they were permitted to take from the kitchen, where it was furnished for them as they returned from the shops. After supper, they can, if they choose, read Scripture undisturbed and then reflect in silence on the errors of their lives. They must not disturb their fellow prisoners by even a whisper (Quoted by Barnes, 1972:136).

Auburn's structural design—inside cells and wings composed of tiers and cell blocks—became the model for most prisons built in the following 150 years. Once they became convinced of the efficacy of these extensive architectural arrangements, early prison builders in America rushed into mass production of huge gothic-style structures. Between 1825 and 1869, thirty-two maximum-security prisons were built, establishing the penitentiary as the primary house of correction (Rothman, 1971).

Today, despite programs in reformatories and individual rooms (not cells), as well as dormitories and less regimentation in minimum-security systems, the monolith prison structure forms the backbone of corrections. These factorylike structures house nearly 300,000 inmates nationwide and reinforce America's deeply entrenched myth about the "convict bogie." A repressive, highly costly, and grossly ineffective system, it is geared to maximize supervision, control and surveillance of the inmate's every move. The history of the prison dramatizes the failures of reform.

> The pragmatic penal leaders in the last half of the nineteenth century began to accept imprisonment as a valid end in itself, rather than a means to reform. This opened prisons up as a dumping ground for America's poor and different masses. Foreign immigrants, blacks, and anyone who did not fit the 'all-American' mold were likely candidates for these remote asylums. The reformers' rhetoric spoke of rehabilitation, but the actions of corrections administrators belied this emphasis. Prisons were built to keep the prisoners in, but also to keep the public out. To justify the imprisonment of such a heterogeneous group of offenders under such rigid control required a theory of uniform treatment and uniform punishment, without regard to individual differences (Allen and Simonsen, 1978:190).

The old prison discipline had a number of components calculated to deny inmates any basic needs. Gill (1970:29-30) outlines the main tenets:

Hard labor—Prison industries or nonproductive punitive labor such as the treadmill and the carrying of canon shot from one end of the prison yard to another. In southern states, the chain gang was a common sight, an unpaid labor force for public works.

Deprivation—Of everything, except the bare essentials of existence. Until the 1930s most prisons even lacked running water and toilets. Bland, unsavory food was typical.

Uniformity—Most prisoners were treated alike, though some were treated worse than others (e.g., frequent punishment, solitary confinement, food deprivation).

Mass Movement—Mass living in cell blocks, mass eating, recreation, even bathing. The loss of individual personality was characteristic; prisoners' faces appear as masks, human animation deadened into dull gray lines of shuffling feet.

Degradation—To complete the loss of identity, prisoners became numbers. Housed in cages, forced to wear "prison stripes," denied civil contact with guards or others, degradation became a way of life. A bizarre form of discipline developed at Auburn was the lockstep formation. Prisoners were required to line up in close formation with their hands on the shoulders or under the arms of the prisoners in front. The line moved rapidly toward its destination as the prisoners shuffled their feet in unison, without lifting them from the ground. Because the steadily moving formation left no room for errors, prisoners who fell out of step could be seriously injured or viciously punished.

Subservience—To rules upon rules upon rules, for their own sake, or the sake of the prison officials. The aim was to *break* the inmates will, eradicate it entirely, so that all discipline could be imposed from outside and from above.

Corporal punishment—Brutality and force prevailed. In Tennessee, the paddle was used, in Colorado the whip, in Florida, the "Sweat Box," etc.

Noncommunication—Silence or solitary confinement was the preferred norm; news of the outside world was limited as were letters, visits, contacts or telephone calls.

Recreation—At first none, later a perfunctory daily hour in the yard with no equipment or inadequate space.

No responsibility—Self-control and choice were totally eliminated as prisoners were relieved of every social, civic, domestic, economic or even personal responsibility for the simplest daily routines.

Isolation—Often 16 hours a day. Psychologically the admonition to "do your own time" implied no social connection with other inmates or guards. This increased the likelihood that the egocentric and dangerous "lone wolves" would assert dominance.

No "fraternization" with the guards—The rule found in many prisons prevented any personal exchange between guards and inmates. This cut off the possibility of developing alternative role models among a conventional group.

Reform by exhortation—Rules specified how the inmates should behave but denied every normal basic need of the human personality. Instead of integration, human dignity and constructive growth, the prison fostered a type of eroded personality: rejection, doubt, guilt, inferiority, inadequacy, diffusion, self-absorption, apathy and despair. "Is it any wonder that men left prison worse than when they entered?" (Gill, 1970:30)

The current rehabilitation phase coincides with the more enlightened conception of corrections adapted from psychological and sociological theories about personality and group life. Employing the same mechanistic conception throughout—diagnosis, classification, uniformity and social isolation—the reformatory suffers from similar problems as the prison. The needs of the institution take precedence over the needs of the individual; treatment programs are inadequate, understaffed and scarce; disciplinary activity is organized around security and provides the dominant motif; and professional staff morale is often low and turnover high. Group therapy is often little more than disguised control devices. Behavior modification, the most popular form of institutional treatment, most recently has come under attack as violating due process.[3]

The treatment ideology that underlies the rehabilitation model is crippled by a fundamental conceptual error. A belief that criminal behavior is simply another manifestation of pathology to be handled by some form of therapeutic activity favors approaching the offender much as one would the mentally ill, the neglected or the underprivileged. The "patient" is informed that he/she is "sick," that treatment will "cure" the "illness," and that dependence upon the wisdom of the "doctor" will correct the problem. Not only does this ignore the ultimate sources of deviance in the social environment—unemployment, alienation, class struggle, powerlessness—but it presumes that the individual is solely responsible for his own "cure." Returning to a poverty-stricken community and resuming the criminalistic life style becomes interpreted as weakness by parole and prison officials. This justifies another round of intervention: surveillance, loss of self-determination and punishment. Rehabilitation concepts that ignore economic and social deprivation are bound to fail. The rehabilitation model, more humanistic on its face than the old prison discipline, betrays a myriad of make-believe states of affairs. It pretends that inmates have rights, rank and good reputations that prison will restore; that prison is the appropriate place to correct antisocial conduct; that only the most serious offenders are in lock-up; that prison programs can provide good health, ability to work, and self-governance; and that failures are the fault of the individual, not the system. With such misconceptions, whether intended or not, is there any doubt why critics of the prison system emphasize its deficiences and failures?[4]

II. CONCEPTUAL FRAMEWORKS AND EXAMPLES

The Politics of Punishment

By the close of the nineteenth century, the "enduring institution" as Rothman (1971) refers to the asylum, had become a place of last resort. Total institutions reverted from their original humanitarian beginnings to become the dumping ground for social undesirables. Because paupers monopolized these places, which were often little more than "legalized cesspools" (Rothman, 1971:292), there was little social incentive to clean them up. Life within, once casual, undisciplined and irregular, had become highly regimented. A total routine prevailed, based on doctrines of separation, obedience and labor, testifying to the nineteenth century concept of a well-ordered society. The military paradigm was augmented with additional ideological supports—the use of biography to establish failure of upbringing. Criminality, insanity, delinquency and deviance were believed to be merely the external trappings that represented something else—the collapse of family and local community control. The total institution's most significant function was to create order in the midst of great uncertainty. But the rationale that carried the most insistence, had the longest history, offered the greatest amount of clarity and consistency and created a visible sign for separation and obedience was *punishment*.[5]

Beginning with the highly organized medieval European societies, punishment is a pervasive theme in controlling errant or suspect populations. The means employed in this punishment may have changed over epochs—from the slow torture of the rack and screw or drawing and quartering to isolation cells in contemporary

mental institutions or prisons. But the underlying cultural principles that provide socially legitimating sources and enable punishment to appear natural, or part of the everyday attitude, are more
similar than we would like to think (see Walkero, 1979).

We need to ask ourselves some fundamental questions about
how social reality and moral order are constructed, maintained and
reconstructed. How do certain symbols maintain a huge symbolic
load (or high-meaning capacity), as when blacks are presumed to
be supercharged with sexuality and violence, or white middle class
professionals, especially men, are believed to be more rational and
unbiased than other populations? Which idioms, or body of language, are used that communicate the social and political experiences of an epoch? How do these idioms present a model of appropriate order and social action? In short, what are the classification
schemes, based on those tacit social conventions, that delineate
appropriate thinking and activity boundaries for members of a
culture? These clarify why punishment regimes are not only so
persistent in modern life, but are actually deemed to be the *more*
legitimate by large segments of citizens for the carrying out of their
order goals than the so-called reform or therapeutic regimes.

One useful guide is the structural theory based upon "diffuse
status characteristics." This enables us to identify the implicit rules
that undergird the contemporary social order and account for
punishment regimes.[6] One is the *status rule*. This stipulates that a
person's net value is based on an averaging out of his or her status
ranks in society. Generally, income, occupation and education are
the major criteria for evaluation, although these interact with race,
gender and age. Importantly, the status rule typically operates
below the level of consciousness so that lower-status persons and
groups being evaluated by higher-status persons and groups lack
both codes and power or even understanding to alter their negative
status evaluation. Conversely, official evaluators may apply a set of
standards that they believe are fair, equal and just, but on closer
examination, through the lens of what Garfinkel (1967) calls "a
stranger to the 'life as usual' character of everyday scenes," turn out
to represent a "special motive" or "perspective" derived from background expectancies. These usually unrecognized expectancies
form the basis for a scheme of interpretation.

The second rule is the *merit rule,* which holds that sanctions in
society should be isomorphic (one-to-one) with a person's achieve-

ments. Rewards go to the deserving. In caste or estate societies, this principle is activated only within clearly bounded groups. Thus, an entire caste or estate may rise or fall in social mobility, affecting all social members within the larger group. The individual person, though, is typically unable to negotiate the hierarchy on a solo basis. Merit is a highly charged category in industrial societies, especially in democratic societies that have elaborate normative theories of social worth and justice. Merit is the source of intense dispute, not on grounds that it is a poor indicator of social worth, but on the basis that there are too many competing criteria for measuring it accurately. This is said to systematically discriminate against certain groups.

The merit rule overlaps with the status rule in significant ways. Because the status rule carries one of the most powerful loadings of all our social conventions, it often predicts who will achieve success. In the United States, vagaries of birth (sex, class, race) often override individual skill and competence. Thus, white male professionals have higher prestige than women or black professionals.

The formal correspondence between these two rules enables us to derive a third rule that demonstrates the coherence of industrial culture. The single idiom that equates status and merit is *work*. As a single measure of evaluation, work impresses its meaning throughout all levels of the classification system. It defines social class, life style and identity. Regardless of how anomic and alienated persons are, work provides an order and a rationale for living. It is thus the central experience for humans in modern life.

In the politics of punishment, therefore, the crucial, unresolvable problem in the total institution is the *absence* of meaningful work. The "time on your hands," the "dead time," the "drag time," the empty space unfilled by labor or meaningful tasks is what creates the violence and the vacuity among controlled populations. Certainly, the absence of loved ones, sexual deprivation, tasteless food, lack of material possessions, and chronic coercion are all acute hardships. But in a society geared around work as the sign of adulthood and power (especially for men) and as the essential symbol for ranking and ordering experience, the failure to provide meaningful work becomes interpreted as an attack on a person's most cherished self-attributes (see Komarovsky, 1940). Conversely, when the total institutional system is liberalized, the first change in institutions is either labor for wages or community-based programs where offenders can pursue a trade (Sykes, 1978).

Whether conceived as patients, dependents, convicts, inmates, retarded, aged, school children or political prisoners, lock-up populations have effectively been declared socially dead. If we consider Durkheim's (1947) thesis that the only viable reality that connects persons to community and the larger society is work, the concept of effectively "incarcerated" can be applied to all those functionless populations who are disconnected from meaningful work activities. Marx (in Avinere, 1968:43-47) referred to this loss of control over work skills as alienation—social and psychological dislocation.

Making Coercion Effective

The punishment regime symbolizes negation. It is effective because it manages the terrors of uncertainty for both the incarcerated and the nonincarcerated. Moral orders depend upon a dual structure: institutions that define what is right, appropriate, just and true, and institutions that stand for what is wrong, inappropriate, unjust and false in the society. The asylum fulfills the latter function. The negating principle, punishment, also renders invisible the potentially volatile implications of status distinctions. Class, race, age, sex, income, prestige and power divisions—all are eclipsed by forcible coercion.

Myths contribute to making coercion effective. They extol the institutional arrangements as natural and normal. One is not allowed to question what is believed to be invariant and eternal. Once terms are locked into opposing institutions, they tend to assume a polar value. Total institutions thus become the mirror-opposite of the free world, as Table 4:1 shows (see Douglas, 1966; Levi-Strauss, 1967).

Table 4:1   Dual Instutional Structure:
The Total Institution and the Free World

Total Institution	Free World
Punishment	Reward
Idleness	Work
Guilt	Innocence
Evil	Good
Nonrational (Insanity, mindlessness or lack of will)	Rational (Sanity, minded behavior and self-determination)
Danger	Safety
Stranger/outsider	Social member/insider

If Mary Douglas (1973) is correct in her assessment that social orders are maintained as much by the purported consistency and clarity of their classification system as by their overt power plays, we may generalize that the punishment regime performs a herculean control task. It not only defines the boundaries of what is permissible in the sense that functionalists have talked about for so long, but more importantly, it gives form and content to the free world by characterizing precisely what it is not. The liberal clamor to release prisoners and provide meaningful work in prisons and mental institutions has fallen on deaf ears. Society apparently prefers to retain these contrasting institutions, as long as status arrangements continue to be based on inequality and injustice.

Needless to say, society pays a heavy price for this mode of ordering the universe. Punishment regimes carry heavy risk. Because they brutalize and dehumanize, they undercut other cherished values such as fair play, egalitarianism, humanism and justice. They lead to periodic violence in men's prisons, and systematic hysteria or apathy in women's institutions. In nursing homes, they induce an early comatose or senile state among the elderly. In homes for the mentally retarded, they encourage unsocialized inmates, many of whom soil their clothes with urine and feces, babble incoherently and break rules with impunity, if unsupervised. Among mentally disturbed persons, the lobotomies, shock treatments, water therapies and other enforced treatments, create not merely dependency, but also an almost animal state of terror. This makes working with advanced cases of schizophrenia or depressive psychosis impossible. The near ubiquity of tranquilizing drugs in this population creates a "Catch-22" situation. There can be no successful intervention for psychotic patients unless they are tranquil or otherwise in a state of psychic integration. But once tranquilized, they are unreachable (vague, indifferent, sleepy, confused, nonverbal).

Why do people tolerate these abuses? Why don't they fight back? Etzioni (1961:23-39) reports that certain socio-cultural environments produce a "tolerance for coercion." In Prussian schools and English public schools (i.e., private boarding schools) students were socialized by their families, classmates and the general community to accept an extensive use of coercion. Preparing for their elite positions in society, students expected fairly high levels of social deprivation. Hence the alienation produced by coercion was less and the negative effect on discipline smaller, Etzioni concludes.

While these data report upper class behavior, similar coercion-tolerance training appears to occur among selective groups in contemporary societies, and may be related to their perceived uncertainty in the environment. For instance, groups that are less status differentiated may be most threatened by onslaughts on the authority system. If this hypothesis is correct, it is possible that lower middle class groups are most likely to prefer order goals over cultural, aesthetic or political ones. Not only as a class, but as a middle management group, the lower middle class experience high levels of "structural strain," to employ Robert Merton's (1957) term, which shapes their discourse. And because this class primarily forms the groups recruited into control occupations—teaching, social work, police work, institutional custodian work and so on—we should expect to see the most favorable attitudes toward repression of social differences.

Other conclusions follow. Persons or groups who experience high levels of uncertainty in their environment will be most likely to instigate or support a range of *excessive* regulations, or rules that are *not* functionally relevant to the specific task. Indeed, rules that humiliate inmates, or force them back into the weak, dependent status of childhood, typical in total institutions, appear to be the products of social groups that lack power and confidence, and perceive their authority to be shaky or tentative (a standard situation among prison guards) (Sykes, 1978:254). In fact, the war of all-against-all that characterizes prisoners can more accurately be described as custodian-induced conflict (e.g., leaving cell doors open so that vulnerable inmates can be attacked by aggressive individuals or groups, denying medical treatment for prisoners in isolation or extending solitary confinement until prisoners react by violence or irrational outbursts).

Jessica Mitford (1972) asserts that persistent branding of lawbreakers as sick or abnormal may be a mask to hide the hatred, fear and revulsion that many white, middle class Protestant reformers and managers feel toward lower class offenders. "Who is sick," Mitford asks. "These courageous men or the society that condemns them to barbarities?"*?[7] The threat principle also leads to excessive concerns about security, which is believed to be undermined by self-governance or politicization among inmates. California's director of corrections is quoted in the *Reader's Digest* as protesting any "revolutionary movement" among inmates. Any efforts to define and shape their own fates are interpreted as revolution.

> What is happening here is a highly organized attempt to destroy our system of correctional justice. These agitators mean to bring anarchy to the prisons, and through them, to the streets of our cities. It is an explosive situation (Adams, 1974:185-186).

A few years ago, Stanley Milgram (1973) of Yale University performed a series of experiments that aimed to test the willingness of persons to obey commands to inflict pain on another person. Here is a description of the laboratory procedure and a transcript of an obedient student.

> The focus of the study concerns the amount of electric shock a subject is willing to administer to another person when ordered by an experimenter to give the "victim" increasingly more severe punishment. The act of administering shock is set in the context of a learning experiment, ostensibly designed to study the effect of punishment on memory. Aside from the experimenter, one naive subject and one accomplice perform in each session. On arrival each subject is paid $4.50. After general talk by the experimenter, telling how little scientists know about the effect of punishment on memory, subjects are informed that one member of the pair will serve as teacher and one as learner. A rigid drawing is held so that the naive subject is always the teacher, and the accomplice becomes the learner. The learner is taken to an adjacent room and strapped into an "electric chair."

> The naive subject is told that it is his task to teach the learner a list of paired associates, to test him on the list, and to administer punishment whenever the learner errs in the test. Punishment takes the form of electric shock, delivered to the learner by means of a shock generator controlled by the naive subject. The teacher is instructed to increase the intensity of electric shock one step on the generator on each error. The learner, according to plan, provides many wrong answers, so that before long the naive subject must give him the strongest shock on the generator. Increases in shock level are met by increasingly insistent demands from the learner that the experiment be stopped because of the growing discomfort to him. However, in clear terms the experimenter orders the teacher to continue with the procedure in disregard of the learner's protests. Thus, the naive subject must resolve a conflict between two mutually incompatible demands from the social field. He must continue to follow the orders of the experimenter and shock the learner with increasing severity, or he may refuse to follow the orders of the experimenter and heed the learner's pleas. The experimenter's authority operates not in a free field, but against an ever mounting countervailing pressure from the person being punished.

> *150 volts delivered.* You want me to keep going?

165 volts delivered. That guy is hollering in there. There's a lot of them here. He's liable to have a heart condition. You want me to go?

180 volts delivered. He can't stand it! I'm not going to kill that man in there! You hear him hollering? He's hollering. He can't stand it. What if something happens to him?... I'm not going to get that man sick in there. He's hollering in there. You know what I mean? I mean, I refuse to take responsibility. He's getting hurt in there. He's in there hollering. Too many left here. Geez, if he gets them wrong. There's too many of them left. I mean who is going to take responsibility if anything happens to that gentleman? (The experimenter accepts responsibility.) All right.

195 volts delivered. You see he's hollering. Hear that. Gee, I don't know. (The experimenter says: "The experiment requires that you go on.") I know it does, sir, but I mean—Hugh—he don't know what he's in for. He's up to 195 volts.

210 volts delivered.

225 volts delivered.

240 volts delivered. Aw, no. You mean I've got to keep going up the scale? No, sir. I'm not going to kill that man! I'm not going to give him 450 volts! (The experimenter says: "The experiment requires that you go on.") I know it does, but that man is hollering in there, sir..."

The Yale experiments not only fail to support findings about coercive structures as specifically class related, but also show that the prestige and legitimacy of science is so widespread that people are willing to suspend their judgment and behavior in ways that would normally be construed as sadistic or "sick." While these data do not support global assertions about conditions under which forcible obedience can be instituted, they do suggest that people are much more compliant than generally assumed (see Blau and Meyer, 1971:154). Rejection of authority is much more the exception than the rule. Most persons do not seriously test authority structures and hierarchies, regardless of how coercively they constrain their members. And institutions often persist for generations and even centuries without basic alterations in their form or structure.

To be effective, coercive compliance must rest on asceticism. As a result of profound cultural changes (many of them induced by the therapeutic model of individualism) the ascetic substructure has gradually been eroded away (Rieff, 1968). What takes its place is at once a more fragmented but individualized system, and an expanding array of do-it-yourself commitment and alternative therapies (considered in later chapters).

Total Institutions and Their Environments

Total institutions remain loosely coupled with their larger environment, effectively sealed off from the larger system of legitimations. As much a part of the social landscape as parks, schools and factories, they are closer to Dante's image of the entrance into the gates of hell: "Abandon hope, all ye who enter here."

The decoupling strategy helps to account for what can only be described as the *spiritual* isolation of the prison, mental institution, nursing home and other large-scale lock-ups. Physical separation from the community is mainly an American (USA) phenomenon. Institutions are located in the country or on hilltops or in other out-of-the-way places, and they are cut off from the local town or city by walls, moats, electric fences or patrol dogs. In cities, they are located in slums that ecologically divide them from respectable residential areas. In some model women's prisons for middle class offenders, gardens or clusters of trees may surround the buildings, leaving inmates free to wander around or away. Most do not, however, because their social location is an internalized reality.

Informants report being "betrayed," "abandoned," "forgotten," "ignored," "too shamed to leave" or use other terms of rejection and defection. If incarcerated for many years, many inmates simply refuse to cope with the outside world. Some actually escape shortly *before* their release, so they can be returned and detained longer. Among older citizens, the nursing home has become a sign of their own degeneracy and impending demise. These modern death houses often have only the most minimal physical, medical and social accommodations, and signal a kind of rehearsal for life's exit, one without dignity or ceremony.

The only genuine connection with their environment practiced by all total institutions is the producing of "output" data. Accountability is the bureaucratic language, and more specifically *evaluation*, a record that shows how goals have been met, and that rationalizes requests for future funding (see Dornbusch and Scott, 1975). Sophisticated analysts observe that most evaluation is ritualistic; the more prestigious the organization, the more fantastic and empty the accounts. This is not to say that organizations do not accomplish genuine goals and make significant contributions in their local and perhaps national environments. What the theory of evaluations emphasizes is that the symbol system (rhetorical language, statistics, categorical imperatives, sense of mission and so on) must be in ritual conformity to societal myths. The more highly legitimated the organization, the more approximate the language should be to the central myth system. Thus, the organizational accounts of physicians and lawyers that find their way into social policy are determined to be "true" renderings of a particular state of affairs. Similar inputs by social workers or nurses are more likely to be viewed with skepticism or ignored.[8]

A standard output measure for total institutions is the number of times a client/patient returns to the institution with the same problem (illness, crime committed, etc.). The *recidivism* or repeat variable is said to measure the effectiveness of treatment—low recidivism, good treatment program; high recidivism, poor treatment program. As a negative measure, it only reflects failure rates and probably does not count these accurately (see Reid, 1979:755-762). Here is an example. A mental patient, let us say, is admitted into the hospital with an acute psychotic episode. If this is a first admittance, elaborate histories will be taken and the patient will be observed some days or weeks before the treatment program (e.g., drugs, behavior modification, electroshock or lobotomy, the latter now an abandoned procedure) begins. During this time, the patient and hospital staff develop a relationship with each other that defines for each party what can be expected. This is usually implicit. But it has everything to do with whether the staff believe the patient is "curable," and whether the patient arrives at a self-definition of "curability." If the interaction effects are *negative,* the patient may go through the treatment process, and once released on a voluntary basis, decide that in the event of future psychotic episodes he or she will assiduously avoid hospitalization because the "cure" is worse than the illness. Relatives and friends may plead in vain—the patient knows that nothing is worth reentering that "zoo." This candidate is counted as a nonrecidivist, a positive output from the hospital's point of view. On the other hand, an individual with the same syndrome may suffer recurrent attacks, find the staff and services helpful during these psychotic lacunas, and voluntarily enter the hospital, perhaps frequently, over a period of years. This patient rates as a high recidivist.

Obviously, the system's accountability data would be highly skewed if these were typical cases, which they undoubtedly are not. But our example suggests that recidivism measures can be highly inadequate methods of evaluation when dealing with human troubles or troubled humans. They are not much better for evaluating prisoners' successes or failures, as they are used politically in contradictory ways: as evidence of both the deterrent success of prisons by conservatives and the failure rates by liberals. The recidivism myth sets up a dual self-fulfilling prophecy. Once labeled as deviant, the person is not only more likely to accept a self-definition as an outsider, but is also more likely to become a systematic target for control agents.[9]

Ironically, prisons may be more successful than the recidivism measures indicate, although we should remain skeptical about these data because of their strong ideological overtones. Perhaps as many as two thirds of first offenders never return to prison. It is apparently the "eternal return" of the one third that keeps the system moving. And among this group, it is also probably safe to assume that less than half are dangerous. This is a far cry from saying, as prison critics stress, that recidivism rates run between 60 and 85 percent. It is also a safe bet to assume that like the mythical patient in our last example, the sophisticated deviant will learn his or her way around the track, and either avoid getting caught or hire more competent counsel to avoid imprisonment, if means are available.

On the whole, though, regardless of what output measures are used, the total institution runs counter to the collective consciousness because it violates common standards of decency, fair play, humanity, and individual responsibility. It homogenizes rather than differentiates evil, and practices a mode of administration that was more appropriately adapted to premodern populations. Based on proscriptive law, it tends to tell people what they cannot do, rather than open up the world to what people can do with their lives, however limited these choices may be.

Social policy should take account of the dreadful paradox of the total institution. On the one hand, it is the most potent source of power society has at its disposal to control deviants, as it clarifies the vast degrees of freedom available in the noninstitutional world. On the other hand, it is a degenerative doctrine that corrupts both controllers and controlled and seriously hampers the individual's efforts to successfully adapt to a more open society. And in another sense, it is a mark of the age; the widespread intrusion of the potentially monolithic state into all of our daily affairs. The total institution is the most extreme form of state control. It introduces stability, predictability and absolutist order into social relations. It thus reduces uncertainty to bearable proportions in a world without faith, without salvation and without a future. Despite its ludicrously misfitting features and unmasked power, it may, indeed, prove to be the most enduring institution.

A Minimum Rationale for Maintaining Total Institutions

Some human problems require confinement. A policy to eradicate all custodial institutions is an ill-advised, if not dangerous, social policy. Alternatives to total institutions—community psychiatry, halfway houses, benign neglect—are not adequate for all cases. How many Charles Mansons can a community absorb? What kind of freedom exists with an unregulated population of drug and alcohol abusers in urban shopping centers who collide into women with shopping carts and children? Do we do a favor to skid-row alcoholics by allowing them to sleep in doorways, as an invitation to predatory juveniles? It is possible that the victims of total institutions—incarcerated men, women and children—could turn around and become the victimizers. A severely retarded child totally dominates a family's life style. Violent gangs keep sizable sections of American cities uninhabitable. The psychotic or incontinent elderly can traumatize a household. These suggest instances where some form of minimum incarceration could intervene.

We wish to clarify our position about total institutions. First, the *principle* of confinement should be limited in scope. For example, dangerous criminals, severely mentally disturbed and very elderly senile persons may require some form of institutionalization. The confinement rule might read: segregate the severely antisocial; restrict the activities of nonserious and nonrepeater violators; and resocialize the careless, subsocial and sociopathic offenders. In certain instances, this may actually *expand* the scope of control, as when traffic accident repeaters are jailed with minimum sentences and no probation, and when wife or child beaters and rapists, once dismissed by the courts as personal problems, are now more likely to be treated as violent offenders.

Secondly, the *use* of confinement should be reduced to extreme cases, and not applied to all deviants in particular classes. For instance, nonviolent property offenders should be treated as civil offenders and sanctioned by restitution such as unpaid work services and fines, or by short-term incarceration with early probation.

Thirdly, basic *reform* of service institutions must be mandated immediately to facilitate the performance of *prosocial* functions. It is assumed here that professional and custodial staff will necessarily be committed to their service function and not to self-perpetuation of their professional and occupational careers. Rather than existing arrangements, which foster managerial and professional interests over public and client groups, reform focuses on meaningful services for inmates' needs and the protection of social members.

Now, there may be a basic contradiction between serving the inmate and deterring serious deviance and disorder in the larger society. Thus, we need a different set of criteria to determine how a conflict between these two interests will be resolved. Substantive and procedural law, Hart (1961:7-12) reminds us, remains the crux of jurisprudence and legal practice. Formal law looks to the adequacy of procedure and determines equity on the basis of technical points. Substantive law, on the contrary, stresses the notion that the basic function of the law is to protect human life, personal integrity and common values. In recent years, procedural law has invaded ever larger sectors of legal practice, as lawyers stand to receive high fees for knowledge of technicalities, whether they serve the interests of life, integrity, and social values or not. Substantive justice clarifies priorities, and places collective rights over individual rights, if those individual rights have been gained primarily through the niceties of procedural technicalities (see Nonet and Selznick, 1978).

The breakdown in substantive justice, characterizing much judicial practice today, has some bizarre consequences. For instance, a weak criminal justice system in Brazil in the 1950s produced the *"esquadrillos de muerte"* (death squads), entailing informal squads of police who went about executing criminals without civilian or government directives. We have a strong suspicion that this goes on today in America's large cities, especially police violence against ethnic offenders. The SWAT program (Special Weapons Action Team), a paramilitary police organization in major American cities, has been equipped with machine guns, bazookas and other highly volatile weapons. In the early 1970s when one of these teams moved against the Symbionese Liberation Army, a radical dissident group, their action took on the trappings of an infantry platoon performing a mop-op operation during World War II. Rather than adopting a more benign policy of tear gas or food blockage, this paramilitary group used total extermination, terrorizing civilian populations and suggesting to some critics that a relatively autonomous urban police may be more dangerous than the unsystematic criminal activities of youthful revolutionaries.

When linked to certain kinds of crimes, an eradication policy actually violates substantive justice. Outraged at the inhumane and shabby treatment of rape victims, feminists have demanded basic reforms. Rape centers counsel victims, encouraging them to report the crime and prosecute the offender. But in the absence of an equal commitment to justice by police and the court, many women experience merely further abuse and degradation. Women reporting rape are accused by dominant groups as being oversexed, or of lying, or of unintentionally inviting rape by thought or deed, or of acting out their revenge against a former boyfriend through the rape charge. It is perhaps the only violent crime where the victim becomes transformed into the offender. Whereas some rape myths describe the offender as simply the "boy next door," an otherwise usually clean-cut American, the data show rape offenders to be systematic criminals, with a number of previous serious crimes on their record. Rape becomes a form of invidious social control, as women are prevented from using the streets or frequenting public places for fear of male violence. In earlier epochs, when women were believed to be a legal extension of their father or husband, the rape revenge might entail the violated possessor (in this case, the male) moving against the violator (the rapist) and either severly injuring or even killing him. The shotgun marriage may be a weak variant of this possession violation. But in an epoch of female independence, without adequate protection of life and integrity, the woman is on her own.

It is not surprising to find among radical feminist groups talk about setting up vigilante committees, or groups of women who actually take the law into their own hands by physically threatening or attacking alleged rapists or other males reported to be oppressors of women (Brownmiller, 1975; Stasz, 1978:169-171; Davis, 1977:247-276).

In the rape case, the paradox of humanitarianism becomes apparent. Whose rights shall be taken into account? Who is the victim and who the offender in this situation? How does the liberal consensus aim to resolve this essential interest conflict? Most rapes are never reported; most rapists are not arrested; and if arrested, few are prosecuted; and only a miniscule percent of those prosecuted ever serve a prison sentence. Doesn't this suggest that the formal rights of men, regardless of their criminality, supercede the substantive rights of women? What the rape case underscores is that an eradication policy—closing prisons down and returning violent offenders to the community—violates substantive justice in two ways: it makes a mockery of fundamental human values, and it promotes indifference for the law.

The application of the eradication principle, a liberal invention, achieves one set of goals—the elimination of a totalitarian order in a civilian state. But it ignores the second set of problems—how to prevent antisocial and socially harmful behavior. It also ignores the special needs of certain vulnerable populations who may require extraordinary human services. The belief in some quarters—"let the deviants do their thing"—increasingly apparent in urban juvenile courts, drug and alcohol nontreatment programs, urban management of unattached psychotics, and some inner city schools —is really an "indifference" policy created by well-buffered bureaucrats and social managers, who remain personally exempted from the consequences of lax regulation. This policy could be called the liberal "alibi hunt" because it has to do with a basic philosophical acceptance of exploitation and oppression, while expressing the secure pieties of a protected class. The "whose right" controversy is intimately related to the "who controls" issue. A minimal rationale for maintaining a drastically updated and reformed service institution might take into account the enormous hypocrisy that governs the liberal consensus. Granted that complexities produce unresolvable contradictions, it nevertheless strikes us as peculiarly unreflective when a governing class determines that "rights" entail no deterrence for violent criminals on technical grounds, though citizens and especially vulnerable populations are exposed to the vagaries of a lax enforcement system. At the same time, such "rights" support closed-shop laws in powerful unions, while leaving the overwhelming proportion of working class populations unprotected in an open labor market.

CHAPTER 4—NOTES

[1] For opposing viewpoints, see, for example, Wilson, 1975; and Quinney, 1975.

[2] Stinchcombe (1965) argues that time of origin fixes the content of organizations.

[3] For discussion of the ethics of behavioral control in institutional settings, see Bermant, Kelman, and Warwick (eds.), 1978.

[4] Criminological theory has shifted over the decades regarding the appropriate role of the social scientist in explaining crime, criminal behavior and social control. For an overview of these issues, see Gibbons, 1979; and Davis, 1980.

[5] Turk (1969) defines punishment as any action designed to hurt or deprive a person or persons of things of value, because of something that person has done or is thought to have done, or has not done, or is believed not to have done. This includes a range of valuables: loss or abridgement of liberty, civil rights, skills, opportunities, material objects, health, identity, life, tangible and intangible forms of wealth, and most crucially, significant personal relationships, including friendship and sexuality. Criminal punishment incorporates many of these as standard techniques (see Packer, 1968).

[6] The following discussion is an application of expectation-states theory, Berger, Cohen, and Zelditch Jr. (1972) and Berger, Conner, and Fisek (eds.), 1974).

[7] Mitford's question is an interesting example of how antiestablishment reformers fall into the sentiment error, i.e., reference to convicts as "courageous." It is not the putative quality of prisoners, (whether brutal, courageous, revolutionary and so forth) that is at issue. Rather, it is the tendency to categorically lump the inmate population into single behavioral attributions.

[8] The relationship between environments and organizations is analyzed by Meyer and Associates, 1978; and Meyer and Rowan, 1977:440-463.

[9] The labeling approach argues that for identified deviants both processes—exclusion and surveillance—operate in tandem (see Davis, 1980).

Chapter 5
Purity and Danger:
The Rise and Fall of the Asylum

Yet surely of two souls, one is said to have intelligence and virtue, and to be good, and the other to have folly and vice, and to be an evil soul...Plato, *Phaedo*

Since Plato, the Western mind has been intrigued by oppositions and paradoxes in social life. Disorder rises in a rule-ordered world, vice and madness intrude on goodness and reason, purity is constantly corrupted, and reason undermined by mindlessness. Among primitives, social anthropologist Mary Douglas (1975) observes, the entire cosmology is organized at the conceptual level into a dual system—right versus wrong, male versus female, adult versus child, health versus illness and so forth—that undergirds fundamental social practices. Marriage, social rights and obligations, work, medicine, and significant social rituals all have a dual structure. What these primitive schemata show, and what can be extrapolated to our epoch, is how the dualistic structure is resolved. Are opposites such as reason and unreason built into the social fabric, thus enabling both principles to exist in some kind of balance? Or are these cultural antimonies silenced or muted by treating one principle, unreason, as barbarous, dangerous and evil, or even nonexistent? Or, a third solution to contradictory principles— does the opposing idea merely get treated as an anomaly, and thus having no approved category, become forced to fit into preexisting concepts even when they are inappropriate? These questions relate to the treatment of madness.

In contemporary society, rationality provides a single accounting system. As the overarching concept and practical guide for action, rationality has snuffed out nearly all serious competitors, and has severely crippled religion. Once medieval cosmology embraced nonreason as part of the human scheme. With the rise of experimental science in the seventeenth century, the dominance of rationality provided an almost exclusive set of legitimating ideas for ordering social life. Rationalization is the major social forma-

80

tion generating industrialization, democracy, socialism and capitalism. Although rationalization has its own contradictions (e.g., the rationality of the economic order negates nonproductive persons, thereby eradicating their human worth), it remains the dominant ethos. Ideas and practices that threaten this cultural hegemony have been systematically attacked as unreasonable, meaningless, nonsense or nonbeing. Thus, unreason in our culture has been consigned to limbo or has declined in silence. In our rational epoch, madness remains the ultimate sign of social danger.

The role of the asylum is to assure the dominance of rationality. It is to keep the underside of rationality—madness, myths, dreams, superstition, faith healing, even impulsive behavior—under control by silencing, repressing and punishing it. The rise of the asylum is linked to Western modernization, particularly its imperative to make an inherent link between rationality and the work ethic. While the medieval Church recognized that both wisdom and madness demonstrated the dual nature of the human soul following the Fall, the modern world view has attempted to banish the concept of the nonrational. At the same time, it seeks to keep dangerously irrational behavior under rationalistic control. The asylum, thus, becomes a metaphor of the dominant moral order. The Fall, a religious metaphor for the limitations of humanity, has been transmuted by the secular vision into the sign of personal degeneracy with madness as the ultimate failure. Why is madness linked to social failure? One major reason is that it represents the inability or unwillingness to carry out requisite work roles.

When we speak of asylums, we are talking about the totalistic state weapon for maintaining conformity. Deviance, especially madness, thus becomes the ultimate evil. The psychiatric discourse rarely touches upon this social danger directly. Instead, the psychiatric profession that has taken over the care and maintenance of the asylum offers a new metaphysic of adjustment, which, on balance, is far less compelling than the medieval religious system despite the brutality of its witch hunts, religious wars, inquisitions and banishments. The new order of universal reson, too, does not come free. It has emerged and flourished through the enforced obliteration of large chunks of human reality. The asylum stands as a pure sign of the costs of modernization.

Madness and History

Cultural hegemony is often a facade—an *appearance* of unity, uniformity and order. What lies behind the social mask may be an entirely different order of things. Certainly, forms of social evil have changed—from medieval witches to contemporary schizophrenia—but the characteristic features of transgression and punishment animate theological and rationalistic world orders alike.

According to Norman Cohn (1970, 1975), prior to the fifteenth century the dominance of a theological order cast collective inversions into forms of heresy. Millenial movements and witchcraft, two characteristic reversals, both drew their ideological sustenance from demonology, a belief in devil possession. The "demonization of medieval heretics" was initially a belief system kept in check by canon law and the accusatory legal mode, which required individual accusers to come up with nearly infallible proofs of transgressions. Both imposed limitations on random lay reactions against nonconformists or suspicious persons.

Stereotypes of heretics or witches (often perceived as a single sect) drew on European myth and folklore. Versions of the devil theory survived and expressed the ultimate in medieval danger. *Maleficium,* a predominant version of occult power through devil possession, provided the doctrine that figured so widely in the witch trials of the fifteenth, sixteenth, and seventeenth centuries. In contrast to the relative power of nature and the powerlessness of humans, the possessed were believed to have almost unlimited power. This was expressed in malicious and destructive ways. They caused death and disease in human beings or animals, impotence in men and sterility in women, raised storms and destroyed crops and promoted a general malice in human relations. Increased social uncertainty (as a result of social change after 1500) fueled the interpersonal hatreds and resentments that led to the sanctification of the witch fantasy. Cannibalistic infanticide, a peculiarly horrible version of generational conflict, also belongs to the traditional heretic-witch stereotype. So do ritual inversions that include orgies, black masses, incantations of the Satan figure materializing as a tomcat or a male goat, and the use of secret ointments that protect wearers from enemies or enable them to move through space. These externalized myths reveal unconscious resentment of Christianity as a total ideological system, of Christ as too stern a taskmaster and of the Church for its rigid interpretation of doctrine. By creating imaginary outgroups through the mass labeling of destitute women and poor peasants, Church members who were acutely aware of their fallibilities could express repressed tensions in conventional and legitimate theological terms. Apostasy, licentiousness, destruction of self and others and institutional transgressions required extraordinary modes of control.

The Inquisition provided a model for containing lay excesses against nonconformity that took the form of lynching and personal acts of malice. But by invoking the awesome and potentially unlimited authority of the Church, it introduced a purity principle that violated the Church's own moral boundaries. Mass witch hunts were carried out with incredible intensity and ferocity in some regions (e.g., Scotland, France, the German States, the Swiss Confederation and later Salem, Massachusetts). Under both Catholic and Protestant authorities, hundreds of women were burned, sometimes collectively, in a messianic mop-up operation that rivals contemporary warfare in guerrilla-entrenched military zones. The corpus of demonological lore proved to be more consistent, however, than the control practices. Everything depended upon the authorities, the ambiguity of the system being related to the degree of cohesiveness or disintegration of the ruling classes. Punishment varied widely. The accused might be executed, tortured, banished, fined or simply required to seek absolution by pilgrimage. The punishment provided proof of the reality of evil. So did legends and reports of nocturnal experiences by neurotic or sexually frustrated women. These features conspired to keep the demonic fantasies alive (Russell, 1972; see also Evens-Pritchard, 1937).

Reminiscent of contemporary psychiatric claims about the ubiquity of madness, late medieval authorities belived that over one third of Christendom was afflicted by demons. The mass fear, hate and persecution that followed this assertion set the tone for the total purge, with institutional demands for purity evoking ruthless and brutalizing tactics. While strategically unsuccessful in that the more intense the repression, the more protracted and determined the oppostion, the purge of the heretics relegitimated the theological world view as the primary ordering principle of social life.

By the eighteenth century, rationalization and science eventually broke through the cultural and institutional barriers and defeated the religious *Weltanschauung*. These silenced heresy through sheer indifference. What arose in its place was a new conception of cultural purity and danger and a new body of knowledge and officialdom to mark the boundaries between order and destruction. Descarte's radical cognition dogma—epitomized in the phrase, "I think, therefore, I am"—signaled a new epoch.[1]

Ostensibly, the world has been liberated from the shackles of theological thought. This renders religious fanaticism obsolete. Or does it? In actuality, new forms of repression arose. Though previous social regulation had been superstitious, arbitrary and brutal, it was softened by inefficiency and Christian charity. Not so in the new order. The Puritan character structure was stark and severe. Its obsession with law and order involved a beating down, restraining, breaking and even destroying of the will, if necessary, to enforce status and work rules (Demos, 1978:157-165). In this repressive regime madness acquired a new identity. It became isomorphic with illusion and alienation, while at the same time, it gained an intrinsic ambiguity. This is what Foucault (1973) calls the terror of "unfettered freedom."

In the preclassical age of Shakespeare and Cervantes, literary works treated madness as essential elements of tragic theatre. Madness was beyond appeal, the character indelibly marked. Lady Macbeth's tragic destiny, which brought a kingdom down, Ophelia's watery solution to ambivalent love, and Don Quixote's challenge to death expressed not merely madness and disarray. Rather, madness worked as a unique medium to communicate the unformed, the shadows that hover on the underside of organized social life.

In the premodernizing epoch, madness was defined as nonfreedom, a sign of falseness seeking truth. To achieve truth, the mad must remain physically free, essential actors in shaping their own destiny. As industrialism proceeded, confinement altered this order. Initiated by the founding of the Hôpital Général in Paris, confinement became the new universal. Madness was defined as socially dangerous, a repudiation of the Calvinist work ethic, a sign of unfettered freedom and possibly a self-imposed plunge into bestiality.

In this regime, the mad lost both their liberty and their identity. These enormous houses of confinement built during the seventeenth century and flourishing to our own day confined one of every hundred inhabitants in Paris within several months of its opening. In 1661, as many as 5-6,000 persons were lodged at one French hospital, including orphans, nursing mothers, school boys, married couples, beggars, unemployed workers, the indigent, the idle, vagabonds, petty criminals and the mad. Tours and Rouen each had 12,000 beggars to control. Indiscriminate institutionalization was deemed necessary to deal with the pressing problems of mendicancy, illness and rebellion brought about by an economic crisis that affected the country through unemployment, low wages and debilitated state coin.

The confinement principle, aimed at controlling a population without resources, without social moorings and without hope, also solved the long-time institutional struggle between Church and state. Foucault (1973) argues:

> In this silent conflict that opposed the severity of the Church to the indulgence of the Parlements, the creation of the Hospital was certainly, at least in the beginning, a victory for the Parlement. It was in any case, a new solution. For the first time, purely negative measures of exclusion were replaced by a measure of confinement; the unemployed person was no longer driven away or punished; he was taken in charge, at the expense of the nation but at the cost of his individual liberty. Between him and society, an implicit system of obligation was established: he had the right to be fed, but he must accept the physical and moral constraint of confinement.

More was expected of the confinement principle than was possible to deliver. Theoretically, confinement was to perform a double role: reabsorb unemployment (or at least mask its visible social effects) and control costs of production through cheap inmate labor subsidized by the state. Multinational economics, even at this early stage, could not be simplified so readily. Curing poverty in one region or community simply shifted the burden to another region or community. The employed resented the subsidized unemployed. The factory owner resisted paying a living wage as long as the state continued to cushion unemployment. As the rolls of the idle able-bodied grew, the confinement doctrine of salvation gave way to a more absolutist, ruthless control structure.

Essentially the asylum failed at its concrete economic roles. It succeeded, however, in establishing the state as exclusive control agent over the surplus populations. In effect, morality and virtue became an affair of the state. Poverty, incapacity for work and inability to integrate with the group became synonymous with madness and incorporated as a state problem. The new importance given to the obligation to work now shaped the experience of madness and determined its course.

When the hospital first opened, madness was perceived to be folly. It attracted the curious, providing a humorous way to spend a Sunday afternoon by visiting the human zoo for a small price. At the end of the seventeenth century, the asylum took on a different sign system. Rigor now replaced the early laxness. Excessive mechanical contraints now typified the homogenous moral order. Chains, cages or prison cells restricted physical movement. Bloodletting, straitjackets, purging, blistering and low nutrition diets were also common treatments to restrain behavior. Such punishment regimes suggested a wish for stability in a world of increasing social uncertainty and collective volatility. Social danger, epitomized by mental disease, was a metaphor for degeneracy and believed to arise from the lower depths of society. To contain this threat, a new regime was proposed that contained madness and ultimately rationalized the detention process. With the unchaining of the insane by the Frenchman Pinel in the late eighteenth century, the era of positive psychiatric medicine had begun.

The intimate link between medicine and society, observed by Oliver Wendell Holmes in 1861, was nowhere more evident than in the first wave of moral management following the "great restraining machine" of New England's mania for asylum building. As a peculiar rendering of eighteenth century Enlightenment, with its belief in the perfectability and educability of all humans, the curability cult ignored social content or unequal social conditions. Cure became the new watchword for asylum managers, driving out both the older medical therapeutics (based on mechanical assumptions of brain lesions) and the therapeutic nihilism of the restraint school. Science and cultism joined forces to inaugurate new treatment modalities. Such newer developments as brain autopsies (which showed a notable *absence* of brain tumor or lesion in the insane), hydrotherapy or immersive baths for soothing the agitated, homeopathy with its emphasis on tiny doses of medicine to combat illness, and other dietary and psychological methods were among the techniques used to restore persons to their normal state. Extravagant claims by asylum superintendents loosened legislatures' purse strings and raised lay hopes that psychiatry could cure everything from hysteria to urban problems (see, for example, Rothman, 1971; Bain, 1964; Deutsch, 1949).

Tackling the immigrant problem, the state asylum opened its doors to the deranged masses, absorbing long-standing chronic cases. Treatment soon differentiated: long-term confinement and constraint for the poor and short-term medical and moral approaches for the respectable classes. The long-accepted linkage between insanity and violence reappeared. This justified the transformation of treatment into various punishment modalities. The water cure, for instance, became mandatory for mania. The patient was blindfolded and immersed, often for hours at a time, in a tub of water, and forbidden to move or speak under pain of total isolation. These early models of sensory and interactional deprivation were further supported by electroshock therapies, and later by surgery (e.g., lobotomy, organ removal). They were calculated to coerce obedience through sheer terror, including the induction of a comatose state. Severe spinal injuries eventually tended to discourage standardized use of the more primitive methods of shock treatment. In many institutions, though, the absence of staff, citizen or peer review led to an assortment of excesses. Popular myth —the figure of the raging maniac—helped to sustain restraining regimes. Despite the preponderance of evidence that showed violence and rampaging to be either relatively uncommon among the insane, or when present, to be induced by brutal, isolating or unpredictable treatment, the punishment models endured.

When reformer Dorothea Dix hostilely criticized the curative program, it was not an attack against confinement or unequal class treatment (Rothman, 1971). It was the scale of hospitalization she rejected, which rationalized a uniform system of custodial care in state asylums, regardless of the patients' varying capacities. Active therapy, Dix said, should substitute for the repressive programs. But this required more well-equipped, small hospitals that would have music, books, games, libraries, and good physical facilities, including abundant land for farming. What reformers could not predict was that such moral crusades, orchestrated with such passion against the abuses of psychiatry and the asylum, merely fed into a cyclical process. The meanings of madness continued to shift back and forth from scientific to moral interpretations. The medical model, as it turned out, was no less crushing than the moralistic one. Unreason had no voice in this dialogue. It was either defined out of existence or treated as something that could not be publicly evoked. This apartheid program, accompanied by a rich mythology, prevailed. Given the reluctance of taxpayers to support the poor and their horror at confronting what they perceived as the violently insane in their midst, the asylum became a separatist system, reduced to a caretaker institution for indigents. Not until the rise of an entirely new therapeutic—psychopharmacology and the invention of the so-called wonder drugs—has there been any substitute for massive incarceration of the mentally troubled and disordered.

Psychiatry and the State

Nineteenth-century psychiatry periodically attemped to shake loose its intimate attachment to moral treatment to become a *bona fide* science. It was impeded by the punishment regime, because of its link with the stigmatized. Mad persons were defined as outside the moral-social-political accountability system. Thus, once incarcerated, the mad person lost all claims to humanity and citizenship. Failing to achieve its primary goal as a serious science because of moral contamination, psychiatry still managed to create a well-defined mandate.

First, it used the trappings of science to create a spurious medical diagnostic system for ordering behavioral disorders. Secondly, it capitalized on urban crime-engendered fears to seek an exclusive legal role; that of determining a suspect's sanity in circumstances of violent crime. Thirdly, during the twentieth century, as a result of world wars and continuous overseas military commitments, it secured the right to identify and exclude the mentally unfit from responsible participation. Fourthly, it acquired control over underclass suspect groups. Finally, in its caretaker function, it adapted Freud's rationalistic doctrine to justify confinement.

The medical model in psychiatry received its major legitimation as a consequence of the extraordinary successes of germ theory and the doctrine of contagion in the field of infectious medicines, and from the equally dramatic success in the prevention of nutritional disorders (Bloom, 1965; 333-338). As an application of biological theory, the medical model relies on taxonomy, a method of disease classification that differentiates diseases by isolating their specific symptoms into coherent syndromes. Because etiology (causes) and treatment are disease-specific, the belief is that the physician must establish a diagnosis before instituting appropriate treatment. Thus, symptoms may "look alike"—fever occurring in both malaria and typhoid—but when bundled in particular ways, they reveal to the discerning physician their unique configuration. This doctrine actually retarded modern medicine in that many dissimilar diseases are related to the same organic pathologies, while seemingly similar diseases, like cancers, are not the same in fact.

In the emotional disorders the medical model has been the course of an extraordinary professional illusion.[2] The diagnostic problems are legion. How is neurosis different from psychosis, a necessary distinction before treatment can be introduced? It is often only a matter of degree. But the model does not allow for such continuums, and so the patient must be placed in one or the other category, whether the behavior fits or not. What of mania, the excitable stage of the manic-depressive syndrome? Obviously, there may be similarities to some phases of other mental disabilities, say schizophrenia, and only time can tell which disease the symptoms reveal. But by then early treatment will be impossible, as the patient will be too far along the course of the disease. Can the schizophrenic diagnosis be determined in the absence of certain symptoms? Without the familiar hallucinations, including the "voices" of an externalized conscience, can the patient's bizarre behavior be explained as common schizophrenia? Or perhaps it is a preschizoid condition. Certainly, if it persists after treatment, it is a regressive schizophrenia, about which nothing can be done.[3]

In psychiatry, the mind-body dualism was a particularly pernicious doctrine. Despite the belief that insanity is a "mental" disorder, patients often exhibit highly cogent intellectual states in the midst of severe emotional disorganization. Thus, the patient could be defined as a "trickster," a "volatile" type or in a temporary remission—in general, one that could not be trusted to fit the category, and hence not susceptible to treatment. The "contagion" concept that psychiatrists use so abundantly to describe such varied collective outbursts as ward violence or mass homocide is a direct descendant of the physical theory of insanity. The relatively easy movement into community psychiatry and preventive psychiatry during the 1960s and '70s probably took its cue from this early belief that mental disease, like the plague and other severe diseases, attacks entire groups and communities unless forcibly checked by a rationalistic counteragent. This role was to be performed by state-directed public health groups (Bloom, 1965:333-338).

While diagnosis continued to confound the field and embarrass its more concerned practitioners, psychiatry entered a new domain —the criminal law court. In the insanity test, the social stakes were high, the human hazards multiple, the professional rewards uncertain. McNaghten Rules, which have been the basis of the insanity plea as a defense in criminal cases throughout most of the English-speaking world, were the result of questions of law propounded by the House of Lords to the fifteen criminal judges of England in 1843 (Bazelon, 1974:18-25). The original case was the murder trial of Daniel McNaghten, who shot and killed Edward Drummond, Sir Robert Peel's private secretary. The accused pleaded that he was being persecuted by the Tories and subsequently pleaded not guilty on the basis of medical evidence. McNaghten was eventually declared insane, a victim of "morbid delusions." The McNaghten test revolved into a determination of reason. If the accused could be shown to be suffering from a "defect of reason," as not knowing the nature and the quality of the act, the person was exonerated from guilt.

The Durham Rule formulated in 1954 in the United States corrected certain deficiences of the McNaghten Rules that presume medical opinion's primary role is to determine guilt or innocence on the basis of cognitive processes. Durham limited this right considerably by stipulating that psychiatrists perform the expert witness role, bringing to the courtroom such knowledge as they have regarding mental disease or defect, but leaving to the judge and jury the traditional function of applying moral responsibility to those accused of crime.[4] The Jenkins case of 1962 extended the range of expertise to psychologists. Despite the absence of medical training, this discipline now competes with psychiatry as equally qualified to give expert opinion (Bazelon, 1974). The model, though, remains a medical one.

What these three cases did is the following. First, they opened up the possibility of psychiatry serving what one critic terms a "star chamber proceeding," when hospital staff usurp the function of the court and possibly impede the adversary process. Secondly, the cases argue that human beings are one-dimensional. Either they are rational or nonrational. If rational, they must by definition make free choices informed by conscious considerations. There is no middle ground. Thirdly, insanity pleas use professional experts who may ignore ordinary common-sense renderings of moral responsibility that are rooted in community meanings and sentiments. This undermines an already fractured consensus. Fourthly, psychiatric information is offered as grounded medical conclusions, rather than as unverified testimony. What psychiatrists have not understood is that labeling a person "schizophrenic" does not make him or her so. It simply has consequences for the person's status and identity. Finally, these cases justify deliberate falsification by psychiatrists, especially in their testimony on "dangerous" (a ground for involuntary confinement) when they believe the suspect is too sick to seek help voluntarily.

Psychiatry has been ill-used by the state, and in return has exploited the public and has been exploited by defendants. On the one hand, serious legal challenges have been needed to surface the hidden agenda—the filling up of empty hospital beds and guild self-protection that resists outside evaluation. On the other hand, the medical model of "sickness" has been perverted to encompass judgment of what is socially and politically unacceptable behavior. The hazard implicit in professional resistance to public scrutiny is well illustrated by the use in the U.S.S.R. of psychiatric facilities for the suppression of political dissenters. Whenever psychiatry has entered the public domain—law, business, schools and other institutions—it has done so as a conflict-ridden profession torn between the therapeutic interests of patients and the institutional interests of private employers or the state. Admittedly, peer review is virtually unknown.

Psychiatry presents a complex face. Like much of social science, psychiatry is an unverifiable knowledge system. It has used available power opportunities, or been used for questionable purposes, in the selecting and sorting of human materials for institutional functions. Sometimes, its end product is a brutal one, such as the locking up of political or criminal suspects without appropriate adversary process. At other times, it offers beneficial outcomes, as in the protection of the vulnerable from institutional pressures.

In its World War II military role, the psychiatric mystique assisted the state's recruitment of military personnel and the treatment of casualties. A profession marked by indecision, confusion, timidity and jealous rivalries was nevertheless charged with wide-ranging moral responsibilities (Deutsch, 1949). Its mission was to:

1. maintain and strengthen civilian morale on the home front
2. formulate techniques for selection of recruits for the armed

forces, and for separating out bad military risks, from a psychiatric point of view, at selection and induction centers

3. offer prompt and efficient treatment of psychiatric casualties in the armed forces

4. maintain optimum mental health and good morale among men in the military ranks

5. rehabilitate rejected draft registrants and military casualties returning to civilian life

6. provide minimum mental hospital standards.

Certainly, this charge alerted governing groups to the widespread existence of emotional and mental disabilities, and greatly accelerated the national interest in mental health. In rejecting well over one million (17 percent) of otherwise physically able-bodied men between 18 and 37 for military service on the grounds of neuropsychiatric disorders, the profession encouraged public outcries against possible malingerers and the "quacks" that supported them. Potential recruits discovered that it was easier to escape military service by psychiatric rather than by military disabilities.

If psychiatry traditionally had been the Cinderella of civilian medicine, as Deutsch (1949) claims, and the object of widespread attacks, it also rose to a position of prominence as a result of its great stimulus to the study and treatment of psychosomatic diseases (notably peptic ulcers and various stress ailments that were formerly considered to be organic in nature). Along with the chaplains' services the profession has certainly helped to cushion the horror of modern war for millions of war-disabled and traumatized persons. It is probably also the case that it has achieved this success mainly outside of standard military regulations, operating as a functional aside, as it were, to its primary role as selection agent.

The use and abuse of mental illness categories is not restricted to military situations. Psychiatric labeling is also an updated version of the premodern almshouse solution to poverty and economic stress. Brenner (1973) claims that psychiatry is intimately tied to dislocations in economic sysems. As such, it performs a kind of malevolent mediation role between economic downturns and individual aberrations that result from economic uncertainty and loss. Not that psychiatry consciously perceives itself as a buffer system, Brenner hastens to add. Psychiatrists appear to be fairly oblivious to economic changes and their impact on group and personality functioning. Both doctrine and practice mitigate against psychiatry adequately dealing with the social context of life stresses. Equipped with an individual adjustment model, the profession emphasizes external activity over internalized meanings. No established criteria for hospital admission exists, and psychiatry has relied almost exclusively on legal or professional certification to determine insanity. Thus, psychiatry has operated unwittingly in a behind-the-scenes fashion as an agent of social repair for large-scale victims of economic and social disequilibria. After reviewing the alternatives and analyzing mental hospital admissions in New York state over 127 years, Brenner (1973) makes the following conclusions about the significance of economic and social factors in the etiology of mental disorder.

1. Economic change is the single most important cause of mental hospitalization. Economic downturns in general—regardless of size or chronological specificity—are associated with an upturn in mental hospital admissions.

2. The higher the social-economic class, the lower the likelihood of mental hospitalization. The conclusion has been verified in other studies as well.[5]

3. Men between the ages of 20 and 54 are most severely affected by rising unemployment, which is directly correlated with important life stresses. Status and career dislocations are the primary causes of mental disturbance in this large group.

4. Females between 25 and 29 are most at risk for mental breakdowns, as important life stresses revolving around marriage and birth, are in significant decline during economic downturns. This is corroborated by New York state census data that show that 63 percent of female first admissions are *not* married—that is, they are single, divorced, separated or widowed.

5. Both males and females who are nonmobile respond similarly to economic upturn by *increased* hospitalization. This finding is related to the relative evaluation of social status.

When psychiatrists ignore problems of social interaction or the implications of social or economic change, they may be missing the root cause for the patient's malady. In such cases mental hospitalization becomes both the psychiatric solution and the social problem. As Brenner (1973) says:

> Hospitalization is not only a psychiatrically inappropriate response to economic stress; it actually compounds the social impact of economic stress enormously. Under conditions of economic stress, mental hospitalization

represents the culmination of a process of disruption and disintegration of family and other close relations. It closes off and isolates an individual from his normal social context, placing him in a situation in which the focus of his life consists of adaptation to the routine of a highly bureaucratic organization... Within the scheme of mental hospitalization, the patient's economic and social careers can be very seriously damaged. (See also, Levinson, et al, 1970.)

Brenner tackles a long-standing controversy in the field of psychiatric epidemiology concerning the inverse prevalence of mental disorder to socio-economic status.[6] Two alternative theories attempt to explain this relationship. The life-stress theory argues that stressful life circumstances increase as one approaches the lower end of the social structure. Low status is hypothesized to be the precursor for a variety of mental and social ills. The downward-drift model posits, contrariwise, that the mentally ill are simply less effective workers who drift downward in social position as a result of their relative incompetence. Brenner asserts that both models are correct. Downward mobility is enhanced by economic downturns, and the lowest socio-economic groups, lacking the resource margin of the affluent, are most vulnerable to even short-term economic slumps.

In a historically capricious and unanticipated way, psychiatry has replaced the priesthood as healer of the unhappy and punisher of the damned. Its rationale for medicalizing deviance has often been *ad hoc*—doctrine following practice—especially since the rise of psychoanalytical theory. Having captured the unconscious, psychiatry now possesses a fool-proof dogma that proves to be nearly as unchallengeable as the religious system it replaces.

Freud (1977 ed.) offered a hard-won doctrine of rationality that presumed living to be an unfinished and conflictful enterprise—a constant struggle between the needs and wishes of the unconscious and the imperatives of the culture. As Freud reasoned, the war between nature and culture has no resolution. Taking the low road, the patient would be subject to the unreasonable and insatiable demands of the unconscious, a never ending cycle of appetitie reduction. Taking the high road implies total cultural dominance over the person, the individual being little more than a cultural artifact motored by built-in censors of conscience placed by early authority figures. Therefore, therapy must be geared to enhancing conscious control over our mental and emotional life. This is not to deny nature, Freud warned, but rather to achieve the highest benefits of the civilized state, a creatively controlled use of the mind. Unlike the therapeutic organicists or nihilists before him, Freud used the monologue of unreason to build his case for the reasoning enterprise as a dialectical process, a kind of perpetual dialogue etween nature, culture and self.

Freud showed therapy to be both scientific and moral. At one level, psychoanalysis is a science. It identifies pain, categorizes symptoms and distributes physical, cognitive and emotional factors in their appropriate taxonomic order. But at deeper levels, psychiatric symptoms are interpreted as codes, requiring the analyst to interpret patients' dreams, symbols, jokes, slips of tongue and other external acts as products of the unconscious. The language of the unconscious requires uncovering and explicating a special grammar of meanings (Lacan, 1966; Rieff, 1966). Relationships between nature and culture, biological past and experiential present are not obvious, but rather yield their meanings through intense interactive work between analyst and patient. As an interactive team, they commit themselves to transcendence through ascendancy of the rational over the locked-in psychic materials. Symptoms, then, are mere externals, however painful they may be to the person, that provide evidence of an underlying structure.

The only solution for releasing the patient from perpetual pain, whether it be the failed repression of neurosis or the rebellion of psychosis, is to make the patient become aware of and even confront the fundamental meanings of his or her own life. Obviously, if repression is "successful," that is, no psychological pain or physical illness accompanies unawareness, there will be little ground for intervention. At the same time, however, there is also no possibility of self-liberation. The patient remains fixated at a precreative level of existence. Except for artists, whose creative process is still unknown, most persons must actively work and suffer through their unconscious processes in order to become free of them. Militant racists, hysterics, the psychosomatically ill, religious and social-movement fanatics, all are simply expressing externalized instances of an unexplored unconscious. Thus, classical psychoanalysis entails a double cyclical movement. It uses the unconscious toward understanding the workings of normal mental processes. And it adapts rationalistic techniques to understand the submerged language of the unconscious.

After Freud, the dialogue between reason and unreason was possible. As it turned out, it was only a short-lived episode in the larger thrust toward rationalization and obliteration of the unconscious. As a suspect medical specialty and a dependent control unit of the state, psychiatry lacks the autonomy (and perhaps the collective intelligence) to follow the master's voice. Instead of developing techniques for releasing locked-in psychic materials, psychiatry uses the lock-up to deny the patient's reality. The hospital regime offers a cuckoo's nest world (Kesey, 1971) or snake pit (Ward, 1955), comprised of a two-class system: inmates and staff. The inmates know they are crazy but resist falling into the professional illusion that cure exists through obedience and restraint. The professionals reject the patients' reality, using the formers' denial as further testimony to their madness. Who can tell the difference between the sane and insane, anyway? Only the patients know for sure, as David Rosenhan's (1966) study shows. Institutional psychiatry continues to bumble along, classifying, judging, rejecting and incarcerating. It is clearly an antiliberation doctrine under the guise of a highly distorted humanistic practice. Its unacknowledged function remains the punishment of the behaviorally incompetent and the politically incorrigible. Freud would hardly have recognized the product of his support therapy in these 20th-century practices.

Inmate Culture

According to sociologist Goffman (1961), who studied St. Elizabeth's Hospital in Washington D.C., institutions are inhumane and personally degrading because they are poorly funded, but more important, because they nourish "institutionalism." This is the process by which the patient internalizes the inmate culture and abandons civilian modes of life (see also Stanton and Schwartz, 1949; Szasz, 1961; Scheff, 1973). Institutionalism begins with the character of the "total institution," symbolized by barriers to social interaction with the outside world and by isolation built directly into the physical plant, such as locked doors, high walls, cages, cubicles, dormitory-style sleeping quarters, a total lack of privacy and so on. Goffman says:

> First, all aspects of life are conducted in the same place and under the same single authority. Second, each phase of the member's daily activity is carried on in the immediate company of a large batch of others (who are required to

do the same thing together). Third, all phases of the days activities are tightly scheduled with...one leading into the next. Finally, the various enforced activities are brought together into a single rational plan purportedly designed to fulfill the official aims of the institution.

Goffman describes the moral career of the mental patient, which begins with the betrayal by family or friends, and continues with a series of assaults on the patient's former identity. In its final phase, the career culminates with the breaking of the patient's spirit to make him or her more manageable. The most common and formerly volitional activities—going to the toilet, smoking, shaving, letter writing—are routinized to keep patients in line. Identity stripping involves mortifying rituals that convince the patient that he or she has no social value other than that provided by the hospital regime. The privilege system entails an elaborate game whereby patients begin on the lowest rung of the ladder, and if appropriately servile, graduate to higher rewards commensurate with the level of patient cooperation. Finally, there is the "secondary adjustment," a process by which the patient expresses a final capitulation to the dominant order. It is the hallmark of institutionalism. Now the inmate's new identity revolves around the "habitual arrangements by which patients employ unauthorized means, or obtain unauthorized ends, or both" to reduce the hospital's control over their life. The incredibly rich underlife, described so poignantly by Goffman, suggests the ironic twist that the only possibility for self-preservation, however reduced, is the "rejection of one's rejectors," expressed by ritual insubordination, while the compliance front is carefully maintained.

Seeking to uncover whether changes had occurred in St. Elizabeth's after Goffman's severe attack on the system, Roger Peel and associates (1977:1077-1081) reexamined the settings. Their study epitomizes how difficult it is to critically penetrate the professional ideology behind the positivistic methodology. Such methodology is totally unsuitable for uncovering the more submerged elements of any meaning system, whether these symbols arise from the culture or from the individual personality.

The study group first differentiated the "secondary adjustment" concept into two parts: institutionalization, measured by observing ward behavior, and the number of structured activity hours per week, and institutionalism, measured by the number of secondary adjustments in the patients for a given program. The concern was to test objectively verifiable characteristics, not merely observers' impressions or hunches. For example, ten categories were developed that were reported to yield Goffman's observed secondary adjustments:

1. wanting to go to industrial therapy to get away from ward programs
2. doing favors for other patients
3. no friends ouside ward
4. bulging handbags, pockets, etc.
5. repetitive "sad stories"
6. unauthorized use of hospital objects
7. panhandling
8. employing or employed by another patient
9. doing favors for staff
10. territoriality

What were the results of the study? First, there was an admittedly rich underlife providing ample evidence of secondary adjustment. Second, the psychiatric wards had a relatively low degree of institutionalization processes (i.e., structure), as compared with programs for alcoholics and drug addicts. The researchers note that in substance-abuse programs, the depersonalization process and the privilege system were elaborated and formalized to a degree exceeding anything described by Goffman. Recruits were completely isolated for hours, house rules were elaborate and formalized, the privilege system contained almost no privacy or free time, activities were blocked out back to back from breakfast to bedtime and the entire system operated on the philosophy that the patient must shed his or her former identity to be "reborn." Yet in these drug and alcoholic programs, compared to the psychiatric programs, secondary adjustments involving rebellious or defensive behaviors were nearly absent. Evidently, there must be an inverse relation between institutionalism, those secondary adjustments by reactive patients, and institutionalization, the degree to which daily activities are highly structured. High structure should imply high reactivity, but the relationship fails to hold in this case.

Acknowledging that they lacked adequate data to test this conclusion, the writers made some qualitative statements. They found diagnostic variation made a difference; psychotics showed a high incidence of secondary adjustment. They also discovered that the institutional population was really distributed across the community—halfway houses, foster homes, nursing homes and patients' own homes all house many patients who were formerly institutionalized. Thus, atypicality in sampling may have contributed to the lack of coherence between institutionalism and institutionalization. This led the study group to conclude that one factor may have caused another: institutionalism could be a product of the lock-step regime. Mental disease itself is a causative factor in secondary adjustment, rather than the product of an inhumane institution. They qualified this evaluation of secondary adjustment by noting that institutional neglect, rather than the structure of the organization, was at fault in creating defensive behavior. And finally, they concluded that the combined effects of diagnosis, length of stay and degree of program homogeneity (i.e., lack of personal choice) were viewed as differentiating those programs that had a great deal of institutionalization from those that did not.

The researchers clearly were puzzled over the problem of institutionalization. Perhaps the regimentation was not as bad as in Goffman's time, they suggested. Since the most publicly admired of the programs surveyed were the most highly structured, institutionalization could not be all that bad. Their resolve was that institutionalization (i.e., bureaucratized, impersonal treatment) is beneficial, or at least not harmful, under conditions of voluntary admission and prompt discharge at the patient's request.

In all fairness, this is a good study design and a clearly written scientific report. In what way, then, does it distort the inmate culture? And how does it help to eradicate the Freudian model of the vital dialogue between reason and unreason that makes possible a higher level of consciousness among the psychically ill and damaged, as well as among the rest of us so-called normals?

These writers wrongly presume that madness and institutionally negating experience can be distilled into a single set of categories. Just as problematically, such categories had been chosen before entering the field. History and social context were left as residual features, rather than critical variables. Certainly, there have been enough changes in the total institution iself to warrant major attention. Hospital population has declined since Goffman's time from 7,000 to 2,700. Many wards have been sexually integrated, enabling more normal relations between adult men and women, and another one third of the wards have been opened up to voluntary movement. Inmates are younger, and the proportion admitted on a voluntary basis has moved from a few percent to about half. In-patient stays, once measured in years, are reduced to weeks, and the final symbol of closure—the walled-in institution—has been reduced in scale or torn down. The study team concluded, though, that "still, none of these figures tell us whether the social phenomena Goffman saw have changed."

What Goffman saw, and what psychiatric sociologists, patients' autobiographical accounts and more critically informed psychiatrists report is a view of the *internal* order of the asylum, as contrasted with its external public relations doctrine (see Stanton and Schwartz, 1949). Only by taking the patients' perspective could this order be perceived, since the hospital regime categorically declared patients' experiences out of bounds unless they fit staff definitions. This internal order, captured by Goffman in his succinct concept of "secondary adjustment," suggested both the possibility of personality eradication if the inmate were to attempt primary adjustment (i.e., obedience to hospital rules) and the viability and creativity of humans to survive against enormous odds and against encapsulation in a negative environment. One is tempted to believe that if Goffman thought the issue could be summarized in ten categories or less, he might have conducted the follow-up study himself. As it is, this well-meaning, but patently wrong, study communicates the impression that mental illness and its manifestations should not be taken too seriously. For after all, it is probably the very sick—those suffering from organic brain syndrome and schizophrenia—who alone engage in secondary adjustment. And like the preinstitutional "village madman" of centuries ago, there is little to be done about it.

This study manifests, then, what is really wrong with psychiatry today. As a pseudoscientific discipline, it serves as an unacknowledged control group that lacks public and peer accountability, is overly dependent upon the state for its healing mandate, and takes a view of madness that is closer to cynical knowledge than curing and compassion. There are now over two hundred distinct therapies and over a dozen professional rivals. Psychologists, psychiatric nurses, vocational counselors, social workers, ministers, sensitivity training centers, masters of the occult, and gurus preaching Eastern mysticism—the list goes on—all contest the right to practice therapy and many groups have pressed for licensing to do so

(Bach, 1971). "Psychiatry's Depression," *Time* magazine (April 12, 1979) sardonically termed this state of affairs. A mandate to control the madhouse may be in the process of being revoked, once society discovers alternative methods of adjustment and restraint.

Hegemony is a standard process of cultural life, a point we emphasized in our initial discussion of the way different societies handle the purity/danger oppositions. Industrial societies extoll pluralism. Indeed, political discourse about diversity, choice, variety, openness and excessive tolerance appears to characterize contemporary renderings of liberal society. But how real are these claims in an increasingly bureaucratized and standardized world? Aren't those homogeneous programs, explicitly calculated to give rebirth to addicts and the insane, and positively viewed by professionals, merely stripped-down versions of the bureaucratic order, embellished by the charismatic hoopla of a religious movement? Even a cursory reading of cloister rules, say St. Benedict's or St. Clare's, should inform the reader how highly personal is the mystic bond between spiritual seeker and God. But a social order that masks itself as a religious one under the rationale of cure is strongly antithetical to personal salvation in any religious sense. It is equally antagonistic to the psychoanalytical model that demands a highly individualized treatment program and an intense, if not a prolonged, spiritual relationship between therapist and patient. The social reality of the asylum cannot be discerned by means of the limited toolbox of positivistic methods, nor by using a single perspective (i.e., psychiatrists' secondhand versions) nor even by the uncritical acceptance of regimented regimes. The asylum yields its meanings by insiders' accounts—inmates, custodians, professional staff and inmates' families. A collection of horror stories, of which there are an abundance, should also be supplemented by success tales. In the current antiinstitutionalizing milieu, it is difficult to get an impartial presentation of those highly personal, yet imperative, social facts.

Deinstitutionalization: The Collapse of the Confinement Principle

By the mid-1960s, the rise of an increasingly well-funded community mental health movement, described in chapter 9 of this book, offered an alternative plan to the unilateral practice of physical incarceration. Institutional costs, public complaints, and former mental patient claims forced psychiatry to change its work habits. In fact, psychiatry itself was is its own worst critic. Although members of the field disagreed on fundamental issues in the social organization of mental hospitals, the most enlightened viewpoint emphasized that taking into account the needs for drastic reform, there are still reasons for continuing the existence of mental hospitals. According to Spiegel (1979) these are:

1. Social protection. The mentally ill person may constitute a threat to others or to himself.

2. Respite for family. The family of a disturbed person, though probably remarkably tolerant of bizarre behavior, is subjected to a great deal of stress. Removing the disturbed person from its midst may permit the family to breathe and regroup.

3. Vacation for patient. Everyone needs a break for social, economic and family pressures once in a while, but not everyone can afford to take off to the golf course or the mountains. A mental hospital is not exactly the French Riviera, but it does offer an environment sheltered from outside strife. At the very least, it offers a change of pace.

4. Setting for intensive diagnosis and treatment. This is obvious, but caution is required in attempting to diagnose and treat outside of the patient's usual social milieu.

5. Availability of self-help. Disturbed persons can learn from each other. And being among more disturbed people may help put things in perspective.

6. Teaching and research.

7. Professional self-help. Mental hospitals provide a setting where professionals can converge to discuss problems and ways of overcoming them.

He closes with Goffman's sobering comment:

"The mentally disturbed person is made into a serviceable object, the irony being that there is so little service to be offered."

The confinement principle has surely collapsed in the face of such a professionally self-effacing commentary. In addition, we can note: (1) the taxpayers' revolt (e.g., California's Proposition 13,) which severely restricts state taxation, (2) the antibureaucratic attitudes of institutional psychiatrists who depart as soon as professionally possible for the more lucrative and autonomous private practice,[7] (3) political resistance to funding "malingerers" and the nonproductive, (4) increasing malpractice suits against private and institutional psychiatry, (5) the haphazard and often humanly destructive diagnostic scheme, (6) systematic exposés in film and press regarding the cuckoo's nest setup—straitjackets, behavior modification, involuntary electroshock, and formerly lobotomy and other surgical treatments,[8] (7) the arbitrary, external and brutal control, the sad and chaotic inmate relations, and finally, (8) the antiintervention movement based on ethical concern over patients' rights and a shift from repressive tolerance to open acceptance of diversity (Bemant, *et al*, 1978). A bold prediction is that we have here a combined set of factors working from all sides to bring about the final collapse of the already toppling institutional structure of the mental hospital.

Until alternative structures are created—and these are in the most tenuous initial stages of development—burial rites may be premature. The total institution is giving way to alternatives, both in-house and in the community. Regimentation is being avoided and new approaches to old human troubles are being sponsored. Extreme forms of institutionalization are now rejected as opposing a sound mental health program. Sometimes, professional staff err in the reverse direction. They refuse patients' institutional help unless they are an extreme danger to themselves or others. A patient must literally be in the process of committing suicide or must have committed homicide for some states to accept an involuntary commitment and sometimes even a voluntary one. Horror stories arise, this time, not from the excesses of institutionalization, but from the agonies of being rejected for care. This leaves the disturbed person and family members distraught, sometimes beyond endurance.

But patients' families, long ignored or persecuted by the profession as causing the harm in the first place (in a distorted version of the Freudian oedipal theme), have in some recent instances been included as essential elements of the therapy program. The psychiatric team has expanded its reach from within the hospital setting to embrace the entire range of community and social services (see chapter 9).

Both buildings and therapies probably need drastic overhaul before an acceptable format can occur. The existing order must be abandoned altogether: massive wings with seemingly endless halls, huge dormitories sleeping dozens of patients, indiscriminate drug therapies, nonlegal involuntary admission policies, rigidly stand-ardized programs, prolonged hospitalization, heavy use of psycho-logical or physical restraints, coercive behavior modification, cold packs and so on. This format is calculated to make the wise mad, and destroy the mad altogether. Organizations must be adapted to fit changing human preferences.

On the one hand, psychiatry can assist in explaining historical and social situations and the way in which these operate to place demands on persons that often lead to maladaptive responses. On the other hand, the profession can shake off its political depend-ence status as a tinkering trade by adopting a kind of R. D. Laing (1960, 1967) political approach—encouraging nonconformity as the only viable human expression in an increasingly standardized and depoliticized society. In a world that denies and falsifies experi-ence, Laing says, the insane are the only sane, an ironic expression that is more than merely a play on words.[9]

If we take Freud's admonition about psychosis as rebellion seri-ously, we cannot help but notice that it is those groups who are most constrained, least powerful, and most victimized, that are most likely to bear mental-illness labels. Powerlessness may have made the labeling easier. Alternatively, being crazy may make more sense in a punishing world than coping with ultimately overly restrictive and eventually false choices. And taking a note from Freud's largely neglected depth psychology, uncovering the complex lan-guage of nonreason could occur in an equal partnership of analyst and analysand. As spiritual seekers together, this could well pro-vide an enriched professional role for psychiatry in the future.

CHAPTER 5—NOTES

[1] Descartes's famous phrase symbolizes the rationalists' focus, an almost exclusive concern with cognition over emotional or value issues. In our current epoch, European structuralism challenges this approach as the primary method of knowledge, and instead argues that the underlying (unconscious) structure is the source for our mental and practical activities. For general analysis and application of this structuralist approach see Levi-Strauss (1967) and De George and De George (1972). For application of structural theory to popular culture, see Leymore (1975).

[2] Korchin (1976) critiques the overdependence on medical metaphors for the conceptualization and treatment of psychological problems, and claims that there are inherent dangers from this approach: it encourages passivity; emphasizes body ills requiring surgery or drugs; creates role inequality between doctor and patient; limits mental health as a professional problem for physicians rather than a shared concern among citizens, patients and other professional and lay groups; leads to a search for specific etiologies, therapies and prognoses that overemphasize diagnosis; entails dangers of labeling and stigmatizing; and fnally, as a disease model emphasizes the pathological themes in life and neglects the sources of competence and strength in personality development. This writer calls for a completely revamped vocabulary in terms other than those traditionally used in medicine.

[3] Schizophrenia (and its related terms) is a disorder particularly resistant to standard therapies, and has received extensive professional attention. What authorities conclude is that the expression of symptoms (e.g., voices, excitability, paranoia, flatness of affect, poverty of speech, slowness, underactivity, social withdrawal, impaired ability to communicate) is directly related to the environment. High-stress environments require more medication than low-stress or highly stable environments. On the whole, mental hospitals do not cure this psychosis, although good environments (and more recently, highly advanced drug therapies) can often restore the severely afflicted to moderate functioning. About half of all diagnosed schizophrenics continue to show symptoms after hospitalization. (For a review, see Wing, 1978:1333-1339; and Silversein and Harrow, 1978:1481-1486.) In China, schizophrenics occupy 80 percent of all mental health beds (Visher and Visher, 1979:28-32).

[4] According to a Wyoming study, legislators appear to believe that the insanity defense is overused, and to grossly overestimate the frequency and success rate of the "not guilty by reason of insanity" plea (Pasewark and Pantle, 1979:222-223).

[5] Hollingshead and Redlich (1958) emphasize that being a mental patient is directly related to low status, especially for men. Except for the lowest socioeconomic class, women are *more* likely to be psychiatric patients, compared to men, whether they are upper, middle or working class. This bias in favor of institutionalizing women for role failure has been attacked by Chessler (1972), who asserts that such practices are related to female powerlessness and dependency, low social integration, and incapacity of women to shape their own social

meanings and destinies. This implies that mental disorder may be a direct result of *conformity* to traditional roles. The wife/mother role not only severely cripples the woman's efforts to achieve autonomy and self-mastery but such roles are also linked to high social loss as the woman ages (e.g., divorce, empty nest, a routine, loveless marriage, severe curtailment on choice-oriented conduct, among others). These findings are corroborated in a recent book by Maggie Scarf (1979), who states that the demands and contradictions of "being feminine" result in a rate of depression among women two to five times the male rate, and growing. Thus, whether women attempt to perform traditional roles or take on nontraditional roles and life styles, the outcomes may be similar with high rates of anxiety, depression and schizophrenia, an increasingly high incidence of alcoholism and drug addition, and other related diseases.

[6] Analysis of prevalence rates (rates of admission to treatment) is mired in ambiguity. Because there is no generally agreed-upon criteria of psychological health or disorder, and because only a small minority of those judged to be psychiatric cases in high-rate studies (self-report data) have ever been in treatment for psychiatric disorder, and finally, because rates of admission vary so widely in different communities (e.g., studies show that there is a variation of one percent to 60 percent in different studies), the prevalence issue remains the least well understood aspect of any psychiatric epidemiology (see Dohrenwend and Dohrenwend, 1972:283-302).

[7] Able psychiatrists apparently find institutional regimes basically unsatisfying, tending to withdraw both from the total institution and the community-care settings in favor of private practice (Winslow, 1979:24-27).

[8] Law suits on behalf of patients who received involuntary surgery are now surfacing (Kneeland, 1979:A14). Other criticisms focus on professionally arbitrary and ill-advised drug dosages that produce severe lethargy or acutely disorientating or physically disabling side effects (Steinmann, 1972:114-121).

[9] Laing (1960, 1967) chooses to emphasize the political nature of deviance to make his point. In doing so, he displays enormous insensitivity to the very genuine problems of the severe mentally disturbed (comment by E. Sagarin in letter).

Chapter 6
Symbolic Offenses:
The Case of the Woman Offender

The sexual caste system is not solely *de facto*. Its rules and restrictions have been enshrined in the legal system since time immemorial and still serve as mechanisms of social control to maintain each sex in its ascribed place. In fact, one can trace the history of caste systems in Western Culture by looking at the legal rules...For the past 150 years, the major caste divisions have been along the lines of age, sex, and ethnic origin; these have been the categories for which special legislation has existed.

Jo Freeman, "The Legal Basis of the Sexual Caste System."

This chapter treats the woman offender as a special case in the symbolic construction of deviance. Sinned against more than sinning, the woman offender performs a kind of scapegoat role. Her crimes are translated into a symbol that expresses some of the profound ambivalences of women and control groups about changing race, gender and occupational boundaries. Women offenders offer a powerful symbol of social control in that they testify to the state's capacity to use punishment to buttress sagging moral and social boundaries.

The Manufacture of Deviance

How do women offenders serve a symbolic function in social control? What rationales, data and myths are brought to bear in this manufacture of deviance?

First, the historically low incidence of female arrest, prosecution and sentencing has undergone sharp increases in both prevalence and variety of criminal arrests. The women's movement is often blamed for this trend. This "new female criminal," supposedly equally adept at committing property crimes and violent crimes, has been personified in media ccounts by such atypical women as Bernardine Dohrn, Susan Sax, Patty Hearst, Emily Harris and Katherine Anne Power, and has been legitimated by criminologists Sir Leon Radcinowicz, Francis Ianni and Freda Adler (see Adler, 1975). The myth of the new female criminal also has gained wide currency among control groups. For example, Los Angeles Police Chief Ed Davis asserts that the women's movement has triggered "a crime wave like the world has never seen before" (Weis, 1976:17). Social control is thus perceived as the appropriate instrument to attack women's social and legal emancipation.

Secondly, female criminality clarifies changing norms and modes of control. Social control is both more legalistic and more expansive. In an epoch that emphasizes increased organizational rationality—efficiency, cost cutting and effective treatment—is it possible that a policy of penalizing female offenders may be out of place? For example, expanding women's prisons for the locking up of prostitutes, drug addicts and petty shoplifters appears to us as highly nonrational. What is the point, we ask, of putting women who commit minor offenses in prison? The criminologists' answers —deterrence, punishment, vengeance, law and order requirements—make some obvious sense for dangerous street criminals, almost all of whom are men. When considering a disciplinary regime for women, though, this rhetoric is not convincing. Instead, a repressive crime-control policy for women runs counter to larger legal and social trends. In this century changing moralities in regard to deviant acts have resulted in narrowing the reach of the criminal sanction or in its elimination altogether (for example, the decriminalization of homosexuality, the legalization of abortion and legal gambling in selected resort areas). Criminalizing women's offenses thus runs counter to this trend.

In sum, under the new conditions of gender-role breakdown, deviance among women has undergone a reclassification from offensive to criminal. In the process, the deviant act shifts from local regulation by kin and community to formal control—police, judges, welfare workers, psychiatrists and other nonkin groups. The criminal justice system functions as a fallback structure. It catches those troublesome populations who occupy tenuous social positions or have limited resources. Over the last decade it has moved rapidly to reestablish gender order by constructing crimes for women and using them as symbolic offenses for validating conventional female roles and punishing deviations from traditional role assignments. In our analysis, crime control is a political reality and women occupy a powerless position *vis à vis* their official caretakers (see Quinney, 1979).

The Political Reality of Crime

Official crime reports, though laden with implicit biases and various numerical misrepresentations, have been used by criminologists for comparison purposes. Drawing on F.B.I. uniform crime reports, other arrest data, and official documents, criminologist report that within a single decade women have entered the crime rolls at an alarming rate. For adult women offenders, arrests went up 85 percent over an eleven-year period (1960-1971) with the under-18-year-old age group having a reported rate increase of 229 percent. Today, women and girls count heavily in arrests for property crimes, and they show continuously high involvement in various victimless crimes, especially drug offenses. If rate increases alone are considered, and these data may mask actual crime involvement, women show high participation for all three major crime categories—violent, property and victimless offenses. Tables 6:1 , 6:2, and 6:3 show trend data as reported by the Federal Bureau of Investigation. The first compares male and female arrests for 1978. Based on number alone, it is clear that females are much less involved in visible crime than males. If we move back a few years to 1975 and consider rates once again, another picture emerges. Here females under 18 show sharp increases in serious crimes, for example, a 27.8-percent increase in criminal homicide, a 51.6-percent increase in manslaughter, a 19.2-percent increase in robbery and a 11.6-percent increase in aggravated assault. These data support the myth of violent women criminals.

Table 6:1 Total Arrests, Distribution by Sex, 1978

[11,872 agencies; 1978 estimated population 207,060,000]

	Number of persons arrested			Percent male	Percent female	Percent distribution[1]		
	Total	Male	Female			Total	Male	Female
TOTAL...........	9,775,087	8,227,228	1,547,859	84.2	15.8	100.0	100.0	100.0
Murder and nonnegligent manslaughter	18,755	16,103	2,652	85.9	14.1	.2	.2	.2
Forcible rape.............	28,257	28,013	244	99.1	.9	.3	.3	(2)
Robbery.................	141,481	131,563	9,918	93.0	7.0	1.4	1.6	.6
Aggravated assault......	257,629	225,018	32,611	87.3	12.7	2.6	2.7	2.1
Burglary................	485,782	455,933	29,849	93.9	6.1	5.0	5.5	1.9
Larceny-theft..........	1,084,088	740,335	343,753	68.3	31.7	11.1	9.0	22.2
Motor vehicle theft.....	153,270	140,488	12,782	91.7	8.3	1.6	1.7	.8
Violent crime[3]........	446,122	400,697	45,425	89.8	10.2	4.6	4.9	2.9
Property crime[4].......	1,723,140	1,336,756	386,384	77.6	22.4	17.6	16.2	25.0
Crime Index total........	2,169,262	1,737,453	431,809	80.1	19.9	22.2	21.1	27.9
Other assaults...........	445,020	384,182	60,838	86.3	13.7	4.6	4.7	3.9
Arson...................	18,114	15,900	2,214	87.8	12.2	.2	.2	.1
Forgery and counterfeiting...	73,269	51,502	21,767	70.3	29.7	.7	.6	1.4
Fraud...................	249,207	157,580	91,627	63.2	36.8	2.5	1.9	5.9
Embezzlement............	7,670	5,742	1,928	74.9	25.1	.1	.1	.1
Stolen property; buying, receiving, possessing........	112,317	99,946	12,371	89.0	11.0	1.1	1.2	.8
Vandalism...............	223,391	204,664	18,727	91.6	8.4	2.3	2.5	1.2
Weapons; carrying, possessing, etc.	149,957	138,482	11,475	92.3	7.7	1.5	1.7	.7

Prostitution & commercialized vice	89,365	28,900	60,465	32.3	67.7	.9	.4	3.9
Sex offenses (except forcible rape, prostitution)	65,666	60,493	5,173	92.1	7.9	.7	.7	.3
Drug abuse violations	596,940	515,230	81,710	86.3	13.7	6.1	6.3	5.3
Gambling	53,066	48,452	4,614	91.3	8.7	.5	.6	.3
Offenses against family & children	54,014	48,502	5,512	89.8	10.2	.6	.6	.4
Driving under the influence	1,204,733	1,103,386	101,347	91.6	8.4	12.3	13.4	6.5
Liquor laws	357,450	304,875	52,575	85.3	14.7	3.7	3.7	3.4
Drunkenness	1,117,349	1,034,412	82,937	92.6	7.4	11.4	12.6	5.4
Disorderly conduct	679,112	570,020	109,092	83.9	16.1	6.9	6.9	7.0
Vagrancy	46,896	33,099	13,797	70.6	29.4	.5	.4	.9
All other offenses (except traffic)	1,788,757	1,530,098	258,659	85.5	14.5	18.3	18.6	16.7
Suspicion	21,650	18,748	2,902	86.6	13.4	.2	.2	.2
Curfew and loitering law violations	78,986	61,890	17,096	78.4	21.6	.8	.8	1.1
Runaways	172,896	73,672	99,224	42.6	57.4	1.8	.9	6.4

1 Because of rounding, the percentages may not add to total.
2 Less than one-tenth of 1 percent.
3 Violent crimes are offenses of murder, forcible rape, robbery, and aggravated assault.
4 Property crimes are offenses of burglary, larceny-theft, and motor vehicle theft.

Source: F.B.I. Uniform Crime Reports, 1978: Published October, 1979, p.197.

Table 6:2   Arrests, by Offense Cha

(5,074 agencies;

	Males		
	Total		
Offense Charged	1974	1975	Percent change
	5,411,175	5,521,491	+ 2.0
Criminal homicide:			
Murder and nonnegligent manslaughter	12,183	12,055	- 1.1
Manslaughter by negligence	2,202	2,195	- .3
Forcible rape	18,652	18,829	+ .9
Robbery	101,531	108,257	+ 6.6
Aggravated assault	140,584	147,912	+ 5.2
Burglary	337,365	362,148	+ 7.3
Larceny-theft	528,972	564,272	+ 6.7
Motor vehicle theft	102,678	97,195	- 5.3
Violent crime (a)	272,950	287,053	+ 5.2
Property crime (b)	969,015	1,023,615	+ 5.6
Subtotal for above offenses	1,244,167	1,312,863	+ 5.5
Other assaults	241,114	260,253	+ 7.9
Arson	10,095	10,968	+ 8.6
Forgery and counterfeiting	31,525	34,618	+ 9.8
Fraud	65,484	74,577	+13.9
Embezzlement	4,709	4,459	- 5.3
Stolen property:buying,receiving possessing	72,587	77,967	+ 7.4
Vandalism	136,282	141,902	+ 4.1
Weapons:carrying,possessing,etc.	107,622	105,148	- 2.3
Prostitution & commercialized vice	11,739	11,677	- .5
Sex offenses (except forcible rape and prostitution	41,117	41,026	- .2
Narcotic drug laws	390,510	366,392	- 6.2
Gambling	40,976	41,698	+ 1.8
Offenses against family & children	33,936	38,498	+13.4
Driving under the influence	609,758	680,272	+11.6
Liquor laws	172,385	190,087	+10.3
Drunkenness	933,763	851,599	- 8.8
Disorderly conduct	378,472	375,178	- .9
Vagrancy	29,678	25,670	-13.5
All other offenses(except traffic)	705,518	729,245	+ 3.4
Suspicion(not included in totals)	28,044	22,087	-21.2
Curfew & loitering law violations	81,951	79,500	- 3.0
Runaways	67,787	67,894	+ .2

(a) Violent crime is offenses of murder, forcible rape, robbery, a
(b) Property crime is offenses of burglary, larcency-theft, and mo

Source: U.S. Department of Justice, Federal Bureau of Investigati
Government Printing Office, 1976), p. 187.

ed, Sex, and Age Group, United States, 1974-75

975 estimated population 145,719,972)

			Females					
Under 18			Total			Under 18		
1974	1975	Percent change	1974	1975	Percent change	1974	1975	Percent change
1,389,617	1,409,358	+ 1.4	1,026,354	1,071,747	+ 4.4	369,741	380,067	+ 2.8
1,313	1,235	- 5.9	2,102	2,214	+ 5.3	108	138	+27.8
218	244	+11.9	316	286	- 9.5	31	47	+51.6
3,698	3,345	- 9.5	160	189	+18.1	60	49	-18.3
34,219	37,763	+10.4	7,447	8,164	+ 9.6	2,545	3,033	+19.2
22,951	25,966	+13.1	21,888	22,571	+ 3.1	4,383	4,892	+11.6
181,060	191,202	+ 5.6	19,066	20,352	+ 7.1	9,897	10,367	+ 4.7
266,699	269,415	+ 1.0	238,582	263,471	+10.4	105,865	109,298	+ 3.2
57,413	52,734	- 8.1	7,132	7,186	+ .8	4,116	4,192	+ 1.8
62,181	68,309	+ 9.9	31,597	33,138	+ 4.9	7,096	8,112	+14.3
505,172	513,351	+ 1.6	264,720	291,009	+ 9.9	119,878	123,857	+ 3.3
567,571	581,904	+ 2.5	296,633	324,433	+ 9.4	127,005	132,016	+ 3.9
43,498	48,411	+11.3	38,743	42,219	+ 9.0	11,548	13,129	+13.7
5,899	6,005	+ 1.8	1,213	1,446	+19.2	618	636	+ 2.9
4,086	4,424	+ 8.3	12,568	14,187	+12.9	1,720	1,843	+ 7.2
2,547	2,905	+14.1	33,606	39,655	+18.0	1,021	1,104	+ 8.1
362	451	+24.6	1,637	1,497	- 8.6	110	119	+ 8.2
25,146	26,233	+ 4.3	8,399	9,302	+10.8	2,326	2,423	+ 4.2
94,631	93,325	- 1.4	11,733	12,525	+ 6.8	7,457	7,617	+ 2.1
18,020	17,729	- 1.6	9,273	9,099	- 1.9	1,067	1,196	+12.1
613	505	-17.6	33,392	33,306	- .3	1,357	1,525	+12.4
8,770	8,398	- 4.2	3,516	3,453	- 1.8	1,237	1,019	-17.6
97,852	86,323	-11.8	63,755	59,050	- 7.4	19,924	16,929	-15.0
1,522	1,502	- 1.3	3,879	3,702	- 4.6	72	81	+12.5
2,698	3,366	+24.8	4,703	5,158	+ 9.7	1,608	2,037	+26.7
8,701	12,678	+45.7	52,170	62,880	+20.5	704	1,092	+55.1
66,203	72,532	+ 9.6	30,555	32,519	+ 6.4	16,466	18,838	+14.4
26,477	28,311	+ 6.9	72,831	67,725	- 7.0	4,071	4,438	+ 9.0
86,465	84,159	- 2.7	107,560	98,721	- 8.2	18,599	16,901	- 9.1
4,514	3,880	-14.0	5,272	5,605	+ 6.3	787	659	-16.3
174,304	178,923	+ 2.6	130,613	135,099	+ 3.4	47,741	46,299	- 3.0
8,156	5,613	-31.2	4,499	3,589	-20.2	1,456	979	-32.8
81,951	79,500	- 3.0	20,269	19,600	- 3.3	20,269	19,600	- 3.3
67,787	67,894	+ .2	84,034	90,566	+ 7.8	84,034	90,566	+ 7.8

aggravated assault.

r vehicle theft.

, Uniform Crime Reports for the United States, 1975 (Washington, D.C.: U.S.

Table 6:3   Arrests, by Offense Charged and Sex, United States, 1977

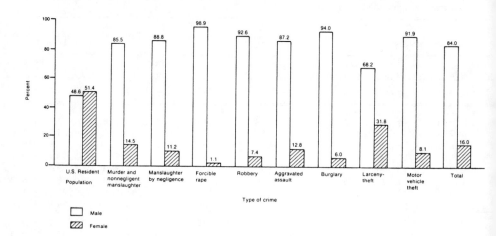

Source: U.S. Department of Justice, Federal Bureau of Investigation, *Uniform Crime Reports for the United States, 1977* (Washington, D.C.: U.S. Government Printing Office, 1978), p. 183; and U.S. Department of Commerce, Bureau of the Census, *Current Population Reports, Population Estimates and Projections*, Series P-25, No. 721 (Washington, D.C.: U.S. Government Printing Office, 1978), p. 17.

Criminologist Rita Simon (1975), who has examined trend data intensively, categorically rejects the women's-move- ment-causes-violent-crime-thesis. Instead, her data support a strong case for near equal participation in property crime involve- ment, as indicated by arrests and prosecutions. Women are selec- tively participating in criminal behavior, Simon asserts, not engag- ing in wholesale deviance or violent crimes. Overall, criminal involvement for women remains a fraction of male involvement. Female arrest for violent crime comprise a little over ten percent. Their relatively higher arrest rates for property crime is mainly for larceny, where they account for 31.8 percent of the total arrests

(1977). This reflects the consumer role played by women in industrial societies. Laws penalizing victimless crimes, long attacked by critics because enforcement procedures violate due process, provide readymade categories for controlling female morality. These account for nearly 60 percent of all female arrests. For example, vagrancy and suspicion are catchall categories for picking up suspects when no more specific charge can be made (*Canadian Journal of Corrections*, editorial, 1968:438-441). Laws against prostitution, another convenient control category, apply for both men and women in all but five states, but men are rarely arrested for this "female crime." To discover what female crime—or, more accurately, arrests—actually are and to pinpoint the status characteristics of persons involved in these arrests, we have reconstructed the *Uniform Crime Reports* shown above to produce six major arrest categories for women—theft, forgery, fraud, prostitution, vagrancy and runaway. By comparing black and white representativeness in arrest statistics, we can draw some telling inferences about criminal statistics and status characteristics.

Table 6:4 Traditional "Female Crimes" — Theft, Forgery, Fraud, Prostitution, Vagrancy and Runaway: Arrest Trends by Race*

	White		Black		% of Female Arrests
	Number	%	Number	%	
Larceny— theft	363,337	63.6	194,949	34.1	31.8
Forgery	38,438	65.3	19,787	33.6	29.1
Fraud	11,939	53.4	10,156	45.4	35.6
Prostitution	32,577	44.3	39,554	53.7	70.7
Vagrancy	21,956	57.0	15,665	40.7	34.2
Runaway	159,996	86.9	19,673	10.7	57.6

* Table adapted from the *Sourcebook of Criminal Justice Statistics* (1979:464, 468, 469).
"Female Crimes" are those in which the number of female arrests are 25 percent or more of the total.
Percents do not add up to 100 because other races (e.g., Indian, Chinese) were not included in this tabulation.

First, it is apparent that breaking down women's crime involvement at the arrest level shows less a picture of serious crime involvement than a rendering of female deviance. Inasmuch as women remain minor offenders, property, sex and status crimes characterize the greatest bulk of women's criminal activities. Shoplifting or larceny is a classic female deviance and heads the list as the most frequent property crime for which women are arrested.

Second, the relative concentration of female arrests among blacks reveals that black women are almost two and one-half times more likely to be arrested than white women (relative to their proportion in the population) for larceny, forgery, and vagrancy, but nearly five times more likely to confront arrest for prostitution. Here they figure in well over 50 percent of all arrests. Other data confirm this picture of low social power and resources as a prior condition for entering the criminal justice system. The Women's Prison Association (1974) reports that two thirds of female offenders are under 30 and almost 75 percent are unmarried (See Glick and Neto, 1976). The largest proportion have less than a high school education, few have advanced job skills, and over half are black. Seventy-five percent have dependent children.

Third, rate analysis distorts the crime picture. Over a 20-year period there has been no discernible change in women's involvement in violent crimes. Between 1953 and 1972 (the most significant change period), the percentage of women arrested for crimes of violence holds firm (Simon, 1975:39). In this urban, industrial society of over 220 million, the real number of violent crimes for youthful females remains low. In 1977, for example, among teenage girls (17 and under), 136 were arrested for first-degree murder; 47 for manslaughter; 2,757 for robbery; and 5,206 for serious assault. Teenage boys continue to murder, rape, rob and assault at numbers that are 5-20 times greater than that for girls (*Sourcebook of Criminal Justice Statistics*, 1979:466).

Fourth, economic crimes, not violent ones, inflate the arrest rates. In 1953, about one in every twelve persons arrested for property crimes was a woman. In 1977, one in every four persons arrested was female. The greater proportion of women arrested for property crimes as compared with men (25 percent of all female arrests versus 16.2 percent of all male arrests in 1977) suggests that if trends continue, female arrest rates for larceny, theft, embezzlement and fraud will be roughly equal to male arrest rates by 1990 (Simon, 1975:46).

Fifth, the greatest rate increase among all arrest categories in the period 1960-73 is violation of narcotic drug laws, where both males and females 17 and under show increases of over 4,000 percent and 6,000 percent, respectively. During the same period, drug arrests for both adult and youthful offenders rose 1,125 percent, while the overall arrest rate increased by only 14.5 percent. Drug arrests represented the most substantial percentage change in any offense category. For example, marijuana accounted for 66.9 percent of the total in 1973 (up from 18.3 percent of arrests in 1963) (Balch and Griffiths, 1975). According to Balch and Griffiths (1975) declining arrest rates for offenses against public morality (e.g., drunkenness) left a gap to be filled by the invention of a new form of deviance; namely the sale and possession of dangerous drugs. As guardians of the moral order, the police serve as the first line of defense against threats to the prevailing social system. One major outcome of the officially constructed "drug crisis" has been an expansion of police staff and budgets.

Sixth, despite the rate jump, females may actually be underrepresented in arrest statistics. In Oregon, police arrest four males for every female picked up. Among Portland adults arrested for narcotic use or sales, almost all are under 30, with women constituting 23 percent of these arrests (Portland Police Statistics, 1975). Though changing sex roles and the women's movement are alleged sources for increased crimes among women, they probably play a less central role in women's increased use of contraband drugs than participation in the youth culture. In this context drugs are a symbolic gesture of defiance against established values and life styles (Robinson and Miller, 1975:101-109).

Seventh, the lower arrest rate for women as compared with men has alternative interpretations. Historically, low rates justified official and scientific neglect—"the forgotten offenders," in Marcia Hovey's (1971) analysis. Enforcement and sentencing policies reflect this invisibility in maintaining custodial programs that foster a "revolving door" system of justice. Contrariwise, even 15 percent of total arrests account for close to one million women, the largest proportion of whom are young, poor and minority. Offenders are generally young. Fifty-five percent of all arrests reported to the FBI are among persons under 25. While the under 18-year-old male group comprises an estimated 20 percent of the male offender population, teenage females 17 and under account for about 33 percent of all female arrests. Greater public visibility as women move out of the home into the marketplace and street as well as open flouting of stereotypical sex roles may explain, in part, this 13-percent differential.

Eighth, other evidence suggests that regulating minorities constitutes the hidden agenda of criminal justice agencies. Minority women, like their male counterparts, provide a highly visible pool of offenders that seem to justify increased police power.

Ninth, social class is the key variable accounting for the "funnel effect" (Blumberg, 1967). This screens out affluent, respectable, middle class citizens who can afford expert witnesses and private attorneys and who have influential community and credit contacts. Those women caught up in the control net form the one percent of unscreenables, the "dregs" of the system. Such persons lack social resources and political clout and provide a ready-made deviant pool for filling correctional and mental institutions. By contrast, middle class offenders, whether male or female, who are potentially able to cause "trouble" for the system, have less negative police contact and tend to be protected rather than exploited by control groups.

Tenth, Wilkins (1965) offers a deviance-amplification model as a more general explanation for rate increases in criminal acts and criminal subcultures. Very low social tolerance of troublesome social groups, Wilkins argues, leads to increasing the total number of proscriptive legal categories, and hence the number of persons defined as lawbreakers. This strategy fosters alienation and, subsequently, a high crime rate among labeled groups. Increases in their criminality cause more forceful action by control groups, who pit conforming groups against nonconformists. As more acts become defined as deviant, a context for exacting harsher penalties is built. Thus, the entire system continues around and around in an amplifying circuit. Stringent control leads to the devaluation of social sanctioning systems.

Finally, the most basic criticism of these trend data is their low statistical credibility. Because crime data represent a type of social production, arrests should be interpreted as an internal accounting system produced by the organization for keeping track of its own activities and for legitimating requests for public funds and personnel. Whatever the actual "hidden figure" of women's crime, it is doubtful if any methodology can be constructed to uncover this concealed social fact. Because of the political nature of crime control, prosecutors tend to choose cases that will reflect favorably on their career. For example, low convictions for rape have been attributed to a limited enforcement mandate for controlling this offense because of low success rates (Schram, 1978). Conversly, lower class women caught for prostitution, petty shoplifting and other fairly trivial offenses, provide easy marks and help to fill necessary organizational quotas with little or no public outcry about these arrangements. (Critical analyses of standard political interpretations are also available in Heidenshon, 1968; Smart, 1976; and Davis, 1977:247-276.)

Statistical trends provide little more than a gloss on the political reality of crime. A more feasible approach is to examine the life fate of women who have experienced arrest and imprisonment, the topic of our next section.

Women Offenders

Who are the women offenders? What are their status characteristics, their work, family and leisure time activities? What problems do they confront as insiders accommodating to the prison regime; and what external constraints act upon them in regard to the labor market, support structures, resources, and their own aspirations? What are the objective features in their lives that contribute to conventional role behaviors, compared with those that encourage deviance and crime? And finally, in what way does the rehabilitation doctrine currently applied to offender groups contribute to a disrehabilitation outcome for offenders.[1]

Status Characteristics and Focal Concerns

Among the 61 imprisoned women we interviewed, we found the expected lower class and caste ranks evident in other prison studies. Whereas middle and upper class groups are never or rarely in prisons or jail, the low-income, unskilled, often minority populations in urban centers are most likely to have negative experiences with police, and many have been in jail for short or long periods (Crawford, 1975:262-272). Among some of the women in our sample, jailing is a new experience. Sixty percent are first-time offenders, although they are relatively older than first-time offenders in national surveys (50 percent are over 25 years old). (For a review of women in prison, see, for example, Giallombardo, 1966; Ward and Kassebaum, 1965; Glick and Neto, 1975; Burkhart, 1973.) Table 6.5 summarizes status characteristics of our sample.

Table 6:5   Social Characteristics of Study Population and Arrest Charge

		%	N
Age	Under 21	22.9	14
	22-25 yrs	27.8	17
	26-30 yrs	26.2	16
	Over 30	22.9	14
Race	White	52.4	32
	Black	39.3	24
	Indian	4.9	3
	Other	3.2	2
Marital Status	Unmarried (Single, divorced, separated, widowed)	80.3	49
	Married	19.6	12
Father's Occupation	White Collar	13.1	8
	Skilled	8.2	5
	Semi-Skilled	47.5	29
	Unemployed	9.8	6
	Don't Know	6.5	4
	No Answer	14.1	9
Subject's Education	Eight Grade or less	11.4	7
	Some High School	34.7	21
	High School	19.6	12
	Some College	31.1	19
	College Degree	1.6	1
	Post-Graduate	1.6	1
No. of Children	None	13.1	8
	One	32.7	20
	Two	22.9	14
	Three	19.6	12
	Four or more	6.5	4
	N/A	4.9	3
*Arrest Charge**	Violent Crime (murder, manslaughter, robbery assault)	18.0	11
	Property Crime (theft, burglary, forgery)	39.3	24
	Drug and Drug-Related Offenses	26.2	16
	Prostitution	13.1	8
	Other (probation violation, conspiracy, concealed weapon, unlawful use of vehicle)	6.5	4
	N/A	3.2	2

* Percent exceeds 100% because of multiple charges in some cases.

Family histories reveal a fairly high level of family and economic instability. For example, as children, 57 percent spent one year or more in foster homes or experienced other long-term separations from parents. The greatest proportion have high school degrees or less, and only 20 percent live in intact marriages. Frequent separations and limited income and education among parents presents a classic picture of both female and male offender groups. Where women differ from men is their double jeopardy: first, by a sex-typed job market, defined by Sullivan (1976) as a dual labor market for black women and a secondary labor market for white women; and, second, by dependent children, for whom many serve as sole economic and social support. For the petty criminal (a term descriptive of 82 percent of these women, most of whom have been incarcerated for minor felonies such as larceny, check fraud, prostitution, drugs and welfare fraud) jailing interrupts an already unstable marital, live-in or boyfriend relationship. Their living pattern usually consists of a relatively steady but low-paying job, a low to moderate parenting commitment and an urban life style oriented around drink, drugs, parties and sex. Let us consider each of these focal life concerns separately: support groups, job, parenting and leisure time.

According to our findings, relationships with men are inconstant affairs. On the whole, men of this class cannot be counted on to support the family, to fill in during crises or to support the woman during her "bad" periods: imprisonment, drug or alcohol abuse (overdose), depression or suicide attempts. Live-in men can usually be depended upon for some domestic assistance—taking care of the car, buying insurance, contributing to food and other household expenses and sharing vacations. But they tend to disappear when the woman is arrested and rarely turn up during the arrest and court period for child care or moral support. Except for the relatively few high-income earners (usually prostitutes), most of these women seek public welfare to tide them over bad periods. About 60 percent of the women we spoke with admitted to having regular contact with community agencies for welfare, medical, counseling or other basic services over the last year. For most of these women, depending upon other persons creates a double bind. Significant others are likely to be men and are often undependable for financial and social support. Women are supportive, but are defined as too emotional or materially deprived to offer sustained support. In times of emergency, an impersonal case worker may be the only viable support person available.

For most women, the job as a focal concern offers a mixed agenda of limited, but significant, social participation, albeit in low income, dead-end jobs. Two work patterns emerge from these data. First, women conform to a segregated labor market that isolates transient, low-status and underpaid jobs into a distinguishable submarket. Gordon (1972) states that the nature of these jobs is to reinforce poor work habits such as nonpunctuality, irresponsibility, proneness to quit and other low performances that justify for management the low wages and high rate of layoffs.

Among our sample, the greatest proportion worked three different jobs over five years, although over one third shifted jobs more frequently. None of the women admitted they were ever fired for poor performance. For most, leaving a job was necessitated by personal family or working conditions (e.g., illness of self or child, graveyard shift, overlong working hours colliding with family responsibilities, objectionable or hassling supervisors or workmates and so on). Many indicated the desire to seek a better job, but few women left a job for mobility reasons. Additionally, they commented that most jobs were not worth returning to after release from prison.

The second pattern shown by these data contrasts with the depressed employment picture and reveals a fairly strong work orientation. Many of these women want more than they are getting, inasmuch as they expressed high work aspirations and made attempts to upgrade skills (43 percent took some post-high-school training). Less than 30 percent indicated a willingness to settle for low-level employment (e.g., domestic or factory work). Middle class career aspirations are evident by the strong response to the question: "Do you think a career is as important for a woman as a man?" (81.9 percent agreed.)

What these imprisoned women wish to receive and what they realistically expect, though, suggests a critical discrepancy. In addition to work aspirations being out of joint with experience, many women tacitly or directly reject sex-typed job positions. Traditional "women's work" (e.g., retail sales, clerical work, waitressing, child care, domestic work) was acceptable to only 36 percent. However, when asked what kind of work they could *realistically* get after release, the traditional women's work category rose to 44 percent.

Life in prison may distort realistic planning or job counseling. For the overwhelming proportion (75 percent), there was little or no information available on vocational or educational programs, or if the women were aware of any in-prison programs, they expressed uncertainty about whether they could qualify.

How do parenting arrangements contribute to or undermine conformity? If marriages and live-in relationships are basically unstable, jobs are segmental, short-term enterprises, and even friendships are fleeting, as these data show, is it possible that parenting provides the core set of values and practices for most women inmates? The answer is mixed: ideally, yes, but practically speaking, no. Commitment is the essential problem in the parenting role. But it is primarily a resource-related problem and only secondarily an emotional and intellectual one. Our evidence certainly shows parenting to be the most demanding and durable focal concern for almost all of the 54 women in our sample who are parents (see also Lundberg et al, 1975). Not only was parenting the primary responsibility of these prison mothers when they were civilians, but few could count on live-in men to handle the child arrangements during arrest and court periods. For example, only four women indicated that their husbands took charge of their children during their most recent imprisonment. Many women had to handle the details themselves or rely on absentee relatives or the court. Relatives and friends are about twice as likely to take over care of children during the mother's incarceration than the woman's husband or children's father (especially when the husband is not the natural father).

Separation from children and inability to shape their destinies may be one of the more frustrating aspects of imprisonment (see also Lundberg et al., 1975). Almost 40 percent of these mothers are thoroughly dissatisfied with the present child placement. Their worries center upon the child's reaction to the mother's separation or fear that the child will discover the real reason for separation. Younger children, especially, are reported to be sad, depressed or fearful (27.8 percent). Their behavior could be best characterized as dependent, passive or negative (36 percent), and occasionally antisocial, aggressive, angry and rebellious (9 percent). Almost half the women indicated that before jailing, their children were primarily dependent on themselves, although another 30 percent shared some of the parenting role with husbands or relatives (21 percent gave no response). Once the women are in prison, the children depend mainly on others—grandparents, their father, the woman's sister or other relatives. For a few, there is loss of the child to foster parents (6.5 percent). Only six women among 54 indicated that their children turned to them for help while they were in prison.

Despite the centrality of the parenting role, separation from children is a fairly common occurrence among women offenders. Among this Oregon-Washington women-offender group, 42.8 percent have been separated from their children two years or more. Prison is not the sole cause of separation, as the largest proportion (over 60 percent) report their prison term to be under one year. Both work and family instability equally promote separation from children (e.g., three women lost their children to estranged husbands who took them while they were in prison).

Prison arrangements also contribute to a sharp decline in communication between the woman and her children. Almost 40 percent never visit or write children, although the telephone enables most to keep in touch with the home base (and is encouraged by the institution, which allows one free phone call a week). The difficulty here is that some mothers (22 percent) do not wish to share the guilty knowledge of their whereabouts, offering either no explanation or lying to their children about their prison stay. Despite these and other practical reservations, 71 percent report that they would like to have regular in-prison child-care arrangements.

Welfare and other agency dependencies often supplement or supplant the informal support system. Before imprisonment, almost 60 percent of the women admitted to having regular contact with community agencies, one third for welfare, and the other for various social services (e.g., medical, counseling). Forty-three percent were agency regulars, having had contact with one or more agencies for one year or more. Prison often exacerbated agency dependency without providing support, as when the Children's Services Division arbitrarily shifted children into foster care while the mother was in prison (five women).

Among these inmate mothers, it is apparent that both personal and structural commitment to parenthood are in jeopardy. Studies show that prisonization and protracted role loss loosen nonprison attachments, identities and obligations (see Quinney, 1979:341-359). When coupled with external constraints, including social pressures in prison that negate conventional role enactment, they contribute to what Johnson (1976) calls "termination procedures." These are specific steps to discontinue a line of action. Relatively infrequent child-mother communication, failure to confide in children about the mother's prison status, discontinuity in modes of childrearing practices between parent surrogates and the inmate mother, little or no opportunity for meeting dependent children's needs and lack of family counseling in and out of prison all may set in motion or exacerbate role withdrawal strategies. Nearly universal institutional expectations that paroled women will "naturally" return to traditional roles of homemaking and children (a rationale that justifies low expenditures for rehabilitation) do not take into account these important variables that undermine conventional role commitments.

Conforming life styles, then are problematic. They are hedged by disparities between preferred values and existential choices, by lack of viable role models and support persons, by role displacement and by a correctional milieu that reinforces feelings of deprivation and worthlessness. Women report that the worst things about prison, ranked in order of priority, are their feelings of powerlessness, boredom, separation from loved ones and a disesteemed self. An Oregon prison counselor with two years of correctional experience takes a critical view of rehabilitation in the following personal communication.

> At least 75 percent of the women are responsible for children. Once in jail they are powerless to keep their family together and have little or no say in decisions that are made. The only thing a woman can do is worry and try to forget by sleeping a lot, getting loaded on contraband drugs or letting herself get caught up in petty hassles and hustles of daily existence. There is a certain amount of maintenance and "busy" work, but for the most part the inmates are idle and tend to be preoccupied with the trivia of the setting. Very little of their activities have any relationship to bettering their life when they get out. Idleness leads to impaired sleep and weight gain and damages the individual's sense of physical well-being. It also increases the felt need for drugs—on the inside to sleep and stop (from) being nervous—and on the outside to lose the fat. The correctional system promotes the problem further by providing very fattening (and dull) food and handing out tranquilizers on demand allowing almost no athletic activities.

Moreover, once in prison, associations and friendships are almost exclusively with other offenders. Most women have few visitors from the outside, and these few often disappear with long-term internment. The use of letters to maintain intensive relationships is rare. Passivity, powerlessness and trivia characterize the woman offender's prison experience. Cherished values of autonomy, sociability, activism and expressiveness must be severely restricted and regimented with prison rules. Role invalidation in prison, then, has several negative consequences. It reduces conventional commitments by depriving the women of meaningful activities. It further enhances the deviant identity by intensive interaction within a segregated deviant world. And finally, invalidating civilian roles promotes ambiguity, or inability to organize self and roles for future action.

Leisure time activities, the fourth focal concern, may substitute for deprivations in other areas. Excitement is a strong value, evidenced by these women's reported preoccupation with parties, dancing, sports, going to bars, heavy drinking, drugs and nonmarital sexuality. Such activities appear to have a compelling influence in shaping identity and role organization because they lead to tolerating deviant activities as an acceptable way of life. Over two-thirds of these women are self-reported regular drug users, 50 percent of whom admit to being seriously addicted. Another 38 percent are probable alcoholics (moderate to heavy use), and over 30 percent have engaged in homosexual activities outside of prison. Prison homosexuality is a standard mode of coping for about one third, and another 55 percent indicated either tolerance or positive acceptance of homosexual persons or life styles. Another 21 percent of the women have experienced mental illness, a few having attempted suicide more than once. Arrest records also show high deviant involvement. About 48 percent have previous records, either as juveniles or adults, and a fair proportion are either tenuously or more firmly linked up with criminal subcultures, where violence, property crimes, drug sales and drug dependency are a way of life.

Do these data confirm Adler's (1975) portrait of the so-called masculinized, liberated female criminal? In one sense, they do. Lacking standard middle-class props of a supportive husband and a stable occupation, many women must assertively seek a niche in a highly competitive, often corrosive urban milieu. Drinking, drugs, lesbian relationships and mental illness may provide "secondary adjustments" (Goffman, 1961) for coping with role ambivalence and identity stripping. Such deviant behavior temporarily simplifies the struggle for survival, although eventually it exposes persons to official intervention and institutionalization. That most of these women remain uncommitted to the deviant life style is also apparent from our research. Other facets of self are equally or more important, as revealed in the conventional attitudes and concerns about job, family life, domesticity and friends. Neither liberated or alienated, these women often remain uncommitted, free to experiment with various unproductive and deviant life styles (see Irwin, 1977).

Now that we have considered statistical trends and offered our interpretation of the life world of imprisoned women, we need to examine in a broader theoretical context the varying explanations of women's criminality.

Social Construction of Women's Criminality

Biological and psychological theories that date back to Lombroso (1920), have dominated discussions of female criminality. These theories allege that biological, emotional or mental disturbances are the primary source for misconduct. In early studies the reasoning was blatantly stereotypical: an "evil-causes-evil" theorem, linking biological inferiority to moral incompetence (Glueck and Glueck, 1934). In this analysis, crime was interpreted as individual behavior; hence, only peripherally affected by economic, social or political factors (Klein, 1973; Klein and Kress, 1976).

Later revisions of the trait-analysis argument emphasized the special nature of female crime. Pollak (1950) believed it to be perpetuated by deceit or manipulation, rather than willful effort. Abortion, infanticide or homicide directed against helpless or sick victims demonstrated women's incapacity for open aggression. However, women could be accomplices of males in the criminal act, according to this view, because they hide behind male leadership.

Two conflicting arguments have been advanced regarding female criminality. On the one hand, women are said to have low criminal participation because of confining gender roles that limit opportunity and expression. Alternatively, they are also said to have relatively high (but invisible) criminal involvement due to crimes being conducted in the privacy of their homes. Thus, most offenses go undetected or unreported (Reckless and Kay, 1967).

Psychological studies have done little to clarify the rate muddle because most analyses have retained the abnormality thesis. This alleges that personality failures are the source of criminal behavior. Investigators' widespread claims to having identified sociopathy, hysteria and drug addiction in female prisoners have merely reinforced official doctrines that conner.ed psychological disorders and female criminality (see, for example, Hoffman-Bustamante, 1973:117-133).

The gender-trait analysis has been the preferred theory in accounting for women's differential criminal participation. This approach starts from the uncritical belief that sex-linked personality differences (male aggression, female passivity) are the chief factors that explain variations in crime patterns between the sexes. Masculine traits, identified as courage, adventuresomeness, strength, daring, leadership and so forth, are presumed to be independent variables causing crime and delinquency (see, for example, Mednick and Weissman, 1976:122-136).

Shover and Norland (1975), among critics of this approach, contend that trait analysis is ambiguous, that it obscures variables and relationships in *ad hoc* assumptions and that it assumes behavioral uniformity about gender traits and conduct that is unsupported by evidence. Instead, they sketch five parameters of criminality that may be different for males and females. Among women, criminality varies by (1) the distribution of offenses across offense categories (i.e., the types of crimes most often committed), (2) the extensiveness of criminal involvement, (3) the distribution of victims across victim categories (i.e., the most typical victims), (4) the *modus operandi* employed in committing offenses or, when more than one offender is involved, the role played in the perpetration of the offense, and (5) the subjective meaning of offenses, or the motives for criminal involvement.

The conception that crime is "masculine" conduct is also disputed by studies of self-reported crime among females. Clark and Huarek (1966:217-227) and associates studied juveniles in Ohio and found no difference in either number or types of self-reported delinquent acts between males and females, but a statistically significant larger number of *official* contacts for the male sample.

On the whole, traditional views of female deviance retain a two-category role prescription. "Normal" women are nonassertive and dependent upon males. Regardless of actual behavior, they are perceived as noncriminal. "Aberrant" females, contrariwise, are self-assertive or aggressive and violate sex-role norms. They are therefore suspect for criminal acts. Moral slippages among usually nonassertive women represent their more impulsive natures, easily swayed by passion or sentiment, as compared with men. This paternalistic doctrine is essentially an adjustment ethic in that it justifies intervention for the "fallen woman's own good." A heavy concentration of female arrests for status and morality offenses has been traced to this source.

A two-fold distortion exists in analyzing the objective figure of female crime. On the one hand, the "chivalry" principle protects "good" women by assigning a lesser charge or diverting them out of the system altogether. On the other hand, visible violations of traditional sex-role conduct results in stringent enforcement. For youthful status offenders, violating curfew, running away, truancy, ungovernability and sex offenses (i.e., "promiscuity") account for 70 percent of all female referrals to the juvenile court. Only 31 percent of all boys were referred to the juvenile court for the same offenses; the remainder were booked for serious crimes—theft, burglary and assault (Report, American Association of University Women, 1969). The "sexualization of female juvenile crime," according to Meda Chesney-Lind (1974:44-46), produces a discriminatory structure since teen-aged women charged with status offenses are:

1. more likely to be incarcerated than those convicted of criminal offenses;

2. twice as likely to be detained over 30 days than other delinquents;

3. more likely to be detained prior to trial;

4. more likely to have a longer sentence than boys.

Imputations of sexual misconduct are apparent in institutional practices that routinely provide vaginal smears for incoming female residents. Regardless of the specific charge, incarcerated girls tend to be treated as sex-norms violators, a definition that reinforces correctional biases regarding female misconduct as moral "deficiencies."

Whatever the actual figure of female crime, the role of official intervention is to reinforce institutional control over female conduct. This approach serves to brake female assertiveness, while also acting as a powerful barrier to equal participation whether in conventional or alternative life styles.

Criminologist Freda Adler (1975), the leading spokesperson for the idea that the women's movement has led to increased crime, has had much public and professional attention. Her thesis, unfortunately, implicitly supports theories of female deviance as issues of sexuality, psychological stability or morality, long the classic trio for explaining this phenomena. Adler's approach treats female crime as a masculine statement; an expression of a rejection of femininity, even of normality. In social-psychological terms, it is a concomitant of "role reversal." In our judgment, the cause of increased arrest rates is not the feminist movement (which is, instead, the *result* of social change); but rather, the dominant myth accepted by control groups and the public that links female deviance to human liberation and both to increased crime trends. Such a thesis, if seriously treated by scholars, tends to distort our understanding of female crime. It presumes that there are no longer genuine role constraints for men and women that mark culturally requisite behavioral categories (e.g., men must *act* in many situations as though they were independent and aggressive, whereas women will continue to be negatively sanctioned if they behave accordingly). The role-reversal thesis also ignores the pervasive class and race inequalities that encourage widespread economic and violent crimes among all classes and groups, some of these crimes remaining invisible (e.g., corporate crime, child abuse, battered wife). Used indiscriminately in this era of the collapse of well-marked sex-role boundaries, this theory could be a highly effective mobilizing myth for an even more repressive legal and correctional regime, especially for poor minority women (see Nagel and Weitzman, 1972:18-25). What were the rationalizations used by control groups to mark the sex-role boundaries before the advent of the women's movement? The next section considers the ideological sources for perpetuating symbolic offenses.

Pollution and Boundary Marking

Until the recent feminist movement, sex-role boundaries were rigid and reinforced by moral-theological means. Control groups, continuing their dependency on individual moral regeneration for women, borrowed the moral technique, style and ideology of an earlier epoch. Moral blemish, stigma, spoiled identity, impure, polluted, fallen women—these terms evoked images of pollution within a sexual context, and they reveal men's deep-seated ambivalences about women's sexuality. The theological language of regeneration used by control groups, although thoroughly inconsonant with secular society, borrowed the Puritan ideal to perpetuate a moral stratification order in which women's behavior served as symbolic markers to give sociological unity to otherwise disparate groups. As Veblen (1899) said, in a competitive social order men use women to broadcast their status and social value to other men. Women as consumers and sex objects mark the external boundaries of men's worlds; women as wives, mothers, daughters and faithful mistresses occupy the inner place. A marketplace conception of the sex role game enables men to measure themselves against other men by the social worth of the women they possess, in terms of their beauty, social class, fecundity, education, sexuality and respectability. These attributes, however, are invariably weighted. A woman's social class, respectability, and purity are defined as more status enhancing for the man than beauty or education. And while fecundity is typically a negotiated order, overt sexuality remains a muted term for wives, mothers and daughters, largely reserved for the "outside" woman in a man's life.

Women's sexuality in this epoch is no longer strictly regulated. Yet sexual promiscuity among females remains as carefully guarded and continues to be an indelible sign (along with homosexuality) of the general corruption of personal and social life—"matter out of place," in Mary Douglas's (1975) terms. Control over women's sexuality, whether by fathers, husbands, priests, reformers, physicians, psychiatrists, police officers, judges or social workers continues, more subtly, perhaps, in the middle classes. This is not the case in the lower classes. Sexual control remains the most formidable weapon in the arsenal of sex stratification, and moral indignation the affective force to reimpose moral standards. As Joseph R. Gusfield (1963) shows in his study of the temperance movement, moral indignation brings into play the quality of disinterested anger and upholds norms where apparently no personal advantage is at stake. Among symbolic offenders, the prostitute offers the classic example.

Among the many social evils of 19th-century America, *the* social evil was prostitution. Eradicating the brothel and prostitute became a reaffirmation of a Puritan ideal of society. Sin had its symbolic expression in the "fallen woman," entailing departure from a state of grace; a "fall" from the pedestal. The fallen woman also symbolized a strategic boundary crossing. Even if "pushed" by others, her sexual misconduct signaled a severe, irrevocable loss of social worth and permanent exclusion from family and marriage institutions that alone gave women status and security (Pivar, 1973).

Transformations in gender roles throughout the twentieth century sent increasing numbers of women out of the home and into streets, working places, cafes, and clubs. This created a shift in the morally stigmatizing language. "Fallen" became thought of as too harsh, indicating a virtual drop out of society and into a déclassé position. Legal, economic and social rights provided women with education and a reform doctrine that emphasized a democratic choice ideology. Whereas the "fallen-woman" metaphor implied coercion and entailed images of white slavery, pimps and inexorable social forces, the newer choice model conjured up a marketplace image. It stressed the woman's individual responsibility to adhere to cultural standards of appropriate feminine-role performance. Failure signifies a "spoiled identity," a cheapening of the moral package, the woman as blemished goods. Instead of making sexually deviant women invisible, this newer stigma signals her as sexually, psychologically and socially inadequate or abnormal. It reinforces existing social relationships between men and women by depicting "good" women as exemplars of feminine cultural standards and "bad" women as morally contaminated. Neither included nor excluded in the social schema, the sexually deviant woman occupies a polluted place (see James and Meyerding, 1977:1381-1385).

Located in a kind of social limbo the sexual offender remains exploited by clients, pimps and control groups; she is virtually ignored by reformers and treated as a pariah by many middle class feminists who reject the permissive life style of sexual anarchy (Davis, 1979).

The prostitute engages in role reversal behavior in that she initiates the sexual encounter. Crass, aggressive and blatant, the streetwalker's interactive style symbolizes the antithesis of the appropriately feminine woman. Whistling at potential clients, running after cars, grabbing at men's clothes, arms, or crotches, and exhibiting a variety of erotic and expressive gestures (e.g., public cursing) are threatening acts. These gestures not only inform interested men (johns) of the woman's sexual availability, but also alert vice-squad officials of her presence.

Visible, indeed highly public, announcements of polluted status have three consequences. First, prostitutes can be easily picked up by police to form part of their normal bureaucratic accounting system. Filling quotas and emptying the street of contaminating sex-sellers is a two-for-one activity for the police. Second, local businesses lure tourists and conference-goers into urban centers by implying how travelers can pursue the sweet, "lush" life. Keeping boundaries intact is important, however. When too many sex-sellers move into a business area and hamper, not help, business, police sweeps then remove the largest tourist "eyesores," the lowest and least resourceful class of street prostitutes. Call girls, party or escort girls, sex sellers in massage parlors and other more discreet forms of prostitution tend to be ecologically segregated and often tacitly protected by police by means of informal exchanges (e.g., money, sex, friendship and information). The streetwalker, forming a relatively permanent deviant pool, operates as a pawn in the law and order game of the prosecutor filling up or depleting arrest quotas, depending on the nature of the variegated moral and political constituencies that impinge on the control situation (Davis, 1979).

Law enforcement groups who detect equivalencies between increased women's deviance and their more expressive life styles are not necessarily misperceiving the signs. What the feminist movement signifies is a severe rupture in the configuration of traditional sex roles—passive female sexuality sustained by male-controlled morality. "Uppity woman," the newest moral construct for women who invade the standard sex-role boundaries, applies to the "liberators" as well as to those underclass and sexually deviant women who are being "liberated." In fact, in some bohemian, feminist and middle class circles promiscuity or sex deviance may be a highly cultivated activity. The chalk marks that once clearly pointed out moral directions have been erased, ignored or multiplied. Sexuality has lost its primordial quality for maintaining the gender system. Only in prison, a sex-segregated, isolating, punishing milieu, do symbolic offenses clearly designate a moral order, however obsolete and maladaptive this may be.

Political Implications

Social control in women's prisons may be described in Foucault's (1977) words as "not controlling less, but controlling better." In recent years the fallen-woman image often takes a more masculine direction. Human behavior as determined by prior socialization implies that women are conditioned by their sexuality, that is by behavior usually considered to be immoderate or excessive in the eyes of professional definers. Persistent vigilance is required to keep such "problems" under control. Overindulgence extends to the entire personality to include alcoholism, drug abuse, promiscuity, illegitimacy and law violations interpreted as unitary phenomena, the singular product of a weak, inadequate character.

In adult-male prisons rational-administrative procedures have a different set of correlates, including rule of large numbers, impersonal imperatives of task and technology, strict chain of command, rigid division of moral organization between staff and inmates and state control over labor power as a replacement for private corporation control. But these characteristics do not define the structure of most women's facilities. Instead, the woman-inmate system appears to suspend standard rational procedures in favor of a personal style. Closer inspection of this contrived regulatory mode, though, reveals it to be surface only. At the depth structure, control works through psychological restraint, and it is at least, or perhaps more, effective than the harsher methods used within male prisons.

What are some characteristic features of the women's prisons we observed? Friendly, amiable counselors, loose structuring of time and task, private rooms instead of cells (in prisons, especially), shared day rooms enabling inmates to enjoy frequent visiting among themselves and physical contact with family and friends. In some respects, the prisons could almost be compared to boarding schools or enlightened mental hospitals where young women deal with the burden of time by dancing, knitting, sewing, writing letters, holding hands, or simply sitting together staring into space until the next meal while pondering unshareable private troubles.

By contrast, men's prisons are volatile structures. Prison eruptions in state penitentiaries across the country, in Attica, New York, New Mexico, Jackson, Michigan, and Walla Walla, Washington, testify to the degradation of inmates and the systematic exploitation of the weak by the strong (for an analysis of men's prisons, see Sykes, 1958; Irwin, 1970, 1980). Ranking orders and rigid scheduling help to maintain superficial order. They also contribute to periodic explosions in which violence breaks the monotony of tight regulation and control.

Rehabilitation, the dominant theme of the correctional system, is a split concept. Inherited from juvenile criminal law, the idea has an individualistic orientation. "Let the treatment fit the offender" was the catchword. This involved a twofold approach: individuating punishment and institutional commitment to change behavior. A split between theory and practice was inevitable, because caste, class and gender differences have been the pervasive, but unacknowledged, forces.

There are really two prison systems, divided by gender. One, the women's system, employs a remedial rehabilitation model. The female inmate is defined as deficient or weak, and she is believed to need socialization, similarly to errant children. Indeterminate sentencing (actually entailing more jail time for the same offense than male offenders) has been one organizational response to this correctional doctrine. The other prison system, the male prison, involves a coercive resocialization program aimed to change what authorities believe is destructive behavior. Male criminals are defined as dangerous, but "serious," offenders. They easily become "habitual" and thus require more careful supervision. And since most offenders are male (the criminal justice system itself offers primarily male imagery), the rehabilitation praxis retains the competitive, often zero-sum exchange found in the political economy. Thus, high-cost, showy prison programs (e.g., computer, photography, accounting), virtually nonexistent in the women's facilities, operate as incentives for the few. But showcase programs are actually available only in "model" prisons, or those containing the nonviolent and nonminority male offenders.

The largest proportion of offenders, both women and men, work in dead-end jobs. Prison kitchen work, factory work and institutional housekeeping fill the inmates' day without providing sustantive job training or effective counseling that could create a postprison model for guiding the felon's life.

The rehabilitation doctrine, expressed in psychological-familial terms for women and vocational-adaptation terms for men, fails on two grounds. First, the praxis violates the manifest principle of the individualistic rehabilitation concept. Both women and men experience categorical lumping, as when women offenders are uniformly defined as immature and inadequate and called "girls" by staff. Yet they are expected to resume traditional family roles after release. Male offenders are generally perceived as antisocial or subhuman and are usually relegated to a barbaric regime that, except for middle class offenders, makes little or no allowance for individual differences. Being a convict entails a highly restricted emotional and social existence. Women are limited to an endless round of idleness and vacuity. Men are exposed to frequent violence and corruption.

Second, failing to relate persons and programs to the outside world—the working class world of often inconstant jobs, financial and personal insecurity and often very limited support structures —is to perpetuate the deviant life style. Third, the middle class staff bias in women's prisons retains the theory of egalitarianism and the praxis of rank. Communication flows downward; deference goes upward. This implies power by indirection, effectively creating confusion and immobility. It also explains in part the reported alienated behavior of women inmates, who often appear to be indifferent to their fate (our interviewing team found many who were passive, silent, withdrawn or apathetic).

For many working class persons, the cell within prison resembles the trap outside prison. Whether inside or out, society bears down ruthlessly (as in Dustin Hoffman's film portrayal of "Getting It Straight"). In Foucault's (1977:228-229) analysis the contemporary prison has become the prototypical modern institution:

> Is it surprising that the cellular prison, with its regular chronologies, forced labor, its authorities of surveillance and registration, its experts on normality, who continue and multiply the function of the judge, should have become the modern instrument of penality? Is it surprising that prisons resemble factories, schools, barracks, hospitals, which all resemble prisons?

Arbitrary, indeterminate detention for frequently minor offenses is, on the whole, more likely to affect women than men. Prisonization, or the process of transforming the individual from civilian to convict, is accomplished by a variety of practices. Social control systematically violates the rehabilitation ethic by categorical treatment. It ignores the principle of individuation of penalties because it is abused in favor of middle-class whites; and in imprisoning lower class women, it also punishes whole families since children are the primary victims of this policy. Under the influence of ostensible penal reform (e.g., due process clause) proportionately more women are entering the justice system through increased arrest, prosecution, and sentencing.

Clearly, the total institution is a power system. Described in negative terms only, prisonization accomplishes the following: "it excludes, it represses, it censors, it abstracts, it masks, it conceals" (Foucault, 1977:194). But it also produces another transformation. It creates a type of human object and a truth system that transforms one relatively plain version of a person into another—a complex deviant being, stigmatized by deprivation of liberty, individual submission to authority and adjustment to a total-control apparatus; an individual separated by captivity; different from his or her normal fellow human beings.

CHAPTER 6—NOTES

[1] This section is based on Davis's study of women offenders, from intensive interviews with 61 women in prison drawn from Oregon and Washington correctional facilities (1976). Data analysis was made possible through a Research and Publication Grant, Portland State University, 1976-1977.

CONCLUSION TO PART II

Total Institutions and Social Control

Durkheim's (1938) vision of social control in the modern epoch entailed an irreversible movement from a repressive system to a restitutive one. In his scheme social control would be less pervasive, more individualized and invariably more benign. Contrary to this hope, the total institution survives as a living testimony to the repressive consciousness of a different age. What are the normative and legal structures that permit, and even encourage, the persistence, and possibly even the proliferation, of the total institution in our epoch?

First, the punishment regime is molded by two institutional forces: the state, in its capacity to create formal rules, and the various enforcement bureaucracies that transform rules into practices. Habermas (1973) argues that the state is increasingly instrumental in shaping culture and total class ideology, an issue we take up in the next chapter. Indeed, it is the single most profound influence for constructing the punishment categories.

Second, for many transgressions, especially those sometimes mislabeled "victimless crimes," where social consensus is in shambles, and where interest group struggles are most likely to concentrate, the state fails to perform its neutral role as translator or compromiser. Instead, it takes a cynical knowledge approach. Some "dead" laws persist (e.g. criminalizing prostitution) that are unenforceable. Certain laws and their administrative machinery tend to be very discriminatory toward poor and minority groups (e.g., drug and gambling legislation). Still other legal consensual agreements between individuals entail serious exploitation by one party over another (e.g., nursing home "rackets"), which remain out of the state's purview.

Third, as a general rule, the law operates proscriptively. It is more likely to define what people *cannot* do, under risk of sanctioning, than what people can do. The more notorious forms of total institutions—prisons and mental institutions—are filled with people who have crossed the forbidden boundary. They have injured another, or themselves, taken another's property, violated a moral code, or simply acted bizarre from the viewpoint of an enforcement agent (which could include family members, neighbors, the police, judges or members of the community). As Sumner (quoted in Barnes, 1948:391-408) reminds us, proscriptive rules originated when the community moved from informal and tacit understandings about social order to more complex social structures that required rules to be spelled out. When most people are related to each other by blood, marriage or ritual ties, casual understandings bond social members. Enter modernism, and the situation changes. Exchange relations tend to supplant the unspoken understandings. Members demand *quid pro quo,* and begin measuring, counting and evaluating relationships in impersonal ways. Elaborate superstructures arise. Market and state act often in opposition to each other. This opens the way for a separate legal structure to reconcile, or at least to perform the official conciliatory role that will keep the Hobbesian vision of a war of all against all from becoming a reality. The modern state ideally operates to stipulate the minimum set of conditions that make possible a human community. Hence, many legal categories and enforcement practices are linked to older forms of moral order (e.g., British common law, poor laws, the workhouse) rather than to current or projected social arrangements.

Fourth, most noncompliant crimes—prostitution, gambling, abortion, drug addiction, homosexuality, drunkenness, public order offenses—are really offenses against the hegemonic, ascetic, work-oriented life styles of the middle class political majority (Schur, 1965). If we add to this crime collection the minor property offenses associated with amateurs (usually youth and women)— petty larceny (shoplifting small items), marijuana use, check forgery, "joyriding" with someone else's car and others—we have the largest number of arrests and prosecutions (well over 60 percent). This excludes of course, serious violent and property crimes, such as assault, rape, homocide, robbery and organized burglary committed by "professionals" (or persons whose life styles are organized around criminal behavior). Today most of the people processed through the criminal justice system, whether for serious or nonserious offenses, fall into the "amateur" category. They are young and inexperienced. As novices in the crime business, they are most likely to be caught. With the demise of traditional morality, the old order of punishment and incarceration for evil and reward and freedom for good has been swept away.

Fifth, the legal categories available for crime and deviance are overly limited. When the 17-year-old black youth George Jackson (to cite one of the more dramatic cases) was imprisoned for being an accomplice in a gas station robbery and stealing $70, the system treated him to the same kind of processing that it offers the major bank robber and the professional gun-for-hire murderer. Jackson's crime was "normalized." It was treated with the definitive classification of a state bureaucracy that has a limited number of categorical slots. This assigns arbitrary bits of behavior to entire classes (ie., dangerous person) and constructs the very reality that its overly limited models allow—the idea of the dangerous social rebel. (For an insider's view of prison, see Shalleck, ed., 1972, and Yee, 1973.)

Sixth, the proscriptive classification system works its greatest hardship on the politically powerless. For example, the aged have also been affected by a proscriptive classification system. Unlike the powerless law breakers who are fairly easy to dispose of, the elderly cover the entire range of social classes and occupational groups. And despite their bad press, the elderly are far from a homogeneous group of "burned-out" citizens. Many have had and continue to have enormous occupational, economic and political power; once organized around certain issues they are a potentially formidable political bloc. In any event, since it is probably impossible to warehouse as much as 10 to 20 percent of this elderly population, the state is shifting its policy abruptly to take into account a different mode of social control.

Seventh, contemporary norms support a responsive law that moves beyond the proscriptive/punishment regime to provide affirmative guidelines for social intervention. As a benefits-centered policy, costs are concentrated upon transgressors, and benefits accrue to the community (see Nonet and Selznick, 1978). Understanding the difference between these two models is essential if we are to adequately come to grips with the organizational characteristics, and the ultimate failure of the total institution.

Modern society often appears to be working at cross-purposes— a seedbed of contradictions. Bureaucracies may be rigid, but there are counterforces that loosen them up and reduce the possibility of premature rigor mortis. Ongoing rules change frequently to adapt to changing pressures and constraints of the environment (if the organization is to survive). In democratic societies especially, hierarchies tend to flatten out. Many rules are based on *ad hoc* arrangements, and authority is more likely to be vested in committees than in individuals. Charisma is reserved for the Christmas party, and the excessive deference and demeanor of the old-line Germanic, militaristic organizations are totally out of style.

What is so unusual, then, about total institutions is precisely their "old-line" character—they are creaky reminders of the early European military model, complete with all the old power symbols— uniforms, vacant-faced, shuffling men, salutes, and external, invariably harsh discipline. They appear excessive for correcting the faults of poverty, racism, classism, ageism and the other miseries and terrors that humans are prone to endure. From the clinking of the multiple locks that seal the culprit within to the cage or dormitory arrangements, which are even more obvious in some of the older jails with their dungeonlike architecture, these institutions seem to be anachronisms.

The system is rational, let there be no doubt about that. The goals are clearly articulated in rules that accompany the inmate wherever he or she goes—from cell to dormitory to cafeteria to shop to therapy session. There is rarely a let-up on rules, except perhaps in the institution's hospital, where there is some accommodation to individual needs. For criminals, prison offers an effective physical and biological constraint. And once released, the offender leaves at best as an older and somewhat physically reduced violator; hence, less aggressive. The total institution resocializes a few offenders, but it is more likely to desocialize others, making reentry into the free world a hazardous enterprise. Though incarceration probably serves as a general deterrent, no one has been able to measure this property with any degree of scientific accuracy. Galtung (1969) observes that prisons satisfy collective needs: retribution, outlets for general aggression and satisfaction of masochistic needs. Once they functioned to provide a cheap labor force. Today they serve to decrease to zero the visibility of selected types of deviants. And most centrally, prisons reinforce the symbols of the power holders. Like other early bureaucratic structures, communication only flows downward, and lower orders are expected to carry out written mandates without question. Sheer size, another characteristic of the early systems, required a highly centralized structure to impose order. "Span of control" (Perrow, 1970:18-19) was often out of balance. There were too few supervisors or workers in relation to the number of inmates, a situation that actually reduced efficiency. A visitor to a contemporary prison, mental hospital, institution for the retarded or nursing home, among others, will detect almost immediately the vast number of clients compared with staff. Sometimes officials reduce potential outbursts or break-outs by drugging inmates, a common practice in mental hospitals and women's prisons, as was demonstrated in the last two chapters. Span of control in maximum-security prisons for men, however, presents such acute and unresolvable problems that these can no longer be covered up. Gang rapes are one byproduct. Another is systematic inmate injury to guards, making correctional work exceedingly dangerous. Excessive use of the "adjustment center" (the "hole") as a standard cooling-off strategy is a temporary pallia-tive. This control strategy makes angry men violent; and violent men highly dangerous. Span of control has an additional feature. Increases in the force necessary to ensure compliance (such as slave systems or concentration camps) make it more essential for manag-ers to select out members from the controlled group to carry some of the control tasks. This undermines inmate solidarity and makes self-help impossible.

Increasingly, maximum-security prisons and mental hospitals resemble castelike structures. This is especially true in the volatile maximum-security prisons that house a high proportion of minor-ity inmates typically policed by rural-based white guards. Here, the line is drawn not by managers and supervisors, but by inmates. Crossing the racial line by an inmate into the enemy camp could result in death or severe injury. Constantly anxious for their safety and well-being, inmates and guards alike live in fear or violence: racial hostility, cruelty, brutal treatment by guards and hostile attacks by other inmates (Williams, 1971).

One striking paradox about the total institution is that while it is the most differentiated of all contemporary organizations *among* ranks, it also tends to be largely undifferentiated *within* ranks. Thus, inmates are treated alike as an undifferentiated "blob" or "mass." Rule infractions by a small minority, or even a single inmate, often lead to ruthless rule tightening for the entire group. (For example, in 1980 when a dozen or so inmates started a demon-stration in Walla Walla, Washington, over the poor diet, prison officials instituted a total lockdown: all men were confined to their cells for 24 hours a day for over six weeks.) This lumping is analo-gous to the first flush of institutionalizing efforts in the sixteenth century. Myriad categories of needy were treated as a single cate-gory, that of social dependent.

Even among more enlightened institutional systems, such as schools for the blind or small, personal therapeutic settings, the underlying patriarchal principle—"father (or doctor) knows best"—serves to infantilize the population (Scott, 1969). This makes the resident population more docile, but at severe costs to their integrity as adults. The subtle humiliations that form the bundle of deference behaviors may cripple inmates' later efforts to adapt in the free world.

Closed-system models spend almost all of their resources on internal and fine-tuned monitoring of their captive populations. Despite the fanfare about rehabilitation and therapeutic regimes, order goals usually become reduced to holding down violence, preventing suicide and minimizing staff turnover and incompetencies.

Among the outstanding deficiencies of the total institution, is its cost. At the turn of the century, prisoners working under contract paid for their own keep and kept the state supplied with additional funding (Rothman, 1980). Prisons and state hospitals no longer retained the contract-labor program after the progressives attacked its exploitative features. Now over 60 percent of prisoners are completely idle (Irwin, 1980); and inmates represent a heavy drain on the public treasury. Thus, the economic feature has proved the strongest catalyst for change. Community corrections, community mental health, small residential settings for delinquent youth (who are expected to work) are some of the current solutions to the oversized, cost-glutted "Big Houses" of yesteryear (Irwin, 1980).

III. Custodial Care

Chapter 7
The Greedy Institution:
The State as Social Problems Monopoly

But the Rights and Consequences of Sovereignty, are the same... His Power cannot, without his consent, be transferred to another: He cannot Forfeit it: He cannot be acused by any of his Subjects, of Injury: He cannot be Punished by them: He is Judge of what is necessary for Peace: and Judge of Doctrines: He is Sole Legislator, and Supreme Judge of Controversies; and of the Times, Occasions of War and Peace: To him it belongeth to choose Magistrates, Counsellors, Commanders, and all other Officers, and Ministers; and to determine of Rewards and Punishments, Honour, and Order.

Thomas Hobbes, *Leviathan*

From Thomas Hobbes's *Leviathan* to James Madison's *Federalist* papers, the classical debate has been waged over the nature and moral function of the modern state. In this early period, the legitimacy conflict occurred between the sovereign and the commonwealth; later it was the crown and the parliament; more recently, the dispute has revolved around the question of state versus society. With the emergence of the modern state, social-contract theories flourished, forming the core of Rousseau's and Locke's political thought. The legitimacy controversy, then as now, concerns the appropriate parameters of the political state; the distinct moral separation between public and private; and the proper balance between law and freedom. Today, that balance appears to be fundamentally shaken.

Expansion of state power is the most remarkable phenomenon in modern life. With the demise of the economy as a patriarchal structure—taking care of workers and their families—the weakening of extended family networks and the secularization of religion, only the state can be counted on to generate the broad range of human services in those areas that the federal government calls, "health, education, and welfare." Modern capitalist societies essentially legitimate themselves by their capacity to "deliver the goods" —providing loans and subsidies to corporations, direct and indirect payments to citizens and government employment for masses of workers. We now recognize that the activities of state enterprises do not merely complement or correct the private market, but largely determine the parameters of economic activity. In the social service area, the state operates a virtual monopoly. There are mildly competitive systems, for instance, fee-for-service psychiatry, private education, church-supported counseling and welfare services. But their survival is largely dependent upon preexisting public institutionalization that sets the pattern for organizational rules, bureaucratic formats and client-professional relationships. Such private service ventures are dependent in a fiscal sense, as well. Without contracts, grants, tax breaks (e.g., nonprofit status), state-subsidized staff (e.g., CETA) and other direct and indirect government funding, many so-called private service ventures would be out of business. The state now has a virtual monopoly over education, welfare, mental health and criminal justice. Control over the fiscal character of the human-services economy does not imply, though, that the state effectively copes with the problem of order and integration in humanistically and constitutionally approved ways. Confronted with legitimation problems, the modern state seeks to control ever larger spheres of social action. The causes for state expansion, the type of professional service workers it produces, its capacity to mobilize resources, its unilateral advantage for constructing social problems, its monopoly on legitimate violence and its overreach into the private areas of family life represent growing areas of concern. The state's inherent deficiencies in implementing policy shape the kind and distribution of community services.

The State as Institution

The state is the prime mover in contemporary society (see Meyer, 1978; Meyer et al, 1979; Boli-Bennet and Meyer, 1978). As part of a world state system that is increasingly homogeneous in structure from one nation-state to another, modern governments support a hierarchical system, based on class, race, occupation, education and income. Because the state controls manpower allocations (through such strategies as taxation, corporate subsidies, federal reserve board rates, manipulation of interest), it can cushion, ignore or deny different populations' needs. Using symbols such as social problems and resource mobilization, the state validates its expanding role. Order and control are its twin values, often carried out in violation of privacy norms in democratic societies. Unlike the economy that fosters individualism and consumer values, the state centers its value claims on entire populations. State myths promote legalizations that justify intervention into every human area—family, sexuality, minorities, the elderly, alternative life styles and so forth. "Government-grown values," Meg Greenfield (1980:88) says, are "by definition and necessity spiritually deformed." Yet, these bureaucratic values are also essential to mobilize the necessary resources to meet constantly increasing demands from citizens. In this way, all the world's a client. Citizens are either servers or servees in this government, service-station-like political economy, which stresses homogeneity through a rule of law.

The state as institution is roughly compared to economic and social institutions in the following table, which contrasts the economy and state as strong structures with family and religion as weak structures.

Once we grasp the idea that weakly institutionalized units such as families, teacher groups, the elderly, minorities, feminists and the poor have no other place to go for support of their cause, we can begin to unravel the repressed contradictions that confound the state and undermine its legitimacy. For example, when President Carter called for a White House Conference on Families after much pressure from profamily groups, he undoubtedly had in mind federal support for a particular kind of family; nuclear, heterosexual, middle class, conventional and the like. The administration failed to anticipate the obvious, that "families" in the United States are pluralistic. There is no single family reality. Political intrusion simply reinforces the lack of unity and the fragmentation in these weakened social institutions.

The state has become the legatee, by default. It inherits social problems thrown up by decaying institutions. During the early liberal epoch of social-contract building, the burden of proof was on the state to show why it interfered in privacy areas such as sexuality, life styles, sexual harassment and so on. In this period of social fragmentation where there is no other institution than the state to care for persistent human problems—the aged, poor, minorities, overpopulation and others—the burden of proof is on those who attack state intervention.

Habermas (1973; 1979), among the most vociferous critics of the state, has attacked unbridled state intervention because it denies

Table 7:1 Institutional Sectors: Comparison of Strong and Weak Structures

	Economy	State	Family	Religion
	Strong Structures		*Weak Structures*	
Symbols	Money, exchange calculability, Gesellschaft association	World state-system organization and distribution of status order; class, race, occupation, education, income; manpower allocations determine populations' adaptation capacities	Uniqueness of person; expressiveness; division of personal power	Mysticism: other-worldliness; commitment ethos: belief, ritual, understanding and experience
Values	Progress, social order, individual-centered or consensus politics; culture of narcissism	Social order and social control; population-centered; culture of bureaucracy	Love, concern, interdependency, dependency; couple-centered (but economy and state structures impinge on weaker system); culture of traditionalism or culture of egalitarianism	Love, hope, renunciation, "communion" of believers, participation reduces anxiety and stress; culture of spiritualism
Metaphor/ Myth	Rationalization of the world; technology saves	Legalization: legal-rational myths justify state intervention in all human areas: family, minorities, sexuality, alternative life styles	Sexual politics; struggle over personal power results in conflict and high rates of dissolution of families and relationships	Personal transcendence – salvation through faith; virtue model (e.g., humility, generosity, self-abnegation, etc.)
Model	Entrepreneurial model	Client model	Romantic model	Faith model
Socialization	Formal education; downplay individual uniqueness; technical capacities emphasized; psychic deflation in competitive marketplace where skills are interchangeable and rendered obsolete.	Rationalized day care; "rationalization of motherhood"; homogeneity stressed; gender and ethnic styles related to manpower needs (as defined by state) *Auxiliary State Institutions* Education Welfare Health (especially mental health) Criminal Justice System Alcohol and Drug Abuse Care for elderly, mentally retarded, minorities, etc.	Learned divisions and subordination; age, gender, economic status	Lifelong education includes formal and informal indoctrination; differentiation by church/sect participation; exclusive systems: interdependency limited to members; in-group/out-group processes

citizens opportunities to genuinely participate in goal-setting and resource allocation. He claims that the state maintains its power not only because it meets ever expanding population needs, but more significantly, because it practices misinformation, false consciousness, ignorance and forceful exclusions. From a normative point of view, this "repressive communication" presents a one-sided political juggling act conducted by governing elites. This seriously lowers the legitimacy of the political order. In practice, however, these strategies also contribute to its integration as a system of power and thus enhance its capacity to deliver human services. Nevertheless, legitimation problems, which haunt the modern sate, entail the following distinct features (see also the review essay by Giddens, 1977:198-212).

1. The market system can no longer be legitimated in terms of its power to mobilize investments, work and spending based exclusively on the ideology of private exchange.

2. The central administrative role of the state in the economy must be legitimated.

3. The administrative role of the state must be maintained independently of the mechanisms of formal participation in democratic politics.

4. The legitimation process requires the mobilization of diffuse mass loyalty without direct participation.

5. The depoliticization of the public realm requires (a) civic privatism, (i.e., the pursuit of consumption leisure and careers in exchange for political abstinence), and (b) the ideological justification of public depoliticization through one of the following means: elitist theories of the democratic process, technocratic justification or professional accounting practices that rationalize administration.

Professionalized accounting practices provide a private language that further excludes citizens. The rationalities of everyday life, expressed in Habermas's (1979) term as citizens' "communication competence," increasingly become treated as irrationalities from this administered viewpoint. A depoliticized citizenry without a voice in the legitimation process in time becomes effectively politically handicapped. Privatism, consumerism, and career are trade-offs for the loss of the shaping of political destinies. In effect, the state takes over the definition of needs and constructs them in light of the expansion of state power and influence.

The state cannot function as a monopoly without strong citizen support. Citizens believe that local communities cannot afford to pay for the increasingly expensive services, programs and technology. They support these large programs as more administratively rational and cost-efficient than small local ones. They rightly perceive that regulation and surveillance of local service distributions by a central authority is necessary to guarantee uniform treatment of clients and accountability in expenditure of funds and program execution. They concede the right to federal and state agencies to expand their influence and mandates, and to obtain more tax funds, personnel and control over their organizational environment. What are the nature and functions of these professional service organizations? How do social-problems construction and management serve as a residual activity and at the same time a primary function for legitimating state power? How does the state's monopoly over social problems aggravate, rather than reduce, its legitimation problems. The next sections examine these questions.

Professional Service Organizations

For social control purposes, the modern state uses a particular type of formal organization as its main instrument, which we call, comprehensively, the professional service organization.[1] These include, for example, social welfare agencies, mental health centers, and family service organizations. At the outset, we may say that these organizations are staffed by *professional* workers and also that they are in part *bureaucratically* organized. The term professional must be used with caution. These professionals are actually not members of high-status groups, like the members of the traditional "learned" professions (e.g., doctors and lawyers). Although they have middle class status, these service workers represent fields of competence within which there is little consensus, and for which there exist only weak institutional criteria for performance. Decisions about the merits of diagnoses, alternative courses of treatment and the nature of the social problems within their spheres of influence are open-ended and disputable issues. Their criteria remains fuzzy because they are not embedded in highly established institutionalized structures, such as courts, law firms, clinic and hospital hierarchies or specialized training programs. Nor do they have rigorous certification procedures and ready access to the various socially elite groups that confer status and professional confidence on physicians and lawyers. Professionals in service organizations work inside clear-cut hierarchies that are characterized by close supervision (Blau, 1955; Blau and Scott, 1962; Scott, 1964). Budgetary constraints produce severe limits on goals and dictate the amount of time and the type of services available. Whereas lawyers and doctors normally charge clients the total costs of service, professionals in service organizations cannot. Heavy client loads, often exceeding the scheduled allotment and not entailing additional pay or time off, reduce service professionals' incentives. Low motivation and cynicism are not uncommon among these professional groups.

Service organizations have limited, specific mandates. In other words, they are nonpervasive. We should expect to see this in a society that adheres to specialization and division of labor, where occupational groups are constantly busy fending off intrusions into their domains. Also, given the strict limits on time and resources, human problems can often be dealt with only in a piecemeal fashion. In a contradictory sense, it is also understood, if not carefully pointed out in rule books, that clients' entire life situations and fields of social relationships may be involved in their problems. But from the state's point of view, it is cheaper to handle problematic groups through nonpervasive organizations. As a cost-efficient measure, this approach negates the total-care package: housing, food, supervision, expenses and the like. Sociologists and lawyers have criticized asylums and total institutions for violating modern conceptions of civil liberties and humanity. Deinstitutionalization, the transfer of treatment to nonpervasive, community-based organizations, represents a fortuitous meeting of the minds of the moral critics and the cost-conscious planners and legislators. Service organizations' mandates emphasize the prevention of trouble, in addition to treatment for those who have already perpetrated it. By contrast, total institutions cannot take preventive action and work only after the fact to correct a problem.

By way of summarizing the roles of service professionals, it is clear that their relationship to clients is bound to be *institutionally weak.*[2] Many hard-core social problems—for example, habitual delinquency or crime, chronic depression and alcoholism—involve the person's entire life style or "life script." To treat such problems, it may be necessary to resocialize and reconstitute the client's entire way of life. The service organization, because of its inevitable structural weakness, is not equipped for such a task. This fact is behind the often observed "revolving-door" (or client-turnover) phenomenon.

Resource Mobilization and the Societal Construction of Social Problems

Above all, service organizations are resource mobilizers and managers. This is how they renew their mandate. Resource mobilization entails the process by which service organizations systematically coordinate their internal activities and those of clients with interested publics and constituents in order to gain influence in legislatures and other decision-making bodies (McCarthy and Zald, 1973:1212-1241). Among the organizational tools used for resource mobilization are fund raising, protests and other symbolic demonstrations, lobbying in legislatures and the creation of alliances with other organizations.[3] Experienced social movements will use all of these with varying emphases. Occasionally an established organization will lend personnel to help organize a less-experienced social movement, often through the Community Chest, but also independently. Social movements are thus intimately related to the functioning of service organizations. If a movement is successful, it effectively expands the organization's mandate for service. If the movement fails, its ideology and practices can be absorbed into mainstream laws and organizations. Grey Panthers, a social movement of the elderly, has had some influence in opening up legal issues and new services for senior citizens.

Fund raising serves the obvious purpose of raising money for the organization's activities, but it also serves to further commit the already interested constituents and to recruit and commit new ones. Making this activity visible on the local community level is a primary goal, because in lobbying for and against legislative measures, it is important for the organization to mobilize its constituents for letter writing and testimonies. Special targets for recruitment are persons who are well known for their standing and involvement in local, state and national communities. Their support helps make the issue legitimate and, by spreading the message, brings in more influentials. Protests and other demonstrations serve to dramatize the issue before the larger public. From the organization's point of view, the public should recognize the seriousness and legitimacy of its concerns. Opposing viewpoints must necessarily be put on the defensive. To a large extent this is how social problems get constructed in society.

Basically, social problems are political *constructions*[4] that involve professional organizations, clients, constituents, the public and decision-makers in complex interactions. Lobbying serves several functions: calling the attention of legislators to the organization's concerns, recruiting their support, influencing the wording of legislation, securing financial appropriations and neutralizing opposing viewpoints and their lobbyists. Because the stakes are larger and often involve the fiscal survival of the organization, direct lobbying has to be supplemented by pressures from clients and constituents through letter writing, direct representations of concerned citizens and press campaigns. Ties with other organizations are essential. One organization can assist another in recruiting constituents, raising funds, turning out bodies for protests and demonstrations and lending friendly support to lobbying.

This is a systemic view of how social problems get constructed. Some needs have to be there in some sense, of course, for the activities to be plausible at all. But much human misery exists without becoming societally defined as a social problem. Problem pregnancies, discrimination against minorities and women, mental troubles, heavy drinking, child and spouse abuse have always existed, but they became social problems, matters for societal concern and action, through coordinated and complex politics. The network of processes that create the social problem will, of course, vary from issue to issue, but generally it will follow the basic model sketched here. A concern in modern society becomes a legitimate social problem when it has become part of public policy, that is, when the state through some agency has made it part of its agenda.

Constructing a Social Problem: The Abortion Case[5]
As a fairly extensive illustration of this social construction process we offer the abortion case, which over the last decade has undergone drastic changes in conception and organization. Five stages occurred in the transformation of abortion: (1) publicizing the problem, (2) dramatizing the problem, (3) networking, (4) legitimating the problem, and (5) backlash. At each stage, the role of service organizations changed. From being on the defensive, professional groups moved to full-scale participation during the legitimating phase to define terms, diagnose needs and propose

treatment. The case study draws on field work conducted primarily in Michigan between 1969 and 1975. Much of the material entails oral testimonies because lack of written documentation typifies nonidentified social problems.

Publicizing the Problem

Contrary to claims of contemporary critics, abortion is neither an innovative nor an unusual solution to unwanted or untimely pregnancies. Since the nineteenth century, women have sought medical abortions, even when the crude surgical procedures of the period left many ill or dead. By the middle 1960s, perhaps as an outgrowth of a general loosening of the traditional sex ethic, more than one million women per year had an induced abortion, most of them illegal. Not until the late 1960s was the public, or even professional groups, aware of the full extent to which abortion was being used (more often by married women with children than by singles), and the heavy social and psychological costs involved. Sunday supplements tended to treat abortion strictly in criminal terms—as a big money-maker for the "Mafia" or as a get-rich-quick scheme for unscrupulous doctors. Little attention was paid to pregnant women or to established medicine and the way in which the criminalizing of abortion deprived both of choice. As participants in an illegal event, the women and their abortion providers maintained a strict silence, broken only by the occasional death of a woman and the subsequent criminal investigation.

Once the black civil rights movement emerged, followed by other ethnic liberation movements and feminism, abortion became part of the freedom dialogue. In most states, however, publicizing abortion had to be done with subtlety and caution, invariably by those groups free from the abortion stigma. In Michigan and elsewhere, abortion-reform clergy members who called themselves "problem pregnancy counselors" took their mandate (in their terms, "covenant") to be the reform of the abortion law and the providing of counseling and referral services for pregnant women in "crisis."

Crisis was the key term used to publicize to interested publics and constituencies, including family-planning organizations, the nature of the problem as a mental health issue. Using ideology borrowed from the women's movement, the Protestant clergy spoke of the abortion issue in terms of "personal choice," "voluntary pregnancy," and, among a few, "abortion on demand." Ideological contradictions aside, it was primarily a moral issue they articulated more than a legal, political or medical one. When the clergy spoke with physicians or legislators, they used symbols of life and death, right and wrong, and good and evil, except that such symbols were usually presented in reverse order. Thus, when these reformers identified "life," they meant the woman's life, her options, her mental health and decisions, not those of the unborn. It was "right" to choose abortion rather than to wrongly endure an unwanted pregnancy, and it was "good," indeed a positive outcome, when problem-pregnancy counseling produced a guilt-free abortion decision. The death of the fetus, being then on the wrong side of the law, and the potential evil of the sexual liberation myth (whereby neither the man nor the woman was really accountable for sexual relationships) were not featured in this discourse.

Service organizations, asked to assist women with problem pregnancy and abortion, often rejected such requests. Clergy reformers were denigrated as "getting on a hobby horse," "crazy," "disgusting," "cranks," "egomaniacal," and "impossible." Some of these early clergy publicizers were denounced by their parishioners, their hierarchy and their boards. Why did they persist in the face of such opposition? "Because there is no one else to do it," they replied. At this stage, family planning centers funded by federal and state governments, and Planned Parenthood groups (supported by United Fund programs) had neither funds nor the professional interest for serving an abortion-seeking clientele. It was left to individual physicians, community persons and these counseling members of the clergy to provide whatever scattered and uncoordinated help they could for their deprived clientele. In heavily populated states such as Michigan, this involved thousands of women annually.

Dramatizing the Problem

As long as abortion was in the "closet," professional service organizations could deny or ignore the problem. When confronted with the growing demand, they could rationalize that, "legally there is nothing we can do." In one sense, it was clients who dramatized their own problem with the help of intermediaries. First, a more permissive social climate gave women the opportunity to seek out professional assistance for an unwanted pregnancy instead of merely accepting it. Second, requests for assistance became translated by service organizations as "pressure," and this information went from professionals and administrators to boards, professional associations and other governing bodies. Third, hospital emergency rooms that had long treated the "septic," or "incomplete" abortion, (euphemisms for illegal abortion) were demanding more outside organizational support instead of doing it alone. Fourth, newspaper editors and columnists, always eager to get a "scoop," found the increasing abortion disputes within and among service organizations good "copy," and among those sympathetic to legal abortion, an opportunity to proselytize. Most dramatic were the sordid stories about "butcher-shop" or "back-alley" abortions where needy women were victimized at high costs, or even paid the ultimate price by dying.

A larger segment of the public began to be affected, and they sent letters to the editor and participated in community volunteer group discussions, church sermons, university lectures and informal talks about abortion. Moral, religious, medical, social and psychological aspects, all were publicly debatable issues. Once clients got their foot in the door, the resistent attitude of service professionals began to weaken. And with "clean" language made possible by the crisis concept, service organizations could ignore the uncomfortable fact that nearly 80 percent of all those counseled by "neutral" professionals were choosing abortion.

Networking

The networking stage during which service organizations, professionals and reform groups constructed an alternative counseling and referral network, followed soon after the demands for abortion became public topics. Certainly, health organizations feared they would be "overwhelmed" by abortionees, which may have been the precipitating factor that led to alliances among reformers. "Control, don't be controlled by the abortion demand," was the implicit message. Clergy reform groups were the chief instigators, forming the working hub of the new service network. But other organizations and community groups were quick to join when they realized that there was little or no legal risk. With members of the clergy in charge, many professionals saw distinct organizational advantages in moving abortion seekers into states where it was legal. By 1970, 15,000 women in Michigan were reported to have moved through the counseling and referral network organized by clergy members and their organizational supporters. To move prospective abortionees from their home base in Michigan to New York, California, Puerto Rico or Mexico, for instance, it was necessary to develop a range of services at different points in the community. Family planning agencies, volunteer women, college and university counseling services and uncommitted Protestant churches were all urged to come forward in this clandestine (though tacitly accepted by law enforcement groups) community effort.

That the network, thus created, was not very efficient should surprise no one. There was much overlap, duplication and deficient care (especially in post-abortion follow-up). From the viewpoint of clients, the referral network was logistically and psychologically complex, even clumsy. There were many professional contacts, too much time to negotiate the service (two to three weeks) and over elaborate rituals of counseling. Physician advice or agency processing angered and frustrated many abortion seekers. In addition, women who moved through this semimedicalized, quasiillegal system became "patients," "counselees" and, in the case of some seekers, "sinners" rather than information seekers in the eyes of a few clergy counselors. Table 7:2 shows a client-centered view of the pregnancy decision process.

Legitimating Abortion

Despite vigorous resource mobilization on the part of reformers to take abortion out of the closet, it continued to retain its traditional stigma among policy makers: images of evil, death and dirt. Viewed as dirty work and relegated to disreputable physicians, established medicine was reluctant to initiate reform. Professional organizations—family planning groups, Planned Parenthood, mental health centers—knew only too well the agency profile of the overburdened, physically disorganized mother and the need for genuine legislative relief for these families. But either the government was legally constrained and, hence, unable to initiate organizational reform, or administators resisted changing their organizations' mandate for various reasons (e.g., board reaction, structural dislocations, costs, lack of consciousness about the problem, etc.). Planned Parenthood and other groups supported by the United Fund and other all-community funding sources often had Roman

Table 7:2   A Model Abortion Referral Network and Its Alternatives

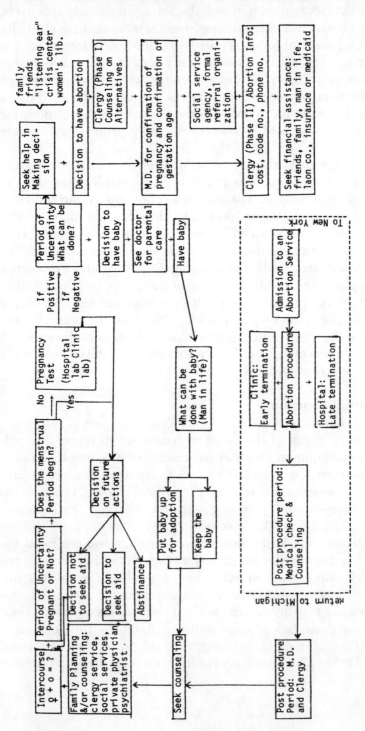

(Flowchart of Client's Decisions: Entrance into the Provision Services at Different Points)

Catholics on their boards, and this group was categorically opposed to supporting abortion in any form. In other cases, service organizations were prepared to provide counseling for problem-pregnancy clients, but refused abortion referrals. Physicians also complained that their offices were inundated with women seeking preabortion pelvic examinations (required in New York City abortion clinics before admittance). Doctors began to limit the number of clergy-referred clients. Clearly, the system was congested. Reformers realized they must tackle the problem at a different level: legislative and community-wide action was required.

Over a five-year period, an enormous amount of work was expended to persuade legislators to change their thinking about abortion. Reformers did not ask for legalization, or a warrant for official action, but merely decriminalization. "Take abortion off the criminal codes, and physicians will take it from there," was their argument. When efforts remained blocked for legislative relief, they turned to the referendum. Let the people decide. The people did. In November 1972, a permissive abortion law was defeated in Michigan in an upset vote of 61 percent opposed to 39 percent in favor. At this point, the State Public Health moved into the regulatory breach and began drafting rules and regulations that would follow if the High Court declared abortion legal.

By late January 1973, the United States Supreme Court shifted the decision to the national level, and declared all states' criminal abortion laws unconstitutional on the grounds that they violated legal rights of privacy and the right of the physician to provide professional medical care. There were no positive abortion laws as such. All the court decreed was the necessity to have an attending physician, a prerequisite that placed the abortion procedure firmly within the medical domain.

Abortion appeared to be a closed issue. It was now a problem resolved by the state, which had passed the regulatory mandate to medicine, and to professional family-planning and counseling services. Reform groups, believing their work finished, soon disbanded. Even the problem-pregnancy clergy counselors closed up shop and left the scene of action to professionals, since abortion became available at local freestanding clinics and hospitals. The legitimate order was restored, or so it seemed at the time.

Backlash

However, once a social problem becomes politicized without losing its contradictory features, it is unlikely to disappear. Instead, the problem assumes new forms, one of which is the "backlash." Backlash may be defined as an opposition reaction to a policy change, and that situation occurred after the 1973 Supreme Court abortion decriminalization decision. Oppositional groups, quiescent or frustrated during the proabortion campaign, moved vociferously against clinics, hospitals and doctors providing abortions. They appealed to state legislatures, the Congress, local hospital boards, mayors' offices and wherever policy decisions were being made to put a stop to what they believed were the horrors of abortion. Right-to-Life or Pro-Life groups formed their own antiabortion counseling, birth referral and adoption organizations. Lobbying intensely aginst community hospitals purchasing abortion equipment (e.g., vacuum aspirators) was one tactic. Others included burning clinics, physically assaulting doctors and clients and disrupting operations. Their violent strategy served to dramatize their own counterperspective to the medicalized one: abortion is murder; it is morally wrong, and it represents an unmitigated social evil.

The current abortion deadlock boils down to this: the abortion problem is unresolvable as long as partisans limit their discourse to political solutions. Politics operates by compromise: the give and take of flexible categories, not the rigid terms of life or death, good or evil. Once a social problem has been cast into the language of backlash morality, the reanimation of oppositional images occurs — in the case of abortion, the stigma, guilt and terror of a world gone amok. The entire antiabortion discourse keys an uncompromising fanaticism and absolutism in a relativistic world where these moral categories are out of place. With the passage of the Hyde Amendment (which forbids federal funding of abortion) in the summer of 1980, the cycle begins another turn. And because professional organizations are powerless to initiate their own service mandates beyond those strictly determined by law, they will be unable to prevent the increased miseries that accompany the unwanted pregnancy, the rejected child and the woman or family under pressure.

The backlash morality *uses* abortion to reconstitute a waning social myth. This holds traditional sex roles to be inherently coherent, family life to be paramount over individual needs and women, unlike men, to be governed by their reproductive roles and family commitments. The opposition ethic is pervasive: sympathy for the encapsulated fetus is opposed to scorn for the free woman. In this impasse, family-centered professional organizations may experience a shift in emphasis—away from woman-centered services to reproductive-birth-adoption services. The already declining birth rate among the affluent may hasten this process.

Legitimating Social Problems

Abortion provides a test case of the failure of the state to successfully depoliticize a social problem. In part, this failure can be attributed to the lack of existing institutional and ideological categories for coping with volatile social issues. Linked to liberation, an irrational category among administrative accounting systems, abortion is caught between worlds. It is neither an approved institutional category nor a deviant one. Rather than closing off debate, decriminalizing abortion creates a categorical anomaly that opens the door to political agitators at the same time that it closes off the possiblility of successful legitimation.

A social problem becomes most easily legitimated if it can be incorporated into well-established institutional and ideological categories. Medicine and education are two examples of approved social categories. For instance, if abortion were only conceptualized as a medical procedure as reformers wanted, it would not evoke the current images of legally sanctioned murder and terror among traditional groups. How have medicine and education managed to successfully legitimate many other social problems? Both have prestige value, surrounded by symbols and practices that buttress their claims for public and state support. Their status accoutrements include: impressive buildings, university credentials of the personnel, the trappings of science, ceremoniously maintained hierarchies and reliance on institutional celebration, for instance, convocations, graduation ceremonies and congresses.

Medicalization of deviance under state direction is a pervasive trend in contemporary societies (Conrad, 1975:12-21). An entire range of problems, once believed to be simply expressions of human misery, aggression or ill will, have reappeared with established medical terminology, diagnosis, treatment plans, and prognosis. For instance, drugs, alcoholism, marital troubles and hyperkinesis have all become problems of mental health, and institutions mandated to deal with these issues have become medicalized. That is, these human services borrow from the legitimacy and prestige of medicine, often in highly selected ways.

Hyperkinesis, one of the more recent medical "discoveries," became primarily a medical problem after observers noted that certain drugs appeared to have beneficial effects on those children exhibiting selected physical symptoms (e.g., restlessness, mood swings, hyperactivity). Extensive drug company advertising, mass-media publicity, validation of drug treatment by HEW medical panels and the educational influence of the Association for Children with Learning Disabilities all interacted to produce and legitimate the medical definition (Conrad, 1975). Shifting to another example, the official credo of the National Council of Alcoholism states:

> Alcoholism is a disease, and the alcoholic a sick person. The alcoholic can be helped and is worth helping. This is a public health problem and therefore a public responsibility.
>
> (Quoted from Chafetz and Demone, 1962:142)

This dogma gains its legitimacy throgh the efforts of many groups, including the medically oriented Yale Center for Alcohol Studies, grassroots organizations and health professionals (see Chafetz and Demone, 1962; Chapter 3; Schneider, 1978). Since the early 1960s, there has been a revolution in mental health, a topic we treat extensively in chapter 9. Despite the inappropriateness of the medical model for correcting problems in human interaction, mental illness survives as the dominant myth (Szasz, 1961).

In the divestment of the criminal process initiated by the treatment ideology, the relinquishing of legal jurisdiction over many forms of traditionally criminal conduct has occurred in the United States over the past century (Kittrie, 1971). The medicalizing of deviance has filled this regulative void. The state prefers this indirect control approach, perhaps because of the professional dominance of medicine, but more likely because it fits the scientific humanitarian values that medicine espouses. Conrad and Schneider (1980) warn that such institutionalization of a medical deviance designation entails a possible overall loss in citizen control. Medicine removes from public discussion judgments of morality. Medical imperialism is an ever constant threat, as when the medical model pervades the courts, workplace and schools. The health insurance industry, already a glutted industry, expands under medicalization politics. This further increases health costs and places medical care out of the reach of increasing numbers of citizens.

Education, the other major social legitimating system, has acquired a less awesome, but still significant, mystique. Unlike medicine, which has its roots in the private sphere, mass education in the United States has always been public. The socialization of lower class and immigrant children into the work ethic and middle class values of society was traditionally accomplished in the name of education. This concept acquired high prestige and legitimacy early in American history (Meyer et al, 1979; Tyack, 1974). In the field of criminal justice, the term "correction," has taken on an oppressive and dubious cast. As penologists struggle with competition over scarce funds, they resort increasingly to "rehabilitation," an educational category. The White House Conference on Families, discussed earlier, agreed on only one goal:

> Delegates...agreed on the vital need for family-life education, and that government at all levels should assist the public and private sectors by providing appropriate courses for children and parents.
> (Quoted in Greenfield, 1980:88)

In one sense, education has an even larger social control mandate than medicine for curing social ills. As a total panacea, it offers what modern information-hungry citizens have come to expect as legitimate solutions for social problems. Designed by professional experts, education fosters a voluntaristic but compelling ideology that promises a painless fix for contemporary ills. That education is a major state mechanism for ordering status hierarchies is rarely considered by advocates.

Service organizations confront countless problems in legitimating their functions, even when supported by master ideologies. In many cases this output is too difficult to evaluate, if evaluation is taken in any strict, cost-accounting sense. Clients come into the organization, receive counseling, financial aid or group therapy, and then disappear. Some return through the "revolving door," but many do not. It is impossible to assess with any certainty if the help and treatment they get has any long-term benefits and still less whether any treatment method is superior to alternative therapy.

The legitimacy of the organization and its practices, hence, cannot be base on its productivity. Instead the credentials of the personnel, for instance, master's degrees and specialized course work and the linkage to legitimating ideological categories become the basis for the community consensus.[6] Sometimes it is cynically understood by state administrators that a program is not likely to affect a serious social problem in any major way. For instance, the city of Detroit instituted a treatment center for alcoholic mothers that could hold less than twenty patients at a time. This is clearly a demonstration or pilot project, a symbolic gesture designed to show that the city is committed to doing *something* about a serious social problem. To attack this problem effectively, it would probably be necessary to set up dozens of similar centers around the city. From the viewpoint of reformers, demonstration projects *are* important. It is better to treat a few persons than none at all, but more importantly, the projects demonstrate the good faith necessary for institutional legitimacy.[7] Demonstration projects are for institutions what marches, sit-ins and picketing are for social movements, namely, symbolic, dramatic affirmations of legitimating myths.[7]

Service organizations pay a price for their legitimacy. Professions have narrow mandates. Defining the social problem they are mandated to deal with in terms of an established professional category, for instance medicine or education, leads to one-sided treatment. But social problems, as we pointed out in chapter 2, are multifaceted. Several components must be tied together in intricate ways to create a social problem. For instance, both alcoholism and hyperkinesis may have physiological bases, but both syndromes are also intimately tied to interpersonal and cultural factors. These are at least as important as the medical ones. When the troubles are "medicalized," it means that the main emphasis of the treatment is medical, although counseling and group therapy are used as supportive, but subsidiary measures. The cultural and interpersonal factors are likely to be dealt with ineffectively, although they, in fact, may be more amenable to intervention and change than the often hypothetical physiological processes.

Social problems, whatever else they are, are issues of *moral integration,* and hence involve troubles in the person's relationships to significant others and community roles; in short, the person's entire role-script. Service organizations seem unable to deal with totalities like role-scripts. In section III of this book, we spell out how various alternative types of organizations have developed in opposition to the professional service organizations. Examples of such organizations are feminist health collectives and counseling centers and Alcoholics Anonymous. It is likely that the practices of service organizations in the future will become influenced by these alternatives. The description in this section is not meant to imply that the community service organizations have reached the end of their evolution, but rather that they are severely limited for their mandated tasks. This inherent limitation is especially apparent in state expansion into the family, our next topic.

The Overreach of the Benevolent State

Jacques Donzelot (1979) examines the managed modern family in *The Policing of Families*. He contends that since the middle of the eighteenth century, the state has actively participated in creating the forms of family life that we know today. The new managerial approach or "tutelary complex" substitutes bureaucratic and medical controls for direct, legislative controls over the family. The "emergence of the modern family and the expansion of psychiatric organizations go hand in hand." Laws and professional precepts have worked in different ways to mold middle class and working class families. Distinct class interpretations of family life, available in infant-care manuals and other source books, drew on the general expansion of expertise—psychiatry, progressive education, marriage couseling, parent education. At the same time the coldness of bureaucratic and professional norms spurred a peculiar concept of sociability formed in the family image: ideal social relations were to approximate the closeness of relations between sexual partners or siblings. Modern educators, psychologists and doctors use the family as the prototype of sociability as a matter of course.

This has two negative effects for family and community functioning. First, it restricts sociability to the myth of the "happy family" (e.g., the I.B.M. corporate family), and, second, it places the family itself in jeopardy as the fimily closes itself off to resist the "destructive temptations of the outside." The "inside-outside" complex of the "advanced liberal" family, described by Donzelot, is related to the family's inherent instability—its dependency on state and professional agencies and its frantic pursuit of sociability in a "good" environment as a primary social value. Donzelot says that the modern family is engaged in:

a sort of endless whirl in which the standard of living, educational behavior, and the concern with sexual and emotional balance lead one another around in an upward search that concentrates the family a little more on itself with every turn; an unstable compound that is threatened at any moment with defection by its members, owing to that relational feverishness which exposes them to the temptations of the outside, as well as to that over-valuing of the inside which makes escape all the more necessary; a half-open place.

The family's instability invites ever increasing rounds of state intervention and manipulation. Placing of the family "outside the socio-political field," and restricting it to social integration through intimacy, neutralizes family authority and transforms the family from institution to social control mechnism. The government works through the family by removing politics and fixating on private concerns.

> The procedures of social control depend much more on the complexity of intrafamilial relationships than on its complexes, more on its craving for betterment than on the defense of its acquisitions (private property, juridical rigidity). A wonderful mechanism since it enables the social body to deal with marginality through a near-total dispossession of private rights, and to encourage positive integration, the renunciation of the question of political right, through the private pursuit of well-being.

Recent attention to the abused child underscores Donzelot's thesis. Children are viewed as helpless and incompetent; but, then, so are their parents. Soloman (1975) estimates 200,000 to 250,000 children in the United States annually who are in need of protective services, over 30,000 of which have been seriously injured. The catastrophic scope of the problem goes well beyond the immediate family, researchers stress. The abused child becomes transformed into a "system" of participants: "the client family, the social worker, the family court, the social service administration, government policy-making agencies and research teams" (Bommer et al, 1977:334). Child-abusers are not "bad"; instead they are described as immature, self-centered, emotionally starved, and having unmet dependence needs (Holter and Friedman, 1968; Morse, 1970). Hostility, anger, impulsivity, pronounced rigidity, lack of warmth and strong feelings of incompetence are other traits of child-abusers. Finally, abusers act out their rage under conditions of accumulated stress in which the abuser feels overwhelmed and unable to cope with his or her problems.

The transformation of human distress into a system of protective services is all accomplished by persons of good faith and sound intentions. Experts identify and categorize needs: education, housing, child care, health, transportation, legal services, socialization, home management, financial needs, employment. The system resocializes parents by a "goal attainment scale" (Bommer, et al, 1977:336) that specifies best to least desired outcomes. The resocialization schedule avoids deadlines for achievement because "this might cause a further stress-producing situation, a condition with which many child-abusers are unable to cope." It is indeed a deadly game, this monitoring and treatment of the violent, and the helpless victims must play by the same ambivalent rules, even if it means their lives or their sanity.

Why not reduce social and economic costs at the outset and seek natural community networks: relatives, grandparents, neighbors, friends (see Speck and Attneave, 1973). This strategy is a last choice. The state evidently prefers to hold on to the remnants of the deteriorating nuclear family with its rituals of intimacy, however barbaric the actual relationships.[8]

Sociability was not always defined as family or family-like intimacy in a cold world. Sennett (1978) tells us that in the Renaissance sociable relations were thought of in terms of citizenship. Cooperation, not closeness, was the mark of sociability. In the contemporary liberal state, the external world is viewed as strange and destructive, and when one's own intimacy capacities are severely marked by negative feelings that make closeness impossible, the individual easily fails. Coupling and parenting, made even more hazardous in modern life, too easily slip into the antisocial end of the spectrum. Then, intimacy breeds violence and despair, a world of shared pain unless interrupted by the clinic or police authority.

A primary source for the current family malaise and state takeover derives from Victorian sentimentality, Ann Douglas Wood (1977) asserts. The "sentiment heresy," initially espoused by affluent women and ministers in 19th-century America, implies that the values a society denies are precisely the ones it cherishes. As a rampant form of false consciousness, the sentimentalization of theological and secular culture was an inevitable part of the self-evasion of a society both committed to laissez-faire industrial expansion and disturbed by its consequences. America lost its Calvinism, a patriarchal and positive culture, without gaining a modern equivalent. In post-Victorian life, male hegemony persisted, but without a religious sensibility, a comprehensive feminism or a humanistic, historically minded romanticism.

Wood (1977) contends that the demise of patriarchal order, because of rapid industrialization, tightened the division of labor between women and men, and between family and outside world. Feminization or a "culture of the feelings" patterned sensibility and family relations, and hierarchical structures dominated relations between men and within work milieus. Proponents of the new order stressed the separation and preservation of the family, and the reformation of the cities by propagating the "matriarchal" values of nurturance, generosity and acceptance. This provoked heroines Dorothea Dix, Jane Addams, Florence Nightingale and others to tackle resistant social structures as though all that were needed was the "woman's touch." But lacking power and toughness, the womanly values merely intensified sentimentality rather than clarifying the fiercely anti-intellectual, humanly trivializing nature of the emerging industrial state. The militant "crusade for masculinity" that followed this feminization of culture and the closing of the frontier signaled new forms of female repression. Sociological theory and political practice exalted Social Darwinism, which justified the right of the strong to trample the weak. Literature took its cues from naturalism with its emphasis on brute instinct and force. Games and athletic events became strategic sites for male competition and violence. Women and the liberal Protestant ministers who were allied with them were further devalued and underwent an enforced self-simplification. Women were uniformly classified as "housewives," an undifferentiated, imprecise and distorted category that masked the enormous variations in women's life styles; while "ministers" came to connote vague, church-bound efforts at "goodness." The power vacuum created by the cultural sprawl, as men concentrated on work and women and ministers on family and privatized charity, was only waiting to be filled. By the early twentieth century, the rationalization of childhood began in the school and juvenile courts and continues today in a revised rendering of *parens patriae* (Meyer et al, 1979:591-613). The therapeutic version of *in loco parentis* eliminates adversary relations between the child and the state, while effectively withering away the remnants of parental authority in the home (Lasch, 1979). Still, the state has only a partial control of the family. In its most fully developed legitimate monopoly, violence, the state demonstrates its potential for total control.

The Violence Monopoly

Among the monopolies the state has acquired over the last three centuries, none is more total, more potentially destructive and more ambiguous than violence. The state is the court of last resort, not only for criminals, but also for all citizens who define their private troubles as issues for state intervention. How did the state emerge as the exclusive apparatus of violence? Paradoxically, the more areas in which the state intervened, the more its legitimacy came under attack. And with this withering away of more benign forms of social control, violence became the generalized substitute (see Geis, 1967:354-358). In democratic societies, though, this violence must be highly masked. It must make few public appearances before middle class and elite audiences; it must be efficient and effective; and it must be adapted to dominant cultural images and practices.

First, the police as the state's ambassadors of violence, theoretically, have a limited arena. Lower class or ethnic communities and disintegrated neighborhoods often serve as a permissible testing ground for coercive control. Thus, the state teaches conformity by selective examples of state action. Social control by terror is rarely explicitly directed against respectable groups, but often the boundaries overlap. As a weapon to regulate suspects and outcasts, it provides general reaffirmation of state authority. State condemnation and persecution does not necessarily stop with the deviants, however. A spillover effect occurs, Michael Brown (1969:33-46) argues. Drawing on the California police attack on the Haight-Ashbury hippie population in San Francisco, Brown concludes that control through violence has unanticipated consequences.

1. Control tends to transcend itself both in its selection of targets and in its organization.

2. As coercive control develops, it is readily institutionalized and finally institutional. Once a more repressive control system emerges, it represents a new stage in social organization and has change-inducing force for social systems.

3. The hallmark of an advanced system of control (and the key to its beginning) is an ideology that unites otherwise highly differing agencies. For example, once social work and the police

united on an ideology of controlling the poor, the specific methods were not disputable.

4. Persecution and terror are acceptable methods of controlling troublesome groups in our society. As more and more deviance is placed in the category of heresy (political opposition), violence and other forms of repressive control become endemic.

Second, the terms *efficient* and *effective* evoke an entire range of symbolic activities that are meant to convey a particular gloss on state violence and arbitrary police action. Case 1—Separation of police and military give the appearance of two distinct orders: civilian militia and military order. But both complement each other. Riots, strikes, crowd behavior and natural disasters that threaten public order are likely to result in the calling forth of auxiliary forces such as the National Guard to support standard police forces. Case 2—Police efficiency is strictly measured by output: number of arrests; crime rates; percent of serious crimes; race, sex and age distributions and other police-blotter information. These crime statistics collected by the Federal Bureau of Investigation and state and local jurisdictions perform the symbolic functions of internal accounting systems for police and provide a mythological apparatus for citizen consumption. That only a small proportion of many serious crimes are ever known to the police, that police neither prevent nor stop crime (but often instigate it, instead), that police characteristically use excessive violence, that enforcement activities increase the schism between police and public, and that police use law as the "fount of legitimacy" (Manning, 1977:100)— all these are conveniently ignored in these reports.

Peter Manning's extensive empirical work on British and American police produced one overriding conclusion:

> *The law serves as a mystification device or canopy to cover selectively, legitimate, and rationalize police conduct.* It does not prospectively guide police action, nor does it provide the principal constraint upon police practices (p. 101).

How, then, can the police as chief arbiters of violence be said to be effective? According to Manning, police present themselves as professionally based experts employing scientific knowledge and technology. With this rationalized crime-control mandate, professional distance from citizens is justified and enhances claims for autonomy. Moreover, the police are agency-interdependent, not citizen-dependent for their functioning. Isolated citizens protesting the overreach of the violence mandate can thus be ignored with impunity.

Third, police also operate within dominant images and instrumental practices that make palatable their mission of violence. They perform a range of public services required in urban societies that also function to symbolically transmit the concern of people to duly authorized persons. After all, the police, along with hospitals, are the primary public service facilities open on a 24-hour basis to persons in need. And police are the line of last resort for many personal and family crises. The police serve a dual role that confounds as well as buttresses citizen support. They serve as advocates of citizens' values, as when they quell riots (see Wilson, 1968), and as adversaries in support of special interests, as when they protect businesses and elite areas, but not poor neighborhoods. Yet their professional demeanor invariably exudes neutrality. In the hegemonious myth, the police, like the doctor, take only one side in the struggle of right against wrong, health against disease. Hence, the difficulty that partisans have in convincing police groups that other perspectives should be considered in a conflict area. For example, the custom of penalizing hookers and petty shoplifters, virtually harmless offenders, operates under the same noncommittal law-and-order rhetoric as that used for serious criminals.

The violence monopoly without adequate citizen input is dangerous. Like Hobbes's 17th-century futuristic image, the modern state's exclusive control of social problems enables it to make final determinants of rewards and punishments, honor and order, life and death. Violence is an open-ended instrument, having no supralegal limits. It cannot be expropriated, traded, shared or discarded. As the ultimate regulative instrument, it can substitute for poor policies, ineffective governing, lax leadership and nonconsent of the governed. The hauntingly perverse echo of the words of the American officer in Vietnam that "in order to liberate the village, we had to destroy it" (quoted in Hofstadter and Wallace, 1970), reminds us that American political culture has gone perilously far beyond the age of innocence.

It should be emphasized that fortunately violence is not a ubiquitous state policy. Certain built-in structural features help to keep violence in check. The implementation of social policies does not flow exclusively from the Leviathan's head, but must be negotiated among various interest groups and agencies.

Policy Implementation

Implementing social policy involves translating objectives into actions, requiring coordination of numerous agencies and individual decision-makers. Too often the accomplishments fall far short of the goals. There are many reasons for this. The policies may threaten the jobs, the power and the budget resources of some agency or personnel group. Affected persons will resist the policy and ignore, sidetrack or reinterpret directives. Other groups, agencies or interests will attempt to co-opt the policy implementation, that is, incorporate it into their own agendas. Students of administration and organizations have dealt at length with such structural obstacles to implementation (see, for instance, Selznick, 1966; Allison, 1971; Bardach, 1977). Implementing a policy is as much a political game, or rather a sequence of political games, as constructing the social problem.

In this section we shall discuss two issues that determine in major ways the implementation of state policies of social control. The first has to do with relationships in the network of agencies, boards, interest groups and personnel groups that are involved in implementation. The second deals with the thought models that are taken for granted in the implementation. Both are easily overlooked.

(1) The agencies responsible for implementing control policies are typically *loosely coupled,* that is, they more often than not act independently of one another, even though there may exist formal charts that mandate consultation, coordination of actions, subordination and other relations. In organizational analysis, the loose-coupling idea has been most often applied to educational organizations (see Weick, 1976; Cohen, March and Olsen, 1972; March and Olsen, 1976). But, it also applies to most social control domains. A careful reading of Cahn's (1970) comprehensive review of the treatment of alcoholics makes it very clear that there simply does not exist a coherently coordinated policy. Instead, a number of competing agencies and organizations routinely deal with alcoholics, and indeed a certain amount of consultation and referral occurs. But many times the actions or nonactions are taken independently. *De facto* decriminalization of public drunkenness

occurred without the development of sufficient resources for detoxification centers and halfway houses. Writing about the alcoholism wards in state mental hospitals, Cahn says:

> For the most part, the hospital's after-care arrangements are not available to its alcoholic patients. They are infrequently placed on leave and are usually discharged outright. The situation is equally unsatisfactory in the case of specialized clinics and halfway houses. Usually, there is not even a per- functory relationship between an alcoholism ward and halfway houses or alcoholism clinics...In a few instances, an alcoholism clinic in a prospective dischargee's home town assigns a social worker to interview him for referral to the clinic; and in a few others welfare departments plan systematically with hospital personnel for discharge. On balance, however, the state hospi- tal system of treatment, no matter ahow good it is, clearly breaks down at the community after-care level.
>
> (Cahn, 1970:95)

In the first section of this chapter we argued that linkage between clients and professionals in community-care organizations tends to be weak. We now see that the links between the various organiza- tions are at best weak also. Individual alcoholics and mental patients very likely fall "between the cracks"; they remain untreated or go in and out of various institutions. Because the primary groups—family, friendship and work groups—cannot deal with alcoholics, drug abusers or the mentally ill very effec- tively, these deviants become socially disconnected in spite of the conscientious care they receive in detoxification centers, commu- nity mental health centers, drug and alcoholism wards, and out- patient therapy groups. Generally, hardworking, well-intentioned and competent persons staff these institutions. The system fails because its *structure* is weak.

(2) The implementatation of social control policies is typically based on an individualistic laissez-faire market model. Following release from mental institutions or alchoholism clinics, patients are expected to rejoin the "community" and avail themselves of its supports and opportunities just like other consumers. But often there is no community for them to rejoin. Also, they are overly vulnerable. Many lack the coping skills taken for granted by healthy persons and end up as isolated residents of boarding houses and converted welfare hotels. Occasional care by under- staffed social work agencies does not meet the totality of needs. The practice of contracting out to private sources for the housing and care of the elderly insane leads to horrendous abuses. Horror

stories are not hard to discover, as any glance at your daily paper will confirm. Here is a local newspaper report of a fire in a New Jersey community, possibly started by an elderly mental patient. It depicts the confusion that surrounds the limits of community care.

> Mr. Chomsky estimated that Asbury Park's population of formerly institutionalized residents was about 1,500. "Asbury Park has always maintained it would accept its fair share of the burden, but not the entire burden," Mr. Chomsky said.
>
> Common "problems" associated with the former patients, he said, were urinating and disrobing in public, jaywalking, panhandling and "walking the streets."
>
> One of the survivors of the Brinley End fire—an elderly woman who left a suicide note in the dining room there sometime before the blaze—was taken to an Asbury Park boarding house after the fire. The woman, who was questioned and dismissed as a possible cause of the fire, spent much of last night wandering near the burned-out inn.
>
> A police captain found her at about 10 p.m. in the neighborhood after she had been listed as missing. The captain said the woman told him she had walked down the oceanfront boardwalk from Asbury Park to the inn because she couldn't sleep. The captain found the woman on a front porch near the inn.
>
> "She has talked about killing herself before, "the captain, who asked to remain unidentified, said. "Her note had absolutely no bearing whatever on the fire. She's looking for sympathy. She wants a place of her own. She didn't want to live in a place like this."

Certainly, community care should mean that the person has some organic tie with others. We know that such ties are necessary for humans because they are social beings in a very real sense. But the natural community has broken down in our metropolitan centers (see, for instance, Connery, 1968 and chapter 9 for a discussion of this in the mental health context).

Instead of the integrated community, we have discussions about updating equipment and rules. For example, commenting on the New Jersey fire referred to in our last illustration, public officials discussed tightening standards of inspection and safety regulations. This is precisely the sort of thing that officials are able to do. Sprinklers and fire doors will undoubtedly save lives. But officials cannot call into existence what may be needed most, namely, a semblance of community.

CHAPTER 7—NOTES

[1] For a historical and sociological description of professions, see Sarfatti-Larson (1977). Crozier (1964) gives a detailed analysis of the workings of bureaucracies.

[2] For a characterization of weak links in social structures see Granovetter (1973).

[3] V.O. Key, Jr., (1962) discusses the political process and the role of lobbying in creating legislation.

[4] For a general theoretical discussion of reality construction, see Berger and Luckmann (1967).

[5] This section is drawn from Nanette J. Davis (1973). It is currently undergoing revision for a book, *Anatomy of Abortion.*

[6] For a fuller discussion of how credentials, requirements and work rules become legitimating rituals in some organizations, see the chapter by Meyer and Rowan in M. Meyer (1978).

[7] A general discussion of the ritual uses of public policy is found in Arnold (1935).

[8] Increasing state interference in family life appears inevitable. As children gain autonomous rights, courts will be increasingly involved as legal referees of disputes between parents and their children. Such intervention far exceeds the judicial limits of state intervention, which is prescribed only under conditions of a "compelling interest" (e.g., protecting a child from harm). (*Seattle Post Intelligencer,* October 19, 1980:D7. See, also, *The New York Times,* October 8, 1980:10.)

Chapter 8
The Opaque Mandate:
Regulating the Poor

> Social policy has been seen as an *ad hoc* appendage to economic growth; the provision of benefits, not the formulation of rights. If we are in the future to include the poor in our societies we shall have to widen our frames of reference. We shall need to shift the emphasis from poverty to inequality, from *ad hoc* programs to integrated social rights, from economic growth to social growth.
>
> Richard M. Titmuss, *Commitment to Welfare.*

The 16th-century Elizabethan poor laws, like the poverty programs of the 1960s offered a set of restrictive concepts and related legislative and administrative practices. "Charity," "dole," "relief" and "welfare"—the words shift with historical context—were measures to buttress the existing social order, while incorporating (at least in theory) the needy, the destitute and the disabled into society. Their influence remains today.

The throwaway image of commodity use, normally associated with market forms of economic organization, is extended to the realm of persons and even communities. Human surpluses are the leftovers of outmoded technologies and changing forms of social organization. Age, sex, social class, race, ethnicity, geography and education are social criteria used to weed out the undesirables from the labor force. At the same time, however, dominant groups recognize that surplus people provide a potential source of social unrest. Consequently, limited public investments in the welfare and rehabilitation of the deprived have been undertaken for the defense of the social order. Moral abhorrence of misery, squalor and destitution combine in the self-interest of dominant groups to produce varying degrees of commitment to welfare measures and policies (for a review of the welfare issue, see Gottlieb, 1974; Steiner, 1971; Ulmer, 1969; Sternlieb and Indik, 1973; Rose, 1972; Gronjerb, Street, and Suttles, 1978).

In this chapter we shall describe the structures of inequality, the facts of life for the poor and the different models of thought, or ideologies, that have been or are currently used to shape social welfare policies. Our aim is to illustrate how failures of social policy, the conservation of poverty, misery and squalor, and even an increased production of deviance can be traced to contradictions in the models of welfare and their masked politics.

Inequality, Work and Poverty

Whatever empirical data is brought to bear—income distribution, measures of health, welfare, mortality and quality of life—the evidence points to the persistence of politically structured inequalities in our epoch. Central among the political structures used to maintain inequality are the *wealthfare* and *welfare* systems (Turner and Starnes, 1976). The wealthfare system consists of those policies and programs, such as government contracts, price supports and tax expenditures, which effectively subsidize the rich. Because the welfare system helps to perpetuate poverty through its low levels of benefits, it does little to eliminate the poor's vulnerability in a competitive job market.

This becomes apparent when we examine income distributions and the proportion of the population who differentially benefit from current policy. In a review essay on the state of inequality in American society, Andrew Hacker (1980) considers income distributions and what these figures tell us about long-term, structured inequality. Table 1, based on census data, shows the classic income-distribution structure typically found in all industrial societies.

First, family incomes exceed individual incomes because they typically include two-spouse—working households (about 50 percent of the time). Second, because 72 percent of the families earn between $10,000 and $50,000 planners and public can ignore the deeply entrenched inequality at both top and bottom. Third, the $50,000 bracket stays rich because they retain almost all the property income, averaging $8,900 per household. This is because tax laws are not progressive; property investment requires an income cushion that only the affluent possess; the rich get regular dividend payments that can be reinvested; there is ready accessibility to capital among the wealthy because of favorable credit, and so on. These structural supports result in total dividend and other property income amounting to 29 percent of the total unearned income category (along with alimony, child support, gifts and pensions). The top group received 28 percent, or all but one percent, of this

Table 8:1   Income Distributions: 1978

	Families	
$50,000 & Over	2,082,000	3.6%
$25,000-$50,000	14,033,000	24.3%
$20,000-$25,000	8,392,000	14.5%
$15,000-$20,000	9,769,000	16.9%
$10,000-$15,000	9,656,000	16.7%
$5,000-$10,000	9.154,000	15.8%
Under $5,000	4,719,000	8.2%
Total	57,804,000	100.0%

Median: $17,640

	Full-time Workers	
$50,000 & Over	1,013,000	1.7%
$25,000-$50,000	5,966,000	9.6%
$20,000-$25,000	6,555,000	10.6%
$15,000-$20,000	11,798,000	19.0%
$10,000-$15,000	16,476,000	26.6%
$5,000-$10,000	16,568,000	5.8%
Under $5,000	3,573,000	26.7%
Total	61,950,000	100.0%

Median: $14,961

From Hacker, 1980:21

amount. Fourth, professionals and executives receive the highest salaries, with physicians remaining the highest-paid professionals, exceeding lawyers two to one. High-income professionals are more likely to be self-employed; high-paid executives earn their high income through salaries. For the over $50,000 income group, 58 percent worked for someone else. It pays to be a high-salaried executive.

Fifth, few women are in the highest income category—only 8,384 in the entire country earned $50,000 or more. Whereas more women are working than in previous decades.—For instance, between 1970 and 1978, 6.5 million men joined the labor force compared to 9.2 million women—their median incomes relative to men remained the same throughout the 1970's, just about 59 percent. By contrast, black men earn 70-75 percent of white male income. This median income holds true for fulltime working women, not only for women who are parttime workers. Women are entering the professional and graduate schools in larger numbers, but no evidence exists at present to support the claim that women are preempting some men's places at the higher-income levels.

Sixth, the status of black Americans has not improved in relation to whites. The most important obstacle to black progress is the increased number of black single families headed by women, which rose from 1.4 million to 2.3 million, a 65 percent increase over an eight-year period. (For whites the comparable rise was 40 percent). Thus, for every black family that moved up to middle class status, three others were added to the bottom rank.

Does this distribution of the wealth imply a hierarchy by merit? No, says Randal Collins (1979) in his analysis of the credentialing society. The myth that higher education is a requirement for wealth or position is dispelled by the fact that 40 percent of top income earners have never attended college, or left before they received a degree. For many persons, education is actually unrelated to what they do; and in a more radical vein, Collins argues that most persons can learn to do almost any job:

> The great majority of all jobs can be learned through practice by almost any literate person. The number of esoteric specialties requiring unusually extensive training or skill is relatively small.

Merit is reduced to a special set of skills: classroom competency with its fixation on memory, testing and quantitative knowledge. In this system, success and failure are predetermined by externally imposed conceptions of abilities, so that whatever the skills required, the method is guaranteed to eliminate poor people and keep them frozen in place.

Inequalities between social classes, a subject only gingerly treated by mainstream sociology as a psychological state or a status system, has been preempted by Marxists as the crucial variable that freezes existing property relations and, hence, reproduces inequality. What are the chances for a working-class or peoples' movement to alter this inequality structure? Examining social class in Britain to illustrate general trends in industrial societies, Westergaard and Resler (1975) conclude that existing social conditions severely reduce the likelihood that a working class movement can emerge and, if started, that it could result in any substantial structural changes.

First, there is no bourgeois model for revolution that can be adopted by the working classes. Models of deference and clearly ranked authority exist, forming the core of a cluster of central values, common in one form or another to all classes in industrial societies. Consequently, intellectuals and professional activists import a model for organization. Once these leaders pull out, rank and file leaders lack the experience to continue.

Second, traditional working class culture is not homogeneous, but split by ethnic, racial and religious affiliations, which can foster or impede solidarity, depending on the issue.

The third theme, arising from the second, postulates that workers are increasingly isolated from one another. Either they have realigned their aspirations toward family and individual goals, rather than collective or class objectives, or they have become primarily fixated on money. Still, tension grows between increasing working class demands on life and the frustrations of members of the working class as inequality persists.

Westergaard and Resler believe that no effective challenge to the established order is likely to result from working class movements as such. The twin antagonism—working class subversion, which undermines worker solidarity, and a reform ideology, which produces worker frustration and discontent—could spin off contradictions that mobilize authorities. Any attempts to redress inequalities, through, are inevitably overly limited.

However, if a different scenario should occur, such as steady pressure by underdogs, this could break down the hegemonious ideology. Despite the unprepared and fragmented state of organized labor, the conditions that undermine their capacity to bring effective force to bear on transforming business rule, the working classes have a diffuse and ambivalent hope for a fraternal society. This works against the capitalist order in two ways. One, concessions by elites can spin off another round of demands. And two, there is always the possibility of unity among blue-and white-collar groups on key issues. Westergaard and Resler hold out for minor victories. The class struggle cannot be dismissed, however defeated each encounter between rulers and ruled, as long as capitalism is gradually undermined by unceasing pressures for change from below.

In *Class, Race and Worker Insurgency,* James Geschwender (1977) analyzes racial exploitation as a dialectical process. A more or less organized system of racial exploitation emerges to fill labor needs in a world capitalist system. Minorities challenge the system through their resistance (e.g., strikes, turnover, sabotage). Not wishing to give up their position, owners and managers move to crush opposition. If resistance is too strong, they may be forced to retreat through a partial abandonment of the system of racial exploitation. Labor retrenchment, resulting in job cutbacks, is the most typical form retreat takes. This strategy usually engenders a new system of racial exploitation, providing many of the advantages of the old system at lower costs. The new structure, in turn, stimulates a collective reaction by the subordinate group against those new groups benefiting from the updated system of racial exploitation.

What Geschwender's argument implies is that specific inequalities are not permanently structured as steady state fixtures of the capitalist order. Instead, oppression results in reaction, an unsettling and destabilizing influence.[1] For example, abolition of slavery in the United States gave way to a new system of peonage — sharecropping, tenant farming and debt peonage. Since World War II, resistance by blacks who joined the Sharecroppers Union and the Tenant Farmers Association forced landholders to make changes. Eventually, black resistance combined with mechanization of agriculture to bring an end to the system of agriculture peonage.

The theorists' perspective, most sociologists agree, is an important element for analyzing stratification structures. For instance, if we take the dialectical approach used by Westergaard and Resler and by Geschwender, that is the observer's stance, the structure appears to be fluid. This entails an ever changing movement of actors, ideologies, and political strategies, created by structured oppositions. Whereas ground structures change in keeping with their technological and political logic, ideological thought among underdogs retains its oppositional quality; it is coherent, programmatic and consistent.

Examined through a different viewpoint, say the participating actors' frame of reference, the internal relations of political ideas look far less integrated. Here political opinions lack goal orientation and creativity; more often they are catch phrases that analysts would depict as stereotypical, noninnovative and weak. This is the premise of the "ideological transmission" school, which interprets political consciousness as a diffusion of "packages" of ideas from ruling groups to masses (Converse, 1964:211 d213). Communication deficiencies cause ambiguity and conflict within the belief system of subordinate groups.

Other writers accept the diffusion idea, but hold that rather than there being communicative deficiencies, the elite-downward dissemination by schools, public institutions and mass media is highly successful (Mann, 1970; Sallach, 1974). These dominant values contradict those shaped by the experiences of everyday life in the lower classes. The result again is a high level of confusion and inconsistency in political opinions of subordinate groups, or what Gramsci (1972 edition) called the result of "domination hegemony."

Considering the British political scene, Cheal (1979) found that subordinate groups lack ideological coherence, Instead, contradictory consciousness immobilizes underdogs and leads to sudden outbreaks of industrial action. Cheal (1979:115) says:

> The tentative conclusion must be that the form of British political culture is consistent with the hegemony thesis. There are two major political ideologies. One is a coherent system of thought concerned with the preservation of traditional class relationships—the ruling ideology. The other is a contradictory set of opinions which partially challenges, but largely accepts, the prevailing balance of economic power—the subordinate ideology.

Thus, class consciousness, contrary to orthodox Marxism, is not a viable concept of analyzing the propensity of underdogs for revolution or self-help. Studies repeatedly show that class structure and class identification are distinct variables. For instance, Great Britain demonstrates a society with a strong class structure—ranks and roles are clearly defined in classic terms—whereas the United States is reported to have a loose class structure, involving more flexibility in moving between classes either in the lifetime of an age cohort or over two or more generations. Yet class consciousness in Britain may actually be lower relative to the United States (Vanneman, 1980:769-789). On social-distance measures and other standard modes of measurement, Americans have higher class consciousness, perceive greater differences between ranks and express greater resentment toward inequalities than their British counterparts. There is no massive "bourgeoisification" of the working class, either in America or Britain. But there is a countertendency. In Britain, more nonmanual workers identify themselves as working class, some two in every three persons surveyed (Westergaard and Resler, 1975:366). This may also reflect little more than the emptiness of the class labels, the diversity of meanings that the persons who use them attach to them. In Western society, the differences in conceptions of class and inequality imply that the Marxist preference for a two-class image, with movement organization aimed at creating hostilities between hgihly structured antagonists, may be greatly oversimplified. In the United States, unionization has *not* promoted equality among the races, but rather the reverse; that is, unionization generally promotes white worker gains at the expense of black income equality. Beck's (1980:791-814) time-series analysis of labor unionism and racial income inequality since the post-World War II period found more support for the white protectionist position than for the class consciousness interpretation. Poor people's movements languish, not only because communities are fragmented and resources are few, but also because there is no strong underdog solidarity that can transcend the various forms of systematic splintering within capitalist societies.

If welfare represents the "last resort" for the chronically unemployed and underemployed in the social service model, what is the nature of the labor market and the productive system that apparently fails so many citizens?

First, there is a dual labor market: a primary one having its base in stable employment, decent wages, benefits and union protection; and another labor market that lacks both stability and a living wage and employs the surplus population—low-or non-skilled people, the young, old, minorities, women and others who lack any collective bargaining power. For example, lower-level service workers—including gas station attendants, nonunionized busboys, supermarket bag boys (who may be men in their forties or fifties), fast-food workers and laundry attendants—receive minimum wage or less, without medical insurance or other benefits; they have no job protection and are expected to work on demand, including night shifts (regardless of personal health risks or family responsibilities). In some states farm labor cruelly exploits entire families. The effort to liberate welfare beneficiaries from the dole through job training is thus a sideways movement (from being jobless to being a member of the working poor). For many job seekers, a major advantage of being on welfare (together with medical benefits, food stamps, psychological counseling, job training and agency assistance for children and family problems) is that the financial cushion enables a more selective job choice. Without welfare funds, the poor must take the first and often the only job available.

Second, welfare actually masks the unemployment policy. Poor people tolerate depressed wages because as surplus workers they are forced to compete with middle class teenagers and college students who are largely suported by parents. The despised class of jobs tends to encourage high turnover, absenteeism and poor job performance. Thus, there is the paradox of the welfare recipient who stays on the relief rolls while the lower-level jobs go begging for workers. But such jobs are not "adult" work; they do not yield a living wage, a decent standard of life, self esteem or human significance.

Third, even in the dominant labor market of manual and white-collar jobs, work in industrial societies may be trivial, boring and insignificant, often breeding alienation and discontent. Work becomes a penalty for the living, a cross that must be endured, regardless of the status or size of the pay check. From discussions with a range of workers, Terkel (1974) concluded that modern work deadens the self and contributes to meaninglessness.

> For the many, there is a hardly concealed discontent. The blue collar blues is no more bitterly sung than the white collar moan. "I'm a machine," says the spot-welder. "I'm a mule," says the steelworker. "A monkey can do what I do," says the receptionist. "I'm less than a farm implement," says the migrant worker. "I'm an object," says the high-fashion model. Blue collar and white call upon the identical phrase: "I'm a robot." *"There is nothing to talk about,"* the young accountant despairingly enunciates. It was some time ago that John Henry sang, "A man ain't nothin' but a man." The hard unromantic fact is: he died with his hammer in his hand while the machine pumped on.
> (Terkel, 1974:xii)

Are citizens in industrial societies drifting away from the work ethic to adopt a new hedonistic ethic—the life style of the narcissist, as Christopher Lasch (1979) describes such self-possessed, alienated persons? While it is difficult to pinpoint such widespread trends as changes in the meaning of work, it is apparent that today's work, which transforms components of persons into technology, seriously reduces commitment. Outside of the family, work has been the dominant mode of integrating persons into society. According to Freud (1961 edition), work gives the person a sense of place and position in the human community. Denigration of work implies the loss of the most significant bonding agent in modern society. And for the larger proportion of working-age adults, there is nothing to take its place.

If work is so coercive and personally destructive, why do women, formerly excluded from the workplace as regulars, so intensely seek their identity, their selfhood, in the world of work (Ruddick and Daniels, 1977)? Is it true, as ideologists of the industrial society argue, that however grim and disreputable many jobs may be, work is sought after because it remains the major interaction link for adults. Isn't it both the sign (and sometimes curse) of adulthood?

The prospect of a life without work appears to be a horrendous idea, a dreadful portrayal of a world without sense. Women are urged to enter or return to the labor market despite their child-care and domestic responsibilities; teenagers discover their self-respect through part time jobs; health retirees retire "to something." Work thus has multiple functions. It connects persons, structures their day, provides sustenance, and gives persons a sense of being involved with an institution larger than themselves ("I work at the X mill." "I'm a professor at Y University.").

The reorganization of work in industrial societies, with a few exceptions in Scandanavia, Yugoslavia and France, remains a fond but distant hope. Critics claim that on the whole schemes for worker control over decisions in the work place have moved little beyond the drawing board, or have turned out to be "wasteful of labor," "often slack on discipline," or arrangements that "primarily benefited management" (Lindbloom, 1977:332-337). Politicians preach full employment, affirmative action for women and minorities and the dignity of work, but make little effort to radically alter the nature of capitalism with its masses of politically powerless laboring classes.

The many faces of poverty, then, reveal an interlocked, dual image; the failure of the economy to produce secure employment and the weakness of the political system to humanize capitalist economic orders.

Identifying the Poor

Who are the poor? What populations are we talking about? Are there industries that serve as "feeder sectors" into welfare? Is welfare a permanent condition, a kind of negative social inheritance carried from one generation to another?

The greatest bulk of the needy poor are drawn from the aged and children, the latter group providing the major population of welfare benefits, up to 80 percent of all beneficiaries under Aid to Dependent Children. Distributions of benefits tend to be clustered in only a few programs. For example, in New York City in 1970, Aid to Dependent Children involved 805,000 cases of a total of 1,093,000 welfare cases. The remaining cases were distributed among simple relief (151,000), old age assistance, (71,000), Aid to Blind (3,000) and Aid to Disabled (63,000) (Sternlieb and Indik, 1973:5). If we count the added costs of subsidized housing (most occupants are elderly or children), Medicaid payments for the indigent poor, a variety of tax-paid social services impacting on the poor including social workers, health workers and criminal justice personnel, and even burial expenses, we can begin to grasp the monumental extent to which poverty affects persons and institutions (see Barrington Moore, 1972:109, for a discussion of government manipulation of welfare expenditures).

Poverty changes forms from one generation to another, according to shifts in political, economic and technological conditions. It can be induced by changing technology. For example, 40.000 persons lost jobs in New York City as a result of the automating of elevators in public buildings and high-rise apartments. Or specific industries may be hit by recession, such as the fishing and logging industries in Oregon and Washington state (1980), throwing large numbers of stable working class persons out of work. Areas like Appalachia are permanently crippled by poverty because the regions are low in resources or represent political backwaters. International competition, in which Americans lose their edge in the world market, is a growing cause of economic dislocation and poverty. The sick auto industry in Michigan, especially the Chrysler Corporation, can be temporarily propped up by large-scale federal and state assistance. But when Japanese auto production turns out a more gas-efficient, lightweight and attractive model than its American counterpart, the cure is a stopgap. A declining industry has the reverse effect of a growing one. As the deficit grows, investments and jobs dwindle. Communities are hit throughout all consumer sectors because increased unemployment dries up expenditures for house buying, food, laundry services, repairs and entertainment. And the number of unemployed workers grows. When Seattle's major industry, the Boeing Company, suffered a recession in the early 1970s, massive numbers of workers, including highly educated professionals (e.g., engineers, Ph.D. lab researchers and technicians), were thrown out of work. If spouses were employed, workers sometimes could slavage their house investment. Many employees, however, were forced to sell their homes at great personal loss and move elsewhere. In addition, many American workers lack even the resources to move. What these examples emphasize is that poverty is not merely an isolated episode affecting the down-and-outers, but rather a permanent and unresolvable problem located in the infrastructure of the economy.

The feeder-sector hypothesis claims that certain financially unstable industries provide the bulk of the welfare population. This oversimplifies the complexities of poverty. While it is true that industries and regions are differentially impacted by recession, there is no clear picture of any specific industrial sector that contributes to poverty and welfare.[2] A Rand study (Abrahamse et al, 1977) examined which industrial sectors were more or less welfare prone but found little to support its premise. Instead, the research found that recipients came to welfare from the lowest rungs of skill and pay ladders. Men's jobs differ from women's jobs, with unemployed female heads of families showing different industrial sector patterns than AFDC mothers. On the whole, though, welfare beneficiaries start poor and end up poor. Even with training, they remain well below the average salary level for the state.

Part of the problem lies in the recipient's low educational achievement. For example, the recipiency rate among family heads who did not complete high school is approximately 30 percent in California. In addition, about 60 percent of welfare clients have moderate to severe health problems (e.g., anemia among black teenage girls).

However residual the welfare system may appear to enlightened social workers (the "last resort" thesis), it is currently the only institutional remedy against temporary or permanent poverty. Case loads reflect this, both in their steady expansion over the last 20 years and in their massive financial support for millions of poor families. In New York City, ADC represents 63.9 percent of all cases and has continued to rise over a ten-year period (Rydell et al, 1974). This means that more dependent children are supported relative to the other programs. In addition, many of the New York City cases are fairly long-term, three years or more. The greater the number of children in an ADC household, the longer the duration and frequency of dependency (on and off welfare over many years).

Because public conceptions of poverty tend to be shaped by the individualistic ethic—conservatives blame the poor for being victimized by the economic system—the problem remains largely out of sight. The welfare poor tend to be ecologically segregated as well, which further compounds their isolation. Clustered into welfare blocks, welfare neighborhoods or housing projects in large cities, the poor remain invisible to working and middle class residents.

Many fulltime workers receive welfare as supplementary wages, a further indication of the failure of the economic order. Thus, low earnings are a major cause of poverty, a situation characteristic both of the United States and Great Britain (Morgan and Morgan, 1972). In effect, subsidizing the free market is the necessary compromise to keep the existing income distribution intact (and this has not changed essentially over a fifty-year period). Persons do not inherit the "welfare mentality." Instead they are "trapped in a hopeless struggle," to borrow a phrase from Sternlieb and Indik's book (1973) on housing and the welfare crisis in New York City. In this metropolis where 20 percent of citizens are currently on welfare, and among whom 60 percent are under 37 years old, it no longer makes sense to speak of welfare as "residual," a "last resort," or of the social worker as the "motivating engine." Rather, we must recognize that welfare is an integral part of American life. It is a "big business," an institution *sui generis* with a growing market, an expanding production system and a viable labor market wherein the college educated find work at the cost of other people's poverty.

In this ill-planned and often irrational system, the human and economic waste is extensive; thirty thousand housing units abandoned in New York City per annum, death at an early age, especially for the minority poor, and cities racked with crime and property destruction.

The poor may not be as invisible as when Michael Harrington wrote his exposé of *The Other America* in 1962. In many ways their influence in American cities is profound. Middle class citizens feel it primarily in their pocketbooks, through the increased costs of welfare, policing and other direct control expenditures. The poor experience their plight more directly as the side effects of government aid become increasingly intrusive or fall below acceptable survival levels. For beneficiaries, intervention remains a mixed blessing. Housing projects are poorly constructed, gloomy and dangerous, far less hospitable than the old-fashioned slum, and at much higher costs to taxpayers. And once caught in the welfare bind, with its invasion of privacy and dependency cycle, it is difficult to extricate oneself (Gottlieb, 1974).

Welfare Ideologies

Welfare ideologies are composed of clusters of beliefs that help shape and define the meanings of various separate institutional arrangements and of the practices of the social work professionals who occupy the regulatory roles in the welfare institutions.

First, the welfare term entails profound division. In the constitutional sense, *welfare* implies universal treatment of all citizens under the direction of a benevolent state. In this context the emphasis is on rights and prerogatives of the governed as opposed to the conditions and obligations for meeting needs by those who govern. Welfare, as in *welfare state,* points to the necessary adjustments government must make to the erratic conditions of the marketplace. This doctrine is most closely linked with John M. Keynes and the "pump-priming" theory, by which government was expected to intervene at critical junctures of the economic cycle (e.g., recession) to stabilize prices and consumer activity (Ulmer, 1969). The concept lends itself to a diversity of government-sponsored social and economic programs, including health insurance, tax credits for the potential investor, public works projects (e.g., highways, parks, schools, conservation, etc.) and federal government support of troubled industries (e.g., Chrysler Corporation). The doctrine has its most favorable impact on middle and wealthy members of the community.

Welfare, as in *public assistance,* the major topic of this chapter, involves the most narrow and rigid government intervention. It represents the state's attempt to segregate and isolate the poor as a special class. Cumming (1968) sums up the public assistance doctrine as "the least services for the fewest persons." Whereas the constitutional and welfare-state doctrines aim for direct impact on the labor market, employment practices and income levels, with such measures as direct legislation or indirect subsidies to corporation and communities, public-assistance welfare has no significant impact on economic institutions. In this sense, public assistance represents a bottom-line remedy; the product of a fragmented policy and failure of constitutional authority.

Second, there are clusters of more or less coherent beliefs about the sources and development of the different social problems that official welfare institutions are mandated to deal with. Welfare ideologies describe the poor, the mentally ill, alcoholics, or criminal or delinquent persons in terms that depict "personality characteristics," and which often shade into moral disapproval (sociopathic, emotionally unstable, unenterprising, weak, lazy, volatile, irresponsible, etc.). Beliefs about typical problem careers depict how personal and moral characteristics separately, jointly and in conjunction with negative social factors (for instance, the nature of families and communities, education and job opportunities, physiological and/or medical factors) often produce individuals that get locked into poverty, subsistence dependence, mental illness, crime or vice.

Under these conditions, the state acts to regulate the images of the destitute classes through its crude and subtle labeling. Its overarching imagery for the unemployed is "idler"—an update on the vagrant concept formerly dominant for unemployed men. "Tramp" entails a double meaning: disreputably unemployed and sexually promiscuous. Both terms are labels used by conservatives against single welfare mothers. These theories about the origins and career of social problems entail or get linked to beliefs about suitable remedies and the measures that bring these about. Elites invariably attempt to restrict the welfare problem to the fewest persons. Categorical assistance, for example, aims to save the taxpayers' money, but it actually serves to eliminate a large, needy population from assistance. Two mechanisms to reduce the welfare roles are the "means" test, which requires proof of poverty, and the "least eligible" principle, which keeps the amount of assistance *below* the lowest-paid jobs in society. Under this system, the prevailing belief is that any job is preferable to any amount of welfare for the employables. Low-paid work serves as an incentive to self-improvement, say the modern Calvinists, and every measure must be taken to reduce the possibility that welfare becomes a permanent way of life (Mandell, ed., 1975).

Third, welfare ideologies contain beliefs about how welfare work is or should be organized. These include notions about the proper credentials of the personnel that carry out welfare policies, the organization of welfare work on a day-to-day basis, the proper allocation of resources, sanctions and incentives, and the facilities needed for treatment and/or incarceration. The business model used in social services presumes that efficiency and effectiveness are primary aims (Whittington and Bellaby, 1979). Hierarchy accomplishes these ends best, it is assumed, because it stresses accountability and control. Since welfare populations are among the most deprived groups in society and suffer from multiple problems of health, mental illness, criminality, delinquency, family desertion, child abuse, poor housing and premature death, close surveillance by properly authorized staff is required. Given these multiple social problems, a compliant client is mandatory under these conditions because only experts can determine needs.

Fourth, welfare ideologies attempt to link policies and organizational practices to societal values and forms of organization outside the welfare field. Within the past two decades, increased concern with civil rights and privacy norms led to changes in welfare policies in the form of increased reliance on "deinstitutionalized" treatment forms (e.g., out-patient day-care for mentally ill persons). In the 1970s, deemphasis on poverty signaled the reduced importance of the welfare issue. This ideological shift can be attributed to a number of sources: increased resentment among the middle class caused by spiraling inflation and generalized fear of the future because of energy scarcities, nuclear pollution and increasing political instability among emerging nations. Pollster Daniel Yankelovich (1975) reports that more than nine out of ten citizens (91 percent) express a generalized mistrust of those in power, covering business, government and most national institutions. This resentment further contributes to what Haines (1979:119-130) refers to as the process of "cognitive enclosure" in social problems. Welfare has become a nondebatable issue, and by extension, this enclosure provides the most effective method of depoliticizing poverty.

Fifth, among the beliefs strongly held by dominant groups is the notion that proper status relations must prevail between welfare recipients and persons who belong to the respectable groups of the community. Status subordination is the price often paid for receiving welfare checks or other forms of public assistance. Hospital personnel at drug and alcohol treatment clinics condescendingly treat and boss patients around as a matter of course. In the criminal justice institutions the status degradation practices are even more explicit and cruel. Historically, the precise contents of the beliefs that make up welfare ideologies have varied greatly. (Significant changes that have taken place over time are described in the next section.) In the 1960s Piven and Cloward (1977a; 1977b; 1977c) began challenging status subordination of welfare recipients through the National Welfare Rights Organization. More recently, Swedish welfare policy reflects a willingness on the part of the established welfare adminstrators to treat recipients as clients and fellow citizens whose needs should be actively served instead of as malingerers.

At any one time different actors in the welfare drama look at the problems in often radically different ways. Police officers, case workers in close touch with the needy, community leaders and administrators concerned with fiscal solvency and accountability, welfare recipients and citizens reluctant to pay taxes do not share in a consensual welfare ideology. And not all the actors in the welfare drama have equal power. When policies are translated into action, the views of politicians and the managers chosen by them matter more than those of welfare recipients, local community spokespersons or client-centered social workers. Hence, it is useful to begin our discussion of the dilemmas, contradictions and inadequacies of welfare policies by briefly considering the management ideologies that have shaped them.

Changing Management Models

Historically, social welfare policies have reflected different management strategies for perpetuating legal and political control over recipients. These are the ameliorative-utilitarian model, a clinical-psychoanalytical model and the structural-sociological model. Several themes connect these disparate management models.

First, a basic assumption among most management groups has been that the poor reflect a pathological (disorganized or sick) condition that is generic to this stratum. Second, defining the poor as unworthy justifies giving them the social minimum, allowing for bare subsistence to ensure institutional stability. Third, the logic of an ethical and economic minimum stipend rationalizes official intervention for determining the dependent poor's eligibility and status worth.

The Ameliorative-Utilitarian Model: Crime, Punishment and the Poor Laws. Transformation of the feudal-estate order to an industrial-class system beginning in the sixteenth and seventeenth centuries gradually generated a variety of irrevocable changes in agricultural and commercial sectors.[3] The laborer, no longer dependent on the landlord, was released to the vagaries of a free market. As a unit of production, workers had values, insofar as they contributed labor. The utilitarian laissez-faire imperative dictated that work was a moral state and ability to work a sign of personal competence.

Economic turmoil during this period created an increasing number of unemployed, a condition seen by many citizens as threatening social stability. Faced with a migratory labor force and accelerating numbers of unemployed, administrators abandoned the earlier classification that distinguished the "worthy poor" (e.g., widows, orphans, displaced workers) from the criminal poor (e.g., thieves, vagrants, beggars). "Salvageables," those qualified for aid, increasingly became lumped with "unredeemables," those unfit for benefits.

By the middle of the sixteenth century, public stereotypes evoked images of the poor as rogues, idlers, ne'er-do-wells, tramps, dangerous classes, despised and drunks. Thus, the worthy-unworthy, needy-criminal, assisted-punished dichotomy gradually broke down. The heterogeneous poor became publicly labeled as a single social type—immoral, incompetent and threatening to public order. Regulatory policies following this uniform labeling included legal restraints, police surveillance and corporal punishment.

The Elizabethan poor laws, orginally constructed to provide short-term relief to a locally stable population, were gradually adopted as deterrence mechanisms to prevent job-seeking outside the local community. These measures, however, failed to stabilize the labor market, for it produced depressed wages as employers confronted surplus labor in some areas, and rising labor costs from shortages in other regions. Poor law administration, tied to the local parish, lacked central direction and trained officials. This organizational incompetence, together with corruption of unpaid overseers, led to restrictive practices that have persisted in modified form to the present era. Some control measures instituted during this period included the following:

1. The *means test* required all relatives of the poor, regardless of

ability, to assume social and economic support. By extending deprivation beyond the worker and his family, social managers shifted the burden of responsibility to an already weakened kinship system.

2. *Residence rules* curtailed free labor movement in an attempt to enhance stability. The effect, however, was to freeze the labor supply and exacerbate rural poverty.

3. The *labor test* forced the able-bodied to work in return for payments. Most jobs, though, had little market value or opportunity for training and did not compete with regular labor.

4. The *billet system* provided an additional compulsory work plan, allotting workers to employers with the parish providing partial wages. This further reduced employers' incentive to provide a living wage.

5. *Poverty was defined as a crime* and included incarceration and correction. In herding the mass of poor persons into unsupervised asylums, the workhouse provided a prison environment in exchange for food and shelter. The unemployed, widows, orphans, diseased, insane, beggars and prostitutes were all penalized for noncontribution, thus ensuring their continued dependency.

6. The *less-eligibility principle* of relief, or assistance below the minimum standard wage, aimed to discourage idleness and extravagance. This was linked to the "limited good" doctrine espoused by Jeremy Bentham, the 18th-century utilitarian theorist. Natural scarcity is a zero-sum situation, Bentham said. Redistributed wealth has no effect; for what one stratum gains, the other loses. "Poverty you have at any rate. How do you like it best? With or without industry? Take your choice." (quoted in Poynter, 1969:126). Under this doctrine, remedial action appeared futile.

7. A *contradictory rhetoric* also stifled reformers' efforts. In one version, the poor were viewed as immoral and evil in neglecting natural work obligations, an assumption that encouraged punishment for correcting moral deficiency. An alternative view held that treating the poor as a special social type led to institutional isolation, including social invisibility and brutal treatment that actually worsened the poor's condition. This approach promoted educational schemes, work incentives and charitable enterprises.

Despite conflicting notions, the main thrust of this policy was to drive the poor out of poverty by eliminating premiums that encouraged dependency. Niggardly assistance (with multiple strings attached) persisted throughout the nineteenth century and linked paternalistic treatment with punitive policies. The Elizabethan poor-law heritage, stressing a crime and punishment conception, persists today. It is most clearly reflected in the conflicted, inconsistent, punitive and discriminatory welfare laws in the United States (Tenbroek, 1964-65; ed., 1966). Political opposition from the underclass is controlled by providing meager benefits in a context of legal repression.

The Clinical-Psychoanalytical Model: Psychologism, Personal Adjustment and Casework. The utilitarian-deterrence image underwent certain modifications when transplanted to 19th-century America. The concept of the "natural criminal," fostered by Lombroso and other European positivists, lumped together the nonsocial poor with the antisocial offender. But an alternative conception, generated by Americans' frontier experience, stressed individualism and an optimistic belief in social progress. This promoted private and public philanthropy. An agrarian ethic also mitigated the harshness of the older approach, for it espoused disenchantment with urban conditions, not necessarily with persons. Depravity, corruption and poverty were all attributed to the "evils" inherent in city life. Despite these ideological changes, the end results were similar to earlier policies. Unassimilated immigrants continued to plague elites and the reformers who served them, once again leading to rejection of the urban poor.[4]

For reformers, the immediate enemy was the political boss. The goal was to reduce ethnic leadership influence and Americanize immigrants. A rehabilitative approach, stressing psychological adjustment, offered one solution. Progressive reformers and an emergent social work profession formed a coalition to lay the groundwork for controlling the discredited urban classes, which institutional elites and managers perceived as requiring special precautions and extraordinary intervention strategies (Matza, 1971: 619-669; and Platt, 1969). The language of personal pathology expressed political elites' distrust of the poor. It emphasized individual therapy and adjustment, rather than political action or structural change (Horowitz and Liebowitz, 1968:280-296).

A clinical model refers to the poor person as a patient—diseased, ill, contagious, chronic and requiring prophylactic measures. Intervention and cure necessitated programs for restoring health and for remedying natural imperfections. Dominant images stereotyped the underclass as uncontrollable, impulsive, degraded, animalistic and morally diseased, justifying control to reshape the offender's character. Psychological individualism personified the philosophy and policy of this reform movement.

By the beginning of the twentieth century, the "Americanization of the unconscious" (Seeley, 1967) pervaded the social-problems ethos. Characteristic rhetoric of people-saving agencies espoused commitment to the uniqueness of the individual, to emotional factors in experience, to unity of personality and to the necessity of dealing with the whole person. Such rhetoric formed the basis for casework as the primary method for managing problem populations. (Chambers in Weinberger, ed., 1969:89-106).

Opposition to prevailing institutional practices was interpreted as personal maladjustment. Platt (1969) describes the invention of delinquency by the "child-savers" (with reformer-social work interests), who successfully imposed their own values and rules on a powerless minority. Overall, care and cure of the poor was directed at saving souls, rather than at salvaging institutions. This system adjusted the client to his deprivation, but did little or nothing to correct the imbalance of power.

The punishment theme, muted in theory, remained viable in practice. Existing welfare laws and administrative practices retain this conception of the poor as undeserving and irresponsible citizens, requiring repressive programs. Legislating for the underclass acts against the interests of this category with assumptions of special needs and programs that ignore structural inequalities. Control rhetoric and strategies have been changed to fit new historical conditions, but the outcomes for the dependent poor remain the same: political and legal exclusion with few organizational options for altering their life fate.

Structural-Sociological Model: Culture of Poverty, Marginality, and the Caretaker State. The shifting of terms to designate the same entity is a familiar phenomenon in social life. The historical continuity of disreputable poverty has been obscured by word substitutions that replace inoffensive names for underlying theories of value. The hard-to-reach, the disadvantaged, the culturally deprived and the multiproblem family are the most recent additions to the nomenclature. Stigmatic labels, however camouflaged, continue to impede problem analysis and treatment.

Contemporary sociological research claims to have discovered a distinct culture of poverty, identifying the poor as protean, marginal persons. In the reconstructed version, theorists reverse the conception of the affluent society to that of the "poorhouse state" (Elman, 1966). This directs treatment at an impersonal enemy, such as ignorance, lower class values, or distinctive life ways. But attributing causes and cures of enduring pauperism to local institutions represents little more than a face-lift for the sagging pathological theme. Reforming poor communities benefits the middle class by supplying employment to thousands of professional workers.

Beck (1967a:101-114; 1967b:258-277) argues that the culture-of-poverty idea leans heavily on folk concepts. By adopting policymakers' and lay publics' rhetorics, social scientists, in effect, have rejected a critical approach to poverty. By avoiding redistribution and equity issues, their analyses point to such issues as living standards, directions of change, human costs of being poor, determination of a "poverty line" and rehabilitation programs. The "we-they" dichotomy clarifies the respectable middle class stance of investigators. The "we" alliance consists of scientists, program sponsors, professionals and a sympathetic public, and "they" refers to the target populations for whom programs and efforts are directed. (For a critique of the theoretical and research work in poverty see *The Journal of Social Issues,* Spring, 1970)

What are some current sociological doctrines written into poverty programs and other welfare measures? One approach is to identify special properties of lower class populations reportedly located in values or behavior. The culture of poverty, which represents negative attributes (e.g., localism, provincialism, apathy, suspicion and the absence of class consciousness), locks the underclass into the dependency cycle (Lewis: 1959, 1961, 1966).

The "culture" concept is seriously deficient on several grounds. It neglects crucial structural characteristics of a stratified order, it oversimplifies and obfuscates the issues of power and control in industrial societies and it focuses on a single stratum rather than on the complex set of transactions between interest groups. Whatever is distinctive about lower class life may consist in no more than situational stresses induced by lack of power, lack of resources and lack of options.

Politics are aimed at eradicating the subculture, but programs actually serve to reinforce social exclusion. Striking at "cultural and environmental obstacles to motivation" (Moynihan, 1969), the federal war on poverty program, for example, attacked symptoms and consequences of deprivation, not generative conditions of poverty located in the political economy.

An alternative approach, known as the "opportunity" thesis, considers institutional deprivation as the crucial problem. Lower class anomie has been described as the lack of fit between cultural goals of success and institutional means to achieve these goals (Merton, 1957; Cloward and Ohlin, 1960). Lacking legitimate opportunity, the underclass chooses alternative, if not illegal, routes to achievement. The deviant is normal, in this analysis, in that the anomic condition of normlessness generates antisocial and illegal acts.

This posits the poor as the most criminalistic element in society, a dubious assumption, if only because deprivation constrains two ways. It narrows illegitimate, as well as legitimate, opportunities. Underclass groups, stratified by ethnic, sex, age and geographical barriers, fail to demonstrate the cultural homogeneity theorists claim. Rather, there is marked diversity of deviant and nondeviant patterns (Rosenberg and Silverstein, 1969).

Despite built-in biases, the opportunity structure formula has generated more concrete proposals for change than any other approach to poverty and its effects (Miller in Moynihan, ed., 1968: 288-296). Morally, these programs uphold negative stereotypes that "blame the victim." They focus on the presumed special needs and shortcomings of the most severely deprived. Economically, the programs channel the poor into dead-end jobs that retain the underclass as a marginal labor force to employers' advantage. Politically, they control social unrest by enforcing rehabilitation, instead of granting political power or money to the powerless, and by training for marginal jobs, instead of inaugurating a redistributive policy. Correcting people, rather than social institutions, maintains the status quo and prevents basic political and economic reform. By effectively denying participation among program beneficiaries, the caretaker state fosters exclusionary tactics that serve to divide social groups.

Countering these approaches, the social-action policy calls for institutional intervention for altering exclusionary policies. Indeed, target populations (e.g., the poor, black, dissident minorities and welfare recipients) are increasingly redefining themselves as victims of class power. Rejecting traditional control by social workers or police, the mobilized underclass seek to correct power imbalances by political action (e.g., promoting self-help, class solidarity, consumer action, and community planning).

As for social workers, teachers, police officers and other control agents serving ghetto populations, these "dirty workers" have few illusions about their regulative function. Many recognize the futility of isolating control strategies that deny target populations and their caretakers opportunities to effectively alter social policy. As a result, problems of recruitment and high turnover are endemic, as are internal rebellion, strikes, sit-outs and other oppositional tactics (Rainwater, 1967; Titmuss, 1968). Itinerant professionalism, involving low commitment and loyalty, are related to alienating working conditions. Social service organizations are too understaffed, inadequately financed and poorly coordinated to transform either persons or social structures.

Some dissident professionals reject "holding action" in favor of militant social change. An unsolved dilemma among strategists, though, is how to mobilize sufficient power for basic reforms without invoking the backlash of dominant groups. Urban crisis, class conflict and turmoil occurring within welfare occupations are inevitable outcomes of this recent welfare phase. High social costs of current management policies include a weakening of social control and the rise of what Habermas (1973) and others term "delegitimating" influences. (See, for example, the *American Behavioral Scientist* issue on "Urban Violence and Disorder," Massotti, ed., 1968.)

The Social Sciences and Welfare Ideology

Studies of poverty shaped the early development of the social sciences, especially sociology and economics. When these disciplines confronted unemployment, crime and deviance, they presumed the cause to be the consequences of industrialization and the growth of big cities. In England the investigations of the poor conducted in the late nineteenth century by Charles Boothe and his associates, and the work of the Fabian Socialist reformers, Sidney and Beatrice Webb, combined careful accumulation of case studies and statistical evidence with proposals for administrative and political reform.[5] These investigations were the forerunners of present-day reports of presidential and "blue-ribbon" commissions and the studies sponsored by Senate and House of Representatives committees or federal agencies. Early in this century, a rich and still viable tradition of studies of deviance and social problems was started at the University of Chicago. The American version of this genre dealt with social problems among newly urbanized people, many of whom were also recent immigrants (Davis, 1980).

Gradually, the social sciences have become the prime sources of contemporary welfare and deviance ideologies, and, accordingly, of the justifications for the measures taken by society to deal with dependent and deviant groups. Various concepts that originated in the social sciences are now part of the common vocabulary of deviance and welfare policy, e.g., labeling, subculture, socialization, matrifocal family and therapeutic community. Also, the methods for fact-finding used by agencies that deal with deviants and welfare clients are patterned on social science research techniques.

In this section we shall study a few representative and contrasting examples of social science treatment of deviance and welfare policy in order to get a better picture of the varieties of the modern ideology.

Four basic orientations, all derived from contemporary social science, have influenced modern welfare and deviance ideology and the related practices of societal response. They include (a) the administrative/regulatory approach, (b) the therapeutic approach, (c) the mobilization approach, and (d) the critical approach.

Administrative-Regulatory

The administrative-regulatory approach is implemented through bureaucratic organizations, staffed by persons who have received professional training in applied social science disciplines such as social work, corrections or juvenile justice. The clients—the poor, the mentally ill and the criminals—are to be efficiently dealt with. They are seen as objects for intervention by experts. The experts initiate, and the clients are expected to follow the experts' suggestions and dictates for their own good. The experts perform in a manner consistent with the rules of the organizations; these, in turn, reflect the thinking of the professional disciplines in which the experts were trained.

The professional doctrine is codified, often in pedantic detail, in handbooks, some of which help form generations of students and which reflect the outlook of the profession. One good example is Mary Richmond's classic book *Social Diagnosis* (1919). This book specifies the steps a professional social worker is to take for gathering data necessary for a correct diagnosis of a problematic case. A correct diagnosis is assumed to lead to appropriate intervention and treatment.[6] Bureaucratically organized activities are conducted according to uniform and highly specific rules.

If Richmond's book reflects the bureaucratic outlook that shaped the consciousness of the emerging social work field, the fullest development of the administrative mentality grew out of President Johnson's "Great Society" programs.

One of the more persuasive spokespersons for administered reform, Daniel Moynihan, contends that social science must take a back seat to the "pragmatic liberal political mind" that produces most of what is to be valued in American society. What institutional role is left to the social sciences, Moynihan (1969:193) asks?

> The answer seems clear enough. *The role of social science lies not in the formation of social policy, but in the measurement of its results.*

No utopian vision, no alternative models, no counterideology. Moynihan's program reduces the knowledge enterprise to a data-crunching activity that depends upon "techniques of evalution." This requires strict separation of research from the political sphere of innovative action.

Not so surprising, policy makers prefer a truncated role for social science. This also fits well with public and professional ideologies of the social sciences as an empirical discipline, rather than a critical one; a fact-finding approach that lends itself to quantification and bureaucratization of data. Divorced from values, the quantification method serves technocratic and elite interests. But its limitations are inherent in its procedures. Either the data are irrelevant from the viewpoint of a poor citizen, such as in the establishment of poverty lines, or the information has a coercive intent, such as in the various work incentive programs for AFDC mothers. In many cases, information is simply inadequate for policy purposes, because the total social ideology works against rational program planning and administration.

We can illustrate this with a well-documented Michigan study of the Work Incentive Program (WIN), based on a sample of 1,184 women recipients (Smith, 1971). The WIN program was specifically established to train and find jobs for AFDC recipients. What administrators found, contrary to their expectations, is that financial costs greatly exceeded benefits. The increases in administrative costs, direct AFDC payments and increased case loads raised the average costs $70 million (or four percent) in the program's first five years of application. For the fiscal year 1974-75, the research anticipated that the net AFDC payments in Michigan would be about 30 million dollars higher and the case load 5,100 larger. Value-free empirical methods provided no clues that the paramount problem for welfare mothers would be twofold: first, the high cost and low availability of childcare, especially day-care for preschool children; and second, availability of work that would pay a living wage. The welfare system has virtually only limited and indirect control over the first issue, and absolutely no jurisdiction over the second.

Other antipoverty programs initiated by the Office of Economic Opportunity (OEO) aimed at rectifying deficiencies in rights and opportunities among poor persons eventually have faltered or failed. The Job Corps for young, unemployed minorities, the Model Cities Program, Headstart Program (for preschoolers), Community Action Program, assistance to migrant and seasonal laborers and other remedies all became merely another form of subsidy. (A review of these programs is found in Ripley, 1972; and Levitan, 1969). What had politicians and planners missed in their utopian conception of massive domestic aid? They ignored the deeply structured obstacles that emanated from various sources of conflict: mayors' offices and professional interests versus poor citizens over control domains; uneven or low commitment by Congress and elites; lack of autonomy (OEO was just another agency in the executive branch and was unable to determine its own priorities); and spurious assumptions about evalutation research. In our view, there are no reliable measurements for making conclusive judgments about program effectiveness. As long as programs become merely one more permanent subsidization of the existing social structure, bureaucratized efforts have little effect.

Therapeutic Approach
The therapeutic approach is rooted in theories and techniques that ultimately derive from psychoanalysis or clinical psychology.

Therapy is intervention into people's lives by trained experts. Some therapists attempt to hide their efforts to shape and direct the lives of others behind such phrases as "working *with* clients" and by refraining from giving them specific directives. Nevertheless, clients are presumed to have less insight than the therapist into their own conditions; the therapist's mandate is presumed to be based on professional training and "supervised practice."

Theories and practices of the therapeutic approach are said to be grounded in the research and data of psychology and those social sciences heavily influenced by psychology, e.g., the study of the family and child socialization; sociological theories about small-group processes, roles and communication; and the comparative study of male and female sex roles. Because they have been taught this "knowledge" in professional schools, the therapists claim expertise, maintaining that they know more about the problems of their clients than the clients know themselves. The knowledge is summarized in authoritative texts. Problem definition is lodged in the categories of experts who "speak for" the client (Grimshaw, 1979:582-598).

Social science inadvertently legitimates the therapeutic ideal. For example, the culture-of-poverty concept, discussed in an earlier section, lends itself to a top-down control. It encourages massive intervention, not only at the level of person, families and communities, but also of entire cultures. Anthropologist Oscar Lewis (1961:347), the leading proponent of this poverty concept, says:

> poverty in modern nations is not only a state of economic deprivation, of disorganization, or of the absence of something. It is also something positive in the sense that it has a structure, a rationale, and defense mechanisms without which the poor could hardly carry on. In short, it is a way of life, remarkably stable and persistent, passed down from generation to generation along family lines. The culture of poverty has its own modalities and distinctive social and psychological consequences for its members. It is a dynamic factor which affects participation in the larger national culture and becomes a subculture of its own.

Therapists take this doctrine on faith. Such acceptance of a fatalistic theory enables experts to exonerate themselves when clients fail or refuse treatment.

Whereas therapists tend to treat poor persons as a homogeneous class, ignoring cultural, economic, social and moral differences, the psychological professions are riddled with organizational and value conflicts. The help myth conveniently ignores the implicit power of therapists, their preference for "promising clients," the rupture of clients' confidentiality and privacy, and the passive role of the citizen/client (Howard, 1969). It misses the fact that the goal of "rehabilitation" essentially implies getting people off the relief rolls. In a farewell to alms message by the Director of the California State Department of Social Welfare, the treatment of welfare as a residual, not institutional, system is clear.

> Welfare constitutes nothing more than a sidetrack on the main line of social and economic developments which affect the lives of people.... As long as the cars are on the sidetrack it doesn't matter much how we dress them up in terms of services and activities; we are not established by the community to maintain a museum or a showcase.... It's up to us to apply the additional motive power that will shove our cars faster down the line and back on to the mainstream.
>
> (Quoted in Howard, 1969:196)

As the engine powering the off-track cars, social work plays the key role in fostering "self-care" and "self-help" along traditional lines through intrafamilial cooperation, mutual aid and marketplace transactions. The "gratuitous" help of welfare agencies is to be perceived by clients as a stop-gap measure, at best. At the same time, social workers must provide the emotional, moral and financial support in a society strongly opposed to dependencies—in critics' words, the "sponges," "mooches" and exploiters who live off the public trough. But because basic support is typically accompanied by denigrating and even punitive practices, therapy comes to be defined by clients as simply another obstacle before receiving the benefits. Therapy, then, is doubly loaded in a negative direction. It serves to reinforce clients' feelings of inferiority because of power and status differences, and in the process tacitly blames the poor for their pecuniary deficiency. Added to this are low self-confidence and strong apprehensions of failure, which further compound clients' dependency and sense of futility.

Both the administrative-regulatory and the therapeutic approaches are based on domination and control of the client by the supposedly expert professional. Stratification colors the relationships. In the administrative-regulatory relationship the domination of the client by the professional is open and acknowledged; in the therapeutic relationship it is often masked by terminologies that suggest openness, flexibility and equality ("working with a client"). Of the two, the therapeutic mode of control may be more insidious and intrusive.

Therapists question people's motives, self-definitions, their modes of coping with the outside world. They intrude into the psychic privacy of their clients. At worst, the regulatory agents, like social workers, correctional and parole officers, intrude into their clients' public roles, forcing them to pay child support, apply for jobs, keep regular contacts with an agency and so on.

Psychological studies invariably support the psychic intervention policy. For example, research on lower class children often presumes pathological behavior, even where the data fail to support this finding or contradict it. In one study welfare children are portrayed as unique in being overly compliant, antisocial, violent or evasive; and even among so-called normal welfare children, the authors predicted increased levels of behavioral disturbances (Eisenberg, Langner and Gersten, 1975). Yet the same study stressed that their findings showed *no* significant differences among samples on various child factors that measure relatively serious impairment (Eisenberg et al, 1975:15). If anything, children of single welfare mothers were more easygoing, related more positively to their parent and had less evidence of fairly serious disturbance than the control group of two-parent children who had considerable interpersonal problems (e.g., conflict with parents and siblings). Welfare children have more reported delinquency and higher dependency, although these behaviors did not cluster for the same child. Patterns vary. The dependent child is a stay-at-home, a nonjoiner; the delinquent youngster is a street operator. Such fixation on the developmental characteristics of the children to the exclusion of the influence of police, courts and neighborhood controls, however, overpsychologizes the welfare process. In this way therapy creates an ever expanding market for its self-created services.

Social service agencies need not be updated treatment mechanisms for "paupers." Instead, help and support can be developed within a body of client-centered norms and values. In Cumming's (1968) study, Catholic welfare servies in Syracuse were fully accessible, of wider scope and less specialized than other agencies. In the Catholic welfare agency, the open-door philosophy was possible because workers and clients related within a "pervasive normative control" (Cumming 1968) that minimized bureaucracy and treated requests for aid as a legitimate and shared problem. Unlike the public system, Catholic welfare had no formal intake processes, no forms, no eligibility requirements, limited record keeping, strict confidentiality and informal solutions to personal and economic problems (e.g., money was loaned by the worker or taken out of current agency funds). Such evidence suggests that help structures are not monolithic and need to be systematically analyzed to discern the precise elements that create client subordination and defeatism.[7]

Mobilization Approach

The third orientation to deviance and welfare differs rather profoundly from both the regulatory and the therapeutic approaches. We call it the *mobilization* or *self-help* approach because it emphasizes the unused but potential strengths of welfare recipients and other traditionally regulated populations. Rather than seeing poor people and deviants as *objects* for regulation by professionals who possess superior knowledge, the self-help approach assumes that many poor persons and deviants are active subjects, quite knowledgeable about their conditions, and that some groups and movements under some conditions are able to tap this knowledge and translate it into collective actions and programs.

In a later chapter we shall discuss at some length one successful and well-known mutual-help organization, Alcoholics Anonymous. Yet there are many tenacious self-help movements and organizations that have received much less publicity than AA. Neighborhoods have organized to fight crime and to pressure absentee slumlords. Welfare recipients have organized to confront city hall. Collectives of women have set up centers, often on shoe-string budgets, to provide couseling for rape victims, battered wives and women contemplating abortions.

Mutual-help movements have been dealt with theoretically by a number of social scientists turned activists. Saul Alinsky was a major theorist of self-help in the 1960s; his doctrines continue to inspire organizers and activists. In a series of studies of the system of public welfare assistance, Francis Piven and Richard Cloward (1971, 1974, 1977a, 1977b, 1977c) have attempted to formulate a theory of poor people's mobilization to challenge the controlling welfare bureaucracy.

In mutual-help organizations the participants pool their

resources, e.g., skills, time and contacts, noncompetitively. If individuals do not withhold resources from one another in order to get a competitive advantage in a struggle for status or power within the group, then the group as a whole is able to mobilize all those resources of its members that may bear on a particular collective task. In a society dominated by the norms of possessive individualism, the mutual-benefit orientation is hard to uphold. Piven and Cloward cite several examples of how locals of the poor-people's movements have achieved at least limited successes.

Some mutual-help groups develop a strong sense of ideological commitment among their members. The members come to define their participation in the daily activities of the movement in terms of a world view that transcends their own personal ambitions. A person's discovery that he or she is part of something larger than a personal striving is often accompanied by emotional fervor and enthusiasm. The self is seen as absorbed into a larger totality. This discovery provides the motivation that makes many members of mutual-help movements devote large amounts of time and energy to the common cause, accepting many personal inconveniences and costs. Sometimes a personality transformation occurs. If one is around groups like Alcoholics Anonymous or St. Vincent de Paul, to mention but two examples, one often encounters men and women who radiate serenity and strength. It has often been observed that dependent and controlled persons have negative self-images and low self-evaluations, and that bureaucratic and other control practices reinforce or stabilize these traits. By mobilizing and using their talents, however humble at the outset, mutual-help movements quite dramatically raise the self-conceptions of their participants. Persons who were used to being treated as incompetents discover that they are indeed capable of helping themselves and others in very substantial ways.

Welfare rights organizations have multiple functions. They teach welfare clients to express their frustration, to cope with bureaucracy, to articulate their needs and to assist other needy persons. Here is what these welfare mothers say (Milwaukee Welfare Rights Organization, 1972).

> "The government's policy of paying the farmers to grow nothing sure is working good, because that's what most of us are getting."
>
> Mrs. Jean Rablin
> Milwaukee, Wisconsin (p. 20)

"The country's had socialism for years, only it's been upside down. The rich have known for a long time that socialism's a good thing, but it's about time they started sharing it with the poor."

Mrs. Margaret Courchaine
Milwaukee, Wisconsin (p. 21)

"This is a country where one of our children goes out and steals $70 and the government makes him spend twelve years in jail and then kills him when he tries to escape. But the same government forces people like him to steal in order to live because it cheats them out of billions in welfare benefits, and no one shoots the government. So what does 'law and order' really mean? It means that the biggest welfare fraud is the welfare system."

Mrs. Olivia Hazelwood
Milwaukee, Wisconsin (pp. 55 and 56)

"We are not an organization of selfish people and we are not out to get things done just for Welfare Rights or members of our organization. We, as an organization, want to see some guaranteed adequate income for all people in the United States of America."

Mrs. Beulah Sanders. (p. 124)

"We have been forced, due to our sick society, to live as we are now. Fathers have been driven from their homes because of our welfare system which won't aid a family if the father is in the home. And then the government says the poor family is breaking up, and it's the one who's causing it."

Mrs. Roxanne Jones
Philadelphia, Pennsylvania (p.85)

Welfare rights groups provide a political language where there was none, and action strategies whose hitherto absence was glaring. In the final analysis, though, welfare rights groups rivet their attention on what recipients say, do, feel and think, and not on what the economy and political order should enact to reduce the inequality burden.[8]

Welfare presents a masked politics that sometimes leaves even critical social scientists baffled. Donzelot attributes much of the conceptual confusion to the state's indirect control. According to Donzelot (1979), this is the "tutelary complex," whereby the state controls through its intermediary professionals, the social service workers, and submits citizens to a "total wardship." In this sense, social work is the tool for an unchecked expansion of the apparatus of the state. We must stop asking ourselves the academic quesion: what is social welfare, Donzelot (1979:99) says, and treat it as a power instrument, which under the guise of prevention is extending its grip on citizens to include their private lives and marking minors and economic dependents, who have not committed the least offense, with a stigmatizing brand. The current economic policy is clear. By sustaining high levels of unemployment and underemployment (which has its greatest impact on the politically powerless), it uses the principles of selectivity—fewest benefits for the least people among the neediest citizens. This maintains the fiction of the benevolent state while at the same time protecting the state against revolution from below.

CHAPTER 8—NOTES

[1] This thesis contradicts the "functions-of-poverty" notion, a conservative ideology derived from structural functional theory and most recently articulated by Gans (1972:275-289). According to this doctrine, poverty contributes to the wealth and well-being of the non-poor members of the society (albeit at great cost to the poor). Our argument is that poverty is uniformly dysfunctional for affluent and poor alike, as it delegitimates public institutions, contributes to a state ideology of massive but ineffective intervention that reduces every citizen's arena of freedom and encourages widespread resentment among citizens (expressed in such diverse forms as income-tax cheating, malingering, crime, domestic violence, corporate malfeasance and generally low citizen capacity to plan for the future or sustain grassroots organizations. The newest conservative angle is "welfare reform" in response to the "welfare crisis" (i.e., increased number of case loads and recipients). This entails "purifying" the welfare system by tightening up the enforcement of eligibility rules and regulations. Some tactics include a 20 percent across-the-board cut in grants in Kansas; a house-to-house search for nonsupporting fathers in Nevada; and temination of grants to families with unemployed fathers in New Jersey (M. Anderson, 1980:155). It is a fairly easy matter for politicians to stir up antiwelfare sentiment, often with devastating results (Ritz, 1966).

[2] Ford automobile industry lost one billion six hundred million dollars in 1981, largely because of Japanese competition. The impact on the economy is profound, not only because the auto industry dominates Michigan's economy, but also because it adversely affects so many related jobs in the national economy as well (e.g., steel, rubber-tire manufacturing, auto repair shops, car upholstery businesses, etc.). It is estimated that about one of every seven jobs in the United States is related to auto manufacturing. The notion that certain industries act as feeding grounds for unemployment and welfare, as described in this section, may be a more fruitful hypothesis during periods of recession, where the full negative impact on the economy can be measured, rather than during so-called normal economic periods when key industrial sectors are flourishing.

[3] Historical sources on the evolution of welfare used in this section include: Wilensky and Lebeaux, (1958); Bruce, (1961); Poynter, (1969); Mencher, (1967);

Eden, (first ed., 1929; reissued, 1971). See also Chambliss (1964: 67-77) for analysis of the laws of vagrancy. These laws represent an early attempt to control migratory labor.

[4] This struggle has been documented by Lincoln Steffans (1904) and Oscar Handlin (1951). See also Bremner (1956) for a discussion of the economic and political conditions giving rise to social work.

[5] See the discussion in chapter 1.

[6] According to Trattner (1974:216), Mary Richmond's dense 580-page work was produced as a sequel to the negative evaluation of social work by the national authority on graduate professional education, Dr. Abraham Flexner, at a 1915 National Conference. In his paper, "Is Social Work a Profession," Flexner concluded that it was not, inasmuch as it lacked a unique method. Richmond's book corrected that deficiency in its pre-Freudian bureaucratic preoccupation, but inadvertently fell into the opposite trap: administration became the *raison d'etre* of social work.

[7] Help has been historically linked to repression. One of the more pervasive contemporary modes of producing subservience is "shelterization." This involves very limited programs of rehabilitation in exchange for food and shelter. This relief policy, aimed at homeless men and described by Sutherland and Locke (originally published in 1936), was based on the assumption that the homeless man was a "pathological individual whose patholgy could be modified by appropriate methods of individual treatment." Most shelters today serve the alcoholic or drug-addicted population, although an unknown number of these are probably ill or elderly exaddicts.

[8] Social scientists have recently begun to critically scrutinize their earlier rapture with poor people's mobilization. Roach and Roach (1979) attack the Piven and Cloward strategy of urging separatist organizations as a "road to a dead end." Their counter solution is a general working class movement, not a series of discrete movements splintered by class, ethnicity, geography, industry and so on that divide and conquer the jobless and working poor. Piven and Cloward oppose this attack by pointing out that prior to mobilization, there were no avenues for action or protest for blacks, welfare recipients and other degraded populations, and if they had not generated their own movements, they would have received no attention. Of course, when Southern blacks erupted, they go on to argue, it was bound to provoke the violent opposition of Northern white working class persons as well. This inevitably widened the breach within the larger working class movement, they admit. But what other possible course of action could have been taken, given the racist and classist nature of the society? Piven and Cloward remain deeply pessimistic about the possibility of working class unity. Mass-based organizations generate oligarchical tendencies, they warn, that facilitate the cooptation of movement leadership by dominant groups. This discourages disruptive tactics (e.g., strikes and demonstrations) in favor of an electoral strategy that wins little (Piven and Cloward, 1979:172-178).

Chapter 9
The Triumph of the Therapeutic:
Community Mental Health

> Bureaucracy transforms collective grievances into personal problems amenable to therapeutic intervention.
> Christopher Lasch, *The Culture of Narcissism*

Twenty years following popularization of Freud's radical doctrine of psychoanalysis for the elite, the antithetical ideology of mental health for the people emerged. As the best-financed and most prestigious of the "intermediate structures" (Berger, 1976: 236) that mediate between the atomized individual and the order of the state, community mental health represents a systematic state policy for providing relief to the problems of anomie in modern society. Neither its theory nor method can fulfill this mission.

Community Mental Health

Community mental health (CMH) began as a social movement and political organization with broad claims for social and economic change. By 1960, mental health professionals were urged to reshape their professional roles and to exert a more direct influence on politicians, educators, judges, lay leaders and local state, regional and federal governments. In the process of acquiring a new mandate, professionsl, administrative and political boundaries blurred. Strange hybrids sprang up: political psychiatrists (Brown and Stockdill, 1972: 681), partisan professionals (Golann and Eisdorfer, 1972:14), administrative strategists and new career minorities (Smith, 1968; Kolb, 1968; Levin, 1970). As mental health services moved into the community, they confronted a host of unanticipated problems. Few mental health professionals were trained in the community or for the provision of mental health servies in community settings. The CMH movement, unguided by theory or overall rules for action, took contradictory approaches. Rules and doctrines established by government agencies often flouted professional standards. The infusion of public health concepts into the mental health field stressed prevention of disorder and optimization of goal effectiveness, clearly *status quo* concerns. And the community concept remained an unexamined entity leading to a tacit acceptance of market imagery (mental health providers, consumers, service delivery programs, etc.) to define rules and roles. Populist rhetoric—freedom, equality and individuality—was also overlaid on mental health programs, producing the confusing contradictions of standardized, homogenized services in the name of "subjectivity," "self," "individualism," "autonomy" and "humanity."

CMH represents the first challenge to the medical profession in its explicit repudiation of the individual pathology model (Hobbs, 1969). Substituting a society-is-the-problem focus with its loosely structured ideology of humanizing and regulating urban populations and institutions, it rapidly demedicalized the growing mental health industry and redistributed services among nonpsychiatric occupations—psychology, social work, nursing, vocational rehabilitation, clergy, paraprofessionals and indigenous volunteers (Schultz, Harker, and Gardner, 1977). Questioning its own repressive practices, psychiatry soon jumped on the antipsychiatry bandwagon. Class-based labeling tendencies (psychosis for the poor, neurosis for the affluent; hospitalization for the powerless and community care for more established members) could no longer be ignored. The growing professional outrage against the role of psychiatry as gatekeepers of the asylum and caretakers of the psychiatrically maimed extended into a general repudiation of theory and of increased absorption with praxis (Arieti, 1975; Leifer, 1969; Szasz, 1967).

Advocates of CMH proposed a concept of community as an ecology of moral games where sociability and participatory democracy could finally be realized. As scientists-servants of massive collectivities (Leifer, 1969:237), they proposed a new *Weltanschauung* in which no human activity would be alien to its all-embracing aims. Not content with intervention in local communities—eliminating poverty, malnutrition and other deprivations, and providing recreational facilities and extending medical care—advocates immodestly proposed to isolate all the social ills so as to interrupt pathogenic trains of events and even to prevent or at least ameliorate stresses and crises in life (Vayda and Perlmutter, 1977). Common events became redefined. Preganancy is no longer a natural occurring event, but a "developmental crisis" requiring mental health intervention (Caplan, 1964). Some psychiatrists envisioned therapeutic applications of their knowledge to world affairs, including the prevention of nuclear war and international conflicts.

CMH is a greedy institution. Advocates claim that because of structural similarities, religion and mental health will converge in the future. Tapp and Tapp (1972:107) say:

> Both have been highly individualistic, focusing upon the person. Each begins with a diagnosis (sin/neurosis), proffers a therapy, and promises a remission (salvation/mental health). Each has its experts, its texts, its institutions, its devoted laity. Each has its enemies. Each has a clearly discernible past and a likely future.

Among modernist religious perspectives, community mental health represents the morally infused, secularized version of a realized "social gospel" movement.

Abandoning Freud's theory of the unconscious as outmoded and doctrinaire, social psychiatry proposed new theories of consciousness grounded in group and community therapy. Positing an isomorphism between the individual and the community, psychiatry lost its theoretical rationale and also its special place as high priest among mental health disciplines. Unable to steer a clear direction with the amorphous community doctrine, social psychiatry split. On one side, it preserved the medical format of the patient-physician with all its problematic elements: interactional power asymmetry, transference, tentative and conflictful interpretations of reality, often protracted and costly cures and, increasingly, a pharmaceutical orientation to healing. On the other side, social psychiatry become the administrative-cousulting arm of the newly established community mental health centers, where it quickly lost both its theory and special method.

A conformist doctrine, CMH retains its regulatory power by denying and forgetting its past, suffering from what Jacoby (1975) calls "social amnesia." Having repressed the theory of the psyche, it is vulnerable to the onslaughts of the social collectivity. According to Marcuse (1965), this leads to a repressive tolerance. Subjectivity becomes suspect; instead there are depersonalized notions of community will (see also Fromm, 1970). Psychiatry may have lost its critical function, and with it Freud's vision of a science of values (Adorno, 1968).

Psychiatry and the State

Because programs are couched in medico-scientific language rather than in moral or political terms, their professional and political ties are disguised. CMH is almost entirely the "child of the state," being largely funded by the government rather than by private persons or endowments. A look at expenditures and organization clearly reveals that government policy, not professional autonomy, dictates terms of service.

The federal government is the nation's largest supporter of mental health research; it supplies over one third of the public tax dollars spent for mental health services (Karan, Ochberg and Brown, 1975). The largest proportion of remaining dollars comes from state and local governments. Under federal grants to the Department of Health, Education, and Welfare, Congress has expanded the welfare function of the state to embrace mental health services. The bulk of the Ntional Institute of Mental Health (NIMH) services budget, the primary source supporting a modernized social psychiatry, has been devoted to construction and staffing grants for community mental health centers.

From the inception of the CMH centers program in 1963 through fiscal year 1970, a total of $265 million was awarded to establish 420 centers, covering "catchment areas" for approximately one quarter of the United States' population. By 1975 there were over 600 federally funded comprehensive community mental health centers and about 400 additional state and local out-patient psychiatric clinics. Ideally, all citizens are encompassed in the geographical area ("catchment area"), including a population of 70,000 to 200,000. From inner city ghettos to farmlands, from affluent suburbs to the poorest counties of Appalachia, the goals of CMH are to bring mental health programs into all cities, towns and villages, including those areas where they previously have been virtually unavailable. Prevention and rehabilitation are the dominant goals. No other human service has as elaborate a conception of prevention as the community mental health movement.

The centers are central in two significant ways (Gruenberg, 1975). First, they are the major source for mental health services, including referral for the entire community. This includes five basic services: (1) in-patient care, (2) out-patient care, (3) four-hour emergency care, (4) partial hospitalization and (5) consultation and education services for community agencies and paraprofessionals. To achieve these five essential services, centers are expected to be develop diagnostic services, rehabilitation services, precare and aftercare services (e.g., home visits and halfway houses), training activities, research and evaluation programs and an effective administration to achieve the intent of the program.

Second, the centers aim to replace the patchwork and low-quality performance of the mental hospital and the various private and usually nonmedical, nonstate-supervised mental health services. From the numbers alone, the centers appear to be a smashing success. In 1969, only four years after the CMH program began, more than 2,000 psychiatrists were working full- or half-time in centers, which accounted for more than 10 percent of all in-patient and out-patient psychiatric patient-care episodes.

Government largess (and dependency) operates in additional ways as well. Both community and academic psychiatrists work within the limits of state-mandated fundings and programs. In contrast to medicine, where the majority of physicians practice privately, the largest proportion of psychiatrists, 73 percent, spend some time working for the government. Only 54 percent have any time allocated to private practice, and of these only 40 percent devote more than 35 hours a week. Academic psychiatrists are more flexible in their time allocations than community psychiatrists; teaching, consulting, private practice and research typically are located in schools of medicine where psychiatrists carry out government-sponsored research in state-supported universities. Mannheim's (1936) idea of the free-floating professional has no place here.

Once associated almost exclusively with deviant individuals and their alienation, the language of intervention stresses defective social environments and their impact on the psychic life of the group. Some psychiatrists consider this trend professionally enhancing for the mental health field. Dr. Gerald Caplan, a distinguished community psychiatrist, welcomes the opportunity to extend psychiatric influence over an ever larger segment of the population. In outlining this new psychiatric outreach, Caplan says:

> The community psychiatrist differs from his traditional colleagues in having to provide services for a large number of people with whom he has no personal contact, and of whose identity and location he has no initial knowl-

edge. He cannot wait for patients to come to him, because he carries equal responsibility for all those who do not come. A significant part of his job consists of finding out who the mentally disordered are and where they are located in his community, and he must deploy his diagnostic and treatment resources in relation to the total group of sufferers rather than restrict them to the select few who ask or are referred for help (quoted in R. Caplan, 1969).

Other psychiatrists are less optimistic about this benignly aggressive approach, and urge caution in professionals' movement into the community. In *Therapy in the Ghetto*, Barbara Lerner (1972) examines the opposing potential of the community movement. In its liberating movement, psychotherapy involves an effort to free and strengthen individuals so that they may more effectively pursue their own goals. In its repressive aspect, it entails crude efforts at indoctrination conducted by reactionaries or zealots who politicize the treatment process while denying politics. Similarly, social therapy has the ideological capacity to help free and strengthen groups seeking to redress gross inequities in the distribution of wealth and power. It also can extend and solidify these disparities by enshrining them in new institutional forms. In the ghetto, troubled individuals live in communities characterized by a lack of autonomy, self-control and self-direction. State mental health programs actually exacerbate the power deprivation by imposing reinforcing structures that are heavily centralized, hierarchicalized and authoritarian. Standardization and relief in poor communities are invariably contradictory terms.

If we are to assess the overall achievements of the community mental health programs rather than concentrate exclusively on their problematic role in minority communities, we need to ask what has been *done*, not what has been intended. What changes would be expected in service organization and delivery if a more equitable and meaningful community organization were primary aims? Or, as critics charge, is community mental health merely the most cost-efficient mechanism for social control of poor and excluded groups?

First, enhanced participation by local citizens in community action programs would represent the widest possible spread of citizens across all relevant groups: class, caste, occupation, age and sex. This is clearly not the case. Top-level business, administrative and governmental interests clearly predominate over both citizens and professionals on boards and in formative citizen groups.

Second, rather than calling for increasing manpower, the community mental health system should be reducing paid staff in favor of volunteers by turning over center-initiated programs to self-help and other grassroots groups. This is also not happening. Volunteers tend to be competitive with professionals, and in many instances serve primarily as a bridge into the larger professional network, rather than the reverse (volunteers as agents to transfer professional programs into the community).

Third, a viable community mental health program—one in which the activities were genuinely community rather than professionally based—would make serious inroads into the number of deviants and the seriousness of deviance. And this is certainly not the experience in most American communities. Instead, the opposite situation prevails. Why are the number of deviants and the seriousness of deviance actually rising? Despite relatively severe validity problems in reporting (Hills, 1980), the data consistently tend to show that there are more abused children, more domestic violence, higher suicide rates (especially among younger persons and women), increases both in conventional crimes and in the seriousness of these crimes (e.g., rape, robbery), more corporate malfeasance (e.g., Ford's cover-up of the Pinto's defective gas tank), higher unemployment among underdogs (especially minority males and single mothers), higher divorce rates and increasingly lower levels of reported personal satisfaction and self-esteem at home, at work, at school, and at play (See Taylor and Soady, 1972; Scull, 1977; Ermann and Lundman, 1978). Formerly, deviance with its troubles was confined to the lower classes; now deviance and the troubled are distributed across all social classes.

In part, this represents a widespread shift in perspectives—a movement away from a narrow theory of social pathology of the underclass to a general theory of institutional order and change. But is it also possible that these negative social trends signal the futility, or at least irrelevance, of the renovated therapeutic doctrine? As a state policy of indirect control that masks the underlying power structure, the therapeutic ethic may offer deprived persons and communities the worst of all possible worlds—decarceration of the bad and the dangerous and a social control doctrine that aims at total domestic pacification and control (Scull, 1977).

Lasch (1979) argues that because the therapeutic ethic borrows from a human-relations model in repudiating hierarchies and

stressing interdependence in all relationships, it discredits authority without fundamentally changing it. At all levels of American
society, hierarchical forms of organization prevail in the guise of
"participation," thus comprising a society dominated by corporate
elites with an antielitist ideology. When the adversary relationship
between superordinate and subordinate is denied, citizens do not
defend themselves against the state, workers do not resist the
demands of the corporation or work place and consumers do not
reject the overinflated promise of the American dream.

The therapeutic ethic clearly is not the only source of such
trends. Deviance has multiple roots, most of which can be traced to
conditions of uncertainty and anomie generated by structures of
economy and state. Where the therapeutic, coercive ethic fails is in
its unexamined and unrecognized dualism. The mental health
field both slips into uncritical acceptance of community power
arrangements and promotes a utopian ethic that ignores existing
institutional structures. Both approaches are ahistorical and
asociological in their conception of culture and social organization.
Contemporary social problems are rooted in social conditions
created by profit-oriented industry, insecure working conditions,
weakened family life, erosion and destruction of values, and other
results of structural transformation (see Lasch, 1980). Such deep-
seated problems resist change by prophylactic or "educational"
reforms. To view social control as a technical problem that needs
the right expert or the correct therapy misses the point. The cooptation of both psychiatry and individual-centered therapy by the
state entails a genuine loss of professional autonomy and severe
status devaluing. Reduced to bureaucrats, community psychiatrists
can examine and advise; they cannot define, categorize or command.

Caught between opposing claims—oppressive or liberating—
and contradictory structures—private versus public—psychiatry is
at the crossroads. To simply claim all state structures as dehumaniz-
ing is not helpful for delineating the peculiar arrangements of the
mental health industry with its multiple interventions at levels of
institutions, organizations, groups, families and individuals. In
reality, a state-dominated psychiatry may have allowed itself to fall
into the error of the "administrator trap" (Caplan, 1969). This
involves trading off innovative doctrines and practices for the safe
role of negotiator for the commonplace.

The "consistency doctrine" discussed by Staw (1979) and Staw and Ross (1979) traps administrators into self-justificatory rhetorics, which encourage inflexibility and dogmatism. This stance rationalizes behavior both to themselves and to other parties within an organization. At the same time it effectively neutralizes or eliminates innovation. At the crossroads, psychiatry lacks its old security as a socializing and social control function. Shoved from its former niche by new state policies of bureaucratic control and a collective-based mental health ideology, its professional power languishes and declines. What replaces it are a cluster of glib new conformist psychology models that fly under the banner of the "new group therapies."

Mental Health Models

Proponents of CMH employ a natural selection model to account for the emergence and flourishing state of nonpsychiatric mental health. Invoking the logic of the ecology model (or "adaptation perspective"), organizational leaders or dominant coalitions scan the environment for opportunities and threats, formulate strategic responses and adjust organizational structure appropriately (Hannan and Freeman, 1978). Using this analysis the demise of traditional psychoanalysis is a failure of adaptation.

Because psychoanalysis caters to a highly verbal and affluent group, and depends upon intensive contact between therapist and client, both impossible conditions in today's mental health scene, it is anachronistic (Goldberg, 1973). The 19th-century conception of scarcity and repression from which psychoanalysis drew its inspiration has yielded to a "new culture." Since the 1950s community mental health has argued from principles of liberation and self-fulfillment. A new therapy model naturally follows.

Two assumptions feed the new therapeutic calculus. One is the norm of change as progress, and the other is the necessity to divorce mental health from its former ideological and therapeutic moorings.

To define change as normal, hence good, and stasis as deviant, therefore bad, treats the environment as over-determined. As a complex, competitive and uncertain state of affairs, the environment remains essentially outside any individual's or organization's capacity to influence. Hence, maximum flexibility on the part of individuals is the only recourse. This leaves therapy with a twofold function: free the individual from capricious, external pressures or teach clients how to live in the present: to be sensual, playful, and body-conscious. Neither rebellion nor creativity have a place in this scheme.

Group therapies are to replace the outdated antierotic and antisomatic regime. The human potential movement played directly into this construct. Repression is out, expression is in, Goldberg (1973:21) notes:

> The new groups attempt to create modern man in a new image. His stance is immediate, playful, and sensual. His 'primary vocation is pleasure not labor.' The new groups have conceptualized their task 'as awakening the senses and returning erotic awareness to the total body.' They have changed Descartes's dictum—knowledge begins not with 'I think therefore I am;' but with 'I sense therefore I am.' In a society with a scarcity of resources, the individual often finds it difficult to satisfy his appetites. In order to survive he must learn to adapt to society. A common psychological mechanism for this is repression, the most ubiquitous of the neurotic's defenses. In times of affluence fewer environmental pressures to repress lead to a greater incidence of character problems.

The new man and woman are said to suffer from emptiness and apathy, the Woody Allen version of modern humans. Sensory awareness methods would free repressed feelings frozen by "body armor," and through a series of techniques (e.g., role-playing, analyzing ego states, transactional games, biofeedbacks, nonverbal approaches), would encourage somatic-behavior changes for "doing," in contrast to traditional therapy, which stressed cognitive processes for "understanding." The old therapy is denigrated as wasteful, its complexity befitting a different set of environmental and cultural conditions. The new model replaces the individual's agonized self-search with a new consciousness forged by experience gained through experimental life styles.

The contrast between traditional psychoanalysis and the new group therapies is profound. Not only are core properties opposed to one another on almost every dimension, but there is also a wholesale repudiation of the traditional mode of intervention. We must go out of our minds to regain our senses. "Trips" from reality in the form of drugs and aberrant behavior provide new avenues of experience. Clinicians such as Ronald Laing (1971) have gone as far as stating that even a psychotic episode may generate a growth experience. Table 9:1 summarizes the competing models.

**Table 9:1   Core Properties of the New Group Therapies in Contrast
With Traditional Psychotherapies**

Traditional Psychotherapies	*New Group Therapies*
1. Class oriented (only wealth can afford).	1. Everyone has the right to fulfill his or her human potential.
2. Society has a scarcity of resources; therefore the individual has to learn to adapt to it—repress.	2. Affluence of resources; no need to repress.
3. Concerned with individual patient.	3. Concerned with group processes and social systems.
4. Relieve patient of symptoms by converting to a less debilitating condition.	4. Make dramatic changes in individual.
5. Therapist's credentials based on scholarship and academic training.	5. Group leader acts as role model; is guru; has attractive life syle.
6. Noncontamination of patient-therapist roles.	6. **Role diffusion; blurring of patient-therapist roles.**
7. Therapist assumes legal-medical responsibility.	7. Group leader assumes personal responsibility for self only, not for patient.
8. Therapy is expert-led.	8. Group experience is almost democratic.
9. Encourages interpreting and reliving past experiences and unconscious material.	9. Confrontation of immediate behavior.
10. Cognitive-attitudinal change = understanding.	10. Somatic-behavioral change = doing.
11. Analysis of behavior, dreams, etc.	11. Expansion of consciousness (seeking radical departures from past and present behavior).
12. Absence of external stimulation for healing.	12. Stimulation by external factors (e.g., drugs for healing).
13. Emphasis on relieving repression of anger and sexuality.	13. Emphasis on expression of tender feelings (including homosexual feelings).
14. Developing a relationship before depth-probing.	14. Confrontation without first developing relationship.
15. Dealing with countertransference through control analysis and outside supervision.	15. Countertransference handled in group; participants assume responsibility for reality testing.
16. Theoretical.	16. Experiential-exploratory.
17. Long-term.	17. Short-term.
18. Secretive.	18. Open for investigation and research.

Adapted from Goldberg (1973:23)

At the extreme, the new therapies romanticize experience and denigrate mastery and ability. What the high culture glorifies — intellectualism, expertise, professionalism and self-knowledge — the new encounter culture mocks. Rather than radical in the political sense, the new group therapies deify the "groovy people," the life-stylers, swingers and self-actualizers. Sometimes therapy becomes reduced to a "scam" produced by the guilt-liberated (see Perls, 1969; 1973; Ellis 1973; 1977).

In its more tolerant phase, the human potential movement perceives the mental health environment as a free market. To operate most effectively, all therapeutic regimes must be left unconstrained to compete equally. Survival need not depend upon professional legitimacy or other external factors, though. Political favoritism, program evaluation or other strategies, whereby nonclients determine choice should be eschewed. Enlightened, free-spending consumers can pick and choose among a variety of therapeutic styles in a kind of "different-strokes-for-different-folks" approach to mental health care. The motto is: whatever endures must be good (i.e., adaptive) or it would be selected out. This message signals "hands off" to professional groups concerned with quality and outcomes. One response to this free-market imagery has been the rise of therapeutic nihilism. This is a belief that since mental illness is a myth, no therapy at all is better than muddled intervention by self-interested professionals (Szasz, 1967).

The splintering of the once unified mental health doctrine has engendered an economic version of mental health. Behavior modification uses scarcity to reinforce competition and compliance. In some mental institutions, a system of tokens is used and inmates must earn some or all of their basic needs through work, group participation and general cooperation (Neubeck, 1978). Failure to comply can lead to the denial of tokens, or subjection to fines that can cause inmates to lose out on opportunities to purchase bed, board and privileges. Unlike the claims of the new therapy movement that promise to relieve such modern maladies as boredom, alienation and pervasive indifference, reinforcement schedules aim only for external compliance and use punishment as incentive. What people think, what they believe, how they feel is deemed irrelevant. Behavioral regimes are patently repressive. They appear to survive as a mechanism for cost reduction in the management and control of incorrigible populations.

The collapse of the "therapeutic community" as an ideal goal probably best demonstrates the adaptation principle. In the early 1960s, dissatisfied with traditional asylum outcomes, Maxwell Jones (1962) extolled the "therapeutic community" as a way of reducing "hospitalism," a condition that results in passive-dependent behavior due to long-term institutionalization. Jones proposed a permissive and communalistic milieu that stressed open communication and active participation in patient-centered encounters. Hope and best efforts could not overcome recalcitrant obstacles, however. The program was doomed to failure. The approach was overly selective—it could accommodate a maximum of only 100 persons, including staff and patients. It created high anxiety among staff, who perceived their traditional roles usurped. It neglected to create a new vocabulary, offering instead a mixed therapeutic metaphor—psychiatry as a "branch of medicine," a "democratizing instrument" and a "treatment" program.

With a shift from the in-patient, long-term incarceration to out-patient crisis intervention, the therapeutic community concept declined. Where it persists in somewhat altered form is in the volunteer drug and alcohol hospital treatment programs. Relatively small, self-selected populations of short-term, nondangerous and never incarcerated deviants voluntarily choose the myth of coequality between staff and patients. In ways similar to middle class work and family structures, persons are rewarded for good behavior, and normalcy can be earned in a participatory group context.

The natural selection model has confronted implacable opposition from mental health critics and funding groups. The loose connections among theory, practice and outcomes baffle some observers and anger others. What are the guidelines for treatment? How do these guidelines affect intervention? And how does one intervention method substantively differ from others in terms of curing sick people or eliminating troublesome behavior. Although mental health research has been unable to produce definitive answers to these questions, organizers have attempted to mollify critics by turning to program evaluation. This articulates basic principles, definitions, therapies and outcomes, often in highly rigorous ways (Blackwell and Bolman, 1977).

The scientific method now enters the scene. Hypothesis testing replaces impressionistic interpretations or doctrinal purity. And the research yields valid, if not philosophically broad, answers. Do human service programs help clients? Bergin (1971) claims that a baseline estimate of the effectiveness of short-term therapy, the primary method in the Community Mental Health Centers, shows 70 percent improved, 20 percent unchanged and 10 percent deteriorated. Other research doubts this rosy picture. For example, some evaluators report that only about 5 percent of intake clients go on to continue a full course of therapy (Hoppe, 1977; Albers and Scrivner, 1977). Other studies are trite, proving what any college sophomore in social psychology could address equally well: people tend to improve when their therapist likes them (Edwards and Yarvis, 1977:211).

The fundamental problem in evaluation remains, however. What goals does human-services intervention seek? And more importantly, from whose perspectives do these ends derive, and whom do the ends serve—therapist, client, administrator, funding group, larger community, institution (e.g., school, state policy, labor market)? No evaluation team can attempt to answer this question. The epistemological problems involved in the helping process remain shadowy issues; their shape and density shift with the movement of what ecologists prefer to consider the fluid environment of competing organizations.

The ecology model's redeeming quality for professionals is in its apparent naturalness, a myth that disguises its ideological content. Social change, competition and survival occur outside the individual professional or organization. This reduces practitioners' responsibility and buffers errors and imponderables. At the same time it self-aggrandizes the professional, who can always blame the client for failure to take advantage of the array of psychotherapeutic products. Taking the appearance of change as positive proof of adaptability of the new group doctrines to an ever expanding body of citizens, professionals uncritically betray the underlying reality of confusion and coercion that surrounds therapeutic intervention. Therapists espouse the ideology of pluralism, with its rhetoric of options and free choice, even where such opportunities are primarily fantasies of planners and academics.[2]

Myth and Ceremony

As systems for gathering in resources, organizations use myth and ceremony to buffer their activities from government and market forces. What organizations really do in terms of objective outputs is not at issue. Meyer and Rowan (1977) argue that for highly institutionalized organizations, such as schools and hospitals, specific accounting procedures, civil service rules, employment policies, environmental impact policies, planning bodies, quality-control units and outcome evaluation research are all largely ceremonial gestures in which conformance is neither expected nor enacted. Since tasks are vague mandates, not highly technical accomplishments, what the organization says about its output is not to be taken at face value. Rather, it propounds accounts or "scripts" addressed to relevant publics in order to maintain a "business as usual" stance (Abelson, 1976). These myths can confound both the public and the organization itself.

The single most distinctive feature about CMH centers, compared with the asylum or traditional versions of private therapy, is the proliferation of occupations. No simple hierarchy prevails, although the typical ranking within the organization holds professional credentials to be the primary criterion of merit. Occupations are strictly ordered: (1) M.D./Ph.D. — psychiatrists; (2) Ph.D. — psychologists; (3) M.S.W. — social workers. The dominant myth portrays psychiatry as the "head," the overarching helping profession in its ideological influence and organization. According to community mental health rhetoric, the medical model reigns. Psychiatrists' control in community mental health care is said to be more profound than in asylums, their impact greater. Moreover, cmmunity psychiatric practice prevents hospital admission of disabled persons because of psychotropic drugs and immediate availability of crisis care.

In reality, psychiatric power has atrophied in the community settings. Psychiatrists are no longer the primary provider of mental health services. Instead they compete with a host of old and new helping professions, which not only confounds the ranking order, but also pits incompatible values against one another. In the final contradiction: the least becomes the most. Administrative power exceeds professional values; funding requirements dictate treatment; psychiatrists "consult" and "educate," while paraprofessional and local volunteers heal. Professionals actually have lower patient contact, compared wiht other mental health workers.

The ideology of community participation itself undermines professionalism. One study of a CMH center compared the telephone couseling effectiveness of volunteers to the effectiveness of the center's professionals (O'Donnell and George, 1977:3-12). Volunteer intervention accounted for 72 percent of all contact; nonpsychiatric professional staff handled 21 percent of all client calls; psychiatric intervention accounted for less than 7 percent of all contacts. Volunteers scored about as high or higher than professionals in counseling effectiveness, especially on the variables of empathy, concreteness and genuineness. As gatekeepers, the various "listening-ear" counseling units have enormous unrecognized power. Is this to the client's advantage? O'Donnell and George (1977:11) insist that it is. They list the practical advantages:

> The emergency and reception service model described here has had numerous practical advantages in that it has allowed for (1) a more precise use of limited professional resources, (2) a heightened capability for community mental health center crisis intervention responsiveness, (3) an increased involvement of consumers in the planning and operation of a community mental health center, (4) an increased contact with many members of the community who would not directly seek assistance from traditional face-to-face helping resources, and (5) a better coordination of the community mental health center's services with cmmunity needs and with other community resources as a function of the hotline's call about any kind of problem philosophy and advertising.

An antiprofessional bias operates in some volunteer programs. Among these biases is the assumption that professional services preempt or ignore the client's "natural resource system," so volunteer services should be as autonomous as possible. Plannners are admonished to avoid having clients channeled into the formal mental health delivery system. In effect, the volunteer programs must steer clear of turning "hotlines" into merely another admissions screening unit to the formal mental health system.

But why should volunteers or other semi-trained citizens necessarily be better or more valuable than the highly trained professional for handling crisis events, such as suicide or severe drug episodes? Why should volunteeers, who operate in the isolated context of a telephone, be more equipped to serve the troubled and the desperate? Critics point out that volunteers exhibit more "warmth," a feature that has been shown to be most potent in predicting successful outcomes than other dimensions of couseling effectiveness (Truax and Carkhuff, 1967). The unspoken assumption—that professional organizations are "cold" and that patient healing requires emotional intensity negated by formal office arrangements—stalks the volunteer programs. What guarantee exists that volunteers are necessarily more open, warm and insightful than professionals? There is none. What are the genuine advantages, versus the surface rhetoric, of an extroverted therapist for a serious life crisis? The data do not reveal this. Instead, this issue suggests still another attack on traditional psychotherapy and professionalism. The CMH myth fails to take into account client variation and the situational nature of mental illness episodes. A suicide attempt, delirium tremens, drug overdose, loss of a child or teenage loss of a parent are neither uniform nor standardized events. The "pop" psychology imagery that clings to these formats undermines this variation as well as the complex responses of clients that depend upon prior social and emotional experiences.

An opposing myth in the mental health field—overglorification of the physician—is merely replaced with an equally distorted doctrine—the disutility of psychiatry and the reifying of community as a homogeneous entity. This leveling version strips professionals of social power and, hence, accountability; it fails to protect clients from charletans and leads to the poverty of professionalism: intensive training without authority, status or esteem.

The structure generates a twofold control problem. First, deviants easily become lost in the system. Disorienting mental and emotional problems are exacerbated by agency shuffling between competing professional groups. Second, deinstitutionalizing deviants reduces the total population under surveillance in asylums, but ignores the harsh reality of modern urban organizations and their deleterious effects on persons.

Deinstitutionalizing Deviants[3]
Despite fairly wide differences in topics and research styles, community psychiatrists rally about one major concern: the issue of how traditional asylum care of the mentally ill uses labels as a will to power, to shore up hierarchies, to aggrandize organizational resources and to control people's reality. Research has exposed the various language games—past, present and future—that involuntarily tie social members into rigid categories that are reinforced by institutionalization or strict role assignment. More recently, interest in declassifying deviant categories has led to analysis of delabeling and relabeling phenomena, especially those meanings that have shifted from one institutional context to another. For example, in

the twentieth century, homosexuality became increasingly defined as an illness; various Freudian, hormonal, genetic, and psychogenic models were proposed, and psychiatrists were recruited en masse for treating the homosexual illness. With the advent of the Gay Liberation Movement, the medical model of homosexuality as an exclusive treatment category has been severly challenged (Thio, 1978).

Women, another group undergoing radical declassification, have lived inside a restricted category system that not only limited their social accomplishments, once almost invariably restricted to kinship roles, but stunted their minds and personalities in ways that are only now, sometimes reluctantly, becoming recognized (Davis, 1977).

Mental disorder, once a salient scourge, a shameful payment for individual or group sins, has become demedicalized and politicized. Mental patients are not only recognized as citizens having legal rights, but among some psychiatrists they are defined as more aware of their existential conditions than so-called sane persons (Laing, 1967).

Community psychiatry waged a much needed struggle against smug asylum control for over two decades. Decriminalization, deprisonization, demedication, and deinstitutionalization—the list goes on—are proposed as the ultimate solution to the problems of modern living. Restoring the shattered person or family requires collective self-help, a participatory ethic that promotes various voluntaristic programs that encourage members, paradoxically enough, to accept the negative stereotype in order to be free from the compulsions of dangerous, antisocial or selfdestructive behavior. Parents Anonymous for child abusers, TOPS for the obese and AA for alcoholics are some examples of this genre. Admitting defeat is the first symptom toward health, these programs attest, and members are expected to identify with the deviant label (I am a drug addict; I will always be a drug addict) before self-improvement is possible. The prinicipal idea is that emancipating individuals from the totalitarian regimes of institutions or bureaucracies enables the individual to carve out his or her own moral career without institutional interference.

This is the myth; the reality may be far harsher. For instance, releasing unemployed and unemployable schizophrenics from hospitalization to shabby or, more likely, nonexistent community-care facilities or dilapidated welfare hotels relocates the trouble; it does not eliminate it. Among indigent populations—the aged, alcoholics, mental patients and others—where the need for human services is most acute, roadblocks prevent these needy persons from negotiating with welfare agencies or professionals. Often the troubled individual remains uninformed as to whether services are available, what they are and the various procedures necessary for connecting persons to institutions. Widespread ignorance about modes of coping in urban worlds leads to maladaptive personal solutions, as when an aged woman literally locks herself into her room to avoid mugging by neighborhood thugs.

Deinstitutionalizing women's role—out of the family and into the street, bar, office, gym, jail and other public domains—has not faciliatated social integration as much as it has led to the spread of what Weber called a "disenchantment of the world." Gender role changes represent profound social and personal dislocations that affect the person, family and community. Behavioral repertories, long taken for granted as natural or biological givens, become rejected outright as "power trips" or "male chauvinism." The myth of personal choice, fostered by the liberal ethos and promoted by labelists in their stripped-down model of institutional order, should be reconstructed as ideology. As a mandate for coping during periods of social turmoil, the choice ideology reflects a privatized, capitalist solution to the problems of collective life. Support structures for needy women—divorced, single parent, unwed teen, empty nest, mentally or emotionally unstable, suicidal, aged —are few in number and inaccessible to most who need them. The woman leaves the family domain at her own risk.

Homosexuals, our final example of a reclassified population, are among the cluster of politicized groups that have sought the social movement solution to private problems. Stepping out of categorical boxes that labeled homosexuality as inherited or derived pathology, the formerly stigmatized are now hypothetically free to negotiate the larger society. The relabeling process, however, must be taken into account as having its own built in restraints. Different forms of social exclusion arise that sometimes foster an equally narrow set of role prescriptions as those that were once imposed. There is an understandably deep distrust of outsiders and a corresponding dependence on the politics and categories of insiders. Nonetheless, the resulting sect mentality, so characteristic of self-help groups, neither tolerates innovation nor liberates believers from privatized views of the world that become reified under conditions of segregated living. Inadequate, unsatisfying or exploitative relations are often endured, especially among aging homosexuals, because the ability to negotiate complex roles declines within exclusive dyad sets.

Deinstitutionalization, a concept drawn from the liberal lexicon, becomes translated into moral ghettoization, a kind of isolation and segregation of life styles that further contributes to a political decollectivization. The "do-your-own-thing" stance reverts to a mandate for alienation and failure to make connections across social boundaries. When considering categorical changes, CMH advocates should remain skeptical, asking such questions as: Does deinstitutionalization serve merely as a convenient rationalization for saving taxpayers' money and legislators' jobs? Such groups justify a hands-off policy as a moral solution, but policy is more likely to be related to economic decisions. What impact does a policy really have on deprived groups? How do specific programs affect different populations (e.g., blindness programs for children versus programs for the aged). What are the social consequences for persons and institutions of liberal myths of individualism and privatism? Sentimentality has shaped a spurious humanistic theory that produces nonhumanistic results.

But the decentralizers and deinstitutionalizers rarely saw beyond the plans "to tear down the walls and open the doors," using Beck's (1978) statement. The return of inmates to communities where they are mistrusted and despised, the ghettoization of the stigmatized, the abandonment of the spiritually lost to their fate and the rejection of communal efforts to integrate victimized populations denigrate whatever is left of the community ideal.

The Cult of Community

Out of dissolution and insecurity emerges the contemporary fascination with the symbols and values of community (Nisbet, 1953). American social scientists have been preoccupied with the community concept since the turn of the century. Seeking the "basic conditions of a common life" (MacIver and Page, 1949:8-9) in the urban context of volatile class and ethnic conflicts, theorists addressed the issue in opposing ways.

Writing since the 1930s and 1940s, functional sociologists studying rural or preindustrial societies have interpreted community as an organic, highly interdependent unit: a grouping of like-minded persons living somewhat permanently in a geographically limited area that serves as a focus for daily life (see Hoult, 1974:99). Community transcends family and occupational groups as the most immediate center for shared consciousness and collective activities.

More concerned with population distributions in industrial societies, social ecologists, dating from the 1920s through the present, have studied community as distinct regions or localities that serve as a focus for particular forms of social organization (Hawley, 1950; Mack and Pease, 1973:235-269). Thus, rural communities have characteristic organizations that differ from town or urban units. In turn, urban social organization involves multiple communities or status groups, including class, ethnic, occupational, religious, neighborhood and others. Modern communities generate multiple cultures, they reasoned. In the first model, community translates into order, and in the second model, it converts into differentiation.

A third approach considers the fragmented community, comprised of class and ethnic conflict groups, and takes its cues from classical thinkers (Weber and Marx) and from the social turmoil of the 1960s and 1970s. Here, industrial societies practice invidious rank distinctions in which status, class, religion, occupation and other relatively permanent fate-determining structures locate persons in unequal positions. Community is a convienient term for population centers where the maldistribution of wealth, power and prestige is apparent. These are generated and perpetuated by dominant structures of state and economy.

Urban populations lead separate and unequal lives, a condition maintained over generations through ideological and state structures of control, including taxation, welfare, law, the military, medicine, criminal justice, education, mental health and other occupational and professional structures.

CMH specialists deny these well-established properties of collective social life. Instead, they offer the myth of the integrated community. According to this myth, a community entails:

1. a unified, interdependent center for shared living;
2. a specified geographical location; e.g., rural, open country, neighborhood, town, metropolitan, or mass community;

3. standardized political units; town, country, urban, state;
4. shared institutions;
5. homogeneous values and culture;
6. organizations whose form and function derive from local needs and expectations;
7. integrative mechanism, i.e., family, religion, political order, media, etc.

The exclusive pursuit of community, while well-meaning, insures its decline. CMH deals with surface variations, not the underlying reality of unresolvable class and social antagonisms. It uses the facade of community—these ecologically situated institutions, businesses, neighborhoods, families, jails, halfway houses, churches—as focal points for intervention in a kind of massive good-neighborhood gesture of administered health.

The ideology of community information, community action and community participation masks the reproduction of a class structure held together by a national, if fragmented, network of agencies that operates outside the consciousness and political control of local participants. Where contradictions intrude, they are perceived as mere reflections of antagonisms in the service delivery program. Servers and servees live in disparate worlds of providers and consumers. Nor are professionals viewed as more superior. As tools for delivery of services, professional staff figure into the community-use structure along with buildings, money or machinery. Staff disinterest, or even antagonism toward clients, protects servers from the hazards of compassion and involvement. The professional, as a mechanism to integrate resistant and deviant elements into the normal community, learns to keep social distance. Thus, bureaucratizing therapy provides a vehicle for locking clients and professionals alike into the system.

The welfare state perspective drains community organizations of vitality. Although modeled on limited participation of local groups, the individual career and interest-group politics prevail. Because the liberal ethos promotes a one-directional exchange—the market influences providers and, in turn, providers determine clients' needs and outcomes—it promotes a demobilizing effect. Welfare and CMH structures reproduce class inequality through symptom alleviation, social control and political acquiescence. They ignore both the larger environment and the immediate need structures of deprived persons. Nutrition, housing, health care, taxes, justice, education, transportation, corporate economy and the organization of work—none are affected by the twin props of welfare and community mental health.

Blindness to the real nature of modern communities—their fragmentation, splintering, and class and group exploitation—produces the social logic of a society that deals in exchange values. How much does mental health cost? What is it worth and to whom? And how can therapeutic effectiveness be measured? Such questions merely reaffirm the dependent and typically isolated space occupied by welfare and mental health institutions compared with market and state interests.

Advocates of radical social services confront institutional controls by positing community as a liberating ideology. "Community organization," "community politics" and "community struggle"—these terms are used in opposition to "institutions," "capitalist society" and "power." Here community retains the essential meanings of the "we" group, an identifiable face-to-face group who share common (repressive) conditions of life. Chester Hartman (1978:41), a social-policy analyst, applauds the grassroots partisan activities because underclass-institutional confrontations sharpen the class struggle.

> Community organization can clarify the nature of class conflicts and heighten class consciousness, while community struggle can expose the contradictions in the dominant ideologies of capitalist societies.

The populist rhetoric and visible good intentions of middle class activity effectively disguise differences in class interest (Grady and Ploss, 1978:48). What cannot be eradicated can be mythologized. As a child of the state, CMH becomes as much a part of poor persons' problems as a problem solution. There is a characteristic sequence to the helping process. Middle class activists initially express concern over material and power deprivations among poor minorities. This leads to calls for action and program planning by experts in which local groups participate as "informants" or "consultants," never as political equals. Next comes standardized administrative aid, and if this is ineffective or unacceptable, the final move is coercive treatment for resisters. Middle class critiques directed against inequalities seek equalization or democratization. But equalizing services universalizes them in the direction of bureaucracy and conformist psychology. The ideological middle class demand for equality, rather than equity, results in proposals for the elimination of all differences, a virtual impossibility in an unchanged social structure.

If the intensification of community is a direct response to its actual decline, it ultimately works to accelerate the decline. Unfortunately, the universal slogans and rhetorics that replace it are as vacant and meaningless as the bureaucracies that throw them up. Angered, fatigued and embittered by paper solutions that only recycle social problems, citizens look elsewhere for relief. Proposals to transform society operate outside the conventional context, offering social movement remedies. Often their utopias are reversals; mirror images of the ideal typical bureaucratic model. Plans for banishing oppression eliminate all status differences, expertise, formal organization and standard accountability. Other solutions favor a more traditional concept of human problems: claims that it's the individual's fault, or the lack-of-will argument. Fat people, drinkers, drug users, gamblers and child abusers are urged to join together in a self-imposed, stigma-producing ceremony to redeem themselves.

CHAPTER 9—NOTES

[1] Rieff (1966) introduced the concept "triumph of the therapeutic" in a radical critique of the medicalization of human need.

[2] Compare this institutional construct with Eaton's (1955) report of the Hutterite response to mental illness. Among these survivors of peasant culture in modern life, community treatment of erratic or aberrant behavior is initially unfavorable. The deviant along with the abnormal behavior is defined as "bad." Once the disturbing individual is perceived as unable to self-correct the behavior, the community is mobilized for aid. What Eaton calls the "therapeutic milieu" involves a virtual absence of psychiatric skills, replaced here by such *Gemeinschaft* features as family nursing, prayer, confession, sacrifice, tolerance for the disturbed person and so on. About 2 percent of the Hutterite population demonstrates severe mental disorder, with the depressive symptoms most common.

[3] This section is taken from Davis (1980).

CONCLUSIONS TO PART III

Community Care Structures and Social Control

In this section we considered community regulatory systems of welfare and community mental health as problems in dominant social structures: economy, state, bureaucracy and professional orders. Whereas welfare represents institutionalized nonsolutions to failures in the political economy, community mental health schemes invite intrusion at the level of families and persons. The expansion of the modern state began initially with regulating the labor market through direct control over the destitute classes, but now has moved to incorporate middle and upper classes as well. Through its regulation of images, it brings together all institutional spheres—cultural, economic, political and familial—to define standards of sanity, order, normalcy and right living. Formerly, the sanctions that followed deviations had a benevolent veneer, a kind of paternalistic enforced nurturance—"the state cares more for you than you care for youself." Bureaucratic anonymity exposes this benevolence as spurious.

Sennett (1980) shows the paradox of the modern state. Using the metaphors of parental love inflated well beyond their natural measures, the state ultimately rules through violence: jail, asylum, bare subsistence doles. Nazi Germany and the experiment with the thousand-year Reich and Stalin's slave labor camps are both outgrowths of delusion; of the promise of false love (Sennett, 1980). The state cannot be a parent, but only an impersonal agent of collective action, after all.

The shift to what Sennett calls "autonomy, an authority without love" in the advanced bureaucratic state is power through indifference—there is blankness on the faces of those in control. Regulation changes from violence to shame. Authority established by the practice of sheer indifference employs the ideology of autonomy; a kind of self-possession or self-mastery that excludes other persons. In an indifference regime, there is neither empathy nor sympathy; rulers and ruled are unable to even confront one another.

Bureaucracy is the dominant mode through which the autonomy/indifference regime operates. Its tactics are fivefold: (1) nearly exclusive use of the passive voice ("it is said that..."), a strategy that masks the speakers and source of decisions; (2) control over categories; the bureaucratic discourse is abstract, impersonal and removed from the realm of direct experience; (3) rigid and secret hierarchies—top-down communication and bottom-up obedience; (4) lack of role exchange—master and servant operate in irreconcilable worlds, wherein conflict merely shores up the chain of command because of inherent misunderstandings and categorical differences; and (5) inability of subordinates to negotiate over nurturance; job benefits, day-care, medical help are all planned according to categories, such as level in the organization, age, family size, and the like, rather than according to need.

Influence attacks human freedom more pervasively, Sennett (1980:115) says, because it masks the true intentions of dominance.

> The idea of influence is thus the ultimate expression of autonomy. Its effect is to mystify what the boss wants and what the boss stands for. Influence directed to making workers more content with their work denies them a similar freedom; the nature of the contentments is designed for them. Pleasure is expected to erase confrontation. However, the influences are not rules but stipulations. It is up to the subordinate to find the design. This is the most extreme example of a saying of Hegel's: the injustice of society is that the subordinate must make sense of what power is.

Flexibility belongs to elites alone; or said another way, only the elite are capable of democratic relations. Management by objective, a system that maximizes self-sufficiency and competence for executives, and professional accountability, self-regulation of work through a colleagueship of equals, are dual practices that loosen the old paternalistic ties. The myth of autonomy for subordinates, contributing to their split consciousness, is that all existing systems of regulation—economy, state, work place, welfare, criminal justice, mental health—allow no negotiation between being controlled and being cared for. Paternalism and influence orders breed a similar pathology—a kind of amorphous dependency that creates the fear of omnipotent authority, a condition resolvable only through extreme reactions: immobility, a muted acceptance of the status quo, or anarchism, a total rejection of all authority. Sennett proposes five ways to disrupt the chain of command, all based on the power to revise through open discussion decisions that flow from the top down.

1. The use of the active voice. ("Mr. Brown spoke today about X decision and said that...") This traces decisions to concrete persons, places and events.

2. A discussion of categorization enabling a penetration of the discourse and its exposure to subordinates' experience.

3. Permitting a variety of obedience responses to a directive; goal-oriented rather than control over means by shame and indifference.

4. Role exchange between higher and lower ranks through role simulations, or actual alternations of roles over time. Coercive role exchange within industry and the professions, as in postrevolutionary China (scholars turned into farmhands), should be avoided, as this violates freedom and undermines authority. Equalizing incomes and benefits based on need would encourage greater role flexibility.

5. Face-to-face negotiation over nurturance. Justifying one's own needs, as in asking for support, both economic and psychological, is something we do by indirection. Nurturance is a veiled game by which subordinates hope to secure something extra (in addition to their regular benefits) out of their superiors; and superiors, in turn, hope to tighten their control over subordinates. Sennett considers the *open* negotiation about nurturance the most disruptive experience that can occur in a modern chain of command. Employees, welfare recipients, the mentally ill, minorities, the aged and the young must come to grips with the first fact of nurturance; a face-to-face encounter marks the beginning toward losing shame through employing democratic tools.

The greatest pretense in modern bureaucracy is the belief that public authority is isomorphic with private authority. Bosses, psychiatrists, judges and fathers are one. This confuses the *limits* of public authority and reduces the capacity of citizens to accurately interpret the necessary restraints that make civilized life possible. The confusion of realms also explains why commitment organizations attempt to recreate social organizations without chain of command. Their denial of authority, though, does not resolve the authority problem, but simply puts it aside.

IV. Self-Help Networks

Chapter 10
Perspectives from the Underlife:
Toward a Theory of Commitment
Organizations

> Viewed from a purely ethical point of view, the world has to appear fragmentary and devalued.... This devaluation results from the conflict between the rational claim and reality; between the rational ethic and the partly rational and partly irrational values.
>
> Max Weber, *Essays in Sociology*
> (H. Gerth and C. Wright Mills, eds.)

Of all concepts essential to an understanding of culture and organization in alternative institutions, commitment is at once the most indispensable and the most ambiguous. Like the respectability term of the Victorian epoch that validated the social superiority of the middle classes to the mass of the population, it can be infinitely extended, and every extension fortifies the mystique of differences. Commitment marks the distinction between social orders; between commonplace organizations that hold members by money, career and status and commitment organizations that bind members by values and ideology. In this chapter we are dealing with fundamentally divergent versions of organizing human services.

In the organizations discussed in this and the two following chapters, the means and ends are related differently to one another. Such value-drenched organizations, of course, have ends—for instance, the liberation of women from sexist roles and conceptions or the cure of alcoholism or drug addiction. The means, however, are not chosen pragmatically for their efficiency but must instead serve to *express and dramatize* the values and views of the world to which members are passionately committed. Hence we use the term *commitment organizations* to distinguish them from bureaucracies and professional organizations.

Social Movement Organizations

Commitment organizations view social reality from an ethical rather than pragmatic perspective. This imposes a structure and cognitive style that make commitment organizations radically different from the other organizational types. Their ideology appeals primarily to groups that stand apart from, in opposition to or outside the dominant, "respectable" order. Members advocate either radical social change or secession from the official order. Joining such an organization often involves going through a conversion experience, analogous to a religious one (Lofland and Stark, 1965). Rejecting the established order entails rejecting one's old self, and by accepting the work of the organization the person acquires a new self. Commitment to the organization is built on intrinsic rewards—trust, self-esteem, affiliation, a philosophy of life, a sense of personal integrity—rather than pecuniary gain, social mobility and other instrumental benefits. Pragmatism in the choice of means is often explicitly rejected. Although the goals are eagerly pursued, it is equally important *how*, by whom and for whom the activities are carried out. If functions are performed inappropriately in the light of the ideology, they lose their vaulue, and the activity or the person may be denounced.[1]

One mode of conceptualizing society is to treat structure as an ongoing process of building up and breaking down—a cyclical event. Rationalization, the legitimate technical mode for organizing modern societies, represents one phase of the structure. This occupies the most visible social space and preempts the most important cognitive categories. The conscious revision and articulation of derationalization, or the "other rationality," comprised of values, morality and meanings (Adorno, 1973; Foucault, 1977a; Habermas, 1979) are also pervasive, but are more likely to operate as illegitimate or *sub rosa* features. Because sentiment and value structures tend to be invisible or at least out of sight, they are more easily relegated to silence or stigma. In American society, death, aging, illegitimacy, addiction, poverty and mental illness have been taboo subjects or have been treated within truncated, distorted discourses. Either they have been ignored outright or treated with embarrassment and shame. It often takes a social movement to fundamentally alter the meanings of stigmatic terms and open up the repressed issues to serious reevaluation. This is accomplished through unmasking the socially constructed nature of rationality, which reveals the passions and values that underlie the seemingly objective considerations of means and ends (Bouchard, ed., in Foucault, 1977b:22).

What appears to be merely a pragmatic rationalization process creates elements of the irrational. Through bureaucracy there is a steadily increasing application of explicit rules and procedures to whole areas of social life. This focuses on clearly definable, technical concerns but leaves out large chunks of social life. Bureaucracy narrows, closes off, and confines elements that fail to fit the stereotypical and inevitably limited categories. Whatever its intent, rationalization has the effect of reshaping the private and political meanings of behavior.

In contrast to such rationalistic structures as state and medical bureaucracies, which are fairly permanent fixtures of modern life, commitment organizations usually have short life-spans and high turnover of membership. (In chapter 11 we deal, however, with a commitment organization, Alcoholics Anonymous, that has proven relatively long-lived.) Challenging the pragmatic, cost-benefit, conscious, rational ways of bureaucracies and professions, commitment organizations articulate anomalies, contradictions and needs that are overlooked and open the discourse to forbidden subject matters. The challenges often amount to allegations that bureaucratic and professional practices exhibit class, racial or sexual biases, or that they ignore the pressing needs of large proportions of citizens. Spokespersons for bureaucracies and professions often see commitment organizations as problematic, annoying or "crackpot." This is understandable since commitment organizations necessarily challenge some of the ideological legitimations of bureaucracies and professions. And often the challenges are expressed with a degree of flamboyance that ill fits the orderly ways of bureaucrats and professionals.

Sociologists have written at length about the rise of social movements (see, for instance, Blumer, 1946, 1957; Heberle, 1951; Smelser, 1963; Zald and Ash, 1966; Gusfield, ed., 1970). Some of their discussions clarify the nature and organization of social movements as systematic social forms. But not all social movements are commitment organizations. Most social movements are probably incipient interest groups and soon learn to model themselves on bureaucracies. They are best studied from the point of view of *resource mobilization* (McCarthy and Zald, 1973, and chapter 7 in this book).

The commitment organizations are social movements in which ideology and myth play dominant roles. Some sociologists refer to them as revitalization movements in order to stress their energizing, personality-transforming character (Wallace, 1956; Anderson, 1968). To understand commitment organizations we must therefore first deal with the factors that give them their ideological appeal.

Commitment movements have a long history as alternatives to established and dominant orders. Historians are increasingly studying them. Millenarian sects or movements in the Middle Ages aimed at restoring the world to a more ethical place and used "salvation" as a central term. Cohn (1970:15) asserts that such movements pictured salvation as:

1. collective, in that it was to be enjoyed by believers as a collectivity;

2. terrestrial, in that salvation was to be realized on this earth and not in some otherworldly domain;

3. imminent, in the sense that it was to come about both soon and suddenly;

4. total, in that the movement was to transform life on earth, and in that such change would not be a mere improvement on the present, but perfection itself;

5. miraculous, in that it was to be accomplished by or with the help of supernatural agencies.

The millenarian sects and movements of medieval Europe were drawn from both extremes of the social structure. Franciscan spiritualists flourishing in the thirteenth century came mainly from the mixture of noble and merchant families that formed the dominant class in the Italian towns. Prayer, mystical contemplation, and voluntary poverty were extolled as means for ushering in the age of the Spirit. At the other extreme were the various millenarian sects and movements that developed among the rootless poor. Involuntary poverty rendered their lives insecure and short lived. Their millenarianism was violent, anarchic and often truly revolutionary (Cohn, 1970:16).

The English seventeenth century was another heyday of counterculture (see, for example, Hill, 1965). Nineteenth-century Europe saw movements among craftspersons and peasants in opposition to modernization and industrialism (Hobsbawm, 1959). And in 19th-century America, utopian and alternative communities—Brook Farm, Oneida, New Harmony and others—experimented with forms of organization and ways of life that stressed cooperation, equality and spiritual development, in opposition to competition, hierarchy and materialism. In reading about commitment movements in different times and places, the observer is struck by how the rhetorics and visions resemble one another. Thus, themes of the modern counterculture are found in 17th-century England and among 19-century reformers and enthusiasts.

Here are some typical movement themes that animate both historical and contemporary commitment organizations.

Primitivism	Spiritualism	Egalitarianism
Sensuous Narcissism	Mysticism	Pacifism
Renunciation	Merging with Nature	Abolition of
Faddism (e.g., nudism,	Desire for Liberation	Nuclear Family
vegetarianism)	Privatism	Naturalism
Anarchism	Collectivism	Self-Involvement

Some polarities—strong/weak; good/evil; purity/pollution—are universal. Evidently, so are some themes, such as organicism, the linkage with nature; spiritualism, the identification with the transcendent; and renunciation, the proposal for a reconstructed world.

Each social movement employs its own distinctive metaphors. During the eighteenth and nineteenth centuries, the free-thought tradition rose as an aftermath of the French Revolution with its ideological stress on equality and liberty. This found expression in utopian communities such as Brooks Farm, transcendentalism, the romantic movement, communalism and communism, and in both early and later versions of feminism and humanitarianism. Commitment organizations in Rosabeth Kanter's work (1972) viewed established society as the anomaly and offered anarchy and humanitarianism as opposing models, especially among cult religious movments. In the late nineteenth century, anarchism, socialism and mysticism united. All shared a sense of revolt against orthodoxy. In the twentieth century there has been an expansion of cults, movements and commitment organizations as a result of the demise of traditional relations. Movements as far apart as Zen and radical feminism incorporate similar themes of world renunciation and selfhood (see Toynbee and Ikeda, 1976:304-342).

Kanter (1972) has examined communes and utopias and concludes that the commitment mechanisms that assure communal survival frequently undermine individualism and personal autonomy. Opposed to Western values of self-reliance, independence, personal achievement, and self-fulfillment, successful American utopias build transcendence through different values: institutional awe, mystery, programmed sacrifice and ideological conversion. Deindividuation mechanisms anchor identity in communal rather than personal experience. Communities are families but of a nontraditional type.

> Exclusive couples and biological families were discouraged through celibacy, free love or group marriage. In Oneida's system of complex marriage, for example, each member had sexual access to every other member, with his or her consent and under the general supervision of cummunity leaders. A man interested in a liaison would approach a woman through a third party; she had the right to refuse his attentions. Couples showing an excess of special love would be broken up or forced into relationships with others... children were raised communally from soon after weaning.
>
> (Kanter, 1970:54)

Themes may be transformed over time. During a movement's early phase, themes may feature antitechnological solutions, transcendental values or self-realization. Its interorganizational phase, however, may stress political ideas. Today, socialism, anarchism and a radical struggle for power replace the other-worldliness of the earlier stage of many social movements. Western categories partly obscure these processes. Similar conceptual elements comprising religious revitalization movements also may be involved in cultural or political movements. Social change frequently depends on religious, transcendental or ecstatic themes for intensifying the message (see Leach, 1966, 1967; Musgrove, 1974; Kanter, 1972; Roszak, 1969). Occasionally, social scientists have contributed to the acceleration and movement of protest into political forms. Taking the underdog perspective, some political theorists have succeeded in transforming protest into legitimate partisan grievances (Skolnick, 1969; Cloward and Piven, 1974; Sears and McConahay, 1973).

Organization of Commitment Movements

Within Western culture an oppositional tradition continues to exist, hidden much of the time, but ready to emerge in times when the dominant order and its beliefs have lost credibility. The last two decades have been such times, and commitment movements have become very visible (Roszak, 1969; Musgrove, 1974). Parallel oppositional organizations tend to develop in specific sectors; cooperatives among farmers, free medical clinics among the urban drop-outs (although organized by liberal professionals) and food cooperatives among students. Gardner (1976) estimates that about 1,000 new alternative institutions are created annually in the United States, including free schools, free medical clinics, legal collectives, alternative newspapers, food cooperatives, researchers' collectives, residential communes, restaurants, bookstores, housing construction, energy installations and so on. Most of these institutions are outgrowths of the antiauthority movements of the 1960s.

Much has been written abut the sociological and psychological origins of commitment movements (for example, Wallace, 1956; Anderson, 1968; Geertz, 1957). Many writers stress factors such as the break-up of traditional roles (for example, between the sexes), alienation from established, often hierarchical institutions that are seen to have lost their legitimacy (as when a church has become worldly or a state wages unjust war) and the loss of faith in established ideologies.

Geertz (1957) outlines two necessary conditions for the emergence of these movements. First, cultural turbulence triggers radical cultural change in which essential roles become altered and affect fundamental social relationships. There is a quest for coherence and meaning in a precarious world. Second, a growing problem of authority arises that threatens the legitimation of rules. The existing political order is perceived as somehow wrong, out of place, disordered, unjust or oppressive.

Social anthropologists Mary Douglas (1966, 1968) and Victor Turner (1964, 1969) further observe that under conditions of role breakdown there is generalized domain confusion and an accumulation of anomalies, odd, disconnected and discontinuous features that fail to fit the cultural categories. Status ambiguity and role uncertainty accelerate identity crisis on the individual level and institutional crisis at the structural level. Such meaning crises represent serious social ruptures, because they not only destroy common understandings—the body of taken-for-granted knowledge —but also let loose the demons in the culture, the systematic repressions, oppressions and horrors glossed over by the institutional orders.

Structural liminality, a term used by Turner to refer to status or cultural ruptures that create periods of social crises, tend to be rectified by appeals to myth and ritual. Ritual, especially, enables a social collectivity to tap into its depth structure. Ritual teaches, signifies, articulates and exposes the depth structure. The passion story acted out in the Catholic mass expresses central ideas of Christianity with its belief in transcendence through salvation. Myth and ritual are not necessarily coherent, though. Nativistic churches in Africa use Christian ritual, but retain the native set of beliefs that organize their daily lives, ideas often incompatible with Christianity (Evans-Pritchard, 1962).

In contemporary societies, myth and ritual have weakened under the impact of rationalization. Social movements now carry on the bulk of the reality-affirming work, but in highly selective and sometimes distorting ways. Norms of efficiency and effectiveness in business, professional and government circles contribute to a dependency on mechanical solutions to personal and social ills. Ritualization replaces ritual. And with these empty gestures, a loss of coping ideation occurs. In this state of profound uncertainty, deviance flourishes. In highly uncertain situations, violence may even become a way of life (Taylor and Soady, 1972; Feagin and Hahn, 1973).

The emergence of a social movement (or more characteristically, a wave of movements) acts to restore boundaries. Categories that were formerly drained of meanings become reinstated and differences highlighted. "Feminist," a term of independence, is opposed to "housewife," a dependency status. Small planet, the ideological cry of the ecology movement, is plotted against global markets and star wars. Despite the cyclical nature of movement sequences, which repeat themselves over decades or even centuries, social transformation can be genuine and often profound. Most of what passes as social change is actually quite superficial and peripheral, though. The surface changes have little impact on the organization of values. For instance, the women's movement has had its greatest influence on the labor market (e.g., flextime and double family incomes) and the ecology movement has directly affected family nutrition (e.g., meat-substitute diet). Neither movement has succeeded in ousting dominant classes or styles of institutional oppressions from their preeminent position.

Alternatives to Bureaucracy

Even with a low economic and political profile, commitment organizations offer a viable alternative to the hierarchical models of work and human services. Joyce Rothchild-Whitt (1979) distills the elementary features of "collectivist democratic organizations," and notes how they provide real choice for participants. A primary emphasis is consciousness of social relations and ideology. Thus, members reject passive consumers who are influenced by advertising that produces an ever expanding spiral of psychic deprivation. Instead, collectives attempt to eliminate false needs by instituting new standards or restoring old ones. "Womencare" among feminists means that women collectively work to improve the health and well-being of women. It is not the medical services or level of expertise that is crucial here. It is the *consciousness* of collective involvement that serves merely as a token of the larger effort.

Rothschild-Whitt sets out eight dimensions that differentiate bureaucracies from commitment or collectivist-democratic organizations, as shown in Table 10:1.

Table 10:1 Comparisons of Two Ideal Types of Organizations

Dimensions	*Bureaucratic Organization*	*Collectivist-Democratic Organization*
1. Authority	1. Authority resides in individuals by virtue of incumbency in office and/or expertise: hierarchical organization of offices. Compliance is to universal fixed rules as these are implemented by office incumbents.	1. Authority resides in the collectivity as a whole; delegated, if at all, only temporarily and subject to recall. Compliance is to the consensus of the collective, which is always fluid and open to negotiation.
2. Rules	2. Formalization of fixed and universalistic rules; calculability and appeal of decisions on the basis of correspondence to the formal written law.	2. Minimal stipulated rules; primacy of *ad hoc*, individuated decisions: some calculability possible on the basis of knowing the substantive ethics involved in the situation.

Table 10:1 Comparisons of Two Ideal Types of Organizations (cont'd)

Dimensions	Bureaucratic Organization	Collectivist-Democratic Organization
3. Social Control	3. Organizational behavior is subject to social control, primarily through direct supervision or standardized rules and sanctions, tertiarily through the selection of homogeneous personnel, especially at top levels.	3. Social controls are primarily based on personalistic or moralistic appeals and the selection of homogeneous personnel.
4. Social Relations	4. Ideal of impersonality. Relations are role-based, segmental and instrumental.	4. Ideal of community. Relations are to be holistic, personal, of value in themselves.
5. Recruitment and Advancement	5.a. Employment based on specialized training and formal certification. 5.b. Employment constitutes a career; advancement based on seniority or achievement.	5.a. Employment based on friends, social-political values, personal attributes, and informally assessed knowledge and skills. 5.b. Concept of career advancement not meaningful; no hierarchy of positions.
6. Incentive Structure	6. Remunerative incentives are primary.	6. Normative and solidarity incentives are primary; material incentives are secondary.
7. Social Stratification	7. Isomorphic distribution of prestige, privilege and power; i.e., differential rewards by office; hierarchy justifies inequality.	7. Egalitarian; reward differentials, if any, are strictly limited by the collectivity.
8. Differentiation	8.a. Maximal division of labor: dichotomy between intellectual work and manual work and between administrative tasks and performance tasks. 8.b. Maximal specialization of jobs and functions; segmental roles. Technical expertise is exclusively held: ideal of the specialist-expert.	8.a. Minimal division of labor: administration is combined with performance tasks; division between intellectual and manual work is reduced. 8.b. Generalization of jobs and functions: holistic roles. Demystification of expertise: ideal of the amateur factotum.

— from Rothschild-Whitt, 1979:519.

Rothschild-Whitt offers the best extant compilation of significant features of egalitarian collective organizations, but the schema is flawed. Identifying structural features of egalitarian organizations as though they were universal to all social movement organizations provides an ahistorical and nonenvironmental model. The outstanding error is the assumption that social movement organizations are necessarily democratic. Many collectivist organizations have a highly stuctured authority in which top-down communication is common; i.e., communication is dogmatic, asymmetrical or even closed (e.g. Synanon). Rules may be maximal, not minimal, and discount choice, because substantive ethics transcend individual preferences (e.g., St. Benedict's monastery rules and St. Ignatius Loyola's authoritarian order both emerged in reaction to moral looseness in the Church). Homogeneity in personnel may occur *after* the fact; i.e., after recruitment and socialization into the ethos. Similar status characteristics on some dimensions, for example, age and sex, could be offset by other differentiating statuses, e.g., social class, ethnicity, geographic region, religion and so forth. To take another example, career advancement, which essentially marks bureaucratic organizations, is said to be inoperative in collectivist organizations. But is it? Leaders in revolutionary movements jockey for position, using the rhetoric of equality and amateurishness. Once entrenched, though, traditional hierarchies, rules, roles and rewards enter the scene. Communist and fascist movements in this century evoke images of the professional revolutionary whose power derives from successful positioning in the movement (e.g., Mao Tse Tung).

One model of the commitment organization, egalitarianism, is by no means the universal one. We need an historical perspective. Because these egalitarian structures tend to characterize those in our own epoch, we presume their naturalness, rather than critically appraising the conditions of their emergence. In our analysis, social movement organizations are preeminently oppositional structures. They arise and flourish in *opposition* to their current cultures and dominant institutions. During periods of moral laxity and loose, permissive institutions, we should expect to have emerge tight, hierarchical and dogmatic organizations. In a differnet time period, for instance, during epochs of moral rigidity (e.g. Puritan New England), movements are more likely to emphasize individual freedom and group participation. When social control is amorphous and fragmentary, as in our own epoch, liberation movements stressing individual expression and self-fulfillment arise in response to or are offset by opposing movements emphasizing order and self-effacement (e.g., Black Muslims *vs.* Black Power). The general rule, by way of a hypothesis is: *commitment organizations model themselves in reverse to what they are reacting against.* Thus, their framework may be an entire culture or society, a dominant institution or social sector, or another social movement.

As a subtype of collective organization, Rothschild-Whitt's schema is useful. What are the virtues of democracy, she asks, in light of some fairly severe organizational limitations? Democracy takes its toll, Rothschild-Whitt admits. It is time-consuming; it demands more self-discipline than standard organizations; it encourages less diversity in recruiting and retaining participants; it leads to heightened emotional intensity, causing "burn-out," and it must cope with nondemocratic participants who resist essential organizational processes. In addition, commitment organizations confront environmental constraints over which they exert little power or influence.

On the plus side, democratic participation can alter people's values, the quality of their work and, eventually, their identities. As behavior-shaping institutions, egalitarian-alternative organizations are probably too limited to achieve their self-appointed tasks. They remain isolated examples of amateur collectivism in the context of capitalist-bureaucratic society.

Social Structure and Ideology

Commitment organizations tend to become highly *pervasive*. Becoming a member entails not only learning specific tasks, but also coming to see those tasks—the activities of the organization in general and the events in its environment—in terms of a more or less coherent ideology. The member is often required to give proof that he or she has acquired the ideology and is able to apply it. Socialization and monitoring of beliefs is most effectively done in tightly knit small groups of members who have regular contact with one another. Group affiliation is a major source of identity, reward and punishment. The group meeting becomes an important arena for social control in commitment organizations. Confrontation, the sanctioning of straying members, and exhortation, the explanation of actions and events in terms of the movement's ideology, are regular features of the "rap" sessions, cell meeting, or "conscience sessions." The public confession of transgressions, self-criticism and denunciations by fellow group members render the psychological climate of such sessions intensely emotional. The indoctrination and the sanctions are effective because they come from persons whom the member identifies with and feels close to.

In bureaucracies leadership is based on formal position in the organization, and in professions, on competence certification. In commitment organizations leaders must embody the ideology and values of the movement; spiritual, charismatic authority may be combined with position and competence to buttress a person's standing in the movement. Invariably, rather than status or authority, values remain the basis of any final appeal.

Many contemporary commitment movements in America are strongly opposed to hierarchy, division of labor and formal rules for the conduct of the organization. Feminist organizations are especially insistent on this opposition. And Alcoholics Anonymous, as we shall see in the next chapter, has little formal structure. But many other commitment organizations show hierarchy, formalism and division of labor to varying extents. Religious orders (e.g., the early Jesuits), secret societies (e.g., the early Freemasons) and militant ethnic organizations (e.g., the Black Muslims) are commitment organizations that contain hierarchies, complex rules and division of labor. As long as organizational position coincides with moral authority, hierarchy may, as in other organizations, help effectiveness by concentrating decision making, skills, resources and information. The rules of commitment organizations may be less specific and explicit than those of bureaucracies. The indoctrinated member is expected to be able to apply the ideology and traditions of the organization to the situations and events that he or she encounters (see, for example, Ouchi, 1980). In many alternative settings, the division of labor is not compatible with ideological indoctrination and monitoring, an issue causing great distress to members. The strong opposition to hierarchy, formal rules and division of labor in contemporary American commitment organizations very likely derives from the countercultures' opposition to an industrial society in which bureaucracy, formalism and specialization have gotten out of hand. Yet, specialization is often necessary to achieve goals, a condition that interferes with the ideological state, according to participants. In the case of feminism, it is easy to see how the opposition to male domination and rigid division of labor in the family gets translated into highly egalitarian and unspecialized commitment organizations. In general, commitment movements arise in opposition to some establishment, and are likely to organize themselves as *reversals* of the enemy. For instance, if the establishment is seen as morally lax, the movement will insist on tight moral norms, and if the enemy is profit-oriented, specialized and hierarchical, then the movement will stress communal values of cooperation and equality.[2] But the movement's environment may render some reversals unfeasible: a commitment organization that operates as a secret society may be forced to adopt a tight hierarchical structure.

We need more studies of how contemporary nonhierarchical commitment organizations are managed on a day-to-day basis. It would seem that the operating units would have to be small, if they are to be run nonhierarchically with shifting incumbents in the positions and without detailed and articulated work rules. How else would activities get coordinated and jobs followed through to completion? Bureaucracies can be large because control and information are concentrated in a small number of points, and most members need only a small amount of information relevant to their tasks. In order for a large, highly decentralized organization without any hierarchy or permanent position for incumbents to run efficiently, it would seem to require an extraordinary amount of indoctrination. Commitment movements vary widely in the contents of their ideologies. But one can discern some similarities in style:

(A) Commitment movements see the world in terms of "either-or," i.e., *dualistic* concepts (Davis and Anderson, 1979). The concepts are *sharply bounded;* that is, one is either black or white—nothing is "gray," or undetermined. For instance, one is a sinner or saved, for or against the movement, inside or outside the group, part of the "problem" or part of the "solution," an alcoholic or nondrinker.

(B) Commitment movements are very much preoccupied with persons' *selves,* since a major task that they set for themselves is the resocializing of members. *Honesty* in self-presentation is a strongly held value, and the member is expected to strip away roles, masks and poses in order to make the true self public, translucent. The self-criticism and denunciations at the hands of other group members often center around whether the member is honest, that is, projects his or her true self, at least to the in-group.

These two ideological features seem to have consequences for the social structure of commitment organizations. Groups that insist on sharply defined categories, on boundaries between the movement and the world, and that spend a great deal of time in a relentless inward search for members' true selves and motives, should generate a great deal of internal strife and factionalism. Dissidents must be expelled, or if a faction fails to convince a majority, it must leave the group. Fragmentation, often defined on ideological grounds, is common in commitment movements. New groups and sects often repeat the break-up process on their own after they have split off from a church or movement. The sect that is closest to one's own becomes the worst enemy, because it is here that the problems of defining the precise boundary are the most acute.

Thes two features, dualistic concepts and honesty, also limit the efficiency of commitment movements in their political dealings with other organizations in the larger society. Fragmented movements typically have a more difficult time mobilizing political strength than unified ones. In making alliances, goals must be left ambiguous and one must agree to let one's own motives and those of others remain masked. Thus, a good deal of hypocrisy and dissimulation is necessary for effective political action, a concept that runs counter to the ideology. The cult of honesty, the belief that one should "let it all hang out," often turns out to be disastrous in bargaining between alliance partners.

(C) Commitment movements often "crystallize" their ideologies around a small number of central images that get invested with much affective content: "Black Power," Aztec eagle emblems (for the United Farm Workers Movement), "reproduction by choice," "total abstinence as the only cure of alcoholism," "a woman's absolute control over her body." Such themes provide dominant *myths* of the movements.[3] Recitation of the myths is central to the movement's liturgy. They legitimate and rally members against oppression by setting a counterimage of power. For example, the farm workers are the heirs of the Aztec warriors and hence invincible. Women's sexuality is entirely their own and does not belong to their husbands or lovers. Some of the stridency of the mythic discourse of commitment movements may be rooted in doubt and even despair. Just as the myth of romantic love is a dominant cultural theme precisely because love and family relationships are transitory and fragile, so does, to cite another example, the slogan "Black Power" mask the economic and political weakness of the black masses. Myths *distort* by concealing the facts that the movement does not want to talk about: that a few alcoholics are able to return to moderate social drinking, that neither women nor men have absolute control over their bodies, that the *compesinos* are not tribal warriors but rural proletarians, whose natural allies are other dispossessed groups in society and that most blacks do not participate in politics even by voting.

(D) Deploring the competition, hierarchy, and goal-oriented focus in bureaucratic delivery of human services, commitment organizations take a strong stand for *separatism* and *self-help*. Separatists make their appeals on grounds of self-improvement and moral superiority. Only "they" can be counted upon to attack existing social arrangements and inequalities. Doing it alone is accomplished in the name of independence, class pride, ethnic consciousness or self-confidence. A radical, working class wife in mid-Victorian England spoke of her faith in the capacity of committed individuals to overcome difficulties:

> I would like to tell you what I think all this teaches us—and it is that all our help, all our salvation lies in ourselves. We have proved it by experience. It lies not with our masters, nor with our churches, but in our cultivation of those higher qualities which are lying dormant in our natures.
>
> (Quoted from Tholfsen, 1977:259)

In projecting an idealized social organization as a means of rectifying social injustices, members are in danger of losing all contact with the enemy forces.

Semiotic Model of Social Movement

Semiotics, the general study of meanings (Eco, 1976; Barthes, 1968), can be applied to the study of social movements to analyze the context of meanings through which movements advocate, implement, resist or sustain social change. Such meanings go beyond a psychology of motives. Rather, they are the nonvisible part of the social structure, or what Charles Lemert (1979) calls the "absent to view" world that must be explicated. The semiotic analysis assumes that the often strident and bizarre rhetorics of commitment organizations point toward collective aspirations, fears and resentments that are often unarticulated or imperfectly articulated and that give the movement its moral energies. The rhetoric serves to rally the members, to challenge the legitimacy of opposing views, to expose injustices, contradictions and biases, and to speak about what has been forbidden or unsayable. The semiotics of the movement is the detailed study of how the rhetoric accomplishes these different tasks.

There are three general questions involved in the semiotic study of a social movement: (1) the level of analysis, (2) the interpretative framework or perspective and (3) the intertextuality, that is, the relationship of the movement's discourse to other discourses.

Level of analysis may be individual interpretive behavior or collective action. At the individual level, analysis may entail studying the discourse of movement participation, such as the body of ideas, values or practices and how persons talk about socialization, identity change and role conflict. At the collective level, analysis focuses on the production and reproduction of themes, and the ways in which these reflect opposition to or identification with larger collectivities. Here we wish to find out how themes are transformed as they move from one social collectivity to another, and what meanings are lost or gained in this transformation process (Foucault, 1973; 1976; 1977a; 1977b).

By the *interpretive framework* we refer to vision, world view, ideology, social and moral insights, the entire metaphysics of understanding. Social movements carry a heavy emotional loading for participants, opponents and investigators. Such moral, social and affective materials cannot be eliminated or wished away, but must be incorporated into the analysis. For example, in the emergent phase of the social movement, how do deviant sentiments—resentment, hostility, hatred or what Nietzsche called the "slave morality" —get translated into a transcendent or higher ethic? And how does the social movement analyst treat these movement appeals to "higher morality" against a lower one—as real or spurious experiences; as a tragic, funny or absurd discourse?

Intertextuality focuses on the comparative semiotics of social movements. Often a movement finds discourses left behind by previous movements and uses them, reinterprets them, adds to them and extends them into new areas. This means that each social movement is an installment in a semiotic process that leaves its *traces* in the collectively available discourse (Chomsky, 1972; Derrida, 1976). Even though any one movement may be short-lived or have minimal impact, it contributes to the available theoretical resources. Such traces include misunderstandings of semiotic remains. Thus, the women's movement came *after* the civil rights movement and used its themes of justice and equality for minorities to build a liberal constituency. That women form a numerical majority having multiple classes, statuses and occupations, and are intimately aligned with dominant men in kin and family ties that foster lifelong interdependencies primarily with men, rather than women, is usually ignored by ideologists. Metaphors of "caste," "social exclusion" and "oppression" used by civil rights protestors provided powerful themes for the feminist movement in the 1960s and 1970s (Freeman, 1973; Hymowitz and Weissman, 1978, 1978; Huber, ed., 1973).

Reexamination of social movement discourses requires a historical and comparative outlook. This shows the source of the movement's themes, more likely borrowed ideas, and the transformation of ideologies over time. For example, the practice of passive disobedience among Hindus in India against Great Britain's colonial rule adopted Christian themes to win freedom from Western rule. When organized Southern black Christian leaders sought a strong myth to launch their civil rights campaign, they drew upon Mahatma Gandhi's writings on civil disobedience. But black power, the Northern urban movement that succeeded the rural Southern Christian version of civil rights, repudiated most of the passive resistance tenets of the earlier movement. Instead, new tactics were adopted, including overt disobedience and urban guerrilla violence, more suited to what urban black leaders believed to be their true social conditions of institutional racism and class oppression (Sharp, 1970; Eisenger, 1973; Gamson, 1975; Lieberson and Silverman, 1965; Tabb, 1970; and Lowi, 1971).

Foucault (1973) draws attention to the *silences* in a culture, the lacunae in the discourse—what can and what cannot be said. Social movements may not be original as much as revelatory. They expose the socially unspeakable and provide terms for talking about it.

Take the abortion reform movement discussed in chapter 7. The wild talk that arose when the tabooed topic was first raised has opened up new ways of expressing the unsayable. Motherhood as a choice, the fear of genocide of blacks through coercive contraception and abortion, male violence against women—these new discourses have been generated out of the original abortion discourse.

Using a trace analysis, we can compare, follow up, and even anticipate movement themes and programs. Within these movements there is a complex but understandable logic. Themes can be unpacked and distributed in terms of equivalence or incompatibility, depending on the context. Sometimes the themes are absurd and communicate the reverse of the speaker's intention. When Ti-Grace Atkinson (1974), a radical feminist and socialist talks about liberating the woman's body from involuntary pregnancy, she borrows the language of capitalism—the terms of private property—an outlook she explicitly rejects.

Looking Ahead: Two Case Studies

In the next two chapters we present two case studies of commitment organizations. The first, Alcoholics Anonymous, is a movement that developed in the 1920s to provide self-help and support among alcohol abusers; the second is concerned with alternative health organizations for women. Both movements must be seen against the backgrounds of the discourses about alcohol use and the bodies of women that have their roots in the nineteenth century. Both alcohol use and women's bodies, especially their sexual functions, were, in the not-so-distant past, stigmatized; one talked about them in terms of suppression, denial and disapproval, using sterotyped concepts.

Among native Christians in 19th-century America, alcohol use was viewed as a sign of social inferiority and animalism. The then lower orders—immigrants, ethnics, Catholics, urban working class-regularly used alcohol as a social and recreative activity (Gusfield, 1963). Nonuse of alcohol among white, higher-status, middle class groups became symbolic of moral rectitude and thus a boundary mechanism that divided insiders, the morally eligible participants, from outsiders, the drinking lower classes. As long as alcohol use carried these meanings, dominant classes could successfully deny underdogs civil liberties. Once drinking became part of the American way of life, no amount of moral crusading about the evils of alcohol was effective for keeping socially inferior groups in line.

Throughout most of the Christian epoch, women have occupied

an inferior status in patriarchal society. Like children, they have been seen but not heard; and like slaves, they were a possession of their master. But unlike children, women legitimately sleep with and intimately share in the life cycle of their oppressor; and unlike slaves, they have willingly identified with and loved those who dominate them. Until recently, legal and civil rights have been nonexistent, inoperative or severly limited for women in democratic states. During the nineteenth century, when the first feminist movement arose, new demands for equality and opportunity were throttled by medical ideology (Wood, 1974:1-22). Women's bodies were subsequently expropriated by the newly emergent medical speciality of gynecology, an all-male domain. Body talk remained an emotionally loaded or silenced arena until first the planned-parenthood movement and then the abortion movement arose with updated rhetorics of choice and self-responsibility within the woman's personal experience, not society's expectations.

CHAPTER 10—NOTES

[1] Heberle (1951) emphasizes the role of the age generation in the development of social movements. Such age strata perceive themselves linked by a community of beliefs, world views and wishes, and thereby define their "politically relevant historical experiences" as a collective morality. This analysis may have special relevance for the youth and ethnic movements generated during the 1960s and 1970s. As an exclusive explanation for the emergence of social movements, though, it ignores other status features (e.g., sex, class, ethnicity, etc.).

[2] This reversal hypothesis seems to fit many cases, but should of course be subjected to cross-cultural tests.

[3] See Barthes (1972) for a discussion of myth; Barthes gives a theoretical analysis, and presents many examples of myth and analysis. Further examples are found in Barthes, *The Eiffel Tower and Other Mythologies* (1979).

Chapter 11
Alcoholics Anonymous:
A Self-Help Movement Without Hierarchies

> We admitted we were powerless over alcohol—that our lives had become unmanageable.
>
> From "The Big Book," Alcoholics Anonymous

This chapter continues our analysis of commitment organizations by discussing one of the most well-known and successful movements for control and rehabilitation to emerge in this century, Alcoholics Anonymous. This voluntary group is an almost pure case of the commitment organization as it was characterized in the previous chapter. From modest beginnings in the Midwest in the late 1920s, this organization has grown into a network of groups that now span the North American continent, and its methods, ideology and forms of organization have been copied in other countries.

Alcoholism and Social Control
In our drug-ridden society, alcohol is the most widely used addictive substance. We lack accurate figures on exactly how much alcohol is consumed by various categories of persons or how many men and women in different age, social, ethnic and religious groups are totally or partially dependent on the frequent use of alcohol. We do know that countless social and personal tragedies result from this dependence. There are a variety of more or less plausible medical, sociological and psychological theories about the proper definition of alcoholism and its roots. Some researchers speculate about biochemical factors that make some persons unable to drink moderately, while others attempt to trace psychological or social causes. (See Robinson, 1976, chapter 3, for a survey of these theories.) Since our discussion focuses on the issues of social control, we need not attempt to take any positions for or against the theories. Whatever its origins, alcoholism is a widely recognized problem, partly real and partly socially constructed.

Alcoholism, in its severe manifestations, is extremely difficult to change. Psychiatrists sometimes confess that they have given up on alcoholics. Physicians report that alcoholics are in and out of hospitals and clinics without fundamentally changing their addiction patterns. Often periods of sobriety alternate with drinking bouts, which may become heavier and heavier, resulting in the loss of jobs and family and, for a few, residence on skid row (see, for example, Wiseman, 1970).

Because of its demonstrated success for believers, its unique structure and its ways of working, Alcoholics Anonymous (AA) is of profound interest to anyone who wants to think seriously about social control. It is impossible to tell how successful the AA program is in comparison with other approaches; claims and counterclaims have been made. Some time ago a study by the RAND corporation showed that following treatment many alcoholics were able to return to stable, moderate drinking. For AA, drinking is an all-or-nothing matter for the alcoholic. Spokespersons for AA and groups influenced by AA hotly disputed the RAND report. Whatever the merits of such judgments and counterclaims, it is clear beyond argument that large numbers of persons with severe drinking problems have been helped by AA, and that many have acquired and are maintaining sober lives.[1]

Excessive drinking used to be defined in moral-religious terms; drinkers were said to be "weak," to have "character deficiencies" and to be in need of moral or spiritual redemption. Saloons and other drinking establishments became the symbols of a social disease. The Prohibitionist movement believed that making alcohol unavailable would cure a major social problem. This moral metaphor only gradually gave way to a presently dominant *disease conception* of alcoholism.

The change from a moralizing to a medical conception of alcoholism was the result of a concerted campaign involving members of AA, the Yale Center for Alcohol Studies and some voluntary organizations. The National Council of Alcoholism continues to educate the public to the medical view through the local community (see Cahn, 1970, and Schneider, 1978).

Alcoholism is characterized as an "allergy," (Alcoholics Anonymous, "The Big Book"), a "disease of the will," a "combined physical and mental condition" or a "problem with the sugar balance in the blood." Members of AA believe that most people can be taught to drink socially in a normal way, but that some 10-12 percent of drinkers have whatever it takes to make them problem drinkers, and eventually, alcohol dependents. Members of AA do not frown upon the drinking of alcoholic beverages, but define *themselves* as persons with a problem. In AA, there is no trace of the moral-contamination metaphor that reigned in the Anti-Saloon League or in the Women's Christian Temperance League (Gusfield, 1963). Many community mental health clinics have alcoholism floors or wards; in these facilities alcoholism or problem drinking are treated as medical syndromes. Codifying interviews with informants who were treated at one community mental health clinic, most of the personnel spoke to them in terms of *disease* metaphors with slightly varying contents. On one occasion, a local clergy member was brought into a session, with mandatory attendance, to give the patients a dressing-down: "I wouldn't trust any one of you. You are all habitual liars," were his opening statements. This throwback to the moralistic definition seems to have embarrassed both staff and patients.

The medicalization of problem drinking does not preclude mandatory and negative labeling. In the alcoholism floor of a community mental health clinic observed by one of the authors, the day's program was geared to rubbing the label "alcoholic" into every patient. Group "therapy" sessions, lectures and graphic demonstrations of the drinker's progress were conducted by the center's personnel, all giving the message, "you are an alcoholic," and, "we will approve of you when you publicly admit that." When a recalcitrant patient finally was made to confess in a group session, "I am an alcoholic," smiles of relief broke out on the faces of the therapists *and* copatients alike. It was clear the "alcoholic" and "nonalcoholic" were strictly binary categories; it was not possible to define oneself as a person with a drinking problem, who was not addicted, but was in need of some treatment. Conversion to the view of the problem in terms of absolutist all-or-nothing categories is, as we argued in the preceding chapter, typical for commitment movements. In order to maintain the commitment, rigorous boundaries between the inside and the outside have to be created for members. Shades of meanings and concepts that admit vagueness and ambiguity cannot be used for such a purpose.

In the clinic, the absolutist, social-movement ideology of Alcoholics Anonymous was given professional recognition at least by being publicly sponsored by the medical staff. Attendance at AA meetings, held at the clinic and at the local AA clubhouse, was ordered. Treatment of patients in hospitals, according to the standard medical belief and value system, is based upon established and tested medical knowledge. Yet, in the case of alcoholism, the beliefs and practices of the lay commitment organization have come to dominate the public thinking of the professionals as well, whatever their doubts about the empirical evidence for the claims of the social movement. This reflects, we suggest, the ambiguous attitudes that the medical professions have toward the problem. It is felt by many professionals that if alcoholism is a disease at all, it is not readily incorporated into the categories of scientific medicine. But since theological and moralistic definitions of social problems are no longer very credible, and since alcohol abuse produces a variety of medical side effects (ulcers, liver disease, psychiatric disturbances and so on) medicine has fallen into the treatment of alcoholics in spite of misgivings. Physicians, in turn, are likely to depend upon the presence of AA with its strongly articulated message as the best possible long-term prospect for the abuse drinker.

There may well be serious unintended drawbacks to this wholehearted acceptance of the AA message among professionals and the agencies concerned with alcoholism. Among the patients in the clinic that we observed, there were persons who insisted that they were not alcoholics in the sense of the absolutist AA definition but admittedly needed help to overcome their excessive drinking habits. By patients and professionals alike such persons were accused of being deniers of what was obvious to others and were told that denial is, in fact, a typical symptom of full-fledged alcoholism. In the group sessions this clearly put the patient at a great disadvantage; he or she could not possibly win. It is likely that many drinkers who need help to achieve a controlled alcohol habit are alienated by such experiences.

One of the most disturbing aspects of the label "alcoholic" is that it is often attached to persons as a convenient way of keeping them in line when other problems — for instance, among family members or in organizations — are too unsettling to face. In the clinic we observed, there were persons who had been brought in through what has been called "the betrayal funnel." Spouses, children and coworkers, supported by the clinic professionals, convinced them that they needed treatment for alcoholism. But since the clinic is dominated by the AA ideology, little search needs to occur for the specific nature of the problem. Does the patient need treatment with behavior modification based on social-learning theory to learn moderate drinking? Or is the drinking a symptom of sexual incompatibility or other strains in a marriage, or stresses at work? Or, does the person suffer from a compulsive craving for alcohol that can be contained through total abstinence? The absolutist, social movement ideology can easily define such questions as evasions. The patients' real troubles consequently remain concealed. Professional medical ideologies have in the past served analogous functions of social control and concealment. For example, Ann Douglas Wood (1974) has shown how the prevailing treatment of women's disorders in the nineteenth century served to maintain women's passivity and submissiveness. Women discontented with the dominant family and gender roles could legitimately be contained through long periods of bed rest, long baths, clitoridectomies or painful cauterizations of the uterus (done in the name of medical knowledge by respected professionals). It is likely that all social control institutions or belief systems become productive of mischief when they become hegemonic. The social and individual problems that they attempt to define and control are not unidimensional, and rarely can be fitted into a few, clear-cut categories. Diagnosis and treatment must be adapted to the specific and concrete contexts and concerns. Policy-makers and those who carry out policies and treatments must be aware of the often initially hidden realities of human and social predicaments, and must resist the temptation to routinely use absolutist categories.

But whatever the drawbacks of making the methods and beliefs of Alcoholics Anonymous the official view of a complex social problem, the organization apparently has succeeded in its primary mission. Tens of thousands of men and women lead sober and productive lives through regular practice of the organization's program and activities.

From the point of view of the concerns dealt with in this book, two aspects of the work of AA assume special importance. First, AA has clearly demonstrated that it is possible to transform persons who have been stigmatized by the community and who have accepted strongly negative labels ("drunk," "loser," "worthless" and so on) into individuals with a sense of self-respect who are highly thought of and lead productive, caring and outreaching lives.

AA is a revitalization movement in the sense discussed in the previous chapter. Briefly, revitalization is the total transformation of a person's self-conception, the categories by which the person defines his or her self-identity and place in the world. Such self-changes must, the sociology of symbolic interactionism teaches us, take place in groups of significant others (Manis and Meltzer, 1972). But not all such groups become revitalization groups. AA accomplishes its task through a combination of distinct beliefs and practices that evolved early in the history of the movement. They seem familiar to a sociologist steeped in Durkheim's ideas about religion and symbolic interactionism, but the doctrine developed out of practice rather than theoretical speculations. In addition, AA is remarkably free from hierarchy and stratification both on the organizational and local-group levels. This is unusual, since, as we have argued, industrial societies duplicate the hierarchical mode in almost all of their organizations. As pointed out in the preceding chapter, critics of the present society use the value-oriented movement to protest against existing structures and often advocate nonhierarchical forms of organization to achieve their ends.

Theory of Alcoholics Anonymous

Alcoholics Anonymous possesses an aritculate set of beliefs about individuals and groups. The prescribed recovery from drinking must follow systematic practices based on this theory. Gregory Bateson, who has written a very perceptive analysis of AA based on his own observations in VA hospitals (Bateson, 1972), correctly shows that the basis of the AA theory involves a distinction between the individual and the social self. The self is not identical with the physical person inside a skin, but is a complex of roles and intrinsic, interpenetrating relationships *to significant other persons.* Alcoholism is embedded in a social way of life, but most traditional treatment fails because the focus is on the single individual in isolation from his or her roles and significant relationships. As a social formation and discourse, alcoholism includes society's ceremonial use of alcohol to reach euphoria, and to signify solidarity and affiliation. The underlying perception, especially for men, is that alcohol is a dangerous substance that a *real* man can deal with; thus, the drinker's self-image is that of being a man who is in control of the substance, and is based upon the approval given to him when he shows that he *is,* while using it to be "one of the boys." *Not* to control the danger is to be less of a man. The alcoholic's problem is, paradoxically, that he tries very hard to be *in control,* but fails, experiencing more and more anxiety, which has to be relieved with more alcohol. For AA members, the solution is not to learn finally to master the techniques of being in control, but to admit that they *cannot* be ("giving up"). Therefore, the user comes to define alcohol as one of many other events that he simply does not claim to control (along with the weather or serious illness). Trying to control becomes uncoupled from self-esteem, approval and status. The alcoholic needs to learn new ways of experiencing and signifying affiliation, emotional satisfaction and coping with pain. A whole interpersonal script has to be redone.

The AA theory is in this respect very reminiscent of one of the basic "organicist" intuitions behind George Herbert Mead's (see Manis and Meltzer, 1972) symbolic interactionist position. There has emerged in recent social psychology a certain amount of evidence that Mead's insight and that of AA are correct. What we are used to thinking of as very private experiences, inaccessible to others—for instance, the interpretation of our emotional states— depends on cues and feedback from others (Schachter and Singer, 1962).

The recovery from drinking must, according to the AA doctrine, consist in a total reorganization of the complex of roles and relationships that make up the person's self.

The most important formulation—the recovery program—is contained in the "twelve steps," but it is supplemented with the twelve traditions and by the case histories in "The Big Book" of AA *Alcoholics Anonymous.* The twelve steps read as follows:

Step One: We admitted we were powerless over alcohol—that our lives had become unmanageable.

Step Two: Came to believe that a Power greater than ourselves could restore us to sanity.

Step Three: Made a decision to turn our will and our lives over to the care of God "as we understand Him."

Step Four: Made a searching and fearless moral inventory of ourselves.

Step Five: Admitted to God, to ourselves and to another human being the exact nature of our wrongs.

Step Six: Were entirely ready to have God remove all these defects of character.

Step Seven: Humbly asked Him to remove our shortcomings.

Step Eight: Made a list of all persons we had harmed, and became willing to make amends to them all.
Step Nine: Made direct amends to such people wherever possible, except when to do so would injure them or others.
Step Ten: Continued to take personal inventory and when we were wrong promptly admitted it.
Step Eleven: Sought through prayer and meditation to improve our conscious contact with God "as we understood Him," praying only for knowledge of His will for us and the power to carry that out.
Step Twelve: Having had a spiritual awakening as the result of these steps, we tried to carry this message to alcoholics, and to practice these principles in all our affairs.

These steps are to be taken in order. The alcoholic proceeds from the acceptance that he has "hit bottom," is incapable of fighting the drinking and craving for alcohol on his own. Accepting and learning to internalize the labels "alcoholic" and "helpless" are essential for the beginning of spiritual and moral regeneration. The person who admits that the self is organized by the two labels is expressing his willingness to abide by the decisions of the group, accept its norms and clean out the debris of the failed existence. Conversion, the rebirth of a cleansed self, can then begin.

The twelve steps prescribe a rigorous self-examination and dependence on the continual guidance of other AA members. Most of the time at AA meetings is spent interpreting the various steps for members, drawing upon the experience of the movement but also on the particular life experiences of the group members. Self-deception, self-pity and resentment are seen as powerful forces that impede recovery, so the group meetings often take on an atmosphere of confrontation. One could expect that this group process leads to self-righteous moralism, scapegoating and victimization. This does not seem to happen very often. The moral authority of members who have spent years in the movement and who are known to have good programs for their own lives suffices to control the zealotry of the newly converted. The phrase "a Power greater than ourselves" is meant to stress the necessity for the alcoholic who desires rehabilitation to submit to the support, experience and practices of the movement. Self-righteousness is interpreted as *pride,* the false individualistic belief that one can go it *alone.* This state of mind, it is argued, is often the first stage in slipping back into drinking. Even members who have a good deal of moral authority are seen as *interpreters* of the wisdom that resides in the movement; efforts are made to discourage dependence on particular individuals in the group. Stories are often told about how even those persons with good programs and years of sobriety have slipped.

Members who do exercise moral leadership at meetings are often closely knit and seem to watch one another for signs of self-righteousness. In conversations with AA members, one often finds them engaging in close self-scrutiny on this point.

AA as a Normative, Pervasive, Social Movement

Having "hit bottom" and yet succeeding with the help of AA to reorganize one's life around sobriety should create a strong emotional bond between the alcoholic and the movement. He or she literally owes everything to AA. Like other movements based on conversion experiences, AA is strongly normative. Yet the members are typically not proselytizers. They are willing to help each other and those outsiders who request help, but do not advocate teetotalism or prohibition. The normative fervor is usually expressed at AA meetings and in contacts inside the movement.

Relationships within the movement are often pervasive. From an insider's perspective, AA approximates a total institution (Goffman, 1962). Once the moral hold on the member is weakened, though, the pervasive feature is lost. Hence, the intense effort by established members toward promoting mutual dependence and combining their AA activities as a comprehensive way of life. Decisions that on the surface do not involve a person's sobriety, e.g., taking a new job, going on vacation, changing marital status or making major purchases, lead to consultations with peers or sponsors in the movement. Many of the very active members have a majority of their social contacts within Alcoholics Anonymous. Many of these persons as true believers have "closed minds" (Rokeach, 1960). Attempts to discuss the program intellectually are met with impatience or ridicule. There are strong norms against "intellectualizing the program." Members are reminded that they have resumed productive lives by adhering to the program after long periods of catastrophic dependence on alcohol. Having seen the changes that the program made in their own lives, they are not willing to tamper with it. The program works and that is enough. And since most members of AA are not intellectuals, but come from a very wide variety of walks of life, the norms against "intellectualizing" and "rewriting the program" guarantee that Alcoholics Anonymous meetings do not turn into debating societies dominated by skillful manipulators of ideas and words.

Many revitalization movements make distinctions between the elect and the nonelect, the saved and the damned, and so on. The insiders are described in strong positive terms, and outsiders in negative ones; there is sometimes hope for the outsiders if they can be persuaded to become insiders. In Alcoholics Anonymous, one rarely encounters this way of thinking. At meetings, one hears strong warnings against self-righteousness. The successful, nonalcoholic, social drinker is not frowned upon; rather, it is the AA member who is a part of that minority that is unable to drink moderately on social occasions that is the members' concern.

To what extent is Alcoholics Anonymous a religious movement? It uses a partly religious vocabulary. Meetings are frequently ended with the Lord's Prayer. "There is a God in these meetings" is an expression heard in AA. But it is not conventional religious reference. Bateson (1972) calls it a "Durkheimian religion." This seems an apt statement. God is seen as immanent in the fellowship of AA and in the program of recovery. The higher power can be identified with the movement, its practices, experience and traditions. Some members will add more conventional Christian ideas to this. It is not surprising that a movement that deals with strong affect, and in which many members come to see their lives completely and dramatically changed for the better (and which also is of Midwestern origin) should adopt some of the vocabulary of Christian revivalism. The vocabulary of revivalism is in American popular culture the only one readily available for speaking about profound and dramatic experiences, personal crises and conversions from a burdensome way of life to a different, serene one. It is no more surprising that AA uses religious terminology than do the revitalization movements among the Blacks, especially those with a religious character.

Social movements must deal with the problem of how to get their members committed to the movement. Alcoholics Anonymous resembles in some ways the utopian communities Rosabeth M. Kanter (1972) analyzes in her discussion of the notion of commitment. Like these communities, AA aims at a reconstruction of the ways of life of the members and possesses an explicit ideology, buttressed with norms about how to go about life on a day-to-day basis. Unlike the communities discussed by Kanter, AA is not spatially localized; instead, the active members form networks, dispersed in the population at large. This has consequences for the commitment process. "Slipping" members of communities would have found it hard to hide from surveillance and confrontation by fellow members. With the exception of persons who live in halfway houses, members of AA expose themselves to monitoring, pressures and confrontations only if they choose to attend meetings or make contact with other members. The AA network also links persons coming from very diverse social backgrounds. The movement cannot count on homogeneity in personal and ethical values, socialization, occupational group interests, political outlook or religious views to sustain the cohesion of the network. Material gains are not used to create commitment, as is done in business, professional groups and labor unions. Personal charisma on the part of leaders held together many of the utopian communities described by Kanter, but this is discouraged in AA. Synanon, which started as an AA halfway house, requires members to sign their property and incomes over to the movement, as was the practice in many 19th-century utopian communities (Kanter, 1972: 82, table 2). Members of AA meetings are asked for small donations (one dollar is a common contribution) to help defray expenses for coffee, rent for the meeting room or janitor services; but these donations are hardly sufficient to create any commitment. Ultimately, the pervasive orientation inside AA is a matter of the person's choices. Those who want to slip out of the groups or only attend infrequently may easily do so. But the core of the movement contains persons whose commitments are based on the conversion experience and maintained through constant self-criticism and criticism from others. There exist no figures, of course, but one can guess that only a rather small proportion of persons who at some point have contact with AA become members of the highly committed core groups.

Some Sociological Aspects of Alcoholics Anonymous

In this section, we discuss Alcoholics Anonymous in terms of conventional sociological analysis by locating the movement in relation to other movements and the typology of control systems. Our evidence comes from informant interviews with members of Alcoholics Anonymous in one Middlewestern location. There is a national organization with headquarters in New York City, a newspaper entitled *The Grapevine* and a central directory of telephone numbers, groups and contacts all over the country. State and national conventions are also held on a regular basis. There are several publications, the most important of which is "The Big Book," entitled *Alcoholics Anonymous*. Also, a variety of other publications are used by members of the movement and referred to at meetings.

Members come into the movement in different ways. Some contact Alcoholics Anonymous on their own or after someone has suggested it, having discovered that their drinking habits are unmanageable. Others go through hospital programs, designed for detoxification and rudimentary education about alcoholism. There are no formal criteria for membership, except as stated in the fifth chapter of "The Big Book": desire to stop drinking. The central metaphor is *disease;* the term "allergy" is sometimes used. For diseases there are treatment programs that have to be rigorously adhered to by those who want to recover. AA insists on a regimen. But Alcoholics Anonymous avoids specifying too closely the definition of an alcoholic. It avoids, for instance, the issue of whether alcoholism always is a physiological (or psychological) addiction. "Alcoholic" is, by and large, a *self-definition.* The metaphor is left vague to accommodate a variety of self-definitions. Any person who believes that he or she has "hit the bottom" of a drinking career, whether sick or socially deviant or not, and is willing to start working the AA program of recovery, is welcome. By making alcoholism a matter of self-definition and willingness to seek help, AA avoids metaphor controversy. There is, for instance, a minimum of arguing among members about who was more or less of an alcoholic before coming into the program. Also, discussions about "the real nature of alcoholism," or of medical or psychological theories of alcoholism are not often encountered in AA. The focus is on the efforts of the individual member to do something about *his* or *her* drinking problem and related problems of personal development, regardless of how serious the drinking problem or problems of recovery.

In its local activities the movement has two units: the *meeting* and the *network.* The meeting is the basic unit of the movement. The meeting is *not* a chapter or a club, in any formally constituted sense. It is simply a group of persons, men and/or women, who come together regularly (once a week is common) for a set period of time to discuss their programs and progress of recovery. One becomes a member of a meeting if one keeps coming. One is also welcome to visit a meeting on a casual basis. But meetings usually contain core groups of members, often persons who have made a public commitment to attend a specific meeting for a given period of time.

There are no prescribed procedures for organizing a meeting. Any group of participants who can find a locale and a time to meet may constitute itself as a meeting. Sometimes such meetings are constituted on exclusionary bases: there are meetings for physicians only, for men only, for women only, for gay people and for nonsmokers. New meetings sometimes come about through fission or break-up of a larger group. As one member once put it, "They usually start new meetings because they are mad!" He did not mean to be derogatory, but found it natural that a group of people who did not find what they were looking for at one meeting would constitute themselves as a new one, a common ground for inclusion or exclusion. The intense face-to-face interactions about personal and moral matters that are typical of good AA meetings are impossible in large groups; therefore, successful meetings, paradoxically, will continuously split. A meeting usually gathers once a week at the same time and in the same place. It lasts between one and two hours. Meetings are held in a variety of places—Alcoholics Anonymous clubhouses, church basements, university residence halls, hospital wards, private homes, halfway houses or even on the premises of police stations.

There are closed and open meetings. The closed meeting is for recovering alcoholics only. Open meetings are attended by members, but also by nonalcoholic members of their families, their friends, their business associates and outsiders. A closed meeting is often opened by a reading from the fifth chapter of "The Big Book" of AA, or by a prayer. The meeting may have a topic specified in advance, for instance, one or two of the 12 steps. Other meetings are discussion meetings. In some meetings the members are asked to speak in order by a chairperson, going completely around the table. At other meetings there is no formal order of speaking; members will seize the opportunities to speak as they present themselves. While such meetings are often unchaired, there is, nevertheless, a good deal of order. Interruptions occur but are discouraged, and as long as a speaker holds the floor the other members pay rather close attention to what he or she is saying. Some persons find it a good deal easier to speak up, and members vary in their eloquence. Those who remain silent are often encouraged to enter the discussion. Meetings in Alcoholics Anonymous contrast favorably with, say, faculty meetings in universities, in terms of orderliness of the proceedings, the attentiveness to the statements of others and the willingness to encourage others to speak. Even in the absence of an agenda a central topic for discussion may emerge in the early part of the meeting. A member may broach a concern, discuss a problem or mention specific troubles, and gradually other members begin to focus their remarks on similar issues in their lives; the concern becoming the agenda of the meeting, without anybody ever having planned it in that way. If a member wants to break away from an agenda constructed in this manner, he is not called to order but allowed to do so. In many cases, after such an interruption, the meeting reverts to the preexisting agenda, retaining its focus throughout the session. But many meetings do not become spontaneously organized in this fashion. Members state a variety of issues and the topic spoken about by each member is sometimes only tangentially related to what the previous speaker has spoken about. But the concern with sobriety and references to the program, as defined by the 12 steps, always provides an underlying organizing principle, regardless of diversity of topics. If a member strays from this underlying agenda, he or she can be brought back "in line" when someone says, "what has that to do with sobriety," or, "I thought this was a program of nondrinking." The intensity of the discussion can become quite high, frequently accompanied by tension release, often in the form of laughter.

Some meetings are convened to deal with the problems or behavior of a particular member. These meetings are sometimes called conscience meetings. Present are the member's sponsors and a few other persons that know the member well. During the session a good deal of hard-hitting criticism may be offered, and rather intimate details of the member's conduct and character are commented upon. The steps and other norms of the movement are used for this interpretative criticism, and suggestions on how the member could improve the conduct of his or her life.

Open meetings are often addressed by a speaker, and there is frequently little or no discussion. The speaker is most often a recovering alcoholic; the speech is a narrative of what happened to the person before coming into the movement and the changes that occurred afterward.

The core network links very active members of AA who live in an area and who attend the same or different meetings. Members of the network stay in telephone contact or drop in on other members; they get together for lunch or dinner or call upon one another for special resources. There are no explicit criteria for inclusion into this core network. Ostensibly, persons get included because of successful participation in the movement, having acquired reputations for having "good programs." It should be noted that this is not a seniority principle: some members in the network are young and carry as much authority in the network as middle-aged or older persons. Around many core members there are small groups of newer members for whom the former act as sponsors or informal counselors.

In addition to the local AA networks, there are network ties among active members or groups of members in dispersed locations. A member who has moved often keeps active ties with persons in his or her former location, recruiting them to come and speak at open meetings in the new location. In this way some old-timers in the movement exercise considerable, if indirect, authority through the far-flung networks.

On an implicit level, status stratification may operate in some locales. Large cities are more likely to have members drawn from similar class, ethnic and religious groups. In smaller cities and towns, status stratification is more likely to be successfully muted, not only because there are fewer members and hence less tendency for differentiation, but also because of potentially higher interaction rates among members who share common groups and services (e.g., shopping, schools, politics, doctors, dentists, etc.).

Position in the local cores and dispersed networks undoubtedly reflects stratification. But in its avowed program, AA stresses that this stratification is based on *moral authority* that has been tested in successful adherence to the AA program. Stratification based on conventional status characteristics, such as age, occupation, sex, possession of wealth or education, is strongly discouraged as an organizing principle. This is true for the interactions that take place at local meetings, but also seems to characterize the network. Such status characteristics get suppressed within AA, in spite of the fact that they tend to determine interaction rates, reputation, the granting of authority and power, interpersonal association and so on in most other groups. (See, for instance, the recent summary and theoretical work quoted in Berger, Fisek and Zelditch, 1977.) It is of course true that some organizations can resort to formal means to eliminate the effects of status characteristics. Such organizations are hierarchical and possess mechanisms for the exertion of power (see, for instance, Dornbusch's (1955) study of the Coast Guard Academy, and Goffman (1962). But AA accomplishes the suppression of outside status characteristics in the *absence* of much formal organization. The following is a list of mechanisms used for suppression work. This is not a definitive set, but reflects the conclusions based on our research.

(1) *Anonymity:* A person can walk into an AA meeting and simply identify himself or herself by first name, which may or may not be the person's real name. Hence, "I am Bill (or Sue) and I'm an alcoholic" is frequently the opening statement that precedes a person's discussion of problems, troubles, progress and so on in the recovery from alcohol dependence. Members of meetings that see a good deal of one another will of course eventually learn the occupations of most other members. But such knowledge has little influence in AA meetings. The use of the first name is a way of indicating that a person's education, wealth, occupation or whatever is not relevant to the task at hand. And the statement "I'm an alcoholic" refers to the *common* problem that the group members share, implying that all other considerations are irrelevant for the moment.

(2) *The Exclusive Focus:* In a meeting it is clearly defined to be inappropriate to discuss any matter other than the program of Alcoholics Anonymous. Other issues may be mentioned only in passing, and no one dwells on them. Occasionally one will hear somebody stray from the topic and somebody else ask pointedly: "What does that have to do with sobriety?" This is a normative orientation that clearly serves to keep the focus on the *joint* project of sobriety and recovery, and eliminates discussions about other topics where different persons may have specialized knowledge or real or presumed expertise. The orientation is reinforced by statements in the preamble to the 12 steps (from the "Big Book") that is often read at the beginning of a meeting. It is made very clear that the *sole* purpose of AA is to help participants stay sober, and that

the organization refuses to take stands on various political and social issues. The single-minded, normatively stressed focus on the overriding problem of the members mutes all but *one* status characteristic. The remaining status characteristic is simply a person's reputation for "having a good program." This is relevant to the purpose of the meeting, and consequently, persons with good programs exercise a good deal of moral authority.

(3) *Status Reversal:* To emphasize the recovery program as a prior commitment, status positions are sometimes reversed. We were told of one case involving a member who was instructed to go to one of the persons he himself had sponsored to receive guidance. The relationship between a sponsor and a sponsoree is clearly a kind of authority relationship. Willingness, a central value in AA, is indicated by a readiness to take instructions from one's sponsor, and to ask one's sponsor for guidance. When Don was told to ask Bob for guidance, the relationship between Bob and Don was suddenly reversed. This deliberate "imbalancing" of the authority relationship clearly serves notice both to Don and to bystanders that even the sponsor, a person with a good program, must be humble, that the reputation for having a good program is not to be taken for granted. In another case a man in his fifties was told to get one in his twenties as his sponsor. In terms of work experience, or knowledge of how to cope with life's situations (excluding alcohol abuse), the older man was considerably superior to the somewhat immature younger man. By instructing him to accept the younger man as his sponsor, both he and other members of the meeting were again told that these experiences do not matter in the sobriety program.

(4) *The Restricted Verbal Code:* If mechanisms 1-3 fail, direct pressure on members may ensue in order to avoid signs of external status characteristics. Thus, members may react jokingly or in tones of irritation if someone uses "fancy words." Language is the prime way in which differences in status characteristics (e.g., education, social class and social origin) get manifested. Such pressures (which, in fact, lead members to adopt a rather basic vocabulary) serve to suppress some external status characteristics. The practice can be quite irritating for educated persons in AA meetings, who may wish that issues of emotions, interpersonal problems and life choices were dealt with in a more elaborated vocabulary. But it is quite clear that these pressures are believed to be necessary to prevent the emergence of a status order based on class and educa-

tion. There is, as we know, a wealth of research that demonstrates that such status orders emerge as a matter of course in *most* other groups (see Berger, Fisek, Norman and Zelditch, 1977). For a sociologist it is surprising to watch how this process is muted in AA meetings.

A price is paid for the egalitarianism of AA meetings. There is a tendency for members to speak in stock phrases, to use a limited number of terms to describe their own emotions and reactions and those of others. This is not said in criticism. But there is a paradox here that must be recognized, although it may be unresolvable. The educated person may find that his or her vocabulary for describing the shades of emotional reactions is severely truncated, because one is not allowed to use "fancy language."

However, it is also clear why AA, like other communitarian movements, needs a strong, normatively enforced, egalitarian emphasis. Just as the feminist organizations discussed in the next chapter must emphasize common sisterhood in the face of powerful distinctions and divisions among women as imposed by the larger society, so does AA have to focus on the common status of being alcoholics if the rehabiliatation work is to get done without being side-tracked by other concerns. Some simple social-psychological principles also reveal related reasons. If persons perceive that they have shared status, affective bonds emerge, developing solidarity within the group. And the norms of highly solidaristic, cohesive groups carry much authority.

Next we turn to the feminist health organizations, which, like Alcoholics Anonymous, are in many ways movements against the current trend. These movements are pervasive, when in almost all other organizations the trend is on members' rights and toward specific controls over members' activities. They are communitarian in the era of the administered state with its emphasis on hierarchy, clearly delineated division of labor, lines of rights, duties and spans of control. They use transcendent symbolism in a secular time, and dare to be normative when permissiveness and doing "one's own thing" are dominant values. Yet, it would be a mistake to write off AA or the feminist health movement as throwbacks. They have clearly shown that they can be effective and very practical in dealing with limited, chosen problems. But the deeper significance of these and other communitarian movements may be that they develop, initially, utopian models for alternative and new forms of social organization. The specialized, hierarchical, formalized model for organization is simply not very effective in such fields of social control as criminal justice, mental health and substance abuse. Like alcoholism, much habitual crime, delinquency, prostitution, chronic emotional problems, drug addiction, and child and spouse abuse seem to involve multidimensional aspects: self-systems, complex roles, life styles and life-scripts. Treatment in pervasive, strongly normative structures with a communitarian orientation that creates acceptance also enables the person being rehabilitated or seeking solidarity to work with others, drawing upon his or her own experience. We do not believe that the exploration of new forms for social organization has advanced very far. After all, it took a long time, a hundred years or more, to perfect the modern professional, administrative and business organizations. Sociological understanding, in the words of the late Marxist Paul Baran, should consist in "the capacity and willingness to see the tree of the future in the tiny shoots barely perceptive in the present" (Baran, 1969).

CHAPTER 11—NOTES

[1] Sagarin (1969) disputes AA's success claims as both wrong and possibly harmful. He attacks assertions that alcoholism is a disease; that it is incurable but can be arrested; that AA has had a 50-percent success rate with its members; and that only an alcoholic can understand—or help—another alcoholic on grounds that these claims remain unproved, self-serving and of doubtful validity.

While we have no objectively testable counterproofs for Sagarin's strong critique, we emphasize the constructed and oppositional reality within which commitment organizations work. If members *believe* a program to be successful (whatever the actual facts), it could influence behavior in a positive way. For example, experiments for terminal cancer patients using programmed images that "fight" the disease appear to extend the life of some very seriously ill persons.

Chapter 12
Beyond Disenchantment:
Feminist Health Movement as Commitment Organization

> Basic to our philosophy and our coming together is the concept of health care as a right (rather than a privilege) on a free or at least a pay-as-you-can basis. Our collective focus is on the demystification of medicine, the professionalism of doctors, and our bodies from "experts," but also to learn technically how to care for ourselves. We want to be treated individually with respect, to be told exactly what our illnesses are, what the treatment is, what medicine we are being given and what it is doing to us. We want to be related to as whole persons, psychologically as well as physically. (Statement of Purpose: Berkeley Women's Health Collective)

Self-help movements in the United States are vigorous outgrowths of the cultural revolution spawned in the 1960s and early 1970s.[1] Their form and content bear witness to a new paradigm of social service. This rejects the tyranny of the expert in favor of peer control over ideology and treatment. "Self-help" is actually a misnomer, because the alternative health idea fosters a communal conception: organizations for radical social change. Generated from the same milieu that produced the "cult of experience" (Back, 1972) and that also nourished the alternative therapy movement and "psychobabble" solutions to social problems, the feminist health movement takes a different direction: political, collectivist and oppositional stance to conventional medicine.

Self-help advocates reject professionalism and all its accoutrements in favor of a commitment system. There are distinct limits, however.

Because alternative systems cannot shape their own environment and are indeed dependent upon powerful institutions for their very survival, they must resort to manipulation of symbols in innovative ways. Feminist health collectives share with other radical movement organizations a polarized ideological structure and a temporizing social structure. The resulting contradictions make these systems highly volatile. Feminist health groups provoke relentless change within a changing health institution (Ruzek, 1978; Peterson, 1976; Taylor, 1979; Fischel, 1973).

Feminist Health Movement[2]

The feminist health movement is one of several contemporary protests against the technically over-elaborated, costly health-care systems (see Kanter, 1972; Kanter and Zurcher, 1973). Scholarly criticism contends that medical care institutions in the United States put the main emphasis on crisis intervention, not preventive health care; that they foster dependencies in a monopolistic care structure (Knowles, ed., 1977; Alford, 1973; Freidson, 1970). Fee-for-service medicine takes care of the affluent, but excludes the poor and ethnic minorities. Even for those who can afford it, health-care delivery is fragmented; referral systems are disjointed, costly and time-consuming. Specialization contributes, ironically, to discontinuity of care. The patient's body comes to be treated as a bundle of separated units instead of as a whole entity. Health care for women, critics claim, fixates on specific body parts and complaints reducing the woman to a diagnostic entity: a vagina, uterus, venereal disease or contraceptive failure. Because medical truth is defined as the application of a technology, many of the patient's needs are secondary or ignored. The hysterectomy scandal, in which large numbers of nondiseased uteri are removed every year in U.S. hospitals for the doctor's or woman's convenience, suggests the excesses of specialization. Repeat abortion, typically treated as the "woman's problem," is the direct result of institutional medicine's avoidance of what is commonly considered a marginal medical practice. Regardless of the medical specialty, critics uniformly complain that the existing fee-for-service medical system fosters an overly rigid set of institutional arrangements (Bazell, 1971).[3]

"Self-help" is the term feminists adopt for their advocacy version of health care: women helping women to take over their own bodies without the dependencies incurred by the standard service delivery model. "Medicine without doctors" is a 19th-century invention, part of a larger female moral reform movement that occupied many middle class, native white, American women. They opposed the sickly, corset-bound, and frail-lady image, replacing it with salvation through nutrition, personal hygiene, changes in dress code and eugenics. Women organized themselves into study groups, "physiological societies," which fostered a sense of community against the isolation of the home (Peterson, 1976). The early 20th-century movement centered around birth control, but was coopted by physicians and *status quo* organizations (e.g., Planned Parenthood).

The "self-help demonstrations" by Carol Downer in 1971 *(Off Our Backs,* 1974) publicly revived feminist body consciousness.[4] In the company of other women, Downer inserted a speculum into her vagina and viewed her cervix through a mirror. The response ignited a national movement that combined the elements of self-help with a communal ideology. Feminist health care was defined as a *collective* project for affiliating women with one another, dispelling the idea that every woman is her own doctor. For example, women were warned against having a personalized menstrual extraction kit.

> The idea of a "kit in each woman's private bathroom" is antisisterhood and anti-women's liberation. By being a select item for one women only, within the confines of her own four walls and without the collective help and support of her sisters, everyone and especially the movement loses. The concept of self-help stresses SISTERHOOD that makes possible the benefits from collective knowledge, collective experiences, collective training and especially the sisterly concern for one another (Quoted in Peterson, 1976:14).

Feminist women's health collectives, as these initial ventures were called, were founded on four feminist principles: self-realization, antielitism, sisterhood and the authority of personal experience. Using a mix of medical tools, home remedies and body sensitivity training techniques, feminist advocates succeeded in setting up a dubious practice in a legally ambiguous zone. This raises several interesting legal questions. Can nonlicensed practitioners, these feminist paramedics, diagnose and treat gynecological problems? Probably not when they use standard medical tools. But how about such remedies as yogurt for vaginal yeast infections or vinegar douches and slippery elm suppositories for personal hygiene? There is no legal clarity here. Some groups went further, offering an entire range of services, including abortion.

Even before abortion was legalized, a few collectives operated in direct contravention to the law, offering a sliding-scale fee schedule or free abortion to poor and black women. Despite police harassment and a few arrests, most of the illegal abortion services continued uninterrupted. One clinic logged 110 calls per week and performed 15-25 abortions for each working day (Peterson, 1976).

Free clinics, distributing health care primarily to "street people" (unattached or unemployed persons), provide the organizational model. This model is based upon an ideology of client participation. It aims to radically politicize medicine and return health care to the people. Currently, about 1,200 feminist health organizations in the country offer a range of services. "Well-women's care," women learning about and participating in their own health care, is stressed. Services run the gamut from pregnancy testing, pap tests, venereal disease screening, vaginitis screening and pelvic examinations to couseling or advising upon contraceptive methods and abortion (Ruzek, 1978; see, also, *Our Bodies, Ourselves,* Boston Women's Health Collective, 1973; 1979).

Clinic Users[5]

Users of feminist health clinics fall into two distinct status groups: the middle class counterculture, and the neighborhood poor. Users are often rejects from the traditional system, involving cases such as obesity, chronic or recurrent vaginal and venereal infections, repeat abortions and general poor health.

Referral follows three patterns: physician referral, self-referral or friend referral. The woman may be seeking objective validation for a deviant life style—for example, the case of the lesbian referred by a neighborhood friend—or a new medical experience—for instance, the "woman's touch"; or clients may simply use the clinic because it is cheap.

Low cost attracts many new users, but it rarely holds them. The self-help ideology is the compelling factor that often repels poor and black females (or what clinic workers prefer to refer to as "third-world women"). In most clinics, furnishings take the appearance of what one informant called "Goodwill chic," a generally dilapidated quality typical of the storefront or low-rent district. And while the clinic front blends well with working class neighborhoods, the decor stands in marked contrast to physicians' luxuriously furnished offices. In some clinics, worn-out chairs with exposed stuffing, ripped linoleum or threadbare carpets signal to working class women a poverty-ridden enterprise. Local residents are quick to take note, and when offered a choice, they generally prefer the traditional system, if only because it looks better or is cleaner.

Most users are one-time clients only, on their way to or from a standard physician's care. The other half can be divided into two groups: clients and committed. Many clients treat clinic services like "any other" medical services, neither recognizing nor acknowledging variations in the concepts or procedures. Some women overtly reject the self-help concept, refusing to scrutinize their own vaginas or do their own breast examinations. Other are mute altogether. At the same time, the traditional client role enables the clinic to realize a higher volume of patient care, a serious consideration for funding groups in this resource-scarce system.

The committed user, comprising the smallest group in absolute numbers, remains the most significant. These women learn not only the health practices—self-examination, use of herbs, natural birth control and menstrual sponges, among others—but also the ideology, with its self-conscious, mythic themes. Getting women in touch with their own bodies, it is believed, helps spread the word that women feel closer to other women as well. Some users are ecstatic over the self-help experience, referring to the cervical canal and cervix in religious terms, (Peterson, 1976). Others, initially turned off by the collective self-examinations, eventually learn the codes through counseling and practice. Clinics recruit new workers from among the committed users. In some instances, the worker-user role become a single totality.

Ruzek (1978) reports that a high proportion of both active members and users are drawn from high-status groups. For instance, 79 percent of the active members of the Vancouver (Canada) Women's Health Collective had completed university or other professional training. Self-help clinic demonstrators also attract the more occupationally stable. Self-help report data show that nearly 52 percent of users are professional or technical workers. Other occupational distributions reveal that 16 percent are students, two percent are housewives, 10 percent are clericals and four percent are managers and officials. Only five percent were operatives or service persons. Fischel (1973) observed similar populations in other self-help clinics. In addition, a disproportionate number are young—in their 20s and 30s—although, the age range extends from the teens into the 80s.

What this status and age distribution for clinic members and users suggests is that alternative health programs, particularly the feminist version, represent a self-sustaining enterprise for a dissatisfied, searching middle class. Rather than defining such persons as "alienated" or "anomic," this social-movement action expresses an incipient form of institution building. The extent to which these commitment organizations shape their environments, rather than being shaped by them, is an open question among movement advocates.

Many inside observers are skeptical about the benefits of the women's health movement for organizing women. Unless health and body issues genuinely cut across race and class lines, critics say, the movement's impact will be limited to the preservation of the image of feminism as exclusively concerned with serving white middle class women. Alternative health care has little to contribute to black women, for instance, whose more serious health needs (e.g., hypertension, poor nutrition, multiple pregnancies, sickle-cell anemia) are neglected by standard medicine *and* the feminist health programs. This has led some critics to conclude that black women regard many feminist gynecological issues as trivial (Ruzek, 1978).

Clinic Participants

Mannheim (1936) reminds us that each generation creates its own version of social reality. For the sons and daughters of the postwar bourgeoisie, the 1960s was the epoch of revolt, the age of the counterculture. This was partly a political generation coming of age in the turmoil of the 1960s; the symbols and themes were race riots and assassinations, Vietnam, Watergate, hippies and women's liberation. It was a generation trained in the rhetoric of participatory democracy and the permissive ethic that "anything goes" (Moberg, 1979: 274-311; Case and Taylor, 1979). Feminist health care remains one of the more vibrant and enduring organizations to emerge from the counterculture community.

Originally, clinic participants were entirely volunteers, supported by odd jobs, local community patrons or well-heeled fathers whose generous allowances enabled young women to experiment with alternative service models. That generation has passed on, and while most workers are still young, white, college students or exstudents, they increasingly draw from lesbians, older women, and poor, third-world women. Federal, county and city funding now substitute for the more informal funding, a situation that tends to introduce a more pragmatic worker into the organization.

Less ideologically centered and more concerned with tasks, wages and opportunites, these new workers require a more intensive on-the-job radical socialization than previous worker groups. Increased heterogeneity also raises the likelihood of collisions between ideologists and task-oriented members.

Generally, informants emphasize the satisfactions of the work, its philosophical and political consciousness-raising qualities, including solidarity, freedom from anxiety because of commitment to a valuable human service and an enhanced sense of competence. More seasoned workers tend to be less rapturous, and even cynical, compared with newcomers; they stress the training aspects instead: new or increased job and social skills, and the importance of clinical experience for entering medical school or other established medical jobs.

Ideally, commitment is total. But the level of idealism required to sustain this commitment induces early departures for some workers; they leave for husband, lover, job, school, or simply to "get out." Others deal with the "burn-out" created by overwork—in a job described by one of the workers as a "bottomless pit"—by recognizing their lack of commitment to the holistic politics and life style. The near ubiquitous storefront image masks the real variation in worker type. In one clinic with a total of 100 part- or full-time volunteer and paid staff, three clinic-worker models emerged: self-problem-centered, reformer and revolutionary.

Self-problem-centered members seek solidarity and values when their personal lives are undergoing disarray. Whatever the initial inducement for participation, this group is most likely to be former clients, and many continue the asymmetrical relationship after assuming a participatory role. During the six months to one year of mandatory service, the problem-centered worker uses participation in various ways. For a short time, work provides an overarching purpose. It fills the days and provides friends, a ready made life style, a daily agenda and a transcendent ethic. These women often leave when the purpose for their involvement wanes, e.g., the divorce is finalized, admission to college or professional school is secured and so on. In larger clinics these women are attracted into the mental health service, where they spend a good deal of time working on one another's psychological problems.

The *reformer* is an expanding category of clinic worker who fits the newer model of the clinic as subculture. The counter culture life is not entirely rejected; it is simply recognized as obsolete or perhaps overly subjective and drug oriented. While still opposed to the established health system, reformers recognize the vast, if not impossible, task of institutional transformation. While power dependency is recognized as a structured reality and is certainly not denied, there is a willingness to temporize, make do and develop secondary adjustments. Reformers are more likely to have satisfying roles in addition to the clinic work. Marriage, a live-in lesbian relationship, children or job means that they must juggle competing involvements. Their tenure is accordingly affected, since they lack both intense psychological and political commitment. Reformers tend to be "liberals," radical feminists assert, and hence a despised category. Their role as mediators and efficient workers, though, helps to offset the more intense or dogmatic factions.

Revolutionary workers identify with the sentiments and ideology of the counterculture, categorically rejecting the politics of compromise. Members are urged to express anger and rage, not as a subjective emotion, but as a collective political act toward mobilizing women to overcome the inertia of oppression. There is a demand for ideological "purity," as when a splinter group at one clinic demanded that staff be recruited on the basis of 50-percent lesbian and 50-percent third world women (a request that was seriously discussed by staff at great length). Heterosexual women, the largest category of both staff and clients, are perceived here as too peace-loving or self-indulgent for the revolutionary task. In a 1978 position paper titled, "Liberalism," adapted from Mao Tse-Tung's "Combat Liberalism" written in 1937, two radical-feminist authors attack liberalism as the basis for collective unity. After defining liberalism as "drift," "self-indulgence" and "political degeneracy," the writers say:

> Liberalism is extemely harmful in a revolutionary collective. It is a corrosive which eats away unity, undermines cohesion, causes apathy and creates dissension. It is an extremely bad tendency.

> Liberalism stems from selfishness; it places personal interest first and the interest of the people's struggle second, and this gives rise to ideological, political and organizational liberalism.

> Liberalism is a manifestation of opportunism and conflicts fundamentally with collectivism. It is negative and objectively has the effect of helping the enemy; that is why the enemy welcomes its preservation in our midst. Such

being its nature, there should be no place for it in the ranks of the revolution.

Ideological purity is a renunciatory act. As negative ideology, it gives clinic workers a bad conscience and contributes to low morale, high turnover and chronic disputes.

Structural Problems

Alternative health structures lack coherence and autonomy. Resource difficulties provide uncertain guarantees for survival. Insecure financing limits social support, which along with low status and questionable legitimacy, conspires to make these weak structures. Alternative organizations are often told by funding groups that they must achieve certain goals, some of which actually contradict their moral and political stances. Clearly, these organizations lack a tested and well-established script of expectations and events. Other groups set priorities and force action: funding groups, community groups (e.g., building codes), city health departments, neighborhood residents or street gangs who "trash" walls with spray paint, break windows or shout obscenities.

Organizational formats lack the elaborated code of standard medicine that buffers activities: well-ordered offices, a clear division of labor, uniformed staff (which also indicates status) and other visible appearances of the well-managed facility. Instead, street noises often bombard clinic visitors, clients and staff. A distraught client or staff person's raised voice is often overheard. Or there are repeated interruptions of on-going interactions to request directives or for casual conversation. Children's play in hallways produces noise and congestion, which when added to the normal conversations in the examining rooms, flimsily covered by curtains, virtually eliminates privacy. For patients who seek a subdued "professional" atmosphere, the clinic offers a reversal setting.

Rather than viewing the informality as intrusive, workers assert that it communicates the desired antiinstitutional and antiprofessional ambience. Clients are reported to prefer the open situation: women sharing knowledge and experience in the intimacy of body talk. The all-female paraprofessional staff creates a "fellow-women aura," which Emerson (1970) and others suggest women seek in gynecology (see, also, Smith-Rosenberg, 1975:1-29). This contrasts sharply with the overrationalized and distancing symbols of professional medicine.

Ideological conflict is a way of life in feminist clinics and involves a number of organizational consequences. First, frequent rule shifts are endemic and reflect the low level of power that alternative clinics have over their environment and technical core. Because these settings propose to radically demedicalize women's health care, and yet are at the same time required to be medical care facilities by funding groups and client expectations, the rules must be very flexible. Rule-making becomes an end in itself. Committees debate numerous topics. One is the merits of gynecological medicine versus the holistic health concept. Another is bringing minority women into clinic services. This requires fairly massive adjustment to standard health models, in opposition to accommodation to the ideological status order and feminist values. A third debate rages over whether heterosexual health care, emphasizing issues such as contraception, natural childbirth and postpartum care, should be stressed over lesbians' different needs. Sometimes, rule negotiation takes up more time than actual clinical services. In some clinics, the fundamental question has not been resolved. Are we a service delivery system or a political organization? The answers lead to wholly divergent organizational outcomes.

Part of the problem lies in the ambiguous or contradictory ideas. Feminist health clinics live on borrowed myths to counteract the instrumental rationality of elite systems. Myths perform multiple duties: covering over a thin meaning system, explaining the ideological message for organizational members, producing reasonable organizational stories for clients, community support groups and funding agencies, and coping with new mandates and programs that result from the movement *success* in the environment. For instance, Hispanic women who come in for service under an outreach program are likely to reject the standard format: self-determinism, body control and sexual liberation. Among these ethnics, family ties are strong, marriage is traditional and husband and child care focus the woman's life. Counselors chosen for their ideological commitment, rather than for human or medical skills, may not be very sensitive to these clients. The combined ethic of self-help and structurelessness often prevents workers from grappling with these moral distinctions. Client withdrawal or failure to identify with the enterprise tends to become personalized. It is the worker's problem. A rule to cover every exception is obviously impossible, and moreover, contradicts the ethos of totalism. The effort to create a single universal myth system usually succeeds only at the level of consciousness-raising. Health services remain incoherent, *ad hoc* and temporary structures. They are the result of small-group processes, rather than an organized policy.

These clinics, comprising workers who are younger, female, radical and counterculture, invite boundary interference. The state can deny a license, a negative press can whip up neighborhood opposition and participating physicians can be penalized by their associations. Clinics have little power to combat these disturbances.

There is a fundamental asymmetry here. When upper-status groups invade subordinate ones, the scenario calls for bargaining, hierarchy and customary dominance relations. When underdog groups attempt to take their beliefs, values and rules into high-status contexts, the interaction may be riddled with paradoxes, contradictions, misunderstandings and violations of each other's assumptions (Anderson and Davis, 1981). On the whole, sanctioning moves from top to bottom, with high-status people perceiving any difficulties to be the "problem" of the low-esteemed group. Thus, radical feminists are viewed as man-hating lesbians who have a pathological affinity for dirty words and immoral living. The ideological feminist who demands improved health care and yet rejects hierarchy and customary professional demeanor is likely to earn only scorn. The organization's failure to export significant elements of feminist health practices over time undermines commitment. Given a hostile or indifferent environment with few external incentives, recruitment efforts and innovation dampen, and most energy goes into low-level maintenance activities.

Examination of the internal structure provides important clues to the essential weaknesses of feminist self-help clinics (see also, Freeman, 1975).

First, the acephalous (headless) organization lacks a division of labor. There are no time or space boundaries around functions, work is passed around and in some significant sense, the work is never done. This produces exhaustion and feelings among workers of being overwhelmed.

Second, the technology is reduced in scope or deemphasized in favor of "natural" cures: herbs, exercise, home remedies, myth themes (e.g., "getting to know your own body") and other non-measurable treatments. Workers have no way to distinguish effective from ineffective measures.

Third, communication is in the form of a "wheel" structure, a system that involves maximum interaction without hierarchy and without boundaries. This system operates effectively in a small group, and thus preserves egalitarian aspirations. As a decision-making tool, though, it is problematic. Issues tend to become personalized. The rejection of experts negates the possibility of a charismatic leader resolving disputes; and yet, conversely, in this power vacuum, often one person can exert veto power. Unlike the hierarchical system, where each person does his or her own job and where problems can be localized, the wheel interaction of the alternative structure makes anybody's business everybody's business. Here poor ideas and practices spread with a brush-fire effect, and easily become unmanageable.

Fourth, the motivations in this structure tend to enhance stereotypical sex-role socialization, rather than to create new, innovative adaptations. Ironically, like the housewife, secretary and nurse roles that radical feminists categorically reject, the organization encourages workers to avoid specific job classifications, and to take on a diffuse, total commitment instead. Nor can they withdraw at will into emotional neutrality—the bureaucrat's final refuge. Emotionality is not only expected, but demanded. Workers must show their identification through physical and psychological gestures (e.g., touching, crying, laughing aloud, etc.). They must relate to other participants and clients as "persons"; hence, professional norms, even when learned and applicable for a situation, are perceived as alienating.

Finally, the "sister" role as ascriptive status exerts a more powerful impact on shaping consciousness than any other criterion (Lockheed and Hall, 1976:114-124; Meeker and Weitzel-O'Neill, 1977:91-105). The high proportion of volunteers who move in and out of these systems may be in part a feature of the alternative life style itself, or a way out of a trapped situation, boredom, sexual restlessness, a smashed marriage or a love affair. The "burn-out" and disillusionment among workers, though, relates more directly to the organizational structure itself. Precarious relations with the environment, compounded by an unbounded internal system, appear to contain the essential ingredients for self-destruction (Freudenberger, 1974:159-163).

Internal Strengths

What saves these marginal enterprises is that everyday activities do not necessarily follow from the ideological structures. Indeed, they are often opposed to them. This produces incalculable problems for ideologists, but not for clinic managers and spokespersons who employ a kind of calculated disjointedness to maximize task output. Clinic managers employ two major mechanisms to maintain commitment: radically disconnecting the organization from its medical environment, and offering a loosely coupled link between ideology and practice (see Weick, 1976). Table 12:1 portrays the fit and disjuncture among these three systems: external environment, organizational ideology and typical practices.

Table 12:1 Environmental and Organizational Relations in the Feminist (Alternative) Health System For Selected Variables

Environmental Constraints	*Ideology − Reversal Decoupled Strategy*	*Practices − Loose or Tight Coupling Strategy*
1. Funding	Self-sufficiency and free clinic concept: "the poor helping the poor."	Dependence on state, wealthy donors, client payment and canvassing (e.g., door-to-door campaign)
2. Professional Credentials	Self-care or collective sharing in mutual care (sisterhood); antiexpertise; knowledge as experience (e.g., "know your body")	Utilization of rotating physician in direct service clinics; outside referral to medical, psychiatric and social service specialists for problem cases
3. Elaborate Division of Labor	Task rotation; no formal boundaries around work or workers	Task specialization and functional separation of services (e.g,. workers in Service A unaware of organizational activities in Service B)
4. Hierarchy-rigid distinctions between ranks	Radical egalitarianism − all sisters are equally valuable	Negotiated equality − some sisters are more equal than others (e.g., conflict between gays and straights, women with and without children; class, race, educational differences)

Table 12:1   (cont'd)

Environmental Constraints	Ideology —Reversal Decoupled Strategy	Practices —Loose or Tight Coupling Strategy
5. Monopoly of Professional Knowledge	Knowledge is shared; women have exclusive control over their own bodies; medical knowledge is oppressive and disease-producing (e.g., drugs, surgery, psychiatric intervention are dangerous to your health)	Utilize natural healing in conflict areas of medicine; standard medical products and services in non-problematic areas (e.g., yogurt for vaginal yeast infection); contraceptive treatment for family planning
6. Complex technology surgery, drugs, radiation, prothesis, etc.	Natural medicine or products (herbs, massage, biofeedback for contraceptive control, sponge for period, etc.); technology as antiorganic and capitalistic	Downplay or substitute technology; selective concern with ideologically informed data —anti-Pill; pro-abortion; self-help (e.g., collective control over womens bodies by and for women); mutually incompatible resolutions are justified by *safety* doctrine (e.g., vacuum-aspirated abortion is not "natural," but it is safer)
7. Specialization	Holistic medicine; the body as natural; flow and interdependence between body parts	Moderate specialization in service clinics (e.g., pediatrics, gynecology) volunteer component and advocate role keeps specialists in line
8. Social Control body as object of professional intervention; sexuality as private and heterosexual	Women control their own bodies; reproductive centered: preoccupation with genitalia and sexuality in myth and metaphor —"the Man" as outsider; adult women as primary companions	Low return to clinics by straight and third-world women; clinic staff often 75% heterosexual; lesbian life style accepted but not treated as major model; 80% of lesbian participants have children; family orientation strong (mother-child unit basic)
9. Evaluation: Quantitative— based on health-care providers criterias; outcome stressed, but usually process analysis	Evaluation —Qualitative; based on client experience; Outcome analysis (clients' reports of services)	Client input; critical evaluation of services by conflict-ridden board; political efficacy *vs.* service orientation.

Organizational Strategies

On a number of organizational variables, then, th clinic appears from a rationalistic viewpoint to be a self-defeating operation. What good is ideology when it bears little impact on practice? How do these ideological structures balance their constructed reality against the visible evidence of contradictions and disparate practices? A number of organizational strategies have been developed to deal with this anomaly.

1. Disconnect activites from ideological activities and separate tasks from one another. The organization achieves this by differentiating staff into volunteers and regulars, workers and policymakers. Because services are radically decentralized without any hierarchy or accountability in a strict sense (although informal hierarchies and accounts are implicit features of the system), contradictory elements of the technology or organization tend to be overlooked by participants.

2. Reduce the technical level of the procedures by eliminating many of the highly skilled practices found in physicians' offices. Thus, clinics fit diaphragms and recommend menstrual sponges, while distributing handouts that criticize the utility of the "pill" and "I.U.D." (which, in any event, are not available in these facilities). The stress on self-help places the primary responsibility for follow-up on the client.

3. Accept male physicians who have the "right" attitude, along with women doctors congenial to clinic practice. Resident physicians, still under medical training and supervison, are usually more available than board-certified doctors, whether female or male. Screening is an on-going process, assisted by client feedback, and depends more on such attributes as "understanding" or "rapport" with women than gender or credentials.

4. Adapt practice to system capacity, and not to standard medical formulas. Peterson (1976) sums up this tendency as follows: a bias toward treatment when medical risk is low, but unlike doctors, a bias toward nonintervention when medical risk is high.

5. Live with inequality. Experienced clinic organizers learn to live with "hidden hierarchies" and latent structures. Inequalities are inevitable at this point in the history of the women's movement, they admit, and too much striving after treatment ideologies restricts or eliminates services. While many members

remain nervous about institutionalizing inequality, they recognize that some workers should have more power to make decisions. Thus, committed regulars have more authority than short-term volunteers and clients in order to establish continuity in practice.

6. Develop a unifying style modeled after the counterculture. Blue jeans, plaid western shirts, T-shirts with political slogans, boots or tennis shoes become a kind of uniform that satisfies the ideologists' need for a separate identity (i.e., avoiding the professional dress code). This marks the sharp divergence in ideological orientations, while freeing workers to adopt necessary features of the standard medical model.

7. Separate conflict groups by splitting service into equivalent parts. From one perspective the system appears fragmented; each segment does its own thing. From another viewpoint the system is a fission, larger units split into isomorphic units with each one capable of reproducing itself. It is a primitive form of social organization, but perhaps an effective one for an acephalous organization. In addition, the fission structure is a reaction to the structurally overelaborate medical institution, and hence adapts well to ideological or resource changes. For instance, when a group wishes to expand its program, e.g., older women's health or lesbian health, it can simply add a unit comprised of interested workers and clients, or establish a subsidiary storefront center. Elaborate referral networks and licensing are not required.

8. Reclassify task or authority roles. Communication flows across, not down, and exists by face-to-face contact, not memo. A staff manager who is displeased with organizational output or conflict brings people together for "consciousness-raising," instead of "briefings" or "orders." The source of a statement is identified as a person, not an authority role (e.g., Susan "feels" or "believes" that X is the case, not the chair "says"). People "leave," they are never placed on probation, fired or terminated. Workers "join," they are not "hired" (even if they work for pay). A loose authority structure inculcates high tolerance for linguistic slippage. Thus, it is not the case that medical procedures are efficient, pragmatic, rational and so on. Rather, the use of certain procedures demonstrates a "good" or "bad" scene, makes one feel "worthwhile" or "shitty," or "helps bring the act

together" or "breaks it apart." The discourse shift downward implies that a restrictive code serves as a unifying symbol, negating class, race, education and other status differences.

Anomalies tend to cumulate. The experienced disjointedness, together with the organizationally imposed commitment ethic, takes its toll. Workers complain of chronic fatigue, exhaustion, frequent illnesses and "burn-out." Having a perception that everything must be done at once, and yet with no clear boundaries around tasks, they see their job as endless. Even when away from the job, there is a nagging persistence of things left undone. It is as if the worker must endure a twenty-four hour, seven-day-a-week work load. And without clear-cut authority or reward structures, who is to say where a task begins or ends? Short-funded and oppressed by overload, the sisterhood ideology wears thin.

An ideology that preaches everything is possible for a brave new world may falter when all existing remedies are rejected by a resisting or indifferent environment. To confront organizational decline, some feminist health centers are beginning the inevitable march toward rationalization. Formal authority, paid staff of experts, tighter division of labor, systematized incentives and rewards, bureaucratized record keeping and client census-taking for funding groups are all being introduced to enhance service delivery. By developing specialities and avoiding overlap with existing medical programs, some of the feminist health centers are turning from collectives to full-scale medical services. What is the fate of ideology when this occurs?

The Ideology of Utopia

The significance of ideology, Karl Mannheim (1936) writes, is not in its specific message, but in the utopias it creates. These are alternative perspectives or world views that act to revitalize declining values and cultures by providing new models for social order (Anderson, 1968). Ideologies flourish in a turbulent environment. Situations of ambiguity and conflict provide rich seedbeds for the formation of new ideologies. The health and medical domain, characterized by technical overelaboration, appears rational from the standpoint of system managers. For clients negotiating that order, the system has a counterreality: top heavy, expensive, mystifying and self-negating. Ruzek (1979) delineates key ideological points in the women's health movement, which we summarize below.

1. A rejection of "gynecological imperialism," the woman's body used as an instrument for exploitation and as an object for professional control.

2. A critical investigation of utilization patterns, whereby poor, minority, elderly and other deprived women are excluded from health care because of inability to pay.

3. An attack on the medicalization of female culture; the "woman-as-reproductive-beast" in medicine that considers its clients as solely a "collection of ovaries, uteri, vaginas and other sexual appurtenances."

4. An overturning of medicalization and control over female biological life events. Menstruation, pregnancy, childbirth and menopause are normal and natural events that women will and must shape.

5. A defense against monopolistic professional control over health by building counterinstitutions and supporting alternative models; e.g., childbirth as a family affair, not a hospital routine.

6. A dismissal of drug and surgical therapies for women, including the excess tendency of American medicine to use anesthetics and surgery (e.g., episiotomy and caesarian section as standard childbirth procedures).

7. A blanket repudiation of the medical institution as a sexist system: patriarchal, capitalistic, oppressive and disease-producing. In its most extreme form, this ideological value denies scientific medicine.

The feminists' body-consciousness, one might suggest hyperconsciousness, is not an isolated conception. In the twentieth century, the human body has become fully politicized. The transformation represents a major shift: from the body as something to be known, an object of research and manipulation by outsiders, (e.g., professionals or state functionaries) to a conception of the body as private, an ultimate symbol of personhood and self-determinism. Reactions against impersonal contact, achievement and bureaucratic organization range widely from a yearning for the traditional *Gemeinschaft* social order to the discovery of the self through liberating communes or mind-altering drugs. This is in basic opposition to *Gesellschaft* society, which stresses relations based on impersonal expertise and science.

The women's health movement reflects a paricular form of the romantic style of thought (see Cotgrove, 1978: 358 d371). Health is used to dramatize women's oppression and subordination. Yet most spokespersons are well-educated and far from economically oppressed, reflecting the time origins of the movement. The women's health movement is a child of the 1960s and in some respects captures the romantic vision of the affluent younger generation.

The movement makes more sense when it is seen against a background of an entire network of feminist ideologies aimed to overthrow four major systems women relate to as areas for radical change: production, reproduction, family and socialization. The women's movement is involved in restructuring all domains: affirmative action in the work place; abortion and contraceptive control over reproduction; reorganizing family roles for greater equity and more equal participation in everyday routines of childcare and housework; and a drastically revised socialization to avoid stereotyped, unconscious gender roles. As a total ideology, the women's movement aims for a fundamental reorganization of culture. While skeptics may find such aspirations amusing or ignorant, Mannheim (1937) clarifies the role of ideology and utopia as a dominant and necessary instrument for revitalizing culture.

The utopian outlook transcends the present and adapts the past to create a new future. Ideologies need not be evaluated in terms of the specific beliefs, values, symbols or programs they produce, since these elements are usually in flux or represent distortions or caricatures of dominant realities. Instead, ideologies are mental productions that should be assessed by what problems they address and the systematic formulations they propose. The crisis in social thought affecting contemporary standards and behavior is the belief that the world is locked into existing technologies and political orders. Such arrangements, viewed as a total, final, closed system, lead to exclusions, partial perspectives and a provincial, nonadaptive outlook.

By contrast, the women's movement remains a vibrant force, creating new values and a new morality, although these are not necessarily coherent or free of distortion (see Nietzsche, 1956). By attacking categories reminiscent or expressive of the patriarchal order, the movement unmasks male ideologies that purport to define reality in exclusively hierarchical and oppressive ways. This opens the possibility of new ideals of equality and social purpose. The self-determination for all persons promised by this and other contemporary utopias enhances our human capacity to shape history and hence our ability to understand it.

Social Control of the Body

Alcoholics Anonymous, a mutual-help system, can be compared with the feminist self-help health organizations through a semiotic analysis. This considers the member's body as the center of control. Both organizations are products of social movements, or more accurately, waves of movements and ideologies. Similarly, these approaches stress group control over the individual's impulses or personal preferences. As such, they offer a powerful tool for self-transcendence. Symbols and values aim to transform the person from an isolated deviant, and essentially incompetent self, into a fully integrated human. A self-hatred theme is evident to be sure: alcoholics, like traditional women, are "lost" persons; engaged in self-defeating behavior. The individual is said to lack will and consciousness; only through identity with the mutual or self-help organization can the individual be saved. Salvation works by faith; the deeds are only witnesses to the beliefs. In this sense, the altruism that undergirds these helping systems is both a virtue and a necessity. it mobilizes the will to self-control as opposed to control by drink or by men; it enables the enlightened person to reach out to others who are in need. As such, it is a self-perpetuating order, but one that has no class distinctions, no caste privileges, no symbols of education, occupation or culture, and no rites of succession that would create invidious distinctions between members. Radical leveling is thus a way of life.

The body serves as a central organizing metaphor for both movement organizations. It is the body's tendency for pollution and dirt that must be overcome by personal control over the inner spaces: the mind or the vagina. Equilibrium is broken once the body succumbs to external influences: drink or medical intervention. A twofold irony prevails. The press for equality mitigates against the rise of a normalizing authority structure. This contributes to social exclusion, loss of personnel and recruits, and organizational entropy. And the intended structurelessness and peer control invites abuse by an ambitious cult leader or faction. Thus, the rise of totalitarian leaders who command a docile following as found in live-in drug therapy centers (e.g., Synanon) or religious cults (Jonestown) (Anson, 1978:28-50; Komisar, 1979:43-50).

What is perhaps more remarkable about these two normative structures is their variation. Organizational analyst Stinchcombe (1965) argues that time of origin is the crucial factor accounting for an organization's culture and structure, and even its survival potential in the environment. Let us review this proposition more carefully for each movement.

Pre-Victorian and Victorian reform movements were primarily addressed to the "crisis of acculturation" and the "crisis of integration," the inability of modernizing society to socialize and assimilate subordinate populations—blacks, women, Catholics and minorities—into the dominant institutions. Mutual-help systems grew out of excluded groups' efforts to cope with a rejecting and harsh environment, and to deal with the rigid social boundaries imposed by nativistic leaders. Throughout the nineteenth century, social movements produced a wave of reform organizations to mobilize opposition to the institution of slavery, various ethnics' and women's political/social roles, and working conditions for urban laborers. The temperance movement was one example of this will to confront changing social power during this epoch. Less visible, but significant for their integrative capacities, were the various ethnic mutual-help societies that offered burial services, newspapers, churches, grassroots political organizations and other parallel institutions created by and for the unassimilated minority.

Gusfield (1966) argues that the temperance movement was a reactive system directed against culture assimilation. A "symbolic crusade," it restored the old status order as opposed to the new world of Catholics, Jews and other non-Protestant, newer urban populations. What it succeeded in doing was to link the urban and unemployment problems with the new populations of "unwashed" ethnics, and both conditions to "demon rum." Life-style variations became translated as depravity and corruption, and when the temperance workers attacked saloons with axes and hammers, saloon-keepers restored order only by closing down, at least temporarily, their beseiged businesses.

The body became the overarching symbol of evil. In its role as a pedagogical instrument, the body contained the lessons of the epoch: reverence, clean living, hard work and self-denial. On this body was engraved the dominant morality: for men—be steadfast, grave, self-reliant, aggressive, restrained, industrious, devout. Self was perceived as an uneasy alliance of soul and body, the latter being an ever present threat to the common enterprise. In an era of urban, industrial, state and economic expansion, where secure definitions about reality were collapsing, the body could signify the complex lessons of control without dealing directly with the prohibitive sexual symbols. Certainly, there was a strong Christian symbolism: the concept of the Fall drenches the entire frame; the body is viewed as nature, and like an animal, was to be subdued and kept under a tight regime.

Whereas we contemporaries perceive the Victorians as "prudish" in avoiding sexuality, there was an elaborate moral polarization centered on the mother/whore axis. Men could consort with whores, and drinking within houses of ill-repute was acceptable (and perhaps expected for the affluent). Men could not drink with wives, and they could not imbibe in public houses; this was low-class behavior. What the temperance advocates managed to pull off was a set of opposed terms: drinking identified as loss of body control, destruction of bodily boundaries and pollution. This was opposed to abstinence: body control equated with self-control and salvation. (Foucault, 1978, traces the origins of the "repressive hypothesis" in the Victorian obsession with discipline and administered knowledge.)

Alcoholics Anonymous, the organization that developed out of this social conditioning, takes self-control as the "God term" in Kenneth Burke's (1964) usage. Organizational ideology remains specifically individualistic. No attempt is made to politicize the program or change social policy (although individual members may take a personal stand or action). Drinking is viewed as a personal problem that requires control over one's inner spaces; never mind becoming a missionary about it. The doctrine, expressed in the Twelve Steps, emphasizes the individual's weakness, the body as a center for its own destruction. Here one reads the Christian litany of dangers: gluttony, sloth, concupiscence, the nature of humans who are prone to error. Only eternal vigilance, with God's help, can curb these carnal tendencies. Humility, renunciation and austerity, long rejected in the dominant culture, continue to mark the deserving person. Alcoholics Anonymous lacks a general ideology, not only because the body lessons stop with the person. AA cures alcoholics; it does not cure society.[6]

The women's health movement entered the world at a different point in time. While the rhetoric of integration continues to be used, the real issue is equality, a doctrine in keeping with the general movement toward status-leveling in the 60s and 70s. The institutional crisis has changed, too, as Habermas (1973) emphasizes. We now confront the "crisis of capitalism," its overuse and misuse of rationality, the "legitimation crisis." A world-wide nation-state system, propelled by multinational economies and administration, has succeeded; or perhaps oversucceeded is more accurate. In the process, social values and traditions, necessary to maintain social order and social control, have been seriously eroded. The society experiences "overload," a phenomenon associated with "steering problems." This occurs when the political and social institutions are unable to cope with the human problems that arise from the overrationalized economic sector. Humans' stake in history is nil.

Politicization of the world—this is the slogan signifying one of the more pronounced side effects of the collapse of social trust and cohesion. All of the noneconomic institutions are thrown into disarray: the meaning system is stretched out and thinned out. Here the body becomes a manifest power instrument that symbolizes the perceived inferior status, the denied privileges, the stigmatic, biological differences of women. The body is isomorphic with the social structures, now stripped barren of meanings and motivations. That men also live in oppressed structures and sacrifice their bodies and minds to meaningless labor is generally ignored. The crisis in meanings is total; hence the belief that a general or total ideology must arise to revitalize, indeed drastically overturn, all institutional structures.

If cultural fragmentation is the cause of modern social movements and their politicizing tendencies, what are concrete outcomes for persons? On the whole, they are not much different than those proposed by the 19th-century, Christian-influenced organizers: pain and self-abnegation. Such renunciation is not a self-transcending experience in the Christian conception, though. Instead, it is the pain caused by futility in the recycling of the search and burn-out, a form of despair.

When the person becomes politicized and collectivized, it is a world without a self. Altruistic sisterhood as an ideal transforms the person from an isolated atom to membership in a meaningful community; in so doing, the individual is required to abjure responsibility for actions and feelings in the interests of the collectivity.

Bonds of loyalty, charity, empathy and love between women in a world where all values and feelings are suspect are accomplished by the familiar in-group/out-group process; that is, internal balance is achieved by external hostility against dominant institutions, and for some, against men as a categorical, oppressive group.

Exclusive systems, such as Alcoholic Anonymous and women's self-help systems, have only limited impact on the environment; because AA is overindividualized and psychologized, there is no polity; when self-help is overpoliticized and ideologized, there is no self. Without a clear authority structure to impact on the dominant institutions, the meanings remain insular and precious, a kind of testimony to the ethic of privacy.

CHAPTER 12—NOTES

[1] This chapter is based on research support for Nanette J. Davis, provided by an NIMH-funded fellowship in Organizations and Mental Health, Stanford University, 1978-1979. I am indebted to Professors W. Richard Scott and John W. Meyer, whose insights and criticisms helped to focus the fieldwork and research issues.

[2] Data on the feminist health movement are drawn from Davis (1973), Davis and Anderson (1979), and more recently from Davis's fieldwork in the San Francisco Bay Area conducted under an NIMH fellowship, Stanford University, Spring, Summer 1979. Joan Kofodimos served as the able and spirited fieldworker. This study is based on observations and interviews in 20 radical feminist health centers. These systems are different from "women's care" abortion centers where standard fee-for-service prevails. Other data collected are more impressionistic, but include a study of the larger range of "holistic medicine" centers which are widely distributed throughout northern California, especially around the San Francisco area. These alternative health center services range from massage to meditation. Most commonly, they offer medical services as *one* component, often the least significant, of a number of health and personal development treatments. The total number of organizations surveyed during this period was 35; substantive data on ideology and practices are limited to 25 alternative health organizations, including 20 feminist health centers, two Health Maintenance Organizations (HMO), one "spiritual healing" center managed by a woman who was an ordained Gnostic priest, one abortion clinic, and one educational-health center, which specialized in such medical alternatives as bio-rhythm feedback, acupuncture and acupressure, hypnosis and other marginal or less-developed treatment programs.

[3] Reactive organizations have sprung up around the world to remedy traditional medicine. Organizations of radical physicians, holistic medicine, free "street" clinics, nonhospital-associated abortion clinics in the United States, and "barefoot doctors" in China share similar aims: "proletarianize" primary medical care and redistribute it to the people (Sidel and Sidel, 1973). Basically, this is the "new careers" concept, in which nonprofessional poor and minority persons are incorporated at lower and middle levels of the health care hierarchy. Medical services become a residual of health care. This is achieved by "leveling," for clients and workers increasingly are drawn from the same social classes. This status homogeneity not only ensures a shared world view and life style, it also mitigates the professional mystique contributed by class, race and sex distinctions in traditional medicine.

[4] Self-Help is a broadly defined program to educate women in the anatomy and self-care of the reproductive and genital organs. It emphasizes women learning from other women without the intercession of professionals. Self-help also refers to the specific practice of a woman's inserting a speculum into her own vagina and with the help of a flashlight and mirror determining the state of her internal genitals.

[5] "Clinic" is a generic term that covers all the feminist health organizations in our sample. Most feminist health groups prefer to use the concept "center" or 'collective," at least until they are securely funded. "Clinic" suggests a more technically oriented set of services than are actually available in some organizations, but the term has the advantage of encompassing a more inclusive set of activities than "center" or "collective," which often denotes health information and educational activities.

[6] Sagarin (1969) elaborates on this social-movement theme of changing the individual versus changing the society.

CONCLUSIONS TO PART IV

Commitment Organizations and Social Control   There are two extreme views of commitment organizations. According to one view they are the redeemers of a stale, stifling social order, while the other opinion insists they are the gathering grounds of assorted faddists and misfits. We want to argue that they are neither. This does not mean that the truth lies somewhere in between, but rather that the question of the significance of commitment organizations often gets misstated. To place commitment organizations sociologically, we need first to bring back some ideas developed in earlier chapters.

The idea of *self-help* through mutual help lies at the heart of the practical activities of functioning commitment organizations. Victims (of poverty, alcohol, sexism and other deviance) band together to help one another. Charles Silberman's statement about self-help among the poor has wide generality for social problems, deviance and addiction:

> "...almost everything in poor people's lives persuades them that they are victims, rather than masters, of their fate. But receiving help from the outside often perpetuates the sense of impotence and powerlessness that is a cause, as well as consequence, of poverty. Independence is difficult when one person is constantly in the position of magnanimous donor and the other in the position of perennial recipient. Receiving help is a submission, one that erodes dignity and destoys the spirit."
>
> (Silberman, 1978: 582-583)

Through mutual help, the time and material resources of the participants are combined, and can be used to help a member or to provide a collective benefit. Volunteers, each of whom donates a few hours a week, can run a crisis center or staff a shelter or halfway house. Small cash contributions can provide simple meals. The social-psychological effects are equally important, as Silberman indicates. Feelings of efficacy, trust and self-esteem result from successful group efforts.

In chapter 10 we pointed out two important aspects of commitment organizations. They stress affiliation, often by using terms like "brothers" and "sisters," and they stress ideological consciousness. Both are important for maintaining the mutual-aid orientation. Solidarity with other members, pleasure in their company, makes the cooperative interactions self-rewarding, regardless of the successes and failures of the outcomes. And performing acts in the manner defined as correct by the ideology defines the person as a good member in the eyes of the others. The ideology may even define failure positively. One learns from the failures, especially if the ideology can define the failure as the result of not carrying out the movement's program correctly.

Organization theorists traditionally analyze members' motives for participating in organizations in terms of inducements and contributions. Inducements are seen by members as benefits to themselves, while the contributions always cost them something (Simon, 1964). In commitment organizations the emphasis on affiliation and the ideology serve for the members to increase the values of the inducements and to decrease the disincentives, i.e., the costs of their contributions (Oliver, 1980).[1]

In chapter 3 we argue that we have come increasingly to live in a world of communities and organizations in which the ties that link members are weak, specialized (nonpervasive), and fragmented. These are the life-worlds of corporations, bureaucracies, professions and metropolitan areas. We said that the developments in this direction are irreversible. We also said (in chapters 3 and elsewhere) that such social structures are inadequate for socialization and social control over youth or for transitions over the life cycle. Communitarian environments are needed for much of the initial childhood and socialization, and also for the resocialization that seems necessary if persons are to be helped out of many destructive deviant roles and identities. The question then becomes: is it possible to build stable and enduring communitarian islands in the larger social structure? And what can we learn about this question by studying the existing commitment organizations?

For a long time sociologists held that *the family* served as a communitarian haven. Professor Talcott Parsons, who put together the last of the classical "systems" in social thought, believed this. He laid extraordinary responsibilities on the nuclear family. But dual-career or single-parent families cannot fulfill the functions demanded of them. How can a family in which both parents work away from the home be expected to resocialize or control a drug-dependent youngster or sustain a mentally ill relative? The family shares in the general fragmentation of social relations, even as romantic love myths spread over the landscape by country-music stations sound increasingly unreal.

Commitment organizations are beset with serious problems. The "burn-out" of the most active members is often mentioned, and also strife and factionalism. Alcoholics Anonymous shows that a commitment organization can survive and expand and work successfully over a long period of time without these problems becoming very visible. What is it then about AA that has enabled it to cope with the strains?

First, AA is a *one-issue* movement. It has to do with drinking and nothing else. Unlike the feminist movement, it is neutral politically, does not as a movement advocate large-scale social change. In AA, there are few issues that can become the symbolics of a bitter schism, but simply the formation of a group that will attend to certain common matters *in their relation to drinking,* for example, homosexuality or race. Members of the new group often continue to frequent the meetings of their orginal group. In short, AA has learned not to make differences into oppositions.

Second, AA has taken the time to formulate its program and ideology very deliberately and carefully. The meaning of the steps and the tradition, and their rationale, are regularly explained to members by members. The ideology is not utopian, but emphasizes what can and should be done in the present. "One day at a time" of not drinking leads to a sober life.

It is by internalizing the theory and by following its maxims in detail that the recovering alcoholic gains the insight into the "illness" that is the main precondition for recovery. Recovery is a program of cognitive development, undertaken in collaboration with others, who are going through the steps or have gone through them in the past. It is of course nothing new that a commitment organization develops a highly articulated *praxis,* a theory that is both to be understood cognitively and performed in a prescribed manner. The early years of the psychoanalytic movement, one of the most successful commitment movements in this century, were largely spent formulating a praxis. Religious movements and organizations in earlier times developed elaborate techniques for self-examination and the questioning of God about His will. The most well-known of these are probably the spiritual exercises prescribed by Ignatius Loyola, the founder of the Jesuit order (Loyola, 1964, also Barthes, 1976 and Steiner, 1978:82-83).

The existence of an institutionalized praxis imposes uniformity on the movement. Disagreements about procedure and policy are often settled by appeal to the common doctrine.

Third, an AA member has available a direct test of performance success or failure. It may not be easy to assess whether someone has attained a liberated feminist consciousness, but it is easy to tell whether AA members manage to stay sober or not. The incentive of day-to-day achievement is thus available in AA, and builds commitments and reinforces the practices of the organization. It is incentives that keep members loyal to organizations. And successful *performance* may be a necessary condition for the *cognitive* restructuring that is the basis for rehabilitation (see Bandura, 1977).

If this analysis is correct, then movements whose ideologies contain many competing issues, which fail to articulate and elaborate the precise meanings of the ideology for the affairs of the movement and which lack commonly accepted pragmatic criteria of success that can provide the incentives for the activities should be expected to be most vulnerable to factionalism and "burn-out."

The mentality that many contemporary commitment movements grew out of may not have been conducive to the hard work of formulating and testing a praxis. The reactions against established institutions often turned into antiintellectualist stances. Careful thinking became defined as "headtrips." A cult grew up around "direct experience." However, disillusionment with earlier movement practices has produced a good deal of reassessment.

Many commitment organizations dedicated to self-help and mutual help are working in a variety of places.[2] They should each be seen as an experiment: it is by codifying their evolving practices that we might gain an understanding of how "alternative" organizations can be run and managed.[3]

The quest for community has its dangers, of course. Commitment communities easily become inward-looking, make a cult of intimacy and see the world in "purified categories." This is the critique put forth by Sennett in *The Uses of Disorder* (Sennett, 1970). The problems of modern societies are complex, messy and ridden with ambivalences and ambiguities, and cannot be cast in rigid, simple terms. This also includes social problems that have to do with social policies and such volatile issues as gender equality.

CONCLUSIONS TO PART IV—NOTES

[1] For theoretical analyses and descriptions of mutual-benefits systems, see K.L. Hansen, M.H. Loukinen, and F. Southard *et al,* in David Willer and Bo Anderson, *Networks, Exchange and Coercion* (1981).

[2] An interesting case study is reported in Anthony Sorrentino, *Organizing Against Crime* (1977). Charles Silberman, *Criminal Violence and Criminal Justice,* Chapter 11, and the notes on pages 676-677, mentions cases and literature. A recent book is Lieberman, Borman and Associates, *Self-Help Groups for Coping in Crisis.*

[3] The standard tests on organizations contain virtually nothing that is relevant for an understanding of commitment organizations. It should be mentioned here that the notion of community lends itself to sentimentalizing, rather than to analysis, in the social sciences and in other forms of literature. The *myth* of community comes to filter and distort reality. A masterly treatment of this topic is found in Raymond Williams, *The Country and the City* (1973, especially chapters 23 and 24).

Chapter 13
The Materialist Fallacy:
A Look at Power and Social Policy

The first constitution will be 200 years old in 1987 — as good a date as any to finish the work of the second constitutional convention which will make possible our Fourth Republic, and first — ah, the note of optimism — civilization.

Gore Vidal, "The Second American Revolution"

Many current policy debates, when they are serious at all, are couched in the politics of despair and anxiety: environmental destruction, the demographic problem, global nuclear horrors, urban decay, crime, ethnic strife and constraints on economic growth dominate the discourse. This bundle of gloom and doom talk leads to expectations of inevitable defeat; the illusion that resources are essentially finite things that run down and then out, rather than creations of human will, skill and imagination, stymies our most intense efforts to regenerate our civilization.

This final chapter recapitulates our main arguments and then takes another look at power and social policy using the critical perspective. Here we show some possibilities for social control in the 80s, that may avoid the failed conventional wisdom.

A recurring theme among critical thinkers about society — from Marx to more recent figures, for example Horkheimer (1976) and Habermas — has been to bring societal evolution under the control of human will and intentions. This may in part be an unrealizable ambition. Because societies are parts of nature, they remain what Marx called *naturwüchsig*. But institutions are also created and reproduced by men and women. It is simply a mystification to pretend that laws of economies and other institutions are part of nature in the same sense as are planetary motions and genetics. Rather than throw up our hands in the face of massive social problems, we need to assess how much social control and how much intervention should guide social evolution toward achieving civilized institutions within a normative framework.

312

Comprehensive approaches to societal guidance are being worked on by some modern thinkers, for example Jürgen Habermas and Niklas Luhmann, from the points of view of both critical theory and systems theory.[1] In German sociology where much of this innovative work is happening, productive confrontations have occurred between humanistic critical theory and technocratic systems analysis. In this chapter we shall present some general remarks about how adequate social controls could be developed within social policy. Our remarks must be very brief. The work on a theory of social policy is high on our agenda but requires a full-length book.

Let us first recapitulate our main arguments in the preceding chapter.

A Summing Up

In the early chapters of the book we assessed the control solution of total institutions as a stunning failure when applied indiscriminately to underclass and vulnerable populations. These highly pervasive and hierarchical systems rely primarily on external controls and sanctions, but have little impact on the heart and minds of the inmates. The institutions are profoundly dualistic in nature. There exists a great deal of opportunistic public conformity with the rules and regulations, but turn to the other side, and there also flourishes an often rich, subtle, largely underground system of evasions, resistances, deviant rules and values, manipulations, informal power networks and exploitations, through which groups of inmates in varying degrees protect themselves from the official order. The social process in total institutions should be analyzed in two ways: *social psychologically,* as a battle between public and clandestine identities, or public conformity and self-maintenance in small solidaristic support groups, and *structurally,* as a complex game of strategies by which the official and underground orders attempt to outwit one another. *Coercion* is a way of life in total institutions: the authorities use it pervasively to obtain conformity with the institutional rules. The inmate groups, too, use it to enforce solidarity, to maintain their own system of leadership and stratification, and to discourage collaborations with the authorities. Resocialization to the norms and values of the outside society, vocational training and other humanitarian goals become casualties of the running institutional battle. Life in the institution becomes constant punishment not only for the inmates, but for the various personnel groups in the control apparatus as well.

The authoritarian hierarchical rule of the total institution corresponds to and is justified by a view of inmates as potentially dangerous, constitutionally inferior or polluted, and irresponsible or not quite human. Elaborate penological and psychiatric doctrines, allegedly founded on empirical research, have been developed to provide biological or psychological justifications for the institutional repression. Unmasking such doctrines that purport to be empirically valid, but are revealed as often racist or sexist pseudotheories, remains one of the more significant contributions in the critical social sciences over the last three or four decades. The most significant single work that completed the demolishing of the total institution ideologies is undoubtedly Goffman's *Asylums*.

Total institutions are costly to maintain; inmates have to be housed, fed and clothed. Expensive staffs are necessary to guard and "rehabilitate" them, and society gets no revenue from them. Cost considerations combine with the widespread realization that prison, mental hospital and other total institutional environments are inimical to rehabilitation and resocialization. They also actively foster dependency and asocial behavior. Widespread disbelief in the intellectual pretensions of their control ideologies have led to a massive shift away from reliance on total institutions for social control in Western Europe and North America. "Deinstitutionalization," "community care" and "mental health" become the new key words for social control. By and large, the diminished role for total institutions has been a gain for humane values. But new problems arose when the paternalism of the total institution was replaced by the bureaucratic impersonality of the new systems.

Total institutions will continue to play a limited role in social control. There are persons who are dangerous to themselves and others. And public opinion continues to insist that incarceration is the only justified punishment for many crimes. In some countries experiments are being conducted with new types of total institutions, usually employing smaller facilities and a higher ratio of staff to inmates, in which the control structures are modified to make them more compatible with resocialization and rehabilitation. This organizational evolution is still in an early stage and the results appear mixed and uncertain.

In the second part of the book, we considered the treatment-oriented, professional organizations of social control as products of movements of social reform and modernization. We noted that one starting point in their emergence was the critique of the total institutions mentioned above. Another impetus for reform was their belief that just as professional, scientific medicine has succeeded in preventing and curing many *physical* illnesses, so could, in principle, a variety of *social* ills be prevented or cured through the application of treatments. Such intervention was to be based on tested principles of individual and social behavior. The clients' predicaments are no longer perceived as a result of biological degeneracy or constitutional inferiority but as the cumulative effects of bad environment and life circumstances. By changing or overcoming such negative factors and their effects through carefully-designed social intervention and therapy, a well adjusted individual or family can result.

This therapeutic way of thinking gained credence from various sources. The social and behavioral sciences have successfully demonstrated that much of human behavior is shaped by learning and other social and environmental influences. It thus seems plausible that undesirable behavior can be eliminated through suitable treatment and new, desirable behavior instilled once the person is subjected to the right social and environmental influences. As the social and behavioral sciences evolve, and as practical therapeutic knowledge accumulates, the professional should become increasingly equipped to set up the right conditions for modifying clients' behavior in socially acceptable directions. In addition, the widespread medicalization of some human behavior within medicine through the use of pharmacological treatments has strengthened the analogy between social ills and disease. This furthers the hope that some form of tested and routinely applicable therapeutic procedures eventually will be found for the various social ills. And finally, the very great prestige that the medical profession enjoys in modern society has made it the most desirable group to emulate for those newer professionally insecure groups that staff the modern treatment organizations.

The typical *modern social problem* is defined and constructed through a complex *political* process that involves interaction among the treatment and therapists, the professionals, the more or less organized clients and client-oriented groups and the state. In this political process the scope and nature of problems are negotiated. Other dimensions of this transaction include the broad outlines of the treatment procedures and their organizations, the training and credentials of the personnel involved, the eligibility of clients and finally, the distribution of available funds.

In terms of human values the community care organizations represent a vast advance over the total institution. The emphasis on treatment offers hope. Clients are not removed from all of their normal community ties and can receive treatment without being massively labeled as a deviant. The personnel are often supportive. Yet, there exist some serious problems with the therapeutic model. To begin with, scientific claims for the therapeutic methods based on the social and behavioral sciences are very often spurious. The medical analogy remains a very loose one. In medicine the efficacy of many procedures can be evaluated in detail because large bodies of experimental and clinical cases can be cited. A well-tested procedure can be objectively described and then taught to anyone who possesses the adequate technical training. By contrast, most counseling and group-therapy techniques are only vaguely codified. The data relevant for their experimental and clinical validation are at best very ambiguous. Success or failure depend to a great extent on the personalities of the therapist and the clients and the relationships they manage to create. Also, the nonpervasive, specialized nature of the treatment organization poses problems. Much socialization and self-development seems to presuppose affiliation with and support by pervasive, closely knit relationships. A professional therapist, however, has limited contact with the client and must remain detached. The therapist must not be a member of the client's intimate community, if therapy is to be successful. And, finally, the treatment easily becomes fragmented and discontinuous. Clients drift away from the therapy, remaining under the influence of those elements that produced the problems in the first place. They receive therapy for only a limited aspect of the problem or finish one treatment phase without having available the necessary follow-up care. In other words, it is easy to fall "between the cracks" in the system.

When we turned to self-help organizations, we found that they are more pervasive, i.e., focus their normative concerns more on the total person than community care organizations, but less so than total organizations. Their values are egalitarian, affiliative, and often oppositional. An internal stratification exists, but in principle is based on *moral authority* rather than position or professional credentials. Professional, e.g., medical expertise, is used in the organizations; but attempts are made to keep professionals marginal to the organizational activities. Egalitarian *ritual* is common, for instance, the use of terms like "brother" or "sister," the mocking enactment of status claims, mutual teasing and rank reversals. Self-help groups try to avoid a "frozen" division of labor. Jobs should rotate among the members rather than being the properties of incumbents.

Efficacy is not unimportant. Self-help groups exist to get specific tasks done, but it is secondary to *expressiveness* and *affiliation* —that is, a "warm" group climate. It is as if self-help groups have gathered in and are trying to overcome the discontent many people feel about the coldness and distance that characterize social relations in both total institutions and the professional and bureaucratic institutions dominating modern societies. The consciousness of being different and of conducting their work differently is very evident in the self-help groups that we have observed.

In attempting to write about self-help groups, the sociologist experiences a peculiar difficulty. They are easy to describe as far as their external structures go. The peculiarly "warm insides" of self-help groups are more difficult to capture in sociological terms, however. One is left with the feeling that the external, structural description radically fails to capture what "really happens" in the groups. When we attempt to describe, for example, a bureaucratic and professional organization, we experience no analogous tension between the external and internal descriptions. In part, the difficulty is that traditional sociological concepts and work habits were modeled on the social relations characterizing bureaucratic and rational-efficient organizations. The result is that the sociological treatment of self-help organizations runs the risk *either* of sentimentalizing or idealizing them *or* of approaching them with the debunking attitudes of cynical knowledge. Either attitude is unproductive if we are to understand the real and potential contributions of self-help groups to social organization and reform.

In this book we limited the problem of social control to an *institutional* point of view. It must be remembered that all *three types of control are in evolution*. The total institutions of the future will be considerably different from most contemporary models. They may, for example, use more refined controls, with brute force giving way to techniques drawn from pharmacology, behavior modification or brain surgery. Combinations of behavior-modification techniques and drugs may make inmates more pliable than isolation cells and beatings. Similarly, the modern data techniques in the future may enable the social services and therapeutic bureaucracies to become more efficient in preventing patients from falling between the cracks and escaping from the system, therby ensuring continuous treatments and surveillance. Self-help and commitment movements, too, are likely to grow in various directions: some will become genuine liberation movements and will perfect the techniques of resistance against coercive controls. Others may grow into totalitarian sects or cults that resemble total institutions, for example, Synanon and Jonestown.

The institutional analysis is not the only important perspective on social control. A *social-psychological* approach, played down in our analyses, focuses more directly on the roles of different kinds of incentives in control, resocialization and rehabilitation. An *economic* analysis, also absent here, would study the costs for society that result from loss of tax revenue or the increased use of social services when the breadwinner is incarcerated or incapacitated. Finally, an indispensable perspective on the workings of social control institutions is given by the literature written from the point of view of those controlled by the various institutions. The anguish of the victims of impersonal power is as equally important a perspective on society's social conrol as dispassionate accounts of the effects of different control techniques depicted by, for example, academic experts on criminal justice. So is, for that matter, the anxiety and abuse suffered by third parties, for instance family members, when societal institutions in the name of doctrines of permissiveness fail to control violence-prone or irresponsible persons.

Power and Social Control

Social control is always, in the final analysis, exercise of power. The *techniques of power* have a long history, and modern societies have available a very wide range of such techniques. Michel Foucault has made them the focus of his wide-ranging investigations. The social control institutions are "packages" of power techniques, from naked coercion to group therapies or medicalized procedures. All techniques of power may involve someone bullying somebody else. The writings of Erving Goffman and Jules Henry (1963) are especially replete with descriptions of power techniques. The bullying may be subtle or crude, hidden or visible, but it is there and usually recognized by most of the participants. We have argued in this book, from the point-of-view of human values, that the transition from reliance on total institutions to community care and mental health organizations and the increasing role of self-help groups, by and large, represents progress. The new packages of power techniques are more benevolent than the old ones. Yet, power is as omnipresent in the newer institutions as in the old ones; it only takes different forms.

Social control institutions are surrounded by, enshrouded in, moral ambiguities and unease. This is because of the dilemmas entailed by techniques of power, when confronted by humane value commitments. Societies need techniques of power, but when they involve overt bullying, they lead to subordination, victimization and guilt. Most modern societies use total institutions too frequently, although there are persons who probably have to be kept in prisons or asylums. More benevolent institutions, e.g., social service and mental health institutions, are clearly hierarchical, in spite of some attempts to play down the obvious symbols of inequality. And the tyranny of the collective in self-help groups is often evident. Societies will continue to employ some mix of the various available control structures. At the same time there is a growing realization that undue advantages accrue to those who wield power; and that powerlessness breeds apathy and resentment among the subjected and guilt and bad faith among the powerful. These sentiments interfere with the treatment goals. In some cases those who control, for example, educational administrators or parents, suffer from a sufficiently bad conscience to experiment with overly permissive doctrines and methods, thereby abdicating their responsibility for socializing the young.

The moral unease about control should, in our view, be dealt with by formulating carefully deliberated social control policies. Such policies must be capable of acquiring legitimacy in terms of articulable, universalistic value commitments. In the next section we shall discuss some features of social policy and attempt to state some criteria that can be used to evaluate policy proposals. No proposals, though, can eliminate the moral ambiguities of social control; such as the objective features of oppressive control systems when confronted by unshared values. Nevertheless, some policies and some control institutions are more palatable, more human and more survival-oriented than others, and we need criteria for making discriminations.

Some Steps Toward Policy Analysis

Earlier, in chapter 2, we argued for a perspectivist orientation to social problems. Briefly put, we argued that any social problem involves a variety of social groups and actors, requiring that the social problem be viewed in very different ways. The first criterion for policy formation emphasizes that the problem should be carefully articulated from the points of view of each one of the different relevant actors. Each perspective should be described in terms of the "facts of the case;" the norms and values used within the group to evaluate the facts and various action priorities. Special attention should be paid to the linguistic codes used by the groups to state their cases. The terms used to describe facts, including the behavior of other actors, will reveal explicit or implicit valuations, cognitive emphases and dispositions to act. Most likely, each group will consider its own version to be the correct one and the others to be wrong-headed, and those of conflicting parties to be absurd. Other points of view are likely to be denied. Nevertheless, the perspectives or definitions of the situations perceived by each group are for the policy analyst important pieces of the social problem. They determine, at least partly, how the groups orient themselves to one another in the social process that reproduces the problem on a day-to-day basis.

The second step calls for a *comprehensive problem analysis* that integrates and confronts the perspectives of the various groups with one another. The analysis should spell out how differences in perspectives lead to clashes and how the perspectives are reinforced, modified or stalemated when the different groups engage one another. The perspectives must also be related to social class, political access and outside supports. A significant issue: how do some groups succeed in having their perspectives articulated in the mass media and elevated to official truths? The social scientist should model the system of perspectives, paying special attention to such power issues. Also, the analyst should remembaber that the perspectives of the less powerful, the underdog groups, may be less accessible than those of the more socially respectable groups. The latter are more readily translated into the analyst's social science vocabulary. "Official truths," differential accessibility and congeniality with the "Haves," represent the main sources of biased descriptions at this stage of the analysis.

The third step applies the *sociology of knowledge* to the perspectives on the social problem held by the diverse groups. The guiding assumption is that the beliefs, ways of speaking about the problem and modes of orientation and action are rooted in the life circumstances of the groups. We use the term "life circumstances" for a variety of predicaments. *Social class* is certainly one set of predicaments that deeply affects people's beliefs, orientations and actions on many issues such as welfare. But people's persectives on other matters, for example, abortion, seem more rooted in religious and sexual traditions than social class. Because such perspectives are rooted in total life circumstances, communications between groups about the social problem become distorted.

The fourth step identifies the *distribution of different power techniques* and their ideological justification among the involved actors or groups. Since power is exercised in many forms, naked, unadulterated domination represents only one technique among many others. Power is also in an important sense always *systemic*. Foucault (1980: 98) provides some useful insights into power:

> Power must be analyzed as something which circulates, or rather as something which only functions in the form of a chain. It is never localized here or there, never in anybody's hands, never appropriated as a commodity or piece of wealth. Power is employed and exercised through a netlike organization. And not only do individuals circulate between its threads; they are always in the position of simultaneously undergoing and exercising this power. They are not only its inert or consenting target; they are always also the elements of its articulation. In other words, individuals are the vehicles of power, not its points of application.

This view of power implies that we should not expect a simple dichotomy of dominators and victims to exist for any given problem area. The weak are sometimes also aggressors, although they use different power tactics than the strong. Take, for example, the case of "problem families" in housing developments as sometimes reported in the press of various non-communistic countries. They are locked in perpetual combat with both housing authorities and other families, whom they see as unresponsive, contemptuous and bullying. Members of "problem" families respond with vandalism, delinquency, drug use and drunkedness, thereby causing protracted troubles for the bureaucrats, who, however, also find good reasons for continuing to label them as "trash." Meanwhile, bystanders suffer abuse by drunken or drugged juveniles, larceny and noise pollution, to which they respond by ostracizing all the members of the "problem" families, including those who are not troublemakers. The neighborhood exists in a sort of stalemate of shifting bullying games. In mapping the dimensions of the social problem we must trace the entire network, or tournament, of power plays. To formulate policy it is clearly not sufficient to use a rule like "always focus on protecting the weak," or "don't blame the victims." It is by no means clear who are the weak and the strong, the dominators and the oppressed in the situation we described. Some of the actors are both aggressors and victims.

Reconstruction vs. Incrementation

What should be the shape and content of social control policies? It is arguable, of course, that only a thorough *reconstruction* of society can solve the ourstanding social problems, eliminate deviance, and gradually render the current types of social control institutions obsolete. Reconstruction is undoubtedly a necessary long-term goal. For example, utopian versions of radical thought assume that during a future stage of transition to socialism the state and its control systems will wither away. But the political realities of American society and other capitalist states are not likely, in the foreseeable future, to permit any radical experiments in social reconstruction. Furthermore, no one has available the kind of reconstructive blueprints necessary for eliminating the institutionally related social problems dealt with in the previous chapters. Even so-called radical solutions cannot eliminate the ageism, sexism, classism and racism that runs rampant in all industrial societies including those in the socialist block. Some solutions would certainly make the problems worse and create new atrocities.

Feasible social policies at this point in history, in our opinion, must be constructed on a *piecemeal, incremental, experimentalist* basis and also be guided by *critical, nondistorting systemic* analyses of the existing structures and their possibilities. We shall first explain what the six key words in this statement mean.

(1) A *piecemeal* approach to policy (Popper, 1967) assumes, contrary to much fashionable rhetoric, that at least some progress can

be made on some problems independently of what happens to other problems. Societies are *not* in all respects tightly integrated organisms or "functional wholes" that can either be *comprehensively* reformed or must be left to linger as they are. For example, it is true that improved safety procedures, police work and prosecution can prevent many rapes; we need not wait for a complete revamping of society's sex-and-gender conceptions to make streets, parks and public buildings safer for women than they are now. Social problem solving can move pragmatically on many fronts, even without a master strategy for coping with society's evils. Indeed, master strategies often fail to respond to local, concrete situations, because they are hampered by bureaucratic inertia.

(2) The *incremental* orientation assumes that it is always worthwhile to make *some* progress on an issue, even though most of what is wrong or evil remains uncorrected. Half-measures should always be preferred to no intervention. For example, if keeping the legal drinking age at 21 prevents some minors from regularly being exposed to alcohol, then such a policy should be adopted, though we recognize that a sufficiently determined teenager who is an incipient alcoholic or addict probably will find a way to buy the substance.

Much of the impetus toward social reform has come from the revitalization and commitment movements dealt with in Part IV of this book. These movements typically demand large-scale social reconstruction. To use a slogan of the 1960s, they argue that "what is not part of the solution is part of the problem." As much as we admire the maximalist sentiments of many of the visionaries who have given their lives to commitment movements, the piecemeal and incrementalist view of policy is different from their proposal. For example, the sexist police officer who is a conscientious patroller may prevent many rapes, even though this individual's unreconstructed attitudes in a larger sense contribute somewhat to preserving gender stereotypes. This person is part of the "solution" and also part of the "problem."

(3) The *experimentalist* orientation demands that solutions to problems should be attempted, rigorously evaluated and continuously modified or discarded on the basis of carefully gathered information. *Diversity* of approaches should be encouraged, and the outcomes comprehensively evaluated with a view to finding the most workable arrangements. Social policy, directed only by central

bureaucracy, will undoubtedly lack the necessary diversity. On the other hand, if there is no central authority that gathers, evaluates and pools the information from many experiments, society will not sufficiently benefit from the large variety of information sources.

(4) Social problems as specific issues should be viewed in as total a societal context as possible. Linkages to a variety of social institutions and processes may be subtle and indirect. A policy analyis should lay out these linkages in a *systemic* manner. This point is the complement of point (2) above. The systemic analysis will reveal in detail how much or how little can be expected of a piecemeal, incrementalist policy option.

(5) The *critical* orientation involves a persistent skepticism toward the institutions that carry out and embody social policies. Hierarchical bureaucratic institutions usually develop routines and ideological stances that protect their habitual ways of doing work or the self-interests of their staffs, rather than to further their mandated tasks. This tendency hampers the experimental orientation to social problems that calls for continuous reevaluations of organizations' procedures in the light of *all* available evidence. What we earlier called *perspectivism* is an indispensable aid in the skeptical orientation; it confronts the agendas of organizational professionals with the definitions and experiences of clients and organized client social movements (such as welfare reform groups, constituents and other relevant groups). At the same time, we should not underestimate the difficulty of keeping such communications from becoming defensive exercises in name-calling. Social problems breed resentment and anger. Social class differences that exist between clients, constituents and organizational staffs further impose barriers.

(6) *Nondistorted communication* (Habermas, 1970) is hard to achieve but is an essential goal in policy development. Clients, the "targets" of social control institutions, are more often than not vulnerable people, very susceptible to power and bullying strategies on the part of official social institutions. Bullying is often done in the alleged best interests of clients and with good, sincere intentions. Any ethically acceptable strategy for developing social policy must make special institutionalized efforts for the voices of the vulnerable and powerless to be heard as clearly as possible.

Social control policies inevitably aim to defend the moral order of society. A functioning moral order is certainly one of the basic necessities if persons are to pursue those innumerable and varied private goals that give meaning to lives. As Max Weber in the early years of this century and Jürgen Habermas more recently have insisted, the legitimacy of a moral order no longer depends on loyalty to traditional values rooted in religion, status-groups, family and kinship systems, social classes or occupations. In the future, control practices and power techniques, necessary as they may be for the social order, will have to *earn* their legitimacy. Habermas speaks of a *legitimation crisis* as the major challenge to contemporary society. The belief by large sectors of the population that society is primarily being run for other people's benefit appears to be a major source of resentment and distancing from institutions. Naked power appears, rightly or wrongly, to be used against the already underprivileged. Cycles of distancing, coercion and legitimacy crisis, if they become stable and endemic, serve to undermine any prospects for a civilized order.

In Search of Equality

The materialist fallacy, our beginning point, works on the assumption that human problems can be treated as "things," units merely requiring resources, personnel, budgets and effective public relations to pull the parts together. For any social problem, a rhetoric and network of experts can be mobilized that will attack the nuisance and rectify departures from the American dream. In our judgment this misses the essential issue, the search for a model of human equality and personhood. The materialist mission and the rhetorics of freedom and opportunity that were generated (sometimes in perverted form) from it—*laissez-faire,* legal rights and individual emancipation—are obsolete guideposts because the message masks the growing moral and spiritual disparities among human groups and persons. We are beset, as the distinguished economist Robert L. Heilbroner recently said, by a "crisis of imagination."[2] Locked into the spirit of capitalism and its rationalistic solutions, we endure a crisis of crippling human prospects, for which the economic crisis, political crisis and the crisis of morale and morality are only surface manifestations. The age of entitlement is upon us—the demand for liberation comes from many formerly silent quarters: minorities, the retarded, the aged, the dying, women, even children. However, what liberation means is not the exclusive materialist preoccupation with larger shares of the pie, although this must be a major element in any revamping of our collective relationships. Liberation offers a new myth, a counterproposal to the narrow economic solution. This seeks to create alternatives, rejecting the overly restricted band of existing possibilities. It aims to increase the power of the individual over the hierarchy and to enrich the human crucible with visions of our shared experiences that transcend the technological limits. The search for *moral* equality, if we may translate these liberation myths into a policy format, is a sweeping, world-wide movement. One nation's freedom, then, cannot be another society's or group's slavery. The old bankrupt policies that look to the isolated nation state and its insular welfare cannot work in today's world. Hence, the need for careful reappraisal to assess how an incremental adaptation in one society could lead to positive or deleterious results in another.

No doubt the public rhetorics of liberation are often overblown and strident rather than reflective or pragmatic in the sense of the dominant political tradition. Not all desires and group demands, however plausible, are rights based on morality and social justice. But the enduring significance of the liberation movements may be their attempts to gradually articulate a basic political right: what it entails to be treated as a *person*. This person category is the basis for *moral equality* and is indispensible for the legitimacy of societies that are highly differentiated in organizational power, access to resources and even wealth.[5] Demands by women, blacks and all other minorities in the United States, for instance, call for a reconstructed set of institutions where persons are treated on their own terms as equally deserving of the right to a self-constructed life. The blueprint for that reconstruction remains to be done.

Our incrementalist solution, admittedly, is a temporizing one. What can be emphasized for any social policy approach is that to deny persons housing, jobs or basic standards of living and transportation because of sex, racial origin, age, sexual preference or other socially imposed categories is to assault their human dignity. It is also to condone society and its control institutions as a terror machine, the reverse of the civilized state.

The search for equality is a contemporary fact of life. It may indeed signal the second American Revolution, in Gore Vidal's terms, if we don't turn our backs on that vision.

CHAPTER 13—NOTES

[1] An overview of the issues are presented by Dallmayer and McCarthy (1977). These arguments are further explicated in Habermas, 1970, 1971.

[2] From a public lecture presented at Portland State University, Portland, Oregon, October 15, 1980.

[3] There is a vast philosophical literature about the concept of person, which includes moral, ontological and epistemological ramifications. A normative theory of social policy could with profit draw on this literature (see, for example, Rawls, 1971:433-446).

REFERENCES

Abelson, R.
  1976   "Script Processing in Attitude Formation and Decision Making" in J.S. Garroll and J.W. Payne,eds. *Cognition and Social Behavior*. Hillsdale, New Jersey: Erlbaun Publishing Company.

Abrahamse, A.F., De Ferranti, D.M., Fleeschaver, P.D. and Lipson, A.
  1977   *AFDC Caseload and the Job Market in California: Selected Issues*. Santa Monica, California: Rand Institute.

Adams, Nathan M.
  1974   "Our Prisons are Powder Kegs" in *The Reader's Digest* (October): 185-186.

Adler, Freda
  1975   *Sisters in Crime: The Rise of the New Female Criminal*. New York: McGraw-Hill.

Adorno, Theodore W.
  1968   "Sociology and Psychology" in *New Left Review* 47:95.

_____
  1973   *Negative Dialectics*. London: Routledge and Kegan Paul.

Albers, Robert J. and Scrivner, Larry L.
  1977   "The Structure of Attrition During Appraisal" in *Community Mental Health Journal*, Vol. 13 (4):325-332.

Alcoholics Anonymous
  1955   New and revised edition. New York City: Alcoholics Anonymous World Service, Inc. ("The Big Book").

Alford, Robert R.
  1975   *Health Care Politics*. Chicago: The University of Chicago Press.

Allen, Harry E. and Simonsen, Clifford E.
  1978   *Corrections in America*. Second Edition. Encino, California: Glencoe Publishing Company.

Allison, Graham
  1971   *Essence of Decision: Explaining the Cuban Missile Crisis*. Boston: Little, Brown and Company.

Andeneas, Johannes
  1974   *Straf og Lovlydighet*. Oslo: Universitetsforlaget.

Anderson, Bo
  1968   "Revitalization Movements." Acta Universitatis Upsaliensis. Uppsala Universitat 17.

Anderson, Bo and Davis, Nanette J.
  1981   "Boundary Crossings in Social Networks. In D. Willer and B. Anderson, *Networks, Exchange and Coercion*. New York: Elsevier.

Anderson, Martin
  1978   *Welfare*. Stanford, California: Hoover Institution Press, Stanford University.

Anson, Robert Sam
  1978   "The Synanon Horrors" in *New Times* (November 27):28-50.

Arieti, Silvano
    1975   *American Handbook of Psychiatry.* Second Edition. New York: Basic Books, Vol.6.

Arnold, Thurman
    1935   *The Symbols of Government.* New Haven: Yale University Press.

Atkinson, Ti-Grace
    1974   *Amazon Odyssey.* New York: Links Books.

Aubert, Vilhelm
    1954   *Om Straffens Sosiale Funktjon.* Oslo: Akademisk Forlag.

Avineri, Shlomo
    1968   *The Social and Political Thought of Karl Marx.* New York: Cambridge University Press.

Back, Kurt W.
    1972   *Beyond Words: The Story of Sensitivity Training and the Encounter Movement.* New York: Russell Sage Foundation.

Bain, Norman
    1964   *Concepts of Insanity in the United States 1789-1865.* New Brunswick, New Jersey: Rutgers University Press.

Balch, Robert W. and Griffith, Curt T.
    1975   "Official Response to the American Drug Crisis: An Examination of Erikson's Constancy Hypothesis." Paper presented to the Pacific Sociological Association, Victoria, British Columbia, April.

Bandura, Albert
    1977   "Self-Efficacy: Toward a Unifying Theory of Behavioral Change" in *Psychological Review,* Vol. 84, No. 2, 191-215.

Baran, Paul A.
    1969   *The Longer View.* New York: Monthly Review Press.

Bardach, Eugene
    1979   *The Implementation Game: What Happens After A Bill Becomes A Law.* Cambridge, Massachusetts: The MIT Press.

Barnes, Harry Elmer
    1948   "William Graham Sumner: Spencerianism in American Dress," Pp. 391-408 in *An Introduction to the History of Sociology.* Harry Elmer Barnes (ed.), Chicago: The University of Chicago Press.

Barnes, Harry Elmer
    1972   *The Story of Punishment.* Second Edition. Montclair, New Jersey: Patterson Smith.

Barthes, Roland
    1967   *Elements of Semiology.* New York: Hill and Wang.

    1972   *Mythologies.* New York: Hill and Wang.

    1976   *Sade, Fourier, Loyola.* New York: Hill and Wang.

    1979   *The Eiffel Tower and other Mythologies.* New York: Hill and Wang.

Bateson, Gregory
    1972   "The Cybernetics of 'Self': A Theory of Alcoholism" in Bateson, *Steps to an Ecology of Mind.* New York: Ballantine Books.

Bazell, R.J.
1971   "Health Radicals: Crusade to Shift Medical Power to the People" in *Science*, 173:506-509.

Bazelon, David
1974   "Psychiatrists and the Adversary Process" in *Scientific American* 230 (June):18-25.

Beck, Bernard
1967a   "Bedbugs, Stench, Dampness and Immorality: A Review Essay on Recent Literature about Poverty" in *Social Problems* Pp. 101-114.

1967b   "Welfare as A Moral Category" in *Social Problems* 14 (Winter):258-277.

1978   "The Politics of Speaking in the Name of Society." 1977 Presidential Address, Society for the Study of Social Problems. *Social Problems* 25 (April).

Beck, E.M.
1980   "Labor Unionism and Racial Income Inequality: A Time-Series Analysis of the Post World War II Period" in *American Journal of Sociology* 85:791-814.

Becker, Howard S.
1962   *Outsiders: Studies in the Sociology of Deviance*. New York: Free Press.

Berger, J., Cohen, B. and Zelditch, M.
1972   "Status Conceptions and Social Interaction" in *American Sociological Review* 37:241-255.

Berger, J. Conner, T.L. and Fisek, M.H.
1974   *Expectation States Theory: A Theoretical Research Program*. Cambridge, Massachusetts: Winthrop.

Berger, Joseph, Fisek, M.H., Norman, Robert A. and Zelditch, M.
1977   *Status Characteristics and Social Interaction*. New York: Elsevier.

Berger, Peter L. and Luckmann, Thomas
1967   *The Social Construction of Reality*. New York: Anchor Books.

Berger, Peter L.
1976   *Pyramids of Sacrifice: Political Ethics and Social Change*. Garden City, New York: Anchor Books.

Bergin, A.E.
1971   "The Evaluation of Therapeutic Outcomes" in A.E. Bergin and S.L. Garfield (eds.) *Handbook of Psychotherapy and Behavior Change: An Empirical Analysis*. New York: Wiley.

Bermant, G., Kelman, H. and Warwick, D.
1978   *The Ethics of Social Intervention*. New York: John Wiley and Sons.

Blackwell, Barbara L. and Bolman, William M.
1977   "The Principles and Problems of Evaluation" in *Community Mental Health Journal, Vol. 13 (2):175-181*.

Blau, Peter
1955   *The Dynamics of Bureaucracy*. Chicago: University of Chicago Press.

Blau, Peter and Scott, W. Richard
1962   *Formal Organizations*. San Francisco: Chandler.

Blau, Peter M. and Meyer, Marshall W.
1971   *Bureaucracy in Modern Society*. Second Edition. New York: Random House.

Bloom, Bernard L.
    1965   "The Medical Model, Miasma Theory and Community Mental Health" in *Community Mental Health Journal* 1:333-338.

Blumberg, A.S.
    1967   "The Practice of Law as a Confidence Game: Organizational Cooptation of a Profession" in *Law and Society Review* 1, June:15-39.

Blumer, Herbert
    1946   "Social Movements" in A.M. Lee (ed.), *New Outlines of Principles of Sociology.* New York: Barnes and Noble, Inc.

Blumer, Herbert
    1957   "Collective Behavior" in J.B. Gittler (ed.), *Review of Sociology: Analysis of a Decade.* New York: Wiley.

Boli-Bennett, John and Meyer, John W.
    1978   "Ideology of Childhood and the State" in *American Sociological Review,* Vol. 43, No. 6, 797-812.

Bommer, M., Goodgion, G., Pease, V. and Zmud, R.
    1977   "Development of an Information System for the Child Abuse and Neglect Service System" in *Community Mental Health Journal,* 13 (4):333-342.

Boston Women's Health Collective, Our Bodies, Ourselves.
    1973   New York. Simon and Schuster. 1979 Second Edition.

Bouchard, Donald F.
    1977   "History of Systems of Thought"in—M. Foucault, *Language, Counter-Memory Practice: Selected Essays and Interviews.* Ithaca, New York: Cornell University Press.

Bremner, R. H.
    1956   *From the Depths: The Discovery of Poverty in the United States.* New York: New York University Press.

Brenner, H. Harvey
    1973   *Mental Illness and the Economy.* Cambridge, Massachusetts: Harvard University Press.

Brown, Bertram M. and Stockdill, James W.
    1972   "The Politics of Mental Health," Pp. 669-686 in S.E. Golann and C. Eisdorfer, *Handbook of Community Mental Health.* Englewood Cliffs, New Jersey: Prentice-Hall, Inc.

Brown, Michael E.
    1969   "The Condemnation and Persecution of Hippies" in *TRANS-action,* 6 (September):33-46.

Brownmiller, Susan
    1975   *Against Our Will.* New York: Simon and Schuster.

Bruce, M.
    1961   *The Coming of the Welfare State.* London: B.T. Batsford, Ltd.

Burke, Kenneth
    1954   *Permanence and Change.* Second revised edition. Los Altos, Ca.

Burkhart, Kathryn W.
    1973   *Women in Prison.* Garden City, New Jersey: Doubleday and Co., Inc.

Cahn, Sidney
    1970   *The Treatment of Alcoholism: An Evaluative Study.* New York: Oxford University Press.

Caplan, Gerald
    1964   *Principles of Preventive Psychiatry.* New York: Basic Books.
Caplan, Nathan
    1970   "The New Ghetto Man: A Review of Recent Empirical Studies" in *Journal of Social Issues* 26:59-73.
Caplan, Ruth B.
    1969   *Psychiatry and the Community in Nineteenth Century America,* New York: Basic Books.
Case, John and Taylor, Rosemary C. R.
    1979   *Co-ops, Communes and Collectives: Experiments in Social Change in the 1960s and 1970s.* New York: Pantheon Books.
Chafetz, Morris E. and Demone, Harold W. Jr.
    1962   *Alcoholism and Society.* New York: Oxford University Press.
Chambers, C.A.
    1969   "An Historical Perspective on Political Action Vs. Individualized Treatment" in Paul E. Weinberger, ed., *Perspectives on Social Welfare.* New York: The Macmillan Company, pp. 89-106.
Chambliss, W.J.
    1964   "A Sociological Analysis of the Law of Vagrancy" in *Social Problems* 12 (Summer):67-77.
Cheal, David J.
    1979   "Hegemony, Ideology and Contradictory Consciousness" in *The Sociological Quarterly* 20:109-117 (Winter).
Chesney-Lind, Meda
    1973   "Judicial Enforcement of the Female Sex Role: The Family Court and the Female Delinquent" in *Issues in Criminology* 8, 2:51-69.
Chessler, Phyllis
    1972   *Women and Madness.* New York: Avon.
Chomsky, Noam
    1972   *Language and Mind.* New York: Harcourt Brace Jovanovich.
Christie, Nils
    1975   *Hvor tett et samfunn?* Copenhagen and Oslo: Christian Ejler's Forlag and Universitetsforlaget. Vol. 1 contains the text, vol. 2 tables, charts and bibliography.
Clark, John P. and Huarek, Edward W.
    1966   "Age and Sex Roles of Adolescents and their Involvement in Misconduct: A Reappraisal" in *Sociology and Social Research* 50, 4:495-508.
Cloward, Richard A. and Piven, Frances F.
    1974   *The Politics of Turmoil.* New York: Random House.
Cohen, Michael D., March, James G. and Olsen, Johan P.
    1972   "Garbage Can Model of Organizational Choice" in *Administrative Science Quarterly,* Vol. 17, 1-25.
Cohn, Norman
    1970   *The Pursuit of the Millenium.* New York: Oxford University Press.

    1975   *Europe's Inner Demons.* New York: New American Library.
Cole, Margaret
    1961   *The Story of Fabian Socialism.* Stanford, California: Stanford University Press.

Collins, Randell
1979   *The Credential Society: An Historical Sociology of Education and Stratification.* New York: Academic Press.
Connerton, Paul
1976   *Critical Sociology.* Hammondsworth, Middlesex, England: Penguin Books.
Connery, Robert H.
1968   *The Politics of Mental Health.* New York: Columbia University Press.
Conrad, Peter
1975   "The Discovery of Hyperkinesis" in *Social Problems,* Vol. 23, 12-21.
Conrad, Peter and Schneider, Joseph W.
1980   *Deviance and Medicalization* St. Louis, Missouri: The C.V. Mosby Company.
Converse, Philip E.
1964   "The Nature of Belief Systems in Mass Publics," Pp. 206-261 in David Apter (ed.) *Ideology and Discontent.* New York: Free Press.
Cotgrove, Stephen
1978   "Styles of Thought: Science, Romanticism, and Modernism" in *British Journal of Sociology.* Vol. 29 (September):358-371.
Crawford, Thomas J.
1975   "Police Overperception of Ghetto Hostility," Pp. 262-272 in Richard L. Henshel and Robert A. Silverman, *Perception in Criminology.* New York: Columbia University Press.
Crozier, Michel
1964   *The Bureaucratic Phenomenon.* Chicago: University of Chicago Press.
Cumming, Elaine
1968   *Systems of Social Regulation.* New York: Atherton Press.
Dallmayer, Fred R. and McCarthy, Thomas A.
1977   *Understanding and Social Inquiry.* Notre Dame, Ind.: University of Indiana Press.
Davis, Nanette J.
1973   "The Abortion Market: Transactions in a Risk Commodity," Dissertation, Michigan State University.

_____
1977   "Feminism, Deviance and Social Change," chapter in Edward Sagarin, ed., *Deviance and Social Control.* Beverly Hills: Sage Publications.

_____
1979   "Prostitution: Identity, Career and Political Economic Enterprise" in James Henslin and Edward Sagarin, eds., *The Sociology of Sex.* New York: McGraw-Hill.
Davis, Nanette J. and Anderson, Bo
1979   "Semiotics, Archaeology of Knowledge and Social Problems: Application of Structuralism to Analysis of the Changing Abortion Discourse with Some Implications for Social Policy," Scandanavian Sociology Meeting, Abo, Finland (August).
Davis, Nanette J.
1980   *Sociological Constructions of Deviance: Perspectives and Issues in the Field.* Second Edition. Dubuque, Iowa: Wm. C. Brown, Inc.   HM291.D34.1980
Davis, Natalie Zemon
1975   *Society and Culture in Early France.* Stanford: Stanford University Press.

De George, Richard and De George, Fernande
1972   *From Marx to Levi-Strauss.* Garden City, New York: Anchor Books.

Deleuze, Gilles
1972   *Proust and Signs.* New York: George Braziller.

Demos, John
1978   "Infancy and Childhood in the Plymouth Colony," Pp. 157-165 in M. Gordon (ed.), *The American Family in Social-Historical Perspective.* New York: St. Martin's Press.

Derrida, Jacques
1976   *Of Grammatology.* Baltimore: Johns Hopkins University Press.

Deutsch, Albert
1949   *The Mentally Ill in America.* Second Edition. New York: Columbia University Press.

Dohrenwend, Bruce P. and Dohrenwend, Barbara Snell
1972   "Psychiatric Epidemiology: An Analysis of 'True Prevalence' Studies," Pp. 281-302 in Stuart E. Golan and Carl Eisdorfer, *Handbook of Community Mental Health.* Englewood Cliffs, New Jersey: Prentice-Hall, Inc.

Donzelot, Jacques
1979   *The Policing of Families.* New York: Pantheon Books.

Dornbusch, Sanford M.
1955   "The Military Academy as an Assimilating Institution" in *Social Forces,* 33,316-321.

Dornbusch, S.M. and Scott, W.R.
1975   *Evaluation and the Exercise of Authority: A Theory of Control Applied to Diverse Organizations.* San Francisco: Jossey-Bass, Inc.

Douglas, Mary
1966   *Purity and Danger,* London: Routledge and Kegan, Ltd.

————
1968   "Pollution" in *Encyclopedia of the Social Sciences,* XII:336-341.

————
1973   *Rules and Meanings.* New York: Penguin Books.

————
1975   *Implicit Meanings: Essays in Anthropology.* London and Boston: Routledge and Kegan Paul

Durkheim, Emile
1947   *The Division of Labor.* Glencoe, Illinois: The Free Press.

————
1948   *The Rules of Sociological Method.* G. Catlin (ed.), Chicago: The University of Chicago Press.

Eaton, Joseph W.
1955   *Culture and Mental Disorders.* Glencoe, Illinois: The Free Press.

Eco, Umberto
1976   *The Theory of Semiotics.* Bloomington: Indiana University Press.

Eden, Sir F. M.
1971   *The State of the Poor.* A.G.L. Rogers, ed., New York: Benjamin Blom, Inc., first ed., 1929.

Edwards, Daniel W. and Yarvis, Richard M.
1977   "Let's Quit Stalling and Do Program Evaluation" in *Community Mental Health Journal,* Vol. 13 (2):205-211.

Eisenberg, Jeanne G., Langner, Thomas S. and Gersten, Joanne C.
1975   "Differences in the Behavior of Welfare and Non-Welfare Children in Relation to Parental Characteristics" in the *Archives of the Behavioral Sciences Monograph Series,* 48:3-33 (October).

Eisenger, Peter
1973   "The Conditions of Protest Behavior in American Cities" in *American Political Science Review,* 67:14.

––––––––
1977   *Handbook of Rational-Emotive Therapy.* New York: Springer Publishing.

Elman, R.M.
1966   *The Poorhouse State: The American Way of Life on Public Assistance.* New York: Pantheon Books.

Emerson, Joan P.
1970   "Behavior in Private Places: Sustaining Definitions of Reality in Gynecological Examinations" in H. Dreitzel (ed.) *Recent Sociology,* No. 2. London: The Macmillan Company.

Erikson, Kai T.
1966   *Wayward Puritans.* New York: John Wiley.

Ermann, M. David and Lundman, Richard J.
1978   *Corporate and Governmental Deviance: Problems of Organizational Behavior in Contemporary Society.* New York: Oxford University Press.

Etzioni, Amitai
1961   *A Comparative Analysis of Complex Organizations.* New York: The Free Press.

Evans-Pritchard, E.E.
1937   *Witchcraft, Oracles and Magic Among the Azande.* London: Oxford Press.

––––––––
1973   "Zande Theology" in *Social Anthropology and Other Essays.* New York: The Free Press.

Feagin, Joe R. and Hahn, Harlan
1973   *Ghetto Revolts: The Politics of Violence in American Cities.* New York: MacMillan Publishing Company, Inc.

Federal Bureau of Investigation
1975   *Uniform Crime Reports,* Washington, D.C.
1977
1978

Fischer, Claude
1972   "Urbanism as a Way of Life: A Review and an Agenda" in *Sociological Methods and Research,* Vol. 1, No. 2, Sage Publications.

––––––––
1975   "The Study of Urban Community and Personality" in *Annual Review of Sociology.*

Fishel, Elizabeth
1973   "Women's Self-Help Movement" in *Ramparts,* Vol. 29 (November):29-31 and 56-59.

Forslund, Anne-Louise
1978   *Vad är Rättssociologi?* Liberforlag: Stockholm.

Foucault, Michel
1965   *Madness and Civilization.* New York: Vintage Books.

1971   *The Order of Things.* New York: Pantheon Books.

1976   *The Archaeology of Knowledge and The Discourse on Language.* New York: Pantheon Books.

1977   *Discipline and Punish: The Birth of the Prison.* New York: Pantheon Books.

1977   *Language, Counter-Memory, Practice: Selected Essays and Interviews.* Ithaca, New York: Cornell University Press.

1978   *The History of Sexuality.* Vol. 1, An Introduction, New York: Random House.

1980   *Power/Knowledge.* New York: Pantheon Books.

Freeman, Jo
1971   "The Legal Basis of the Sexual Caste System" in *Valparaiso University Law Review,* 5:207.

1975   "The Origins of the Women's Liberation Movement" in *American Journal of Sociology,* Vol. 78, No. 4.

1975   "The Tyranny of Structurelessness" in A. Koedt, E. Levine and A. Rapone (eds.) *Radical Feminism.* New York: Quadrangle/The New York Times Book Company: 285-299.

Friedson, Eliot
1970   *Profession of Medicine.* New York: Dodd, Mead and Company.

Freud, Sigmund
1977 ed.   *Civilization and its Discontents.* New York: W.W. Norton and Co., Inc.

Freudenberger, Herbert J.
1974   "Staff Burn Out" in *Journal of Social Issues,* 30:159-163.

Friedmann, Wolfgang
1949   *Legal Theory.* London: Stevens and Sons.

Fromm, Erich
1941   *Escape from Freedom.* New York: Rinehardt and Co.

1970   *The Crisis of Psychoanalysis.* New York: Holt, Rinehart and Winston.

Galtung, Johan
1969   In L.E. Hazelrigg (ed.) *Prisons Within Society.* Garden City, New York: Anchor Books.

Gamson, William A.
1975   *The Strategy of Protest.* Homewood, Illinois: Dorsey Press.

Gans, Herbert J.
1962   *The Urban Villagers.* New York: The Free Press of Glencoe.

1972   "The Positive Functions of Poverty" in *American Journal of Sociology,* 78 (September):275-289.

Gardner, Richard
1976   *Alternative America.* privately published.

Garfinkel, Harold
    1967   *Studies in Ethnomethodology.* Englewood Cliffs, New Jersey: Prentice-Hall.

Gartner, Alan and Reissman, Frank
    1972   "Changing the Professions: The New Careers Strategy" in R. Gross and P. Osterman (eds.), *The New Professionals.* New York: Simon and Schuster.

Geertz, Clifford
    1957   "Ritual and Social Change: A Javanese Example" in *American Anthropologist,* Vol. LIX:32-54.

Geis, Gilbert
    1967   "Violence in American Society" in *Current History* (June):354-358.

Gerth, H.H. and Mills, C.W.
    1946   *From Max Weber: Essays in Sociology.* New York: Oxford University Press.

Geschwenders, James A.
    1977   *Class, Race, and Worker Insurgency.* Cambridge: Cambridge University Press.

Giallombardo, R.
    1966   *Society of Women: A Study of a Women's Prison.* New York: Wiley.

Gibbons, Don C.
    1979   *The Criminological Enterprise: Theories and Perspectives.* Englewood Cliffs, New Jersey: Prentice-Hall, Inc.

Gibbs, Jack P. and Erickson, Maynard L.
    1975   "Major Developments in the Sociological Study of Deviance" in *Annual Review of Sociology.*

Giddens, Anthony
    1977   "Review Essay: Habermas' Social and Political Theory" in *American Journal of Sociology,* 83, Pp. 198-212.

Gill, Howard B.
    1970   "A New Prison Discipline: Implementing the Declaration of Principles of 1870" in *Federal Probation* (June):29-30.

Glick, R. Ruth and Neto, V.
    1976   *National Study of Women's Correctional Programs.* Washington, D.C.: U.S. Government Printing Office.

Glueck, Eleanor and Glueck, Sheldon
    1934   *Four Hundred Deliquent Women.* New York: Alfred A. Knopf.

Goffman, Erving
    1959   *The Presentation of Self In Everyday Life.* Garden City, New York: Doubleday and Company.

    1961   *Asylums.* Garden City, New York: Anchor Books.

    1967   *Interaction Ritual.* Chicago: Aldine Publishing Company.

    1971   *Relations in Public.* New York: Harper and Row.

Golann, Stuart E. and Eisdorfer, Carl
    1972   "Mental Health and the Community: The Development of Issues" in *Handbook of Community Mental Health.* Englewood Cliffs, New Jersey: Prentice-Hall, Inc.

Goldberg, Carl
    1973   *The Human Circle.* Chicago: Nelson-Hall Company.

Gordon, D.
    1972   *Theories of Poverty and Under-Employment.* Lexington, Massachusetts: Lexington Books.
Gottlieb, Naomi
    1974   *The Welfare Bind.* New York and London: Columbia University Press.
Grady, John and Ploss, Charlotte
    1978   "The Compromise: Dilemmas of Community Organizing: Mission Hill in Boston" in *Social Policy,* Vol. 8 (May-June):41-48.
Gramsci, Antonio
    1972   *Selections from the Prison Notebooks.* Edited and translated by Quintin Hoave and Geoffrey Nowell Smith. New York: International Publishers.
Granovetter, Mark
    1973   "The Strength of Weak Ties" in *American Journal of Sociology,* Vol. 78, No. 3, 1360-1380.
Greenfield, Meg
    1980   Editorial comment, *Newsweek* (May 12):88.
Greven, Philip, Jr.
    1978   "Family Structure in 17th Century Andover, Massachusetts," *Pp. 20-37* in M. Gordon (ed.) *The American Family in Social Historical Perspective.* Second Edition. New York: St. Martin's Press.
Grimshaw, Allen D.
            "Social Problems and Social Policies: An Illustration From Sociolinguistics" in *Social Problems,* 26:582-598 (June).
Gronbjerb, Kirsten, Street, David and Suttles, Gerald D.
    1978   *Poverty and Social Change.* Chicago: University of Chicago Press.
Gruenberg, Ernest M.
    1975   "New Methods for Assessing the Effectiveness of Psychiatric Intervention" in *American Handbook of Psychiatry,* Pp. 791-810.
Gusfield, Joseph R.
    1963   *Symbolic Crusade: Status Politics and the American Temperance Movement.* Urbana: University of Illinois Press.

    1970   *Protest, Reform and Revolt.* New York: Wiley.
Habermas, Jürgen
    1970   "On Systematically Distorted Communications" in *Inquiry,* Vol. 13.

    1970   *Toward a Rational Society.* Boston: Beacon Press.

    1971   *Knowledge and Human Interests.* Boston: Beacon Press.

    1975   *Legitimation Crisis.* Boston: Beacon Press.

    1979   *Communication and the Evolution of Society.* Boston: Beacon Press.
Haines, Herbert H.
    1979   "Cognitive Claims-Making, Enclosure and the Depoliticization of Social Problems" in *The Sociological Quarterly,* 20:119-130 (Winter).
Handlin, O.
    1951   *The Uprooted.* New York: Grosset and Dunlap.

Hannan, Michael T. and Freeman, John H.
    1978   "The Population of Ecology of Organizations." Marshall W. Meyer and Associ-
            ates, *Environments and Organizations*. San Francisco: Jossey-Bass Publishers,
            Pp. 131-171.
Hansen, K.L.
    1981   "Black Exchange and its Systems of Social Control" in David Willer and Bo
            Anderson, *Coercion, Networks and Social Exchange*. New York: Elsevier.
Hart, H.L.A.
    1961   "The Use and Abuse of the Criminal Law" in *Oxford Lawyer*, 4.
Hartman, Chester
    1978   "The Context: Dilemmas of Community Organizing: Mission Hill in Boston"
            in *Social Policy*, Vol. 8 (May-June):41-42.
Hawley, A.H.
    1950   *Human Ecology: A Theory of Community Structure*. New York: Ronald Press.
Heberle, Rudolf
    1951   *Social Movements*. New York: Appleton-Century-Crofts, Inc.
Heidenshon, Frances
    1968   "The Deviance of Women: A Critique" in *British Journal of Sociology*,
            19:160-175.
Henry, Jules
    1963   *Culture Against Man*. New York: Random House.
Hill, Christopher
    1972   *The World Upside Down*. New York: The Viking Press.
Hills, Stuart L.
    1980   *Demystifying Social Deviance*. New York: McGraw-Hill Book Co.
Hobbs, N.
    1969   "Mental Health's Third Revolution" in B.G. Guerney, Jr. (ed.) *Psychotherapeutic
            Agents: New Roles for Nonprofessionals, Parents and Teachers*. New York: Holt,
            Rinehart & Winston.
Hobsbawn, E.H.
    1965   *Primitive Rebels*. New York: W.W. Norton.
Hoffman-Bustamante, Dale
    1973   "The Nature of Female Criminality" in *Issues in Criminology*, 8 2:117-136.
Hofstadter, Richard
    1963   *Anti-Intellectualism in American Life*, New York: Knopf.
Hofstadter, Richard and Wallace, Michael
    1970   *American Violence: A Documentary History*, New York: Knopf.
Hollingshead, August B. and Redlich, Frederick C.
    1958   *Social Class and Mental Illness*, New York: John Wiley & Sons.
Holmes, Oliver Wendell
    1861   *Currents and Counter-Currents in Medical Science*, Boston: Ticknor and Fields, p.
            7.
Holter, J. and Friedman, S.
    1968   "Principles of Management in Child Abuse Cases" in *American Journal of
            Orthopsychiatry*, 38:127.
Hoppe, Edward W.
    1977   "Treatment Dropouts in Hindsight: A Follow-Up Study" in *Community Mental
            Health Journal*, Vol. 13 (4):307-313.

Horkheimer, Max
    1976   *On Critical Theory.* Edited by John O'Neill. New York: Seaburg Press.
Horowitz, I.L. and Liebowitz, M.
    1968   "Social Deviance and Political Marginality: Toward A Redefinition of the
            Relation between Sociology and Politics" in *Social Problems 15 (Winter):280-
            296.*
Hoult, Thomas Ford
    1974   *Sociology for a New Day,* New York: Random House.
Hovey, Marcia
    1971   *The Forgotten Offenders.* Published by Manpower Administration, United
            States Department of Labor (January):38-41.
Howard, Donald S.
    1969   *Social Welfare: Values, Means, and Ends.* New York: Random House.
Huber, Joan
    1973   *Changing Women in a Changing Society.* Chicago: The University of Chicago
            Press.
Hughes, Everett
    1972   *The Sociological Eye: Selected Papers.* Chicago and New York: Aldine-Atherton.
Hymowitz, Carol and Weissman, Michaele
    1978   *A History of Women in America.* New York: Bantam Books.
Irwin, John
    1970   *The Felon.* Englewood Cliffs, New Jersey: Prentice-Hall, Inc.

    _____

    1977   *Scenes.* Beverly Hills: Sage Publications.

    _____

    1980   *Prisons in Turmoil.* Boston: Little, Brown and Company.
Jacoby, Russell
    1975   *Social Amnesia: A Critique of Conformist Psychology from Adler to Laing.* Boston:
            Beacon Press.
James, Jennifer and Meyerding, J.
    1977   "Early Sexual Experience and Prostitution" in *American Journal of Psychiatry,*
            134:1381-1385.
Jameson, Fredric
    1972   *The Prison-House of Language.* Princeton, New Jersey: Princeton University
            Press.
Johnson, M.
    1979   "The Role of Commitment in Social Problems Theory." Paper presented at
            the Annual Meeting of the Society for the Study of Social Problems. New York
            City (August).
Jones, Maxwell
    1962   *Social Psychiatry: In the Community, In Hospitals, and In Prisons.* Springfield,
            Illnois: Charles C. Thomas, Publishers.
Kanter, Rosabeth Moss
    1970   "Communes" in *Psychology Today,* 4 (July):53-57, 58.

    _____

    1972   *Commitment and Community: Communes and Utopias in Sociological Perspective.*
            Cambridge: Harvard University Press.

Kanter, Rosabeth Moss and Zurcher, Louis, Jr.
    1973   "Alternative Institutions" in a special issue of *The Journal of Applied Behavioral Science,* 9 (March-June).

Karan, Lorrin M., Ochbert, Frank and Brown, Bertram S.
    1975   "The Federal Government and Mental Health" in *American Handbook of Psychiatry,* Pp. 960-976.

Kesey, Ken
    1971   *One Flew Over the Cuckoo's Nest.* New York: Viking Press.

Kett, Joseph
    1977   *Rites of Passage.* New York: Basic Books.

Key. V.O., Jr.
    1962   *Politics, Parties and Pressure Groups.* New York: Thomas Y. Crowell Company.

Kittrie, N.
    1971   *The Right to be Different: Deviance and Enforced Therapy.* Baltimore: Johns Hopkins University Press.

Klein, Dorie
    1973   "The Etiology of Female Crime: A Review of the Literature" in *Issues in Criminology,* 8 (Fall):3-30.

Klein, Dorie and Kress, June
    "Any Woman's Blues: A Critical Overview of Women, Crime and the Criminal Justice System" in *Crime and Social Justice,* 5:34-39.

Kneeland, Douglas E.
    1979   "Chicago Suit Says Mental Patients Were Used As Guinea Pigs" in *The New York Times* (April):A14.

Knowles, John H.
    1977   *Doing Better and Feeling Worse: Health in the United States.* New York: W.W. Norton Company.

Kogon, E.
    1960   *The Theory and Practice of Hell: The German Concentration Camps and the System Behind Them.* New York: Berkley Publishing Corp.

Kolb, L.C.
    1968   "The Community Mental Health Centers: Some Issues in Their Transition from Concept to Reality" in *Hospital and Community Psychiatry,* Vol. 19:335-340.

Komarovsky, Mirra
    1940   *The Unemployed Man and His Family.* New York: Dryden Press.

Komisar, Lucy
    1979   "The Mysterious Mistress of Odyssey House." New York (November).

Korchin, Sheldon J.
    1976   *Modern Clinical Psychology.* New York: Basic Books.

Kuhn, Thomas
    1970   *The Structure of Scientific Revolutions.* Chicago: University of Chicago Press.

Lacan, J.
    1966   "L'instance de la lettre dans l'inconscient ou la raison depuis Freud" in *Escrits.*

Laing, R.D.
    1960   *The Divided Self.* London: Tavistock Publications.

    1967   *The Politics of Experience.* London: Penguin Books.

    1971   *The Politics of the Family.* New York: Ballantine Books.

LaPiere, Richard T.
1954   *A Theory of Social Control.* New York: McGraw-Hill.

Larson, Magali S.
1977   *The Rise of Professionalism.* Berkeley and Los Angeles: University of California Press.

Lasch, Christopher
1979   *The Culture of Narcissism.* New York: Warner Books Edition.

————
1980   "Life in the Therapeutic State" in *New York Review of Books,* Vol. XXVI, No. 10 (June):24-32.

Laslett, Peter
1977   *Family Life and Illicit Love in Earlier Generations.* New York: Cambridge University Press.

Laumann, Edward O.
1973   *Bonds of Pluralism: The Form and Substance of Urban Social Networks.* New York: John Wiley.

Leach, E.R.
1966   "Ritualization in Man in Relation to Conceptual and Social Development." Philosophical Transactions of the Royal Society of London, CCLI. Ser. B. No. 772:403-408.

————
1967   *The Structural Study of Myth and Totemism.* Association of Social Anthropologists, Monograph 5. London: Tavistock Publications.

Leifer, Ronald
1969   *In the Name of Mental Health: The Social Functions of Psychiatry,* New York: Science House

Lemert, Charles C.
1979   "Language, Structure and Measurement: Structuralist Semiotics and Sociology" in *American Journal of Sociology,* Vol. 84, No. 4:929-957.

Lerner, Barbara
1972   *Therapy in the Ghetto: Political Impotence and Personal Disintegration.* Baltimore and London: The Johns Hopkins University Press.

Levi-Strauss, C.
1967   *Structural Anthropology.* Garden City, New York: Anchor Books.

Levin, H.
1970   "Psychologist to the Powerless' in Korten, F., Cook, S. and Lacey, J. (eds.) *Psychology and the Problems of Society.* Washington, D.C.: American Psychological Association.

Levinson, H., Weinbaum, L. and McLean, A.
1970   *Mental Health and Work Organization.* New York: Rand McNally.

Levitan, Sar A.
1969   *The Great Society's Poor Law: A New Approach to Poverty.* Baltimore: The Johns Hopkins Press.

Lewis, O.
1959   *Five Families: Mexican Case Studies in the Culture of Poverty.* New York: Basic Books.

————
1961   *The Children of Sanchez.* New York: Random House.

1966   *La Vida: A Puerto Rican Family in the Culture of Poverty —San Juan and New York.* New York: Random House.

Leymore, Varda Langholz
1975   *Hidden Myth.* New York: Random House.

Lieberman, Morton A., Donald Borman and Associates
1979   *Self-Help Groups for Coping with Crisis.* San Francisco: Jossey Bass.

Lieberson, Stanley and Silverman, Arnold R.
1965   "The Precipitants and Underlying Conditions of Race Riots" in *American Sociological Review,* 30:887-898.

Lindblom, Charles E.
1977   *Politics and Markets: The World's Political-Economic Systems,* New York: Basic Books.

Lockhead, Marlaine E. and Hall, Katherine Patterson
1976   "Conceptualizing Sex as a Status Characteristic: Applications to Leadership Training Strategies" in *Journal of Social Issues,* Vol. 32:114-124.

Lofland, John
1966   *Doomsday Cult.* Englewood Cliffs, New Jersey: Prentice-Hall.

Lombroso, C.
1920   *The Female Offender* (translation). New York: Appleton. Originally published in 1903.

Loukinen, M.M.
1981   "Social Exchange Systems" in David Willer and Bo Anderson *Networks, Exchange and Coercion.* New York: Elsevier.

Lowi, Theodore J.
1971   *The Politics of Disorder.* New York: Basic Books.

Loyola, St. Ignatius de
1964   *The Spiritual Exercises of Saint Ignatius.* Garden City, New York: Image Books.

Lukes, Steven
1973   *Emile Durkheim: His Life and Work.* New York: Harper and Row.

Lundberg, D., Sheekley, A. and Voelker, T.
1975   "An Exploration of the Feelings and Attitudes of Women Separated From Their Children Due to Incarceration." Unpublished paper, School of Social Work, Portland State University, Portland, Oregon.

MacIver, R.M. and Page, Charles H.
1949   *Society: An Introductory Analysis.* New York: Rinehart.

Mack, Raymond W. and Pease, John
1973   "Ecology and Urbanization" in *Sociology and Social Life.* Pp. 235-269. New York: D. Van Nostrand Company.

MacKenzie, Norman and MacKenzie, Jeanne
1977   *The First Fabians.* Weidenfield and Nicholson.

Mandell, Betty Reid
1975   *Welfare in America: Controlling the "Dangerous Classes."* Englewood Cliffs, New Jersey: Prentice-Hall, Inc.

Manis, Jerome G. and Meltzer, Bernard N.
1972   *Symbolic Interaction.* Boston: Allyn and Bacon, Inc.

Mann, Michael
1970   "The Social Cohesion of Liberal Democracy" in *American Sociological Review,* 35:423-439.

Mannheim, Karl
1936   *Ideology and Utopia.* New York: Harcourt, Brace and World, Inc.
Manning, Peter K.
1977   *Police Work: The Social Organization of Policing.* Cambridge, Massachusetts and London: MIT Press.
Manuel, Frank
1956   *The New World of Henri Saint-Simon.* Cambridge, Massachusetts: Harvard University Press.
March, James G. and Olsen, Johan P.
1976   *Ambiguity and Choice in Organizations.* Bergen, Norway: Universitetsforlaget.
Marcuse, Herbert
1965   *A Critique of Pure Tolerance.* Boston: Beacon Press.

1968   *Negations.* Boston: Little, Brown and Company.
Mathieson, Thomas
1965   *The Defense of the Weak.* London: Tavistock.
Matza, D.
1971   "Poverty and Disrepute" in Robert K. Merton and Robert Nisbet, eds., *Contemporary Social Problems.* 3rd Edition. New York: Harcourt, Brace, Jovanovich, Inc., Pp. 619-669.
McCarthy, John D. and Zald, Mayer N.
1973   "Resource Mobilization and Social Movements: A Partial Theory" in *American Journal of Sociology,* Vol. 82, No. 6, Pp. 1212-1241.

1973   *The Trend of Social Movements in America.* Morristown, New Jersey: General Learning Press.
Mednick, Martha T. and Weissman, Hilda J.
1976   "The Psychology of Women," Pp. 122-135 in Sue Cox, *Female Psychology: The Emerging Self.* Chicago: Science Research Associate, Inc.
Meeker, B.F. and Weitzel-O'Neill, P.A.
1977   "Sex Roles and Interpersonal Behavior in Task-Oriented Groups" in *American Sociological Review,* Vol. 42:91-106.
Meisel, C. Anthony and del Mastro, M.L.
1975   *The Rule of St. Benedict.* New York: Doubleday.
Mencher, S.
1967   *Poor Law to Poverty Program.* Pittsburgh: University of Pittsburgh Press.
Merton, R.
1967   *Social Theory and Social Structure.* New York: The Free Press.
Meyer, J.W. and Rowan, B.
1977   "Institutionalized Organizations: Formal Structure as Myth and Ceremony" in *American Journal of Sociology,* 83:440-463.
Meyer, John W.
1978   "The World Polity and the Authority of the Nation-State" (MS:Department of Sociology, Stanford University).
Meyer, John W.; Tyack, David; Nagel, Joane; Gordon, Audri
1979   "Public Education as Nation-Building in America: Enrollments and Bureaucratization in the American States, 1930-1970" in *American Journal of Sociology,* Vol. 85, No. 3, 591-613.

Meyer, Marshall W. and Associates
    1978   *Environment and Organizations,* San Francisco: Jossey Bass Publishers.
Milgram, Stanley
    1973   *Obedience to Authority: An Experimental View.* New York: Harper and Row.
Miller, S.M. and others
    1979   Articles in *Social Policy* (September-October).
Miller, W.B.
    1958   "Lower Class Culture as a Generating Milieu of Gang Delinquency" in *Journal of Social Issues,* 14 (Fall):5-10.
Milwaukee County Welfare Rights Organization
    1972   *Welfare Mothers Speak Out: We Ain't Gonna Shuffle Anymore.* New York: W.W. Norton and Company.
Mitchell, Juliet
    1966   "Women: The Longest Revolution" in *New Left Review* (November-December):11-37.
Mitford, Jessica
    1972   "Prisons: The Menace of Liberal Reform" in *New York Review of Books* (March 9).
Moberg, David
    1979   "Experimenting with the Future: Alternative Institutions and American Socialism," pp. 274-311 in Case and Taylor, *Coops, Communes and Collectives.* New York: Pantheon Books.
Modell, John and Hareven, Tamara K.
    1978   "Urbanization and the Malleable Household: An Examination of Boarding and Lodging in American Families," pp. 51-68 in *The American Family in Social-Historical Perspective.* M. Gordon (ed.). Second Edition. New York: Harper Books.
Moore, Barrington, Jr.
    1972   *Reflections on the Causes of Human Misery and Upon Certain Proposals to Eliminate Them.* Boston: Beacon Press.
Morgan, E. Victor and Morgan, Ann D.
    1972   *The Economics of Public Policy.* Edinburgh, Scotland: Edinburgh University Press.
Morse, C.
    1970   "A Three-Year Follow-Up Study of Abused and Neglected Children" in *American Journal of Diseases of Children,* 120:430-446.
Moynihan, D.P.
    1969   *Maximum Feasible Misunderstanding: Community Action in the War on Poverty.* New York: The Free Press.
Musgrove, Frank
    1974   *Ecstasy and Holiness: Counter Culture and the Open Society.* Bloomington: Indiana University Press.
Nagel, Stuart S. and Weitzman, Lenore T.
    1972   "Double Standard of American Justice" in *Society,* 19, 5:18-25.
Neubeck, Kenneth J.
    1977   "Capitalism as Therapy" in *Social Policy* (May-June):41-45.
Nietzsche, Friedrich
    1956   *The Geneology of Morals.* Garden City, New York: Doubleday.

Nisbet, Robert A.
 1953 *The Quest for Community: A Study in the Ethics of Order and Freedom.* New York: Oxford University Press.

Nonet, Phillippe and Selznick, Philip
 1978 *Law and Society in Transition: Toward Responsive Law.* New York: Harper Colophon Books.

Nordhoff, Charles
 1966 *The Communistic Societies of the United States.* New York: Dover Publications. Originally published by Harper and Brothers, 1875.

O'Donnell, John M. and George, Kathi
 1977 "The Use of Volunteers in a Community Mental Health Center Emergency and Reception Service: A Comparative Study of Professional and Lay Telephone Counseling" in *Community Mental Health Journal, Vol. 13(1).*

Off Our Backs
 1974 "What Is Feminist Health?" (June).

Oliver, Pamela
 1980 "Rewards and Punishments as Selective Incentives for Collective Actions" in *American Journal of Sociology,* Vol. 85, No. 6, 1357-1375.

Olson, Mancur
 1971 *The Logic of Collective Action.* Cambridge, Massachusetts: Harvard University Press.

O'Neill, John
 1972 "The Hobbesian Problem in Marx and Parsons" in O'Neill, *Sociology as A Skin Trade.* New York: Harper and Row.

Ouchi, William G.
 1980 "Markets, Bureaucracies and Clans" in *Administrative Science Quarterly,* Vol. 25, No. 1:129-141.

Packer, Herbert L.
 1968 *The Limits of the Criminal Sanction.* Stanford: Stanford University Press.

Parsons, Talcott
 1937 *The Structure of Social Action.* New York: McGraw-Hill.

———
 1954 "A Revised Analytical Approach to the Theory of Social Stratification" in *Essays in Sociological Theory* (revised edition). New York: The Free press.

Parsons, Talcott and Bales, Robert F.
 1955 *Family, Socialization and Interaction Process.* Glencoe, Illinois: The Free Press.

Pasewark, Richard A. and Pantle, Mark L.
 1979 "Insanity Plea: Legislator's View" in *American Psychiatric Review,* 136:2 (February):222-223.

Peel, Robert and Associates
 1977 "Asylums Revisited" in *American Journal of Psychiatry,* 134-10 (October):1077-1081.

Perls, Fritz
 1969 *The Gestalt Approach and Eye Witness to Therapy.* Ben Leonard, CA: Science and Behavioral Books.

———
 1973 *In and Out the Garbage Pail.* Lafayette, California: Real People Press.

Perrow, Charles
1970   *Organizational Analysis.* Belmont, California: Wadsworth Publishing Company.

1978   *Complex Organizations.* Glenview, Illinois: Scott, Foresman and Company.
Peterson, Karen Jean
1976   "Creating Division of Labor: A Case Study of Nonprofessionals Professing Self-Help." Dissertation, Northwestern University.
Pivar, David, Jr.
1973   *Purity Crusade: Sexual Morality and Social Control, 1868-1900.* Westport, Connecticut: Greenwood Press, Inc.
Piven, Frances Fox and Cloward, Richard A.
1971   *Regulating the Poor.* New York: Vintage.

1974   *The Politics of Turmoil.* New York: Pantheon.

1977a   "The Urban Crisis as an Area for Class Mobilization" in *Radical America,* 11:9-17.

1977b   *Poor People's Movements.* New York: Pantheon.

1977c   "Dilemmas of Organization Building" in *Radical America,* 11:39-60.

1979   "Social Movements and Societal Conditions: A Response to Roach and Roach" in *Social Problems,* 172-178.
Platt, A.M.
1969   *The Child Savers: The Invention of Delinquency.* Chicago: The University of Chicago Press.
Pollak, Otto
1950   *The Criminality of Women,* Philadelphia: University of Philadelphia Press.
Popper, Karl R.
1964   *The Poverty of Historicism,* New York and Evanston: Harper and Row.
Poynter, J.R.
1969   *Society and Pauperism.* London: Routledge and Kegan Paul.
Quinney, Richard
1979   *Criminology.* Second Edition. Boston: Little, Brown and Company.
Rainwater, L.
1967   "The Revolt of the Dirty-Workers" in *Transaction,* 5 (November): 12, 64.
Rawls, John
1971   *A Theory of Justice.* Cambridge, Mass.: Belknap Press of Harvard University Press.
Reckless, Walter C. and Kay, Barbara
1967   *The Female Offender.* President's Commission on Law Enforcement and Administration of Justice. Washington, D.C.: U.S. Government Printing Office.
Reid, Sue Titus
1979   *Crime and Criminology.* Second Edition. New York: Holt, Rinehart and Winston.

Rhodes, James M.
1980   *The Hitler Movement: A Modern Millenarian Revolution.* The Hoover Institution Press.

Richmond, Mary
1965   *Social Diagnosis.* New York: The Free Press (Originally printed for the Russell Sage Foundation, 1917).

Rieff, Philip
1966   *The Triumph of the Therapeutic.* New York: Harper.

Ripley, Randall B.
1972   *The Politics of Economic and Human Resource Development.* Indianapolis: The Bobbs-Merrill Company, Inc.

Riska, Elianne and Buffenbarger, Nancy L.
1980   "Primary Care Delivery: Is Family Care the Solution?" forthcoming in Roth, Julius A. (ed.) *The Changing Structure of Health Care Occupations,* JAI Press, Inc.

Ritz, Joseph P.
1960   *The Despised Poor: Newburgh's War on Welfare.* Boston: Beacon Press.

Roach, Jack L. and Roach, Janet K.
1979   "Mobilizing the Poor: Road to a Dead End" in *Social Problems,* 160-171.

Robinson, David
1976   *From Drinking to Alcoholism: A Sociological Commentary.* John Wiley and Sons.

Robinson, Gerald L. and Miller, Stephen T.
1975   "Drug Abuse and the College Campus" in *The Annals,* 417 (January): 101-109.

Rokeach, M.
1960   *The Open and Closed Mind.* New York: Basic Books, Inc.

Rose, Stephan M.
1972   *The Betrayal of the Poor.* Cambridge, Massachusetts: Schenkman Publishing Company.

Rosenberg, B. and Silverstein, H.
1969   *The Varieties of Delinquent Experience.* Waltham, Massachusetts: Blaisdell Publishing Company.

Rosenhan, D.
1966   "On Being Sane in Insane Places" in *Science* 179:250-258.

Ross, E.A.
1901   *Social Control.* New York: MacMillan Co., 1901 and later editions.

Roszak, Theodore
1969   *The Making of A Counter Culture.* Garden City, New York: Doubleday.

Rothman, David J.
1971   *The Discovery of the Asylum.* Boston: Little, Brown and Company.

———
1980   *Conscience and Convenience: The Asylum and Its Alternatives in Progressive America.* Boston: Little, Brown and Company.

Rothschild, Emma
1981   "Reagan and the Real America" in *The New York Review of Books,* Vol. XXVIII (February 5):12.

Rothschild-Whitt, Joyce
1979   "The Collectivist Organizations: An Alternative to Rational-Bureaucratic Models" in *American Sociological Review,* Vol. 44 (August):509-527.

Roucek, Joseph S.
1980   *Social Control for the 1980's.* Westport, Connecticut: Greenwood Press.

Rubin, Lillian Breslow
  1976   *Worlds of Pain.* New York: Basic Books.

Ruddick, Sara and Daniels, Pamela
  1977   *Working It Out: 23 Women Writers, Artists, Scientists, and Scholars Talk About Their Lives and Work.* New York: Pantheon Books.

Rule, James, McAdam, Douglas, Stearns, Linda and Uglow, David
  1980   *The Politics of Privacy.* Mentor Books, New American Library.

Russell, J.B.
  1972   *Witchcraft in the Middle Ages.* Ithaca, New York: Cornell University Press.

Ruzek, Sheryl K.
  1978   *The Women's Health Movement: Feminist Alternatives to Medical Control.* New York: Praeger.

Rydell, C.P., Palmerio, T., Blais, G. and Brown, D.
  1974   *Welfare Caseload Dynamics in New York City.* Department of Social Services, City of New York: The New York City Rand Institute.

Sagarin, Edward
  1969   *Odd Man In.* Chicago: Quadrangle Books.

Sallach, David L.
  1974   "Class Domination and Ideological Hegemony" in *The Sociological Quarterly*, 15:38-50.

Sarfatti-Larson, Magali
  1977   *The Rise of Professionalism.* Berkeley and Los Angeles: University of California Press.

Scarf, Maggie
  1979   "The More Sorrowful Sex" in *Psychology Today* 12 (April).

Schachter, Stanley and Singer, Jerome
  1962   "Cognitive, Social and Physiological Determinants in Emotional States" in *Psychological Review*, Vol. 69:379-399.

Scheff, Thomas J.
  1975   *Labeling Madness.* Englewood Cliffs, New Jersey: Prentice-Hall.

Schneider, Joseph
  1978   "Deviant Drinking as Disease: Alcoholism as a Social Accomplishment" in *Social Problems*, Vol. 25, No. 4:361-72.

Schram, Donna
  1978   *Rape Complaints.* Published by Battelle Law and Justice Study Center. Study funded by Law Enforcement Assistance Administration, Seattle, Washington.

Schultz, Cynthia L., Harker, Phillip C. and Gardner, James M.
  1977   "A Comparison of the Community Psychology and Medical Models" in *Community Mental Health Journal*, Vol. 13 (4):268-276.

Schur, Edwin H.
  1965   *Crimes Without Victims.* Englewood Cliffs, New Jersey: Prentice-Hall.

Scott, Robert A.
  1969   *The Making of Blind Men.* New York: Russell Sage.

Scott, W. Richard
  1964   "Theory of Organizations," Pp. 485-529 in Robert E.L. Faris (ed.) *Handbook of Modern Sociology.* Chicago: Rand McNally & Company.

Scull, Andrew T.
  1977   *Decarceration: Community Treatment and the Deviant.* Englewood Cliffs, New Jersey: Prentice-Hall.

Sears, David O. and McConahay, John B.
1973   *The Politics of Violence: The New Urban Blacks and the Watts Riot.* Boston: Houghton Mifflin.

Seaver, Richard and Wainhouse, A.
1966   *The Marquis de Sade,* New York: Grove Press, Inc.

Seeley, J.R.
1967   *The Americanization of the Unconscious.* New York: J.B. Lippincott Company.

Selznick, Philip
1966   *TVA and the Grassroots.* New York: Harper and Row.

Sennett, Richard
1970   *The Uses of Disorder.* New York: Random House.

————
1977   *The Fall of Public Man: On the Social Psychology of Capitalism.* New York: Alfred A. Knopf, Inc.

————
1980   *Authority.* New York: Knopf.

Shalleck, Jamie
1972   *Prison Interviews by Leonard J. Berry.* New York: Grossman Publishers.

Sharp, Gene
1970   *Exploring Nonviolent Alternatives.* Boston: P. Sargent.

Shover, Neal and Norland, Stephen
1975   "Sex Roles and Criminality: Science or Conventional Wisdom?" Paper presented to the Society for the Study of Social Problems, San Francisco, California (August 24).

Sidel, Victor W. and Sidel, Ruth
1973   *Serve the People.* Boston: Beacon Press.

Silberman, Charles E.
1980   *Criminal Violence and Criminal Justice.* New York: Vintage Books.

Silverstein, Marshall L. and Harrow, Martin
1978   "First Rank Symptoms in the Post-Acute Schizophrenic: A *Follow-Up* Study" in *American Journal of Psychiatry,* 135:12 (December:1481-1486).

Simon, Herbert A.
1964   "On the Concept of Organizational Goals" in *Administrative Science Quarterly,* Vol. 9, No. 1:1-22.

Simon, Rita James
1975   *Women and Crime.* Lexington, Massachusetts: Lexington Books.

Sjöström, Kurt
1976   *Socialpolitiken i det kapitalistiska samhället: Inledning till en marxistisk analys.* Stockholm: Arbetarkultur.

Skolnick, Jerome K.
1969   *The Politics of Protest.* New York: Simon and Schuster.

Smart, Carol
1976   *Women, Crime and Criminology: A Feminist Critique.* Boston: Routledge and Kegan Paul.

Smelser, Neil
1963   *Theory of Collective Behavior.* Glencoe, Illinois: The Free Press.

Smith, M.B.
1968   "The Revolution in Mental Health Care—A Bold New Approach" in *Trans-Action,* Vol. 5:19-23.

Smith, Robert Ellis
  1980   *Privacy: How to Protect What is Left of it.* Garden City, New York: Doubleday
          Anchor Books.
Smith, Vernon K.
  1975   *Welfare Work Incentives.* State of Michigan, Michigan Department of Social
          Services.
Smith-Rosenberg, Carroll
  1975   "The Female World of Love and Ritual: Relations Between Women in
          Nineteenth-Century America" in *Signs,* 1:1 (Autumn):1-29.
Solomon, R.
  1973   "History and Demography of Child Abuse" in *Pediatrics,* 51:773-776.
Solzhenitsyn, Aleksandr J.
  1978   *The Gulag Archipelago, 1918-1956.* New York: Harper and Row.
Sorrentino, Anthony
  1977   *Organizing Against Crime.* New York: Human Sciences Press.
Sourcebook of Criminal Justice Statistics
  1979   U.S. Printing Office, Washington, D.C.
Southard, F.
  1981   "The Theory of Mutual Benefits Systems" in David Willer and Bo Anderson
          Coercion, Networks and Social Exchange. New York: Elsevier.
Speck, Ross V. and Attneave, Carolyn L.
  1973   *Family Networks: A New Approach to Family Problems.* New York: Vintage Books.
Spiegel, David
  1979   "Society and Mental Illness." Class lecture notes, Department of Psychiatry,
          Stanford University (Winter).
Stanton, Alfred H. and Schwartz, Morris S.
  1949   *The Mental Hospital.* New York: Basic Books.

_____

          "Medical Opinion and the Social Context in the Mental Hospital" in *Psychiatry*
          XII:243-249.
Stasz, Clarice
  1978   *Female and Male: Socialization, Social Roles and Social Structure.* Second Edition.
          Dubuque, Iowa: Wm. C. Brown Publishers.
Staw, Barry M.
  1979   "Rationality and Justification in Organizational Life" in B. Staw and L.L.
          Cummings, ed. *Research in Organizational Behavior: An Annual Series of Analyt-
          ical Essays and Critical Reviews.* Vol. 2. Greenwich, Connecticut: JAI Press.
Staw, Barry M. and Ross, Jerry
  1979   "Commitment in an Experimenting Society." Unpublished paper. Depart-
          ment of Organization Behavior, Graduate School of Management, North-
          western University, Evanston, Illinois.
Steffans, L.
  1904   *Shame of the Cities.* New York: Hill and Wang.
Steiner, George
  1978   *On Difficulty and Other Essays.* New York and Oxford: Oxford University Press.
Steiner, Gilbert Y.
  1972   *The State of Welfare.* Washington, D.C.: The Brookings Institution.

Steinman, Marion
1979   "The Catch 22 of Antipsychotic Drugs" in *The New York Times Magazine* (March 18):114:121.

Sternlieb, George S. and Indik, Bernard P.
1973   *The Ecology of Welfare: Housing and the Welfare Crisis in New York City*. New Brunswick, New Jersey: Transaction Books.

Stinchcombe, Arthur
1965   "Social Structure and Organizations" in *Handbook of Organizations*. James G. March, ed., Chapter 4, New York: Rand McNally.

Stoll, Clarice Stasz
1968   "Images of Man and Social Control," *Social Forces* 47:119-127.

Strömholm, Stig
1972   *Allmän Rättslära*. Stockholm: Nordstedt.

_____
1972   *Sverige 1972: Forsok till en Lidelsefri Betraktelse*. Stockholm: Nordstedts.

Sullivan, T.
1976   "Black Female Breadwinners: Some Intersections of Dual Market and Secondary Worker Theory." Paper presented at the 71st Annual Meeting of the American Sociological Association.

Sutherland, Edwin H. and Locke, Harvey J.
1971   *Poverty, U.S.A.*. New York: Arno Press and the *New York Times*. Originally published as *Twenty Thousand Homeless Men* in 1936.

Suttles, Gerald D.
1968   *The Social Order of the Slum*. Chicago: University of Chicago Press.

Sykes, Gresham
1958   *The Society of Captives*. Princeton: Princeton University Press.

Sykes, Gresham M.
1978   *Criminology*. New York: Harcourt Brace Jovanovich, Inc.

Szasz, Thomas
1961   *The Myth of Mental Illness*. New York: Harper.

_____
1977   *The Manufacture of Madness*. New York: Harper.

Tabb, William K.
1970   *The Political Economy of the Black Ghetto*. New York: W.W. Norton and Company, Inc.

Tapp, Robert B. and Tapp, June L.
1972   "Religious Systems as Sources of Control and Support." Pp. 107-126 in S.E. Golann and C. Eisdorfer, eds. *Handbook of Community Mental Health*. Englewood Cliffs, New Jersey: Prentice-Hall, Inc.

Taylor, Karl K. and Soady, Fred W., Jr.
1972   *Violence: An Element of American Life*. Boston: Holbrook Press.

Taylor, Rosemary G.R.
1979   "Free Medicine." Pp. 17-48 in Case and Taylor, *Co-ops, Communes and Collectives*. New York: Pantheon Books.

Tenbroek, J.
1966   *The Law of the Poor*. San Francisco, California: Chandler Publishing Company.

Terkel, Studs
1974   *Working*. New York: Pantheon Books.

Thio, Alex
1978   *Deviant Behavior.* Boston: Houghton Mifflin Company.

Tholfsen, Trygve
1977   *Working Class Radicalism in Mid-Victorian England.* New York: Columbia University Press.

Thompson, E. P.
1964   *The Making of the English Working Class.* New York: Pantheon Books.

Titmuss, R.M.
1968   *Commitment to Welfare.* New York: Pantheon Books.

Toynbee, Arnold J. and Ideda, Daisaku
1976   *Man Himself Must Choose.* Tokyo: Kodansha International, Ltd.

Trattner, Walter I.
1974   *From Poor Law to Welfare State: A History of Social Welfare in America.* New York: The Free Press.

Traux, C.B. and Carkhuff, R.R.
1967   *Toward Effective Counseling and Psychotherapy: Training and Practice.* Chicago: Aldine.

Turk, Austin T.
1969   *Criminality and Legal Order.* Chicago: Rand-McNally.

Turner, Jonathan H. and J. Starnes
1976   *American Society: Problems of Structure.* Second edition. New York: Harper and Row.

Turner, Victor
1964   "Betwixt and Between: The Liminal Period in *Rites of Passage*" in the *Proceedings of the American Ethnological Society,* Symposium on New Approaches to the Study of Religion: 4-20.

———
1969   *The Ritual Process.* Chicago: Aldine Publishing Company.

Tyack, David
1974   *The One Best System.* Cambridge, Massachusetts: Harvard University Press.

Ulmer, Melville J.
1969   *The Welfare State: U.S.A.: An Exploration in and Beyond the New Economics.* Boston: Houghton Mifflin Company.

Vanneman, Reeve D.
1980   "U.S. and British Perceptions of Class" in *American Journal of Socioloy,* 85:769-789.

Vayda, Andrea M. and Permutter, Felice D.
1977   "Primary Prevention in Community Mental Health Centers: A Survey of Current Activity" in *Community Mental Health Journal,* Vol. 13 (4):343.

Veblen, T.
1899   "The Barbarian Status of Women" in *American Journal of Sociology* 4 (January):503-514.

Vidal, Gore
1981   "The Second American Revolution" in *The New York Review of Books,* Vol. XXVIII (February 5):36-42.

Visher, John S. and Visher, Emily B.
1979   "Impressions of Psychiatric Problems and Their Management: China 1977" in *American Journal of Psychiatry,* 136:1 (January): 28-32.

Wallace, Anthony F.C.
    1956   "Revitalization Movements" in *American Anthropologist*, Vol. 58.
Ward, David and Kassebaum, Gene
    1965   *Women's Prisons: Sex and Social Structure*. Chicago: Aldine Publishing Company.
Ward, Mary Jane
    1955   *The Snake Pit*. New York: New American Library.
Webb, Beatrice
    1979   *My Apprenticeship*. Cambridge: Cambridge University Press (first published in 1926).
Weick, Karl E.
    1976   "Educational Organizations as Loosely Coupled Systems" in *Administrative Science Quarterly*, Vol. 21, No. 1:1-19.
Weis, Joseph G.
    1976   "Liberation and Crime: The Invention of the New Female Criminal" in *Crime and Social Justice*, 6 (Fall-Winter):17-27.
Wellman, Barry
    1979   "The Community Question: The Intimate Networks of East Yonkers" in *Aamerican Journal of Sociology*, Vol. 84, No. 5, 1201-1231.
Westergaard, John and Resler, Henrietta
    1975   *Class in a Capitalist Society: A Study of Contemporary Britain*. New York: Basic Books.
Whittington, Colin and Bellaby, Paul
    1979   "The Reasons for Hierarchy in Social Services Departments: A Critique of Elliott Jaques and His Associates" in *The Sociological Review*, 27:513-539.
Whyte, William Foote
    1955   *Street Corner Society*. Second Edition. Chicago: University of Chicago Press.
Wilensky, H.L. and Lebeaux, C.M.
    1958   *Industrial Society and Social Welfare*. New York: Russell Sage Foundation.
Wilkins, Leslie T.
    1965   *Social Deviance: Social Policy, Action and Research*. Englewood Cliffs, New Jersey: Prentice-Hall. London: Tavistock Publications, Ltd.
Williams, Bob
    1971   "Prisons in Crisis" in *Sacramento Bee* (February 9).
Williams, Raymond
    1973   *The Country and the City*. New York: Oxford University Press.

    1977   *Marxism and Literature*. Oxford: Oxford University Press.
Wilson, James Q.
    1968   *Varieties of Police Behavior*. Cambridge: Harvard University Press.

    1968   "Why Are We Having A Wave of Violence?" in *New York Times Magazine* (May 19).

    1975   *Thinking About Crime*. New York: Basic Books.
Wing, J.K.
    1978   "The Social Context of Schizophrenia" in *American Journal of Psychiatry*, 135-11 (November):1333-1339.
Winslow, Walter
    1979   "The Changing Role of Psychiatrists in Community Mental Health" in *American Journal of Psychiatry*, 136:1 (January):24-27.

Wiseman, Jacqueline
  1970   *Stations of the Lost: The Treatment of Skid Row Alcoholics.* Englewood Cliffs, New Jersey: Prentice-Hall.
Women's Prison Association, Washington, D.C.
  1974
Wood, Ann Douglas
  1974   "The Fashionable Diseases: Women's Complaints and their Treatment in 19th Century America" in Mary S. Hartman and Lois Banner, *Clio's Consciousness Raised.* New York: Harper and Row.
  1977   *The Feminization of American Culture.* New York: Avon Books.
World Almanac
  1979   Published for the *Seattle Times.*
Yankelovich, Daniel
  1975   "The Status of Ressentiment in America" in *Social Research,* 42:760-777 (Winter).
Yearley, C.K.
  1973   "The 'Provincial Party' and the Megalopolises: London, Paris and New York, 1850-1910" in *Comparative Studies in Society and History,* Vol. 15, No. 1:51-88.
Yee, Min S.
          The Melancholoy History of Soledad Prison. New York: Harper's Magazine Press.
Young, M. and Wilmott, P.
  1957   *Family and Kinship in East London.* Baltimore: Penguin Books.
Zald, Mayer and Ash, Roberta
  1966   "Social Movement Organizations: Growth, Decay and Change" in *Social Forces,* 44:327-341.
Zeldin, Theodore
  1973   *France, 1848-1945.* Oxford: The Clarendon Press.
Zuckerman, Michael
  1970   *Peaceable Kingdoms.* New York: Random House.

SUBJECT INDEX

AUTHOR INDEX